Foreign Direct Investment in South Asia

Pravakar Sahoo • Geethanjali Nataraj
Ranjan Kumar Dash

Foreign Direct Investment in South Asia

Policy, Impact, Determinants and Challenges

Springer

Pravakar Sahoo
Institute of Economic Growth (IEG)
Delhi University Enclave
Delhi, India

Geethanjali Nataraj
Observer Research Foundation (ORF)
Delhi, India

Ranjan Kumar Dash
Indian Council for Research on International
Economic Relations (ICRIER)
Delhi, India

ISBN 978-81-322-3494-4 ISBN 978-81-322-1536-3 (eBook)
DOI 10.1007/978-81-322-1536-3
Springer New Delhi Heidelberg New York Dordrecht London

Printed on acid-free paper

Springer is part of Springer Science+Business Media (www.springer.com)

Foreword

Inflows of foreign direct investment (FDI) to the Asian region—insignificant until the mid-1980s—increased since the mid-1990s as FDI shifted from the traditionally important locations in the developed world. South Asia has been a beneficiary of this shift. In fact, FDI has played a leading role in the economic development of many South Asian countries and has been an important source of foreign capital. Since the 1990s, and more so in recent years, governments of South Asian countries have realised the benefits of FDI and changed their FDI environment.

Flows of FDI are among important driving forces of globalisation. South Asia has recently been a preferred destination of FDI due to its robust economic growth in services and exports, its large domestic market, and the positive perceptions of foreign investors. However, South Asia receives relatively low FDI flows when compared to other parts of Asia and emerging economies in Central and Latin America. This book has made an excellent attempt to understand and explain how poor business climate, underdeveloped infrastructure, rigid labour laws, and weak regulatory systems have restricted FDI inflows to the region.

The book lays out the FDI policy and its evolution over the past three decades for five South Asian countries—India, Pakistan, Bangladesh, Sri Lanka, and Nepal. It comprehensively describes and analyses the volume, pattern, and composition of FDI inflows to the region. The book discusses China's FDI policy which has been more comprehensive compared to the piecemeal approach followed in India and other South Asian countries.

The rigorous empirical analysis of determinants and impact of FDI inflows in South Asia is relevant for policy formulation. The econometric investigation of impact of FDI contributes to the debate on whether FDI promotes exports and overall growth and crowds in or out domestic investment.

The book not only details the constraints to FDI inflows to the region but has also proposed reforms required to further liberalise and promote it. It urges South Asian countries to build regulatory and policy frameworks to enhance inflows and project South Asia as an attractive FDI destination. Hence, the book is a fine blend of both descriptive and empirical econometric analysis and encompasses all aspects of FDI inflows relevant to policy.

This interesting and insightful book analyses the overall FDI environment and policy in the South Asian region in depth. I complement the authors on bringing out this timely and policy-relevant book. I sincerely hope that students, academicians, and policymakers with an interest in the South Asian economy will find the analysis in the book valuable and illuminating.

Director, Institute of Economic Growth (IEG) Manoj Panda
Delhi, India

Expert-Comments

'The volume represents a novel attempt to capture the FDI policy environment in South Asia instead of the run of the mill individual country based treatment of the issue. It is based on rigorous empirical research and draws out some very relevant policy recommendations. It is good addition to the literature on FDI and a useful reading for all scholars and policy makers interested in South Asia'.

–Rajiv Kumar
Senior Fellow, Center of Policy Research and Ex-Secretary-General, FICCI

'This book explores comprehensively the macroeconomic determinants and impacts of FDI on South Asia countries. It is required reading for those interested in this important issue and in designing suitable policy recommendations'.

–Pravin Krishna
Chung Ju Yung Distinguished Professor of International Economics and Business, John Hopkins, DC, USA

'This timely book provides a comprehensive analysis of the determinants of FDI flows to India, a country that continues to lag its competitors in this area, and provides sensible policy prescriptions. It should appeal to students are researchers interested in the role that FDI can play in its development, as well as policy makers that can help make it happen'.

–Jayant Menon
Lead Economist, Asian Development Bank

'With comprehensive reforms underway toward an inclusive and sustainable growth by most of the governments in the region, South Asia is likely to become one of the most attractive FDI destinations in the world in the 21st century. The authors of this book with expertise on South Asia's economic development and its external FDI linkages provide very comprehensive empirical studies of the

FDI regimes prevailed in the continent with some comparative analysis on other emerging countries, especially China, and address some challenging policy issues to realize more FDI friendly countries. This book is a must reading for academics, businessmen, and policy makers to understand the impacts of FDI to play in shaping up new development history in this important part of the world economy'.

–Choong Yong Ahn
Foreign Investment Ombudsman, Korea/ Distinguished Professor,
Chung-Ang University, Seoul, South Korea

'The authors have produced an excellent research work on FDI – exports – economic growth nexus in South Asia. While carrying out the empirical analyses, they have used appropriate advanced estimation techniques. The book will certainly be an asset in every researcher's and policy maker's libraries'.

–K. Kalirajan
Professor, Crawford School of Public Policy,
Australian National University, Australia

Preface

South Asia is one of the fastest-growing regions in the world. Despite conflict and strife, it has managed to pull through and is well set on the path to growth and prosperity. Most of the countries in the region undertook economic reforms, albeit gradually, since early eighties. However, despite reforming all areas of trade, industry, and the financial sector and creating a congenial environment for foreign investment, the region attracts less foreign direct investment (FDI) than emerging economies in East and Southeast Asia and Brazil.

For each South Asian country and the region as a whole, this book describes the FDI policy, situates it against its trade and structural adjustment programme, analyses the FDI reform process and the evolution of FDI policy, and presents the prospects and reforms required. The book also describes the Chinese experience with FDI and draws policy lessons for the South Asian region. It empirically analyses the determinants and impact of FDI inflows in South Asia using both time series and panel methodology. The book establishes the impact of FDI on output growth, domestic investment, and exports—a point of debate among both academics and policymakers in South Asia. The empirical exercise tries to answer some of the debatable questions such as whether FDI promotes growth, crowds-in domestic investment, or crowds it out, and the link between FDI and exports. Hence, the book blends descriptive and empirical analysis and encompasses all aspects of FDI inflows that are relevant to policy.

Given its comprehensive nature, it is hoped that this book will help policymakers, academicians, and all interested in the region to understand the complex nature of FDI policies in South Asia and the reasons for the relatively low inflows.

This book would not have been possible without the kind support and help of many individuals and organisations. First and foremost, we would like to extend our sincere thanks to Prof. Manoj Panda, Director, Institute of Economic Growth, New Delhi; Mr. Sunjay Joshi and Mr. Samir Saran, Director and Vice President, respectively, Observer Research Foundation, New Delhi; and Prof. Rajat Kathuria, ICRIER, New Delhi, for their kind cooperation and encouragement in completing this project. We take this opportunity to show our greatest appreciation to Dr. Rajiv

Kumar, Prof. B. Kamaiah, Dr. Shekhar Shah, Prof. Rajesh Chadha, Prof. Shashanka Bhide, Prof. Arup Mitra, Prof. M. R. Narayana, Prof. Pushpagadhan, Dr. Jayant Menon, Dr. Douglas Brooks for their support over the years. We are grateful to our colleagues in respective organisations for their encouraging words. We would like to express our sincere thanks to Dr. Ashwani at Central University of Haryana, Mahendergarh; Mr. Prabhu Prasad Mishra at IEG; Rohit Sinha at ORF; and Ms. Sakshi Chawla and Manish Chauhan at FICCI for their research support. We would like to place on record our gratitude to Mr. Surit Das at IEG for patiently going through all the chapters. We thank Sagarika Ghosh, Sahadi Sharma, G. Shanthy, and Nupoor Singh from Springer for all the help. Last, but not the least, we would like to express our heartfelt love and gratitude to our parents, families, and friends for their help and best wishes for the successful completion of this book.

New Delhi, India Pravakar Sahoo
New Delhi, India Geethanjali Nataraj
New Delhi, India Ranjan Kumar Dash

Contents

List of Figures

List of Tables

Authors Bios

Dr. Pravakar Sahoo is an Associate Professor at Institute of Economic Growth (IEG), Delhi University, New Delhi, India. Earlier he has held Senior Fellow position at Indian Council for Research on International Economic Relations (ICRIER). He teaches macroeconomics to high-level government officials and policymakers like Indian Economic Service and Indian Statistical Service officers. He has worked and published more than 50 research papers in refereed international and national journals such as *Economic Modeling*, *Journal of International Trade and Economic Development, Journal of Policy Modeling, International Trade Journal, Journal of Developing Areas, Journal of Asian Economics, Journal of Asia Pacific Economies, International Economic Journal, Singapore Economic Review, Journal of Economic Policy Reforms,* and *Economic and Political Weekly* on issues related to macroeconomics, development economics, international trade and investment, regional cooperation, infrastructure, and FDI. Dr. Sahoo has wide international exposure and has served as Consultant to several international and national organisations including Government of India.

Dr. Geethanjali Nataraj is a Professor and Senior Fellow at Observer Research Foundation (ORF), New Delhi, India. Before joining ORF, she was a Director at Federation of Indian Chambers of Commerce and Industry (FICCI) heading the Defence and Capital Goods sector along with providing inputs to FICCI's international division on China and Japan. Prior to joining FICCI, Dr. Nataraj was a Senior Economist at the National Council of Applied Economic Research (NCAER), New Delhi, India. From 2001 to 2006, she was a faculty at the Indian Institute of Foreign Trade, New Delhi. She has held visiting faculty/researcher positions to the Institute of Finance Management, Tanzania; Foreign Trade Training Centre, Egypt; ADBI, Tokyo; and Policy Research Institute, Ministry of Finance, Japan. She has completed number of policy relevant research studies for different ministries of the Government of India and also other national and international organisations. She has published more than 30 research papers in reputed refereed journals in and outside India such as *Journal of Asian Economics, Journal of Economic Development, Economic and Political Weekly,* and *Savings and Development.*

Dr. Ranjan Kumar Dash is a Fellow at Indian Council for Research on International Economic Relations (ICRIER). He obtained his Ph.D. in financial economics from Jawaharlal Nehru University (JNU), New Delhi, India. He also holds M.Phil. from JNU. Dr. Dash has previously worked at National Council for Applied Economic Research and Institute of Economic Growth. He has more than 10 years of research experience in macroeconomics, financial economics, international economics, econometric modelling, and development economics. His areas of research interest are financial economics, international trade and finance, applied econometrics, and development economics. He has published more than 20 academic articles in reputed international refereed journals such as *Economic Modelling, Journal of Policy Modeling, the Journal of International Trade and Economic Development, Singapore Economic Review,* and *International Journal of Economic and Business Research.* He has also contributed several articles in editorial books. He has presented papers and delivered lectures in many national and international conferences.

Chapter 1
Overview

One of the remarkable features of globalisation in the 1990s was the flow of private capital in the form of FDI, which is an important source of development finance and which contributes to productivity gains by providing new investment, better technology, management expertise, and export markets. Given resource constraints and lack of investment in developing countries, market forces and the private sector are increasingly been relied on as the engine of economic growth. In the neoclassical growth model, FDI promotes economic growth by increasing investment and its efficiency. Therefore, all countries, particularly developing countries and least developed countries (LDCs), seek FDI for the benefits it brings to the host economy. Foreign investment, especially FDI, both supplements domestic investment resources and acts as a source of foreign exchange and can relax the balance-of-payments constraints on growth. Considering the economic benefits and importance of FDI for promoting economic growth, most countries, including South Asian countries, have formulated wide-reaching changes in national policies to attract FDI.

The World Bank expects South Asia to play an important role in the global development story in the Asian century. It has the world's largest working age population, a quarter of the world's middle-class consumers, the largest number of poor and undernourished in the world, and several fragile states of global geopolitical importance. With inclusive growth, South Asia has the potential to change global poverty. The economic reforms launched in almost all the countries of the region have positively impacted economic growth—it averaged 6 % a year over the past 20 years—and FDI is likely to be a key factor of further growth and development in the region. Although South Asia was selectively receptive to FDI before the 1990s, governments of South Asian countries realised that FDI is an important determinant of investment, economic growth, and employment and acted as 'facilitators' during the 1990s to attract FDI. As a result, FDI inflow increased, and South Asia has become an attractive destination for foreign investors, although not as attractive as China, Singapore, or Brazil. This is because of South Asia's poor business climate: poor infrastructure; restrictive labour laws; lack of policy coordination; a dormant special economic zone (SEZ) policy; lack of institutional

P. Sahoo et al., *Foreign Direct Investment in South Asia*,
DOI 10.1007/978-81-322-1536-3_1, © Springer India 2014

reforms; corruption; and cost and time overruns in infrastructure projects due to contractual and institutional failures, often caused by a lack of coordination among central and state government departments on land acquisition and environmental clearance. This is borne out by its low position on the World Bank's *Doing Business* index. The subindices suggest that South Asian firms encounter serious obstacles in getting reliable access to infrastructure, effective governance, flexible labour laws, paying taxes, and enforcing contracts.

However, foreign investors' perception is becoming progressively more positive, and South Asia has great opportunities for increasing FDI if it meets a few prerequisites: macroeconomic and political stability, appropriate policy and regulatory frameworks, infrastructure development, accelerated development of small- and medium-sized enterprises (SME), flexible labour laws, availability of skilled labour, and enhancement of regional cooperation.

Against this backdrop, the book asks and attempts to answer a few questions relevant to FDI policy in South Asian countries:

- Which major reforms have succeeded?
- What are the factors determining FDI inflows?
- What has been the impact of FDI on macroeconomic performance?
- Which pending policy priorities/reforms are required to sustain and increase FDI inflows to the region?

These questions and answers should interest policymakers, academics, and all interested in FDI and the South Asian region. The book is based on research that blends theory, evidence, and policy. The analysis covers five countries in South Asia—India, Pakistan, Bangladesh, Sri Lanka, and Nepal.

The following section briefly describes each chapter in this book. Apart from the overview (Chap. 1), there are nine chapters.

Chapter 2 presents the economic reforms and economic performances of the five major South Asian countries and of the South Asian region. It analyses the pattern, composition, and sectoral development of South Asian economies in detail and relates these to policy in the last three decades, particularly reforms initiated in the past two decades. Except Pakistan in the past decade, South Asian countries have performed well on all macroeconomic indicators in the past two decades of reforms despite a decline in the contribution of agriculture to GDP. During the post-reform period, there has been improvement in important macro indicators (per capita income, gross domestic savings, gross domestic capital formation, trade, current account balance, capital account, and foreign exchange reserves) in all these countries except Pakistan. The analysis emphasises the need for second- and third-generation reforms to sustain their high growth rates. Prospects look bright for higher growth and foreign investment inflows provided the region works to improve political instability, security, and intra-regional economic cooperation.

To understand the volume, pattern, and composition of FDI inflow, it is necessary to analyse FDI policy and reforms in South Asian countries (Chap. 3). The analysis details the evolution of FDI policy and reforms in each South Asian country. Several measures have been implemented to keep up the pace of FDI inflows: single window clearance, encouraging private sector participation through PPPs, incentives to foreign investors (including tax sops), setting up SEZs, investment promotion zones, and BOIs. Most sectors have been opened to foreign investment, and there is little variation across countries. The chapter details the measures and reforms each country needs for FDI inflows to sustain growth and to keep up the FDI momentum.

To understand the success and failure of FDI policy, it is necessary to understand their impact on FDI inflows. Therefore, Chap. 4 details the inflow, outflow, and sources of FDI; the sectors that attract the most FDI; and the importance of intra-regional FDI and shows that the source of FDI differs for each country, by its political–economic relationship with the source economy. It highlights heterogeneity in the sectoral decomposition of FDI in South Asian economies, partially due to domestic, external, and foreign policy initiatives. Sometimes, the heterogeneity is due to market potential and resource availability. The chapter relates policy with outcomes where FDI inflows, trends, distribution, and pattern (both flow and stock) in South Asia are compared to major economic blocs with reference to GDP, capital formulation, and FDI potential. Additionally, it disaggregates FDI flows by sector and country and highlights the types of FDI inflow. The inflow of FDI to the manufacturing and services sectors has been examined to understand whether it is oriented towards the domestic market or concentrated in export-oriented industries and export-seeking. Robust economic growth, the region's large domestic markets, and foreign investors' positive perception have induced greater FDI inflows recently, although lower than other emerging market economies in and outside Asia.

China is the most successful developing country in the world in attracting foreign investment. Many factor endowments are common between South Asian countries and China and more so between China and India. Therefore, Chap. 5 presents FDI policy reforms in China and draws lessons for South Asia and India. South Asia's approach to FDI has been piecemeal and compartmentalised. In contrast, China's approach has been comprehensive: has created world-class infrastructure, is able to supply cheap labour and power, labour laws remain flexible and the business environment congenial, gives preferential treatment and single window clearance to FDI and SEZs, and makes FDI export oriented. China's centralised political system lets it implement reforms quickly and easily; India's decentralised structure makes that difficult.

To understand why South Asian countries receive less FDI than China or Brazil, Chap. 6 analyses the determinants of FDI inflows by using both time series and panel methodology. The chapter considers economic conditions and macroeconomic fundamentals, including host country policies, and comprehensively analyses methodology and modelling. Overall, the analysis shows that the determinants of FDI for South Asia can be grouped into

1. Economic conditions such as market size, rate of return, labour cost, human capital, physical infrastructure, and macroeconomic fundamentals such as current account balance

2. Host country policies such as trade openness, exchange rate, and governance
3. Trade agreements

Developing South Asian countries have always debated if FDI (1) benefits growth, (2) crowds in domestic investment or crowds it out, and (3) helps host country exports. This book answers these questions in three empirical chapters (Chaps. 7, 8, and 9). These chapters present causality tests performed to supplement the empirical results by finding out the direction of feedback between (1) FDI and growth, (2) FDI and domestic investment, and (3) FDI and exports. The empirical exercise uses both the latest time series and panel econometrics framework. The book highlights existing empirical studies on the nexus between FDI and growth, domestic investment, and exports. With regard to the link between FDI, trade openness, domestic demand, exchange rate, and export performance in South Asian economies, the book presents dynamic empirical analysis to find out the channels of the spillover effect of FDI. All three chapters (Chaps. 7, 8, and 9) have sections on China for comparison.

Chapter 7 analyses the FDI–economic growth relationship in the growth accounting framework. The framework considers the most important growth variables (such as labour, capital, trade openness, human capital, infrastructure development, financial sector development, quality of institutions, macroeconomic instability, and productivity of investment). The chapter tests the absorption hypothesis that the growth impact of FDI on a country depends on that country's overall economic health. Both time series country and regional panel results reveal that FDI has a positive impact on economic growth in South Asia along with other variables such as trade openness, human capital, gross capital formation, financial development, and infrastructure development.

Investment is a crucial intermediate variable for economic growth; therefore, the relationship between FDI and domestic investment (DI) is widely debated in economic literature. Using both time series and panel data analysis, Chap. 8 empirically analyses the dynamic relationship between FDI and DI for five South Asian countries. In previous empirical studies, the evidence varies from country to country and region to region because of differences in national/regional policies, response of domestic enterprises, the type of FDI inflows in the recipient country, and the econometric methodology used for the study. This chapter estimates the investment function for South Asian countries, both individually and jointly, based on the theoretical foundation to find out the contribution of FDI to DI. The same analysis has been done for China for comparison. Overall, results show that FDI crowds in DI in both short and long run. This suggests complementarities between FDI and DI. Panel results also support the time series evidence that FDI has played a significant complementary role to DI in developing South Asian countries. Therefore, these countries must make every effort to get FDI and, thereby, improve DI—which is crucial for sustaining high economic growth.

Through an equation derived after solving the export demand function and the export supply function for equilibrium state, Chap. 9 examines the impact of FDI on the export performance of five South Asian countries, including both demand and supply side factors. The empirical exercise is conducted for the total exports and manufacturing exports of each country and jointly for all five countries. The coefficient of FDI is positive and significant, which means that FDI promotes exports in India, Pakistan, Sri Lanka, and Bangladesh. On the other hand, FDI does not promote exports in Nepal. Panel data analysis also shows that the impact of FDI on export supply in South Asia is positive and statistically significant. The causality test, performed using both time series and panel methodology, indicates that FDI in India, Pakistan, Sri Lanka, and Bangladesh leads to increased export; the causality runs one way. If India emulates the policies followed by China and Singapore, and with the right mix of domestic policies for FDI by South Asian countries, India can substantially enhance its export competitiveness in the international market and total exports.

To suggest feasible future reforms, Chap. 10 attempts to understand the constraints to FDI inflows by asking two key questions:

- What are the major constraints to FDI inflows into South Asia at present?
- What policy priorities/reforms can enhance FDI in the region?

Chapter 10 examines some of the debatable issues like dispute resolution mechanism in infrastructure sector, land acquisition, unification, and harmonisation of the labour laws, making SEZ policy effective, non-governmental facilitation services for foreign investors and pending reforms with respect to FDI policy in each of the countries to help the region move forward as a whole. The chapter explores difficulties arising out of economic stability, tax and other incentives, labour regulations, work ethics, social and economic infrastructure, and costs of production, potential domestic market, and an overall assessment of political and economic conditions. Finally, the study comes up with suggestions for larger inflow of foreign investment into South Asia for sustained exports, investment, and economic growth.

Chapter 2
South Asia: A Macro Overview

2.1 Introduction

South Asia consists of eight countries—Afghanistan, Bhutan, Bangladesh, India, Maldives, Nepal, Pakistan, and Sri Lanka. These countries share social, cultural, linguistic, and economic practices. India is the largest country in the South Asian region by land area, population, and economy; Pakistan and Bangladesh are the second and third largest countries, respectively. India occupies over 70 % of the landmass of the region. Its territorial and maritime boundary touches all South Asian countries except Afghanistan. Bhutan and Nepal are landlocked; Maldives and Sri Lanka are island states.

South Asia has contributed significantly to the world population—mainly dominated by India—and has the world's largest working age population. The World Development Report 2012 estimates the world economy at US$75,803 billion in terms of purchasing power parity (gross national income). South Asia's share is $5,103 billion. The compositional analysis of output for South Asian economies in 2012 reveals that the services sector (55 %) dominates industry (27 %) and agriculture (18 %).

Most countries in South Asia were under British rule and won independence only between 1945 and 1950. After independence, like most developing economies, South Asia adopted closed macroeconomic policies with import substitution (IS) industrialisation policies to varying degrees, under which self-reliance and indigenous efforts were encouraged.[1] This is because South Asia's economic policy after independence was influenced by the colonial experience—which many

[1] The Prebisch–Singer thesis—of the secular deterioration of terms of trade—for developing countries drew their attention. Developing countries had learned from developed countries that they needed to orient their economies towards industrialisation to improve their terms of trade. Accordingly, they designed IS policies to protect all sectors of the economy. This meant high tariffs and various forms of licensing to control entry into domestic 'infant' industries and increase savings, foreign exchange savings, and investment (Dornbusch 1992).

P. Sahoo et al., *Foreign Direct Investment in South Asia*,
DOI 10.1007/978-81-322-1536-3_2, © Springer India 2014

leaders considered exploitative—and by those leaders' exposure to British social democracy and the progress achieved by the Soviet Union's planned economy. Domestic policy tended towards protectionism. There was strong emphasis on import substitution industrialisation, economic interventionism, a large public sector, business regulation, and central planning. Trade and foreign investment policies were relatively liberal. For instance, the five-year plans of India resembled central planning in the Soviet Union. At the same time, the state was assigned a dominant role in the economy, particularly in the infrastructural sectors of communications, transport, and power (Srinivasan 2002). These import substitution strategies, coupled with the large public sector, resulted in rent-seeking activities[2] and uncompetitive production processes (Bhagwati and Srinivasan 1975).

India allocated imports on the basis of firm capacity, which led to rent seeking through capacity expansion (Krueger 1974). But the dominance of the public sector and of the licence-based system might have hampered the full swing of competition under the IS policy and thereby made the economy relatively uncompetitive. A select group of individuals and companies accumulated illicit wealth through political patronage, favouritism in appointments and award of contracts, tax evasion, acquisition of state and private land, allocation of public resources such as spectrum, mining rights of oil, and gas concessions—to the detriment of the larger population. The growing trend of alliances between public office holders, bureaucrats, and big businesses in South Asian countries has caused large-scale corruption and, consequently, frustration, resentment, and disenchantment among the middle classes, which in turn threatens the policies that unleashed the potential of South Asian countries. With the exception of Sri Lanka, which had undertaken significant liberalisation in the late 1970s, anti-trade policies remained dominant in the region for nearly four decades.

The IS policy severely affected economic performance in the South Asian region, which was among the slowest-growing regions in the 1960s and 1970s. As per the World Bank database, GDP grew at 4.2 % per year in the region during the 1960s; world GDP grew at 5.4 %. However, since the early 1980s, liberalisation efforts have been made and deregulation aimed at eliminating incentives for rent-seeking activities.

The decade-wise growth of South Asian economies has been very impressive—over 5 % during 1980–2000 and around 7 % over 2001–2010. Growth has averaged around 6 % per annum over the past two decades. Real GDP growth in the region is forecast to be a little over 5.5 % for the financial year 2012 and improve thereafter. This strong growth has lowered poverty and improved human development. Yet, poverty remains widespread—more than 500 million people in South Asia live on less than $1.25 a day.

[2] See Krueger (1974) for rent-seeking activities in India.

East Asian economies performed poorly in the 1960s. Beginning in the mid-1970s and until the 1990s, their exports and economy grew.[3] This persuaded policymakers to liberalise trade and investment.[4] The literature holds that important ideological factors for change in this region were the collapse of the former Eastern Europe bloc and the transformation of former socialist planned market economies (Bandara and McGillivray 1998; Tendulkar and Bhavani 2007). In the second half of the 1980s, trade policies began to be unilaterally liberalised; such liberalisation became more systematic in the 1990s.

The outcomes of the reform measures are broadly positive. South Asian countries have achieved higher per capita income growth, trade growth, and investment growth in the reform period.[5] The present chapter briefly reviews economic reforms and economic performances of five major South Asian countries. This chapter is structured as follows. Section 2.2 discusses the economic reforms in South Asia. Section 2.3 reviews economic performances of South Asian countries. Section 2.4 deals with major issues or difficulties to growth.

2.2 Economic Reforms in South Asia: Country-wise Analysis

During the 1970s, South Asian countries faced various economic challenges—low level of economic growth and per capita income, growing fiscal imbalances, balance of payments problem, and declining foreign exchange reserves (Bandara and McGillivray 1998; Tendulkar and Bhavani 2007; Rodrik and Subramanium 2004). During the 1980s, South Asian economies realised that the inefficiency in their economic system arose from their closed-door policy and rent-seeking activities and began reforming their economy, including trade and finance. In the 1980s and 1990s, the region learned from many developed and emerging economies and moved away from a purely socialistic model of development—based on the planned model—and adopted market reforms to make the business environment in South Asia congenial and to integrate with the rest of the world.

Except in Sri Lanka, which began market reforms in the late 1970s, the pace of reforms in India, Pakistan, and Bangladesh accelerated only in the 1990s. The reform process in all these countries followed the so-called Washington Consensus

[3] During 1981–1991, GDP grew annually at 9.1 % in the Republic of Korea, 5.7 % in Malaysia, and 8.2 % in Thailand; exports of goods and services grew annually at 11.3, 11.8, and 15.5 %, respectively. The 1997–1998 economic crisis reduced GDP and export growth in the 1990s. During 1991–2001, GDP grew annually at 5.4 % in the Republic of Korea, 6.1 % in Malaysia, and 3.2 % in Thailand; exports grew annually at 15.9, 10.5, and 8.5 %, respectively.

[4] The empirical evidence from recent literature suggests that the potential gains from trade liberalisation are substantial (e.g. Francois et al. 2003; Laird et al. 2003).

[5] All these countries have major socio-economic problems like poverty, unemployment, income inequality, and regional imbalances, and all are dependent on external aid/assistance.

of the IMF and World Bank. However, and naturally, the relative emphasis on the components of the reform agenda differed. Although the reform process in South Asia is gradualist and incomplete, economic performance has been impressive overall. The following section gives a brief overview of the reform process in each of the countries.

Overall, the reforms followed in South Asian countries[6] can be divided into two parts: domestic reforms and external sector reforms.

On the domestic front, the agenda included:

- Fiscal reforms[7]
- Disinvestment and privatisation of state-owned enterprises (SOEs)
- Privatisation and opening up sectors to private sectors
- Financial sector reforms leading to deregulation of interest rates
- Development of infrastructure
- More generally, enhancing the role of market forces in the economy's resource allocation processes (Srinivasan 2002; Rodrick and Subramanian 2004)

The external sector reforms included:

- Removing import-weighted average tariffs
- Abolishing quantitative restrictions on imports
- Exchange rate reforms
- Easing capital flow
- Allowing FDI gradually

On the South Asian regional front, the movement towards the regional economic integration from the South Asian Association of Regional Cooperation (1985) to South Asian Preferential Trade Agreements (1995) to South Asian Free Trade Agreement (2004) witnesses the higher level of intra-regional trade liberalisation and economic cooperation among the member countries.

2.2.1 Economic Reforms and Developments in India: A Brief Review

2.2.1.1 Overall Policy Reforms

India's growth experience had invited the serious attentions of policymakers, as the economic growth averaged a modest 3.6 % and per capita growth of meagre 1.4 % per year during 1950–1980. The poor economic performance was considered an

[6] Here we are only focusing on five South Asian countries such as India, Pakistan, Bangladesh, Sri Lanka, and Nepal.

[7] Fiscal reforms include rational tax reforms such as rationalisation and simplification of tax rates and slabs, debt management policy, and fiscal consolidation.

outcome of state-led import substituting industrialisation (Ahluwalia and Little 1998; Joshi 1998; Acharya 2009). In the late 1970s, India suffered from a grossly overvalued exchange rate because of tight import controls as well as a varied, but generally very high, tariff structure. There was a consensus that quantitative restrictions on imports were dysfunctional and should be phased out. In addition, tariffs had to be reduced over time, and the exchange rate had to be devalued to provide incentives for domestic production as tariffs were cut. The 1980s saw some partial steps to address this problem. The exchange rate was managed in a way that achieved a steady depreciation in real terms, eroding the impact of quantitative restrictions. There was also some limited relaxation in quantitative restrictions but little progress on tariffs. In fact, where quantitative import licensing was reduced, tariffs were actually raised to shift from quantitative restrictions to tariffs.

Economic reforms started in the early 1980s. In July 1991, in the middle of a crisis of balance of payments and foreign exchange liquidity, a comprehensive liberalisation and privatisation process started. Import licensing was abolished for capital goods and intermediates, which became freely importable in 1993, simultaneously with the switch to a flexible exchange rate regime. In 1991, the fixed exchange rate was devalued by 25 % (in two successive steps) to a more reasonable level. Since import controls were to be liberalised, it was logical to shift to a system that allowed greater exchange rate flexibility. This was done in two stages. In 1992, a dual exchange rate was introduced. There was one fixed rate, at which exporters were expected to surrender 30 % of export earnings. This was used to finance essential imports such as petroleum and to meet government debt servicing obligations. And there was a floating rate, at which all other transactions took place based on the demand and supply of foreign exchange. In 1993, the dual exchange rate was replaced by a single exchange rate, which was effectively market-determined. Quotas and nontariff barriers were also reduced. Since then, there have been attempts to integrate the Indian economy with the rest of the world in a variety of ways—removing quantitative restrictions,[8] reducing tariffs,[9] and making the exchange rate flexible.[10]

Starting in February 1994, many current account transactions were also permitted at the market exchange rate. The pace of reforms gathered momentum over the period 1991–1996 when controls over trade were relaxed extensively. Some of the major reform measures included:

- Reduction of the fiscal deficit
- Flexible exchange rate system
- Phased reduction of import licensing (quantitative restrictions)
- Policies to encourage direct and portfolio foreign investment
- Build-up of foreign exchange reserves

[8] In 2001, quantitative restrictions, which were in place for most consumer goods, were abolished.

[9] India has reduced tariffs considerably—from 35.3 % in 1997–1998 to 20 % in 2003–2004.

[10] The exchange rate system was transformed in less than 2 years from a discretionary, basket-pegged system to a largely market-determined unified exchange rate.

- Virtual abolition of industrial licensing and promoting more competition
- Freer access to foreign technology
- More remunerative procurement prices for cereals
- Reduction in protection to the manufacturing sector
- Phasing in of Basel prudential norms
- Reduction of reserve requirements for banks (CRR and SLR)
- Deregulation of interest rates and setting up of institutions like SEBI and NSE (Rodrick and Subramanian 2004; Ahluwalia and Little 1998; Joshi 1998; Tendulkar and Bhavani 2007; Acharya 2009)

Recently, India has taken several steps to enhance its economy's growth, including:

- Initiating the process of enhancing the scope of the Fiscal Responsibility and Budget Management Act,[11] 2003
- Announcing the New Manufacturing Policy
- Promoting more export-oriented units
- Allowing more foreign investment in retail sector
- Setting up the Financial Sector Legislative Reforms Commission

The reform process in India centred on fiscal reforms, trade and industry policy reforms, and financial sector reforms. A few major initiatives are explained below.

Fiscal profligacy was seen to have caused the balance of payment crisis in 1991 and a reduction in the fiscal deficit. Therefore, it was an urgent priority at the start of the reforms. The combined fiscal deficit of the central and state governments was reduced from 9.4 % of GDP in 1990–1991 to 7 % in both 1991–1992 and 1992–1993, and the balance of payment crisis was over by 1993. Reforms in industrial and trade policy were a central focus of much of India's early reform effort. Prior to the reforms, industrial policy was characterised by multiple controls over private investment. These controls allowed private investors to operate only in some areas and often determined operation scale, new investment location, and even technology. The industrial structure that evolved under this regime was highly inefficient and needed to be supported by a highly protective trade policy, often providing tailor-made protection to each sector of industry. Industrial policy has seen the greatest change, with most central government industrial controls being dismantled. Previously, only the public sector could operate in 18 industries, including iron and steel, heavy plant and machinery, telecommunications and telecom equipment, minerals, oil, mining, air transport services, and electricity generation and distribution. Now, only defence aircraft and warships, atomic energy generation, and railway transport are reserved for the public sector. Industrial licensing by the central government has been almost abolished, except for a few hazardous and environmentally sensitive industries. Previously, under the Monopolies and Restrictive Trade Practices Act, industrial houses needed clearance

[11] Under this Act, the central government to eliminate revenue deficit by March 2009 and to reduce fiscal deficit to an amount equivalent to 3 % of GDP (0.3 % annually) by March 2008.

to make large investments. That requirement, to discourage the concentration of economic power, was abolished. The Act is to be replaced by a new competition law, which will attempt to regulate anticompetitive behaviour in other ways.

India's financial sector reform programme included early, wide-ranging reform in banking and capital markets.[12] Reforms in insurance were introduced later. Banking sector reforms included:

- Measures for liberalisation, like dismantling the complex system of interest rate controls, eliminating prior approval of the Reserve Bank of India for large loans, and reducing the statutory requirements to invest in government securities
- Measures designed to increase financial soundness, like introducing capital adequacy requirements and other prudential norms for banks and strengthening banking supervision
- Measures for increasing competition like more liberal licensing of private banks and freer expansion by foreign banks

These steps have produced some positive outcomes: the share of nonperforming assets in the portfolio has dropped sharply, and over 90 % of banks now meet the new capital adequacy standards.

2.2.1.2 External and Trade Reforms

Trade policy reform has also progressed, although slower than industrial liberalisation. Before the reforms, trade policy was characterised by high tariffs and pervasive import restrictions. Imports of manufactured consumer goods were completely banned. For capital goods, raw materials, and intermediates, certain lists of goods were freely importable. But for most items where domestic substitutes were produced, imports were possible only with import licences. The criteria for issue of licences were non-transparent; delays were endemic and corruption was unavoidable. The economic reforms sought to phase out import licensing and to reduce import duties (see Nataraj and Sahoo 2006a, b, 2007). Although India's tariff levels are significantly lower than in 1991, they remain among the highest in the developing world—because most other developing countries have also reduced tariffs in this period.

Liberalising norms for FDI was another important part of India's reforms. This was driven by the belief that this would increase the total volume of investment in the economy, improve production technology, and increase access to world markets. The policy now allows 100 % foreign ownership in a large number of industries and majority ownership in all except banks, insurance companies, telecommunications, and airlines. Procedures for obtaining permission were greatly simplified by listing industries that are eligible for automatic approval up to

[12] Extensive financial sector liberalisation was started following Narasimham Committee Report in 1991.

specified levels of foreign equity (100, 74, and 51 %). Potential foreign investors investing within these limits only need to register with the Reserve Bank of India. For investments in other industries or for a higher share of equity than is automatically permitted in listed industries, applications are considered by a Foreign Investment Promotion Board with a record of quick decisions (see Chaps. 3 and 4 for details).

India has accumulated over US$200 billion worth of foreign exchange reserves in recent years and freed many capital account transactions. In 2002, second-generation reforms focused on reducing the fiscal deficit, improving infrastructure, reforming labour laws,[13] and energising states to accelerate reforms.[14] Since 1991, India has also substantially liberalised trade in services. In 1999, foreign investment was allowed in the insurance sector. India raised its FDI limits in many important sectors including telecommunications, banking and insurance, and civil aviation.

India had committed to the WTO that it would remove all BOP-related quantitative restrictions in phases by the end of March 2001. Accordingly, it rationalised tariff rates during the 1990s. The maximum import duty rate on certain items before the 1990s was over 300 %. The peak import duty on nonagricultural imports was gradually reduced from 150 % in 1991–1992 to 10 % now (subject to certain exceptions). The government has continued to reduce applied MFN tariffs on nonagricultural products to meet its goal of reaching ASEAN tariff levels on these products by 2009. As a result, the overall average applied MFN tariff has fallen from over 32 % in 2001–2002 to less than 16 % in 2006–2007, widening the already large gap between the average tariffs for nonagricultural products (12.1 %) and agricultural products (almost 41 %). The use of import restrictions maintained under GATT Articles XX and XXI has declined; around 3.5 % of tariff lines are subject to such measures. Since 2002, India's use of antidumping and countervailing measures has declined, although it is still one of the largest users of these instruments (Nataraj and Sahoo 2006a, b, 2007).

2.2.2 Economic Reforms in Bangladesh: A Brief Review

Bangladesh was established in 1971. Its government followed an inward-oriented policy by nationalising all large manufacturing units and introducing various regulations and controls on the economy. From the early 1980s, the government began withdrawing food and agricultural subsidies, privatising SOEs, liberalising the financial sector, and withdrawing quantitative import restrictions (Ahmed 2002). These were a part of structural adjustment policies under the auspices of the World Bank and the IMF in the 1980s and early 1990s. The effort started with the

[13] Domestic labour laws no longer apply to special economic zones (SEZs) in India.

[14] Rodrick and Subramanian (2004) distinguish the reforms of the 1980s and 1990s by describing the former as 'probusiness' and the latter as 'pro-market'.

World Bank structural and sectoral adjustment loans (SALs and SECLs) in 1980. The IMF introduced a 3-year structural adjustment facility (SAF) in 1986. Major reform initiatives were undertaken in agricultural, trade, fiscal, and industrial policy; the financial sector; public enterprises; and privatisation. These reforms gained momentum in the 1990s. The broader economic reforms are listed below.[15]

Agricultural policy reforms include:

- Liberalisation of input markets
- Curtailing the role of government agency in input distribution
- Deregulation of input prices
- Reduction of subsidies on agricultural inputs
- Liberalisation of agricultural import
- Liberalisation of output markets with producers' price incentive
- Gradual elimination of distribution of food at subsidised price
- Price stabilisation through procurement policy
- Liberalisation of import of food grain

Privatisation and public enterprise reforms include:

- Denationalisation
- Reduction of excess labour in SOEs
- Rationalisation of jute mills
- Improving operational performance of public utilities
- Privatisation of selected public manufacturing and commercial enterprises

Fiscal policy reforms include:

- Expand the base of the value-added tax (VAT)
- Reform personal and company direct taxes
- Strengthen the tax administration
- Adjust prices for public goods and services while improving their operational efficiency
- Limit the growth of current expenditures to less than the growth of nominal GDP
- Reduce subsidies and administrative costs
- Improve project aid utilisation
- Reduce the operating deficit of Bangladesh railway

Financial sector reforms include:

- Implementing reforms aimed at a market-oriented system of monetary management
- Privatisation of NCB and allowing banking in the private sector
- Interest rate liberalisation
- Strengthening commercial bank loan recovery programmes

[15] A research proposal from the Institute of Development Environmental and Strategic Studies (IDESS), Understanding Economic Reform: A Case Study on Bangladesh.

Bangladesh's economy has grown in the past decade despite the global volatile environment. It is considered that the growth is due to prudent macro fiscal and monetary policies. Recently, the government has prioritised high growth by formulating policy to:

- Reduce infrastructural deficit
- Implement massive reform in priority sectors such as education, health, social security and welfare, ICT, and public financial management[16]

Trade and industrial policy reforms include:

- Reduction of maximum tariff rates
- Rationalisation and simplification of the tariff structure
- Elimination of quantitative restrictions on imports
- Simplification of industrial regulations

Bangladesh substantially reduced tariff and nontariff barriers starting from the mid-1980s. It became one of the fastest liberalisers in the region (World Bank 1999). The country reduced tariff slabs from 24 in 1986 to 12 by 1993–1994, 6 by 1996–1997, and 4 by 2005–2006. It reduced the maximum tariff rate from 350 % in 1991–1992 to 50 % in 1995–1996, 42.5 % in 1997–1998, and 25 % in 2005–2006. As a result, the average tariff protection fell from 89 % in 1990–1991 to 25 % in 1995–1996, 22 % in 1999, and 17 % in 2003. Other major reforms included further relaxation of restrictions on private investment, financial liberalisation with deregulation of interest rates, and fiscal reforms including the introduction of the value-added tax and reduction in subsidies (World Bank 1997).

Political uncertainty in recent years in Bangladesh has constrained economic growth and reform, especially in governance. Whether political priorities will be dictated by economic motives is an open question.

2.2.3 *Economic Reforms in Pakistan: A Brief Review*

During 1960–1980, Pakistan's economy grew at almost 6 %—better than other South Asian economies. The performance is mainly attributable to widespread initiatives by the private sector, sound economic management, substantial capital inflows, etc. Also, the economy moved towards liberalisation, deregulation, and privatisation during 1980. But, in 1990, the economy faced major challenges—stagnant tax-to-GDP ratio, double-digit inflation, low levels of investment, deteriorating infrastructure, poor social sector indicators, and poor governance of institutions—and could not sustain its high growth trajectory.

[16] Ministry of Finance, Government of Bangladesh, Bangladesh: Sustaining Growth Amidst Adverse External Environment.

Given the problems of macroeconomic fundamentals, the economy introduced major structural reforms in the agricultural, industrial, external, and financial sectors. The agricultural sector reforms included enhanced availability of water and its efficient use, more market-based environment for input and output prices, providing physical infrastructure and support for research and extension work, and improving farm-to-market links. Other reforms were allowing foreign equity participation up to 100 %, liberalising the foreign exchange regime and import policy, convertibility of rupee on current account, and removing quantitative and nontariff barriers. On the financial front, monetary management was reformed and changed to a market-based system. It included abolition of credit ceilings and credit deposit ratios, phasing out of directed and concessionary credit, removing of caps on interest rate, and initiation of auction of public debt (Mahmood 1999; Mahmood et al. 2008). Notably, there was a general reduction of direct regulation of prices, greater dependence on the market for resource allocation, and a reduction in the public ownership of the means of production in favour of the private sector, via denationalisation and privatisation of manufacturing units and banks (Mahmood 1999).

Financial sector reforms in Pakistan were also initiated early in the 1990s when private domestic banks were allowed to set up shop along with the nationalised commercial banks. Further reforms were undertaken since 1999 when nonperforming loans were tackled in a decisive manner and minimum capital requirements raised (Hussain 2004). Although several reform measures were carried out prior to 2001, the economic reform programme had its formal genesis in 2001—when Pakistan signed a 3-year arrangement with IMF under the Poverty Reduction and Growth Facility (PRGF) programme. Since then, eight programme reviews have been completed successfully. The key to restoring growth has been the authorities' determined implementation of sound financial policies and structural reforms including tax reform, financial sector reform, investment policies including FDI policy, and enterprise reform. These policies have reduced distortions and increased efficiency and lifted uncertainty off the future course of economic policies.

Pakistan's economy is in a crisis. Pakistan's central bank has expressed concerns over increasing government borrowing, inflationary pressure, lack of government interest in economic reform, and reduced export competitiveness, which in the medium term might impact the ability to earn foreign currency for spending on direly needed imports.

Like other countries in South Asia, Pakistan undertook limited reforms in the 1980s. Since the mid-1980s, Pakistan has considerably liberalised its trade regime and rationalised its tariff structure. Quota restrictions were removed in the 1980s and the restricted list in the 1990s. During 1983–1984 to 1993–1994, 724 items were removed from the negative list. As part of the IMF structural adjustment programme and ADB commitments, Pakistan reduced its maximum tariff rate from 125 % in 1989–1990 to 45 % in 1997 and to 25 % in 2007. Many other reforms accompanied trade and foreign investment reform.

Pakistan needs some reforms immediately: reducing government expenses and stopping unchecked hiring in public sector organisations, reducing internal and external debt, checking inflation, improving employment opportunities, and providing the private sector a competitive market to play its role in national development. The challenge might be to bring political parties on a common ground for economic reform and improve the government's willingness and capacity to deal with such issues.

2.2.4 Economic Reforms in Sri Lanka: A Brief Review

In Sri Lanka's economic history, the 1970–1976 period is considered the worst phase and popularly called the closed economic period, or a trade-restricted period, or a period of socialist orientation. In 1971, Sri Lanka experienced its lowest ever growth rate—0.2 %. In 1977, Sri Lanka became the first among all South Asian economies to open up its economy to the outside world; it remains one of the most outward-oriented economies in the region.[17] The first round of reforms during 1977–1979 included significant trade and financial reform, a public enterprise privatisation programme, exchange rate realignment, and incentives for nontraditional exports (Athukorala and Jayasuriya 2004). The dual exchange rate system, which had been in operation since 1968, was abolished, and the new uniform rate was placed under a managed float. The other elements of the macroeconomic policy mix included significant interest rate reform and a number of measures to ensure fiscal prudence. During the 1980s, the second wave of liberalisation was initiated with a major reduction in import tariffs. The Fiscal Management Responsibility Act, approved in 2002, established the objective of reducing the budget deficit to 5 % of GDP by 2006. Current applied tariffs for most goods range between zero and 15 %; the tariff is 30 % for agricultural and food products, consumer goods, chemicals, and other intermediate goods. Further, Sri Lanka requires the least import documentation in the region.

In addition, Sri Lanka's investment regime is relatively open to foreigners, with a few exceptions—where investment either is subject to non-automatic approval or is reserved for Sri Lanka nationals. Full foreign ownership is permitted in banking, insurance, finance, construction, mass transportation, telecommunications and information technology, and petroleum distribution (TPR 2010).

Despite a brutal civil war that began in 1983, economic growth has averaged around 5 % in the last 10 years. Due to the global recession and escalation of violence during the final stages of the war, GDP growth slowed to 3.5 % in 2009 and foreign reserves fell sharply. 'Mahinda Chintana' (Mahinda's Thoughts) guides government economic policy. Mahinda Chintana policies focus on poverty alleviation and steering investment to disadvantaged areas, developing the small and medium enterprise (SME) sector, promoting agriculture, and developing Sri Lanka to become the regional hub of ports, aviation, commerce, knowledge, and energy. The government has developed a 10-year development framework to boost

[17] Its trade as a percentage of GDP (more than 40 %) is the highest in South Asia.

growth through a combination of large infrastructure projects. Sri Lanka's economy is pursuing its post-war resurgence and is expected to grow strongly in the immediate term. It is all set to enact important policy reforms to reach its full economic potential. Sri Lanka has set the goal of improving its business climate but must follow through with reforms to decrease bureaucratic red tape; increase transparency, particularly in government procurement; and increase the predictability of government policies. Sri Lanka must also continue to improve its fiscal discipline. The 26-year conflict and high government expenditure have contributed to Sri Lanka's high public debt load (83 % of GDP in 2009).

2.2.5 *Reforms in Nepal: A Review*

Until the 1980s, the economy was guided through industrial licensing and commercial, fiscal, and financial and foreign exchange regulation policies. After three consecutive years of BOP deficit (1982–1983 to 1984–1985), Nepal went for the SAF programme with the IMF in 1986 for 3 years along with the structural adjustment loan (SAL) programme of the World Bank and initiated most of its economic reforms. It has carried out various components of economic reform policies including fiscal, trade, and FDI policies during the past decade.

Nepal also initiated financial sector reforms: removal of entry barrier, enactment of Finance Companies Act 1985 and its amendment in 1992, abolition of preemption of bank resources in the form of statutory liquidity requirement, and establishment of prudential norms of the Basel Accord. Reforms in the conduct of monetary policy are also carried out. In the reform process, all types of subsidies including fertiliser, irrigation, food transportation, and interest were completely withdrawn. Nepal completed its accession to the WTO and became the 147th member in April 2004. Now, Nepal is among South Asia's most open and trade-dependent economies.

2.2.5.1 External Sector Reforms

Quantitative restrictions on imports have been fully removed. Customs duties have been rationalised and substantially reduced. As a result, trade-weighted nominal rate of protection indicates a substantial fall in protection, from about 80 % in the mid-1980s to about 40 % by 1993–1994 and further to around 15 % by 2007–2008. Reforms have also been executed on the foreign exchange front. The Nepalese rupee is fully convertible on the current account and capital account is partially liberalised. As a result, Nepal obtained the status of IMF Article VIII in 1994.

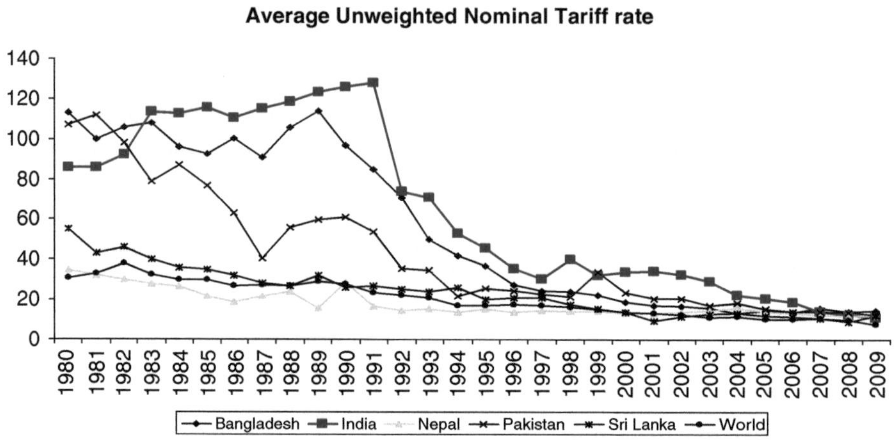

Fig. 2.1 Unweighted average nominal tariff rate (%) (*Source*: Author's compilation from various sources)

Overall economic reforms, particularly external sector reforms, have been significant in reducing trade/import barriers in South Asia. This is indicated in reduction in both unweighted nominal tariff rate[18] and average applied tariff rate[19] (reference). Unweighted nominal average rate across South Asian countries varied considerably during the 1980s and 1990s but declined since the mid-1990s following widespread trade liberalisation and reduction in tariff rate. During the 1980s and 1990s, India and Pakistan had a higher nominal tariff rate than other South Asian countries; recently, the unweighted average tariff rate has been converging among South Asian countries (Fig. 2.1). This shows that the South Asian region has been slowly integrating with world economy.

Similarly, the average applied tariff rate which was close to 50 % (highest in the world) during 1985–1990 in South Asia has fallen to average 15 % during 2001–2009. Compared to other regions, applied tariffs in South Asia are still high. Even sub-Saharan Africa has lower tariff protection for domestic industry. Europe and Central Asia have the lowest tariff protection compared to other regions. Therefore, tariffs in South Asia can be reduced further (Fig. 2.2).

Similarly, the trends in applied tariff rate, most favoured nation (MFN) also has come down significantly from around 45 % in 1985 to around 14 % in 2009 (Fig. 2.3). However, among South Asian countries, Sri Lanka and Nepal have the lowest average MFN tariff rates in the region (WTO 2012).

---

[18] The unweighted average tariff is a measure of the overall degree of protection in the tariff schedule. It is a useful overall measure but can disguise very high protection levels in some sectors. The tariff is defined as a percentage, so the average can range from 0 to ∞.

[19] The average applied tariff rate is the unweighted average of effectively applied rates for all products subject to tariffs calculated for all traded goods.

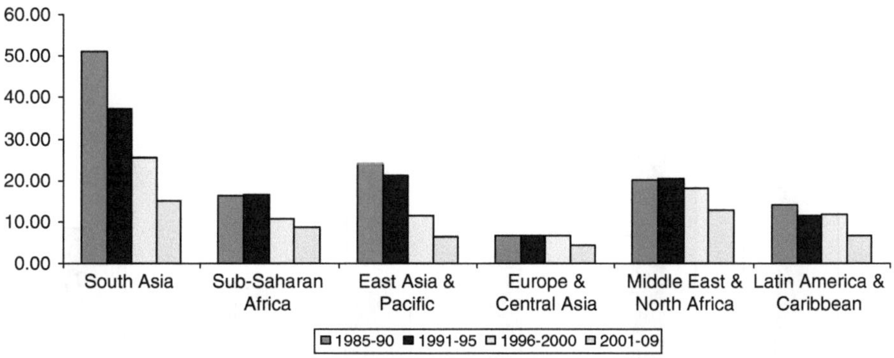

Fig. 2.2 Average applied tariff rate, all products (%) (*Source*: World Development Indicators 2011)

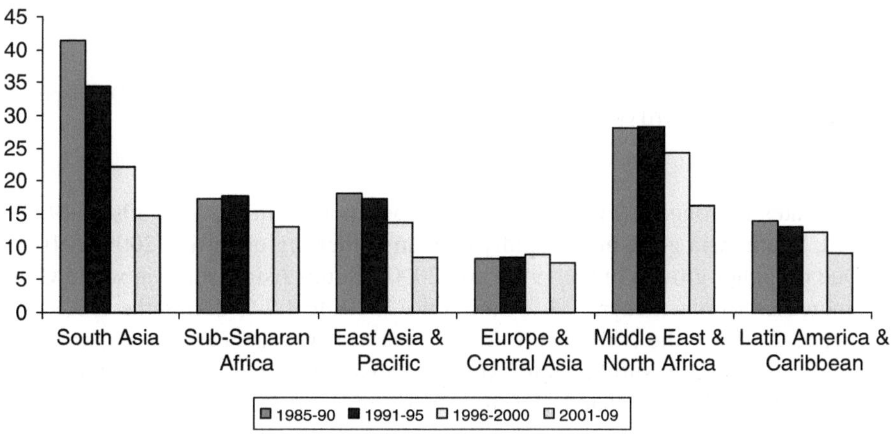

Fig. 2.3 Average applied tariff rate MFN, all products (%) (*Source*: World Development Indicators 2011)

2.3 Macroeconomic Performance of South Asian Countries

Evidently, all five South Asian countries have been consistently following economic reform policies that emphasise the market economy and integrate their economies with the rest of the world. This section reviews the economic performance of South Asian countries vis-à-vis other regions over 1980–2010.

South Asian economies enjoyed rapid growth from 1990 until the onset of global financial crisis in 2008. The growth rate improved steadily and was the highest in the world for 2000–2010 (Fig. 2.4). During the 1980s and 1990s, East Asia and Asia Pacific had higher GDP growth than other regions. South Asia was the second highest growing region. But during the 2000s, the trend reversed in favour of South Asia. As shown, during the period 2000–2010, South Asia increased their GDP

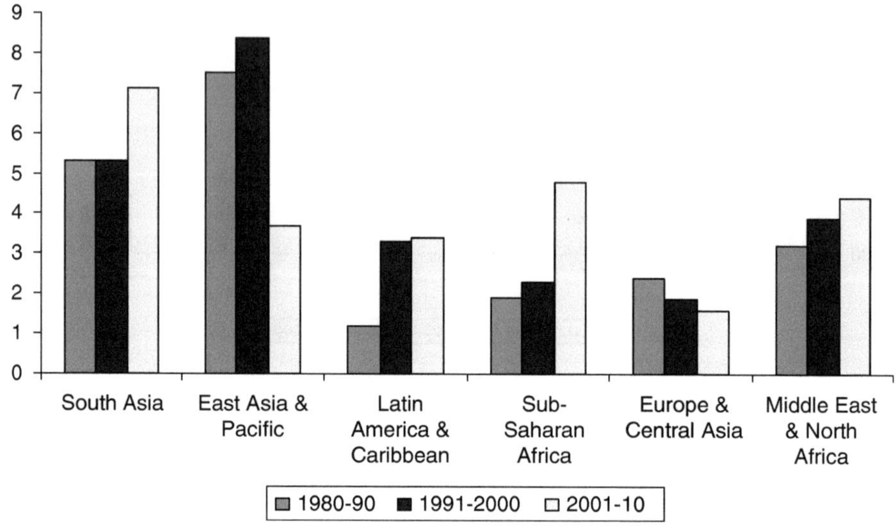

Fig. 2.4 Decade-wise annual average growth rate across regions (*Source:* World Development Indicators, World Bank 2011)

growth rates by roughly 2 percentage points per more than in the 1980s or 1990s. Indeed, South Asia grew more rapidly than any other region during 2000–2010.

Due to higher growth in the 1990s and 2000s, South Asia's share in world GDP has increased from a meagre 1.4 % during the 1980s to 1.7 % during the 1990s and further to 2.4 % in the 2000s. Still, South Asia's share has been lower than other regions'—except for sub-Saharan Africa, whose share has been constant over 1980–2010. On the other hand, the share of Europe and Central Asia has declined steadily over time. East Asia and Pacific countries have increased their GDP share from 22 % in the 1980s to 26 % in the 2000s (Fig. 2.5).

Although South Asia is now one of the fastest-growing regions in the world, its per capita income is one of the lowest (except that of sub-Saharan Africa) but increasing over time. Comparative figures of per capita income across region (at US $2000 price) are presented in Fig. 2.6. It is evident that real per capita income for South Asia increased from around US$290 in the 1980s to US$390 in the 1990s and further to US$600 in the 2000s. Europe and Central Asian countries are ranked first, and Latin America and Caribbean are second; they are followed by East Asia and Pacific regions. Per capita income in sub-Saharan Africa has stagnated.

Notwithstanding significant economic reforms, the global competitiveness of South Asian countries is low. According to the Global Competitiveness Report 2010–2011, the rank of India, Pakistan, Sri Lanka, Bangladesh, and Nepal out of 139 countries is 51, 123, 62, 107, and 139, respectively (Table 2.1). Similarly, they have performed poorly on infrastructure, institutional development, and labour market efficiency. Therefore, the region needs to implement a few quick reforms in the coming years to sustain its growth.

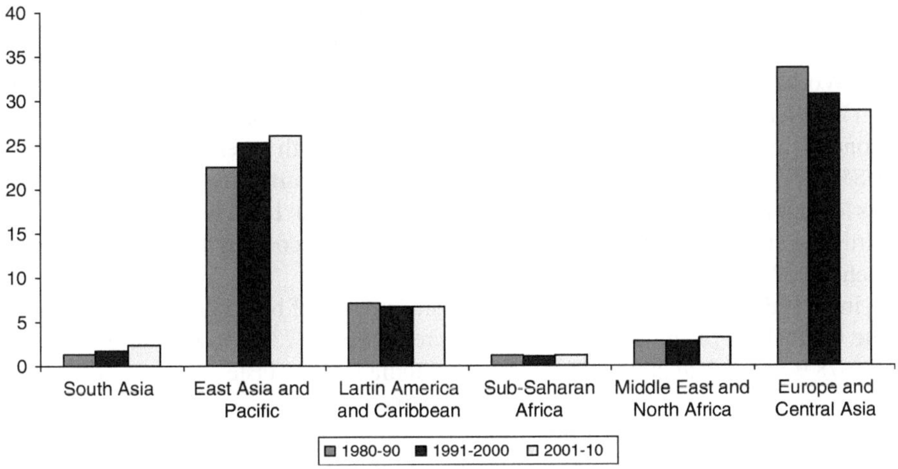

Fig. 2.5 GDP share, across regions (*Source:* World Development Indicators, World Bank 2011)

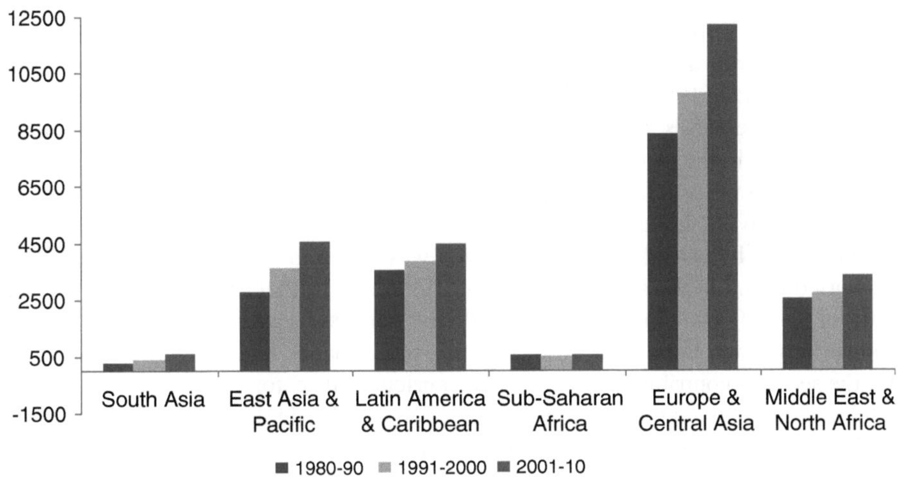

Fig. 2.6 Per capita income level across various regions (at US$2000 price) (*Source:* World Development Indicators, World Bank 2011)

Table 2.1 Global competitiveness ranking of South Asian Countries 2010–2011

Indicators	India	Pakistan	Sri Lanka	Bangladesh	Nepal
GCI	51	123	62	107	130
Institution	58	112	55	115	130
Infrastructure	86	110	70	133	139
Labour market efficiency	92	131	104	108	126
Financial market development	17	73	52	66	106

Source: Global Competitiveness Report 2010–2011, World Economic Forum

2.3.1 Macroeconomic Performances of India

The World Bank (2011) ranks India second in the world in terms of both population (1.17 billion) and arable land (12 %). In 2010, India was ranked the eighth largest economy in terms of real GDP (US$963 billion) and ninth in terms of nominal GDP (US$1,727 billion) (World Bank 2011). It is also the fourth largest economy in the world with respect to the purchasing power parity (PPP). India is expected to be the third largest economy by 2035 and the second largest economy by 2050 (Goldman Sachs 2007).

India is the largest economy in South Asia in terms of both GDP and population. The GDP share of India in South Asia increased from 73 % in the early 1990s to over 78 % in the late 2000s. This is because India was the fastest-growing economy during the 1990s and 2000s in South Asia. India's average economic growth, which was 5.5 % in the 1980s, increased to 6.5 % during 1995–2000 and further to nearly 9 % in the last half of the 2000s. As a result, average real GDP of India (at 2000 price US$) increased from US$291 billion during 1990–1994 to US$797 billion over 2005–2010. Similarly, average per capita income in US dollar almost doubled during the same time (Table 2.2). Therefore, economic growth has been substantial in India in the reform period.

The industrial and services sectors were the main drivers of growth in India, particularly in the 1990s and 2000s. The agricultural sector grew at 5.8 % during the first half of the 1980s, declined to just 1.8 % during 2000–2004, and then bounced back to 3.6 % in the last half of the 2000s. Therefore, the agricultural sector growth rate remained most volatile over 1980–2010.

Comparatively, industrial performance improved steadily, except in the first half of the 1990s. Industrial growth rate which was 5.3 % in the first half of the 1980s increased to 6.2 in the second half of the 1990s and further to 8.8 % in the second half of the 2000s. On the other hand, the services sector growth follows the industrial growth trend. The results of this performance had a significant bearing on the sectoral contribution to GDP. The agricultural sector's contribution to GDP declined gradually in the previous three—from 33.92 % in the first half of the 1980s to 26.2 % in the last half of the 1990s and further to 17.84 % in the last half of the 2000s. However, the industrial sector's contribution to GDP remained more or less constant over 1980–2010. Similarly, the manufacturing value added as a percentage of GDP stagnated, at roughly 16 % over the past three decades. On the other hand, the declining contribution by the agricultural sector is replaced by increased contribution from services sector (Table 2.2).

Further, both domestic savings and capital formation as a percentage of GDP rose over 1980–2010. The gross capital formation as a ratio of GDP increased from around 20.6 % in the early 1980s to above 35.7 % in the last half of the 2000s. Domestic savings also show a similar pattern. However, it is important to notice that the savings–investment gap has also widened during the 2000s, compared to the 1980s and the 1990s. On the fiscal front, India has not done well. Both inflation rates (CPI) and fiscal deficit have remained high, although the inflation rate was

Table 2.2 Key macroeconomic indicators for India

Indicators	1980–1984	1985–1989	1990–1994	1995–1999	2000–2004	2005–2010
Population (in millions)	718.47	798.77	882.78	965.51	1,048.23	1,132
GDP growth (%)	5.47	5.91	4.70	6.55	5.94	8.53
GDP (2000 constant US$, billion)	175	227	291	392	516	797
Share in South Asia (%)	73	73	73	75	76	78
Per capita GDP (2000 constant US$)	238	276	319	391	473	673
Agriculture, growth rate (%)	5.8	3	3.3	3.1	1.8	3.6
Agriculture, value added (% of GDP)	33.92	30.06	29.07	26.20	21.46	18.3
Industry, growth rate (%)	5.3	6.3	5.2	6.2	6.8	8.8
Industry, value added (% of GDP)	25.50	26.36	26.29	26.60	26.44	27.90
Manufacturing, value added (% of GDP)	16.64	16.49	16.17	16.41	15.30	15.33
Services, growth rate (%)	5.5	7.4	5.7	8.9	7.6	10.2
Services, value added (% of GDP)	40.58	43.58	44.64	47.20	52.10	53.59
Gross domestic capital formation (% of GDP)	20.6	23.17	22.93	24.2	26.6	35.7
Gross domestic savings (% of GDP)	18.30	21.52	22.44	22.82	25.39	31.8
Inflation (%)	10.51	7.83	10.24	8.85	3.93	8.00
Fiscal deficit (% of GDP)[a]	NA	−7.81	−7.62	−7.29	−9.29	−6.70
Current account balance (% of GDP)	−1.13	−2.06	−1.37	−1.24	0.45	−1.71
Total forex reserves in months of imports	5.96	4.89	4.06	5.50	9.50	8.96
Trade over GDP (%)	14.51	13.42	18.34	23.49	30.31	45.87
Manufacturing exports (% merchandise exports)	54.2	68.8	74	75.8	74.4	64.3
Short-term debt (% of total reserves)	28.6	60.9	70.6	18.4	6.20	14.3

Source: World Development Indicators, World Bank 2011
[a]International Monetary Fund, Economic Outlook

lower during the first half of the 2000s. The rate of inflation reached its lowest level in the first half of the 2000s (3.93 %) and increased to 8 % in its last half (Table 2.2).

On the external front, the performance is mixed. Trade as a ratio of GDP has increased steadily from around 14 % in the 1980s to over 45 % during 2005–2010. Similarly, the total foreign exchange reserve in terms of months of imports has also increased steadily from around 5 months in the 1980s to over 8 months during the 2000s to over a year now. However, current account deficit as a ratio of GDP has been negative and deteriorated during the last half of the 2000s. The growth experience of India's economy over the past few decades has been well elaborated with great economic insights by prominent studies like Ahluwalia (2002), Panagariya (2004), Virmani (2004), Bosworth et al. (2007), and Acharya (2009), among others. Most of the studies have highlighted the positive impact of economic reforms, which has led to dent poverty levels; a few have lamented India's gradualist approach to reforms and delay in implementing the reform measures announced.

2.3.2 *Macroeconomic Performance of Pakistan*

Pakistan is the second largest economy and second populous country in South Asia. In terms of population, Pakistan is the sixth largest country in the world, and it is the second largest Muslim country after Indonesia. Pakistan's GDP (at 2000 price) increased from around $32 billion in the first half of the 1980s to $106 billion during the last half of the 2000s. In 2010, Pakistan's economy was the 47th largest in the world in nominal terms and 27th largest in PPP terms.

The GDP share of Pakistan in South Asia increased from 13 % in the early 1980s to over 14 % in the first half of the 1990s; it declined to 11 % during 2005–2010. Economic growth was better in the 1980s than in the 1990s or 2000s. The GDP growth rate in Pakistan was 7.3 % during 1980–1984 but 3.41 % in the first half of the 1990s.[20] However, the growth rate recovered moderately to around 4.5 % in the 2000s. As a result, the GDP share of Pakistan in South Asia increased from 13 % in the early 1980s to over 14 % in the first half of the 1990s; it declined to 11 % during 2005–2010.

The industrial and services sectors have largely contributed to the deceleration of growth in the 1990s and 2000s. The former grew by an average annual rate of 8 % in the 1980s, slowed to an average of 4.5 % in the 1990s, and thereafter increased to 5.7 % in the 2000s. Similarly, the services sector also slowed from an average growth of 7.5 % in the first half of the 1980s to 6 % in the second half of the 1980s and further to 4.5 % in the 1990s. In the 2000s, the services sector growth

[20] The economy recovered during the 1980s via a policy of deregulation as well as an increased inflow of foreign aid and remittances from expatriate workers.

remained low compared to the 1980s with the average of 5 %.[21] The slowdown in GDP growth rate over 1990–2010 compared to the 1980s was attributed to internal conflict, serious lapses in implementation of stabilisation policies and structural reforms, adverse law and order political instability, social insecurity, and the interrupted business climate (Sahoo 2006, 2012).

The sectoral contribution to GDP has undergone significant change over time in Pakistan. Like India, the share of agricultural sector's contribution to GDP has come down by around 10 % during 1980–2010. The share of both industry and services has increased by the same percentage. Table 2.3 reveals that the industrial sector's contribution to GDP (on a 5-year average scale) increased gradually, increasing from a 23 % in 1980–1984 to 26 % in 2005–2010, except the period of the 1990s. Similarly, the services sector's contribution to GDP has demonstrated an increasing trend over time, increasing from 47 % in 1980–1984 to 52.8 % in 2006–2010. A similar trend is also shown for the industrial sector's contribution to GDP over the last three decades. As a whole, in Pakistan, the sectoral contribution to GDP has moved away from the agricultural sector to the industrial and services sectors.

Further, both domestic savings and capital formation as a percentage of GDP have shown a volatile trend over 1980–2010 compared to India. The gross capital formation as a ratio of GDP has remained constant during the 1980s (17.5 %) and declined in the second half of the 1990s and early 2000s. However, domestic savings also show an upward trend from the early 1980s until the last half of the 2000s. The current savings rate and capital formation of Pakistan are much lower than India. Moreover, it is important to notice that the savings–investment gap has declined over time except in the last half of the 2000s. On the fiscal front, Pakistan has done well compared to India. However, the inflation rate was high during the 1980s and 1990s; it was well above 12 % in recent times.

Pakistan performed worse than India on the external. Trade openness also demonstrates a moderate level of economic openness (expressed as trade over GDP) over time; it stagnated at 34–37 % in the three-decade study period. On the other hand, Pakistan has had a persistent current account deficit, except for the period of 2000–2004. Similarly, the State Bank of Pakistan's foreign exchange reserve, which fluctuated widely in the 1990s and could finance only 2.90 months' imports in the 2000s, can finance less than 2 months' imports. Short-term debt as ratio of total foreign exchange reserve was very high during the 1990s. Low foreign exchange reserve, high foreign debt, and a continual current account deficit created a macroeconomic imbalance for Pakistan during the 1990s and 2000s. Over the years, various empirical studies such as Kemal (2004), Zaidi (1994), and Looney (2012) have tried to explain the economic strengths and weaknesses of Pakistan's economy.

[21] A steady decline in gross capital from the second half of the 1990s also contributed to the slowdown in economic growth.

Table 2.3 Key macroeconomic indicators for Pakistan

Indicators	1980–1984	1985–1989	1990–1994	1995–1999	2000–2004	2005–2010
Population (in millions)	87.48	100.00	113.63	128.52	144.99	166
GDP growth (%)	7.30	6.43	4.54	3.41	4.34	4.81
GDP (2000 constant US$, billion)	31.4	42.9	55.5	67	79.3	106
Share in South Asia (%)	13	14	14	13	12	11
Per capita GDP (2000 constant US$)	363	419	470	499	527	637
Agriculture, growth rate (%)	2.92	5.9	3.95	5	2.1	3.75
Agriculture, value added (% of GDP)	30.02	27.08	25.73	26.53	23.78	20.92
Industry, value added (% of GDP)	22.91	23.62	24.93	23.80	24.42	26.3
Industry, growth rate (%)	8.6	7.8	5.5	3.9	5.7	5.8
Manufacturing, value added (% of GDP)	15.52	16.45	16.97	15.91	15.77	18.4
Services, value added (% of GDP)	47.07	49.30	49.34	49.66	51.80	52.8
Services, growth rate (%)	7.5	6.04	5.06	4	4.62	5.4
Gross capital formation (% of GDP)	18.72	18.63	19.72	17.75	16.8	19.90
Gross domestic savings (% of GDP)	7.37	9.26	15.42	14.83	16.68	12.78
Inflation rate (CPI, %)	8.43	6.10	10.54	8.89	4.23	12.07
Fiscal deficit (% of GDP)[a]			−5.7	−5.3	−2.6	−5.1
Current account balance (% of GDP)	−2.63	−2.82	−3.98	−4.07	2.25	−4.53
Total forex reserves in months of imports	3.04	1.90	1.72	1.47	5.10	3.89
Trade over GDP (%)	34.44	34.59	37.29	35.53	30.44	35.27
Manufacturing exports (% merchandise exports)	60.4	70.6	81.5	84.6	84.6	76.8
Short-term debt (% of total reserves)	47.2	158.7	216.2	140.1	28.2	12.4

Source: World Development Indicators, World Bank 2011
[a]International Monetary Fund, Economic Outlook

2.3.3 *Macroeconomic Performances of Bangladesh*

Bangladesh is the third largest economy and third populous country in South Asia after India and Pakistan. The size of Bangladesh's economy (at 2000 price) increased from around \$22 billion in the first half of the 1980s to an average of \$72 billion during the last half of the 2000s. Bangladesh won independence from Pakistan in 1971 through a war that had major impact on institutional and physical capital. The economy was ravaged by acute food shortages and famines during the early years. According to Faaland and Parkinson (1976), Bangladesh was designated a 'test case' for development.

Table 2.4 provides the macroeconomic performance of Bangladesh over 1980–2010 and indicates that its GDP growth rate was constant at an average of 3.2 % during the 1980s. However, it increased to 4.6 % in the first half of the 1990s and further to 5.01 % in the second half of the 1990s. In the 2000s, the GDP growth rate of Bangladesh improved to above 6 %. In spite of some fluctuations in agricultural growth rate, the volatility in long-term GDP growth in Bangladesh is found to be remarkably low among developing countries (World Bank 2003).

Therefore, growth of GDP has been accelerating in each successive period since the latter half of the 1980s. The relatively low GDP growth rate during the 1980s was caused by low growth in the agricultural and services sectors. The higher industrial and services growth are also reflected in their increasing sectoral contribution to GDP. For instance, the industrial sector's contribution to GDP increased from 21 % in 1980–1984 to above 28 % in the 2005–2010 and by over 7 % during 1980–2010. Similarly, the manufacturing value added as a percentage of GDP increased from 14 % in the 1980s to above 17 % in the 2000s. On the other hand, the services sector now contributes over 52 % to the GDP. Therefore, like India and Pakistan, Bangladesh is now also led by the industrial and services sectors. Although Bangladesh has achieved consistent higher growth over time, its per capita income remains quite low. The per capita income of Bangladesh at 2000 price increased from US\$257 in the first half of 1980–1984 to over US\$330 during 1990–1995 and further to over US\$496 during the last half of the 2000s.

The higher GDP growth rate in the 1990s and 2000s resulted from the higher savings rates, higher capital formation, lower level of inflation, and higher trade growth. The average gross domestic savings rate in the period of 1980–1984 was only 6.28 % of GDP; it increased to 15 % in the second half of the 1990s and further to 17.4 % in the first half of the 2000s (Table 2.4). In fact, domestic savings rate in Bangladesh is second highest after India.

Similarly, gross capital formation steadily increased from around 16 % in the 1980s to above 24 % in the last half of the 2000s. The savings–investment gap[22] was higher during the 1980s—10.27 % of GDP in 1980–1984 and 7.21 % of GDP in

[22] The savings–investment gap is calculated here by deducting the gross capital formation (percentage of GDP) from the gross capital formation (percentage of GDP).

Table 2.4 Key macroeconomic indicators for Bangladesh (5-year average)

Indicators	1980–1984	1985–1989	1990–1994	1995–1999	2000–2004	2005–2010
Population (in millions)	85.1	97.4	110	122	136.3	144.7
GDP growth (%)	3.24	3.20	4.60	5.01	5.43	6.16
GDP (2000 constant US$, billion)	22	26.3	32	40.4	52.2	72
Share in South Asia (%)	9.2	8.5	8	7.7	7.7	7.1
Per capita GDP (2000 constant US$)	257.8	270	291	330	388	496
Agriculture, value added (% of GDP)	31.48	31.71	28.38	25.89	23.03	19.2
Agriculture, growth rate (%)	2.66	0.56	3.5	3.35	3.5	4.0
Industry, value added (% of GDP)	21.13	21.20	22.76	25.11	26.10	28.2
Industry, growth rate (%)	3.44	5.68	6.9	7.18	7.6	7.70
Manufacturing, value added (% of GDP)	14.05	13.47	14.12	15.62	15.73	17.5
Services, value added (% of GDP)	47.39	47.09	48.86	49.00	50.87	52.6
Services, growth rate (%)	3.9	3.66	3.8	4.7	5.5	6.5
Gross domestic savings (% of GDP)	6.28	9.20	11.98	14.63	17.88	17.4
Gross capital formation (% of GDP)	16.55	16.41	17.52	20.73	23.34	24.4
Inflation (%)	13.38	8.84	4.89	6.50	4.48	7.55
Trade over GDP (%)	20.27	18.19	20.89	30.29	34.79	44.8
Fiscal deficit (% of GDP)[a]	−7.4	−5.9	0.3	−2.1	−3.4	−3.4
Current account balance (% of GDP)	−2.90	−2.24	0.23	−1.23	−0.09	1.75
Total forex reserves in months of imports	1.44	2.35	4.81	2.80	2.23	3.3
Manufacturing exports (% merchandise exports)	64	72	83	90	92	88
Short-term debt (% of total reserves)	74.1	18.5	13	10	25.6	27

Source: World Development Indicators, World Bank 2011
[a]International Monetary Fund, Economic Outlook

1985–1989—than in the 1990s and the first half of the 2000s. This indicates domestic savings are inadequate to finance domestic investment.

Inflation was higher during the first and second halves of the 1980s than in the first and second halves of the 1990s and 2000s. Moreover, a lower fiscal deficit as a ratio of GDP in the 1990s and 2000s accompanied the lower inflation rate. In fact, compared to other countries in South Asia, Bangladesh had a budget surplus during 1990–1994.

Trade has contributed significantly to GDP. Total trade as a percentage of GDP increased from around 20 % during 1980–1984 to 30 % during 1990–1994 and further to 44.8 % during 2004–2010. The current account balance improved steadily in the 1990s and 2000s. The foreign exchange reserve increased from 1.44 months in 1980–1984 to 4.81 months in 1990–1994, declined to 2.33 months during 2000–2004, and increased to 3.3 months.[23] More importantly, external vulnerability represented by short-term debt also shows constant improvement over time (Table 2.4). Therefore, the wide-ranging policy reforms since the beginning in the 1990s have positive impact on the economic growth of Bangladesh.

2.3.4 Macroeconomic Performances of Sri Lanka

Sri Lanka, a small island country situated to the southern tip of India, became independent in 1948 from the British government. It is the 4th largest economy in GDP terms in South Asia. From US$7 billion in the early 1980s, GDP in 2000 constant prices increased to US$10.8 billion in the early 1990s and to US$23.3 billion US$ during 2005–2010. Sri Lanka's GDP share declined steadily from 3 % in 1980–1984 to 2.7 % during 1990–1994 and further to 2.3 % in the last half of the 2000s. However, its per capita income is the highest in South Asia—it rose from US $463 (at 2000 prices) over 1980–1984 to over US$613 during 1990–1995 and further to over US$1,146 during the latter half of the 2000s.

The internal and external shocks the country faced made its pattern of economic growth irregular. Average economic growth was better in the first half of the 1980s than in the last half (Table 2.5)—due to civil unrest during 1987–1989. However, average economic growth increased since the 1990s, except for 2000–2004 due to external shocks. Over 2005–2010, GDP growth increased by over 6 %—higher than in the 1980s. Per capita income in Sri Lanka increased from US$257 (at 2000 prices) during 1980–1984 to over US$330 during 1990–1995 and further to over 496 US$ during the last half of the 2000s.

The services sector has been the highest contributor to GDP in Sri Lanka over the past three decades. Its contribution increased from 44.98 % in 1980–1984 to 57.8 % in 2005–2010 (Table 2.5). Likewise, both the manufacturing and industry

[23] The increase in foreign exchange reserve in Bangladesh is due mainly to higher inflow of remittance.

Table 2.5 Key macroeconomic indicators for Sri Lanka (5-year average)

Indicators	1980–1984	1985–1989	1990–1994	1995–1999	2000–2004	2005–2010
Population (in millions)	15.38	16.45	17.52	18.36	19.01	20.0
GDP growth (%)	5.12	3.17	5.58	4.94	3.96	6.36
GDP (2000 constant US$)	7.1	8.8	10.8	14	17.1	23.3
Share in South Asia (%)	3	2.8	2.7	2.7	2.5	2.3
Per capita GDP (2000 constant US$)	463	528	613	763	892	1,146
Agriculture, value added (% of GDP)	27.71	26.74	25.47	21.82	16.00	12.3
Agriculture, growth rate (%)	3.44	1.14	3.4	1.9	0.56	4.9
Industry, value added (% of GDP)	27.31	26.73	25.79	26.94	27.83	29.9
Industry, growth rate (%)	3.76	4.8	7.2	6.3	3.3	7
Manufacturing, value added (% of GDP)	15.46	15.33	15.10	16.25	17.71	18.55
Services, value added (% of GDP)	44.98	46.52	48.74	51.24	56.17	57.8
Services, growth rate (%)	7.3	2.8	5.9	5.7	5.4	6.4
Gross fixed capital formation (% of GDP)	28.80	22.91	23.97	25.25	22.56	27.08
Gross domestic savings (% of GDP)	12.11	10.43	13.44	17.51	16.08	17.17
Inflation rate (CPI, %)	17.1	8.56	13.0	9.46	8.8	11.55
Fiscal deficit (% of GDP)[a]	NA	NA	−7.7	−7.6	−8.44	−7.62
Trade over GDP (%)	73.79	62.17	73.04	79.58	80.14	63.0
Current account balance (% of GDP)	−9.37	−5.99	−5.03	−3.69	−2.53	−4.2
Total forex reserves in months of imports	1.97	1.54	3.10	3.47	2.56	3.57
Manufacturing exports (% merchandise exports)	27.4	48.8	69.8	73.8	73.8	69.5
Short-term debt (% of total reserves)	66.7	112.8	43	30.7	41	42

Source: World Development Indicators, World Bank 2011
[a]International Monetary Fund, Economic Outlook

value added as a percentage of GDP rose over the past three decades, except for 1990–1994. In fact, Sri Lanka had the highest industrial sector's contribution to GDP in South Asia. Recently, its industrial value addition to GDP increased to 29.61 %. In contrast, the agricultural sector's contribution to GDP shows a significant reduction (around 15 %) in the past three decades. For instance, in 1980–1984, the agricultural sector contributed 27.71 % of GDP, but it reduced to 12.3 % in 2005–2010. Therefore, the services and industrial sectors have taken over from agriculture to lead Sri Lanka's economy now, as in Bangladesh, India, and Pakistan.

Other macroeconomic indicators such as gross fixed capital and savings show a mixed trend. For example, gross fixed capital formation as a ratio of GDP has declined from the peak of the early 1980s (29 %) drastically in the later periods because of the ethnic war that continued until 2002. Sri Lanka has been unable to return to its early 1980s peak. Besides, the savings–investment gap in Sri Lanka over the past three decades was very high over 10 % on average and the highest in South Asia, except during 2000–2004. Inflation rate and fiscal deficit were high over three decades in Sri Lanka; this performance is not better than in India and Pakistan.

On the external front, the performance of Sri Lanka is comparable to other South Asian countries. For instance, trade openness ratio for Sri Lanka shows a fluctuating trend over time although it has remained very high. Trade openness ratio which was very high in the early 1980s (74 %) declined to 62 % in the last half of the 1980s, but thereafter it increased to 80 % in the period 2000–2004. In recent times, it has again declined to an average of 63 % of GDP. Further, Sri Lanka has had a persistent current account deficit and low foreign exchange reserves. Both high current account deficit and fiscal deficit have been the major contributors of high inflation rate in Sri Lanka.

2.3.5 Macroeconomic Performances of Nepal

Nepal is a landlocked country between China in the north and India in the south. It is one of the least developed countries in the world, with an unemployment rate of 46 % and a poverty rate of 24.7 % (CIA Fact Sheet 2011). Nepal is predominately an agriculture-based economy, although the agricultural sector's share has come down from 61 % in the 1980s to 35 % during 2005–2010 and by 26 % overall in the past three decades. In 2000, GDP in constant prices increased from an average US $2.3 billion in 1980–1984 to an average US$3.4 billion during the early 1990s and, further, to US$7.2 billion on average in the last half of 2005–2010. Nepal is the poorest in South Asian per capita income terms. Real per capita income increased from US$145 in the beginning of the 1980s to above US$210 during the last half of the 1990s and further to above $251 during 2005–2010. The macroeconomic performance of Nepal is presented in Table 2.6.

Economic growth was better in Nepal than in other South Asian countries over 1985–1995. During the 1990s, GDP growth rate was higher in Nepal than in the 1980s and 2000s. Its GDP growth rate was 3.95 % in the first half of the 2000s—far

Table 2.6 Key macroeconomic indicators for Nepal (5-year average)

Indicators	1980–1984	1985–1989	1990–1994	1995–1999	2000–1904	2005–1910
Population (in millions)	15.80	17.79	20.08	22.7	26.1	28.63
GDP growth (%)	3.30	4.89	5.44	4.25	3.95	4.23
GDP (2000 constant US billion $)	2.3	2.9	3.7	4.7	5.8	7.2
Share in South Asia (%)	0.98	0.95	0.95	0.91	0.87	0.71
Per capita GDP (2000 constant US$)	148	165	187	210	220	251
Agriculture, value added (% of GDP)	61.00	51.04	45.80	41.18	38.73	34.5
Agriculture, growth rate (%)	3.8	3.4	2.8	2.4	4.1	2.7
Industry, value added (% of GDP)	12.51	15.90	19.28	22.57	19.64	16.85
Industry, growth rate (%)	4.4	11.1	9.2	5.4	3.4	2.4
Manufacturing, value added (% of GDP)	4.44	6.04	8.00	9.53	8.85	7.5
Services, value added (% of GDP)	26.50	33.07	34.92	36.25	41.63	48.6
Services, growth rate (%)	2.5	4.56	6.8	5.5	3.8	5.35
Gross capital formation (% of GDP)	18.2	21.5	20.8	24.6	22.6	29.8
Gross domestic savings (% of GDP)	10.07	11.89	9.74	14.28	12.01	9.5
Inflation (%)	10.55	11.13	11.36	7.91	3.35	8.8
Fiscal deficit (% of GDP)[a]	NA	NA	NA	NA	−1.81	1.20
Trade over GDP (%)	30.97	32.68	41.24	58.25	49.21	46.20
Current account balance (% of GDP)	−3.21	−5.54	−7.16	−5.23	0.49	1.91
Total forex reserves in months of imports	5.66	3.73	6.08	5.16	7.34	6.62
Manufacturing exports (% merchandise exports)	47	68	84.6	74.4	72.2	69.2
Short-term debt (% of total reserves)	9	2.5	1.4	1.2	1.2	1.6

Source: World Development Indicators, World Bank 2011
[a]International Monetary Fund, Economic Outlook

below that in the 1990s. Although it has increased to over 4 % in 2005–2010, it is lower than that of India, Bangladesh, Pakistan, and Sri Lanka. While agricultural growth has been stable, the growth rate of both industry and services fluctuated over time. The average agricultural growth rate, which was 3.8 % in the first half of the 1980s, dropped to 2.7 % in the last half of the 2000s. On the other hand, the average growth rate of industry and services peaked in the last and first half of the 1980s and 1990s, respectively—although both sectors have grown much more than the agricultural sector over three decades. In terms of contribution to GDP, agriculture's share declined significantly, while that of services increased by the same margin. Industry share fluctuated between 12 and 19 % over the period 1980–2010.

Likewise, the savings rate in Nepal is the lowest among the economies in South Asia. It declined from a high of 14 % in the second half of the 1990s on a 5-year average basis to only 9.5 % of GDP now. On the other hand, gross capital formation remained quite high compared to savings rate. Average gross capital formation as ratio of GDP increased from around 20 % in the 1980s to 22 % in the 1990s and further to above 29 % during 2005–2010. Like other countries in South Asia, Nepal has a high savings–investment gap—almost 11 % during 2005–2010. On the other hand, it demonstrates the lowest inflation rate and fiscal deficit among South Asian countries over time.

On the external front, Nepal has performed better than Pakistan and like Sri Lanka, India, and Bangladesh. Nepal is better than Pakistan in trade openness. Its average trade ratio increased from 31 % during the first half of the 1980s to above 58 % in the second half of the 1990s but declined during the current decade. At present, Nepal's total trade represents 46.20 % of its GDP, which is higher than that of Bangladesh, India, and Pakistan. Its foreign exchange reserve is comfortable, as is the ratio of its short-term debt to foreign exchange reserve.

2.4 Concluding Remarks

Overall, we find that Bangladesh, Sri Lanka, and India had higher GDP growth rates during the reform period compared to the 1980s. Both Pakistan and Nepal had higher growth during the 1980s. While the higher growth in India during 1991–2002 was accompanied by substantial growth in the services sector and a marginal improvement of the agricultural sector, the growth in Bangladesh, Sri Lanka, and Nepal was supported by both higher industrial and services sector growth. However, per capita income growth also slowed down in Pakistan during the 1990s, whereas it improved in India, Bangladesh, Sri Lanka, and Nepal. Other important macro indicators like gross domestic savings and gross domestic capital formation improved in all these countries except Pakistan. Following economic reforms, particularly trade reforms in these countries during the 1990s, export and import growth has substantially improved. Further, India, Bangladesh, Sri Lanka, and Nepal have improved considerably on the external sector front such as the current account balance, capital account, foreign exchange reserves, and overall improvement in BOP during the post-reform period.

There has also been an improvement in most of the macro indicators except the fiscal deficit, on both the domestic and external sector front. Indeed, the South Asian region has been one of the fastest-growing regions in the world in recent years. The above analysis suggests that with the exception of Pakistan, the South Asian countries have registered higher trade growth during the 1990s than the 1980s. Though Pakistan failed to accelerate its export growth in the 1990s, it has managed to maintain a constant rise of exports in absolute value. All the countries except Pakistan have also experienced higher economic growth during the 1990s, with more open macroeconomic policies emphasising export promotion.

In the second half of the twentieth century, South Asia's economic growth lagged far behind that of Southeast Asia and Northeast Asia. The lesser performance of South Asian economies is attributed to inward looking policies, statist policies, poor economic management, and political drawbacks. An eminent economist described India's slow growth of the past as 'the Hindu rate of growth', implying that there were inherent weaknesses in India that did not enable it to move faster. India was also characterised as 'the sleeping Elephant' in contrast to the 'Asian Tigers'.

This changed when India and other South Asian economies adopted outward looking economic policies. Sri Lanka was the earliest to undertake structural reforms in 1977. India's later move in the 1990s changed India's growth momentum. India undertook significant economic reforms and opened its economy. The economic growth increased rapidly to reach 10 %. This uplifted the growth momentum of the region, and South Asia was viewed as the new and emerging growth centre together with China. However, the global slowdown and the lack of a new wave of economic reforms have retarded growth in the region and in India in particular. One of the glaring weaknesses of India's economic growth was the continued persistence of a high level of poverty. Even Pakistan, Bangladesh, and Nepal initiated wide-ranging reforms to enhance their growth and development.

Most studies on South Asia in recent times, including by the World Bank, are confined to economic policy measures affecting the growth of the region. In fact, the factors holding back economic growth in South Asia are broader issues of political economy. State control of many economic activities requires to be relinquished. Loss-making state enterprises need to be reformed or privatised. More incentive structures for investment are needed. In brief, second and third waves of reforms are needed in South Asian countries to release their growth potential.

There is serious political opposition and ideological resistance to undertake pragmatic economic policies. Nepal, for instance, is unable to exploit its vast hydropower generation potential due to political protest. Ethnic and religious conflicts continue to distract the state from economic policy changes. The lack of law and order and the rule of law deter foreign investment.

Economic growth in South Asia can be sustained only with reform of these political economy factors that have a direct bearing on economic policies and performance. This is especially pertinent for both Sri Lanka and Pakistan. It is evident from the analysis above that the success of the economic reform measures in South Asia is widespread. Even though the contribution of agriculture to GDP across the region has declined, the industrial and services sectors have continued to drive the growth prospects of the region. Despite the many challenges faced by the region, there is enormous potential and the future prospects look bright. South Asia's growth trajectory is all set to be one of the defining stories of the world economy in the near future.

References

Acharya S (2009) India's growth: past and future. In: Dinello N, Wang S (eds) China, India and beyond: development drivers and limitations. Edward Elgar, Cheltenham

Ahluwalia MS (2002) Economic reforms in India since 1991: has gradualism worked? J Econ Perspect 16(3):67–88

Ahluwalia J, Little IMD (eds) (1998) India's economic reforms and development essay for Manmohan Singh. Oxford University Press, Delhi

Ahmed S (2002) The political economy of reforms in South Asia: Bangladesh and Pakistan, South Asia Region, Internal discussion paper No. 183. World Bank, Washington, DC

Athukorala PC, Jayasuriya S (2004) Complementarity of trade and FDI liberalization in industrial growth: lessons from Sri Lanka, ASARC working papers 2004–10. Australian National University, Australia South Asia Research Centre, Canberra

Bandara SJ, McGillivray M (1998) Trade policy reforms in South Asia. World Econ 21(7):881–896

Bhagwati J, Srinivasan TN (1975) Foreign trade regimes and economic development: India. Columbia University Press, New York

Bosworth B, Collins S, Virmani A (2007) Sources of growth in the Indian economy. India Policy Forum 2006 3(1):1–69

Central Intelligence Agency (2011) The world fact book-Nepal, Office of Public Affairs, Washington, DC

Dornbusch R (1992) The case for trade liberalization in developing countries. J Econ Perspect 6(1):69–85

Faaland J, Parkinson JR (1976) Bangladesh: the test case of development. C. Hurst, London

Francois JF, van Meijl H, van Tongeren F (2003) Trade Liberalisation and developing countries under Doha Round, CEPR discussion paper No. 4032, August. Available at SSRN: http://ssrn.com/abstract=458960

Goldman Sachs (2007) "BRICS and BEYOND" – Goldman Sachs study of BRIC and N11 nations, 23 November 2007. New York City, NY, USA

Hussain I (2004) Financial sector reforms in Pakistan. Paper presented at Italy-Pakistan trade and investment conference, Rome

Joshi V (1998) India's economic reforms: progress, problems, prospects. Oxford Dev Stud 26(3):333–350

Kemal AR (2004) Pakistan's economy: performances and future prospects. South Asian J Apr/June (4)

Krueger AO (1974) The political economy of the rent-seeking society. Am Econ Rev 64:291–303

Laird S, Fernandez de Cordoba SF, Vanzetti D (2003) Market access proposals for non-agricultural products. UNCTAD, Geneva

Looney R (2012) Shifting development paradigms: sequencing Pakistan's new growth framework. J South Asian Middle East Stud 35(2):1–47

Mahmood Z (1999) Pakistan: the impact of economic liberalization on poverty. Sustainable Development Policy Institute, Islamabad

Mahmood, T., Hafeez ur Rehman, & Rauf, S. A. (2008). Evaluation of macro economic policies of Pakistan (1950–2008). *Journal of Political Studies, 14,* 57–75.

Nataraj G, Sahoo P (2006a) A decade of trade reforms in India (co-author: Nataraj G). Synergy, Delhi

Nataraj G, Sahoo P (2006b) India's external sector: performance and prospects. ICFAI J Appl Econ V(3):61–67

Nataraj G, Sahoo P (2007) India and WTO: regionalism and multilateralism. South Asian J (15), 184–195

Panagariya A (2004). India in the 1980s and 1990s: a triumph of reforms. Economic and Political Weekly, June 19, 29

Rodrick D, Subramanian A (2004) From Hindu growth to productivity surge: the mystery of the Indian growth transition, NBER working paper, no w10376. National Bureau of Economic Research, Cambridge, MA

Sahoo P (2006) FDI in South Asia: trends, policy, impact and determinants. Asian Development Bank Institute discussion paper series, No. 56. Asian Development Bank Institute, Tokyo

Sahoo P (2012) Foreign direct investment in India: unfinished agenda. In: Philippa D (ed) Economic reform processes in South Asia: toward policy efficiency. Routledge, New York, pp 109–136

Srinivasan TN (2002) Foreign trade policies and India's development. In: Kapila U (ed) Indian economy since independence. Academic Foundation, New Delhi

Tendulkar SD, Bhavani TA (2007) Understanding reforms. Oxford University Press, New York

Virmani A (2004) Foreign direct investment reforms, Occasional policy papers, Indian council for Research on International Economic Relations, New Delhi

World Bank (2003) World development report 1991. Oxford University Press for the World Bank, New York

World Bank (1997) World development report 1997: the state in a changing world. Oxford University Press for the World Bank, Washington, DC

World Bank (1999) Poverty reduction and the World Bank: progress in fiscal. World Bank, Washington, DC

World Bank (2011) World development indicator, 2011. World Bank, Washington, DC

World Economic Forum (2010) Global competitiveness report 2010–11

World Trade Organization (2012) Tariff profiles. United Nations, Geneva, Switzerland

Zaidi SA (1994) Structural adjustment program and Pakistan: external influences or internal acquiescence. Pak J Appl Econ 10(1 & 2):21–46

Chapter 3
Foreign Direct Investment Policy in South Asia

3.1 Introduction

South Asian countries had a restrictive regime in the early years of their independence, and it is only in the last decade that they have opened up and made their FDI policy environments conducive to foreign investment. Initially, FDI was allowed in a restrictive manner and on mutually advantageous terms with the majority stake held by domestic firms. However, all five South Asian countries tried to encourage FDI more aggressively in the 1990s, by making changes in their macroeconomic policies along with trade and FDI policies. At the same time, the inception of liberalisation policies and more integration of South Asian economies led to conducive environment for businesses from the developed world to take advantage of the South Asian economies. FDI is a key driver of a country's socio-economic development. The developing countries have a common industrial plan to attract the FDI to their countries, and South Asian countries have been promoting themselves for more FDI. Undoubtedly, FDI is a vital requirement for sustained economic growth in South Asia. Expectations of significant future domestic demand, especially in countries with large populations such as those in South Asia, can result in FDI from foreign countries establishing large production bases for these domestic markets. Such FDI will expand product variety and consumer choices and promote technology transfers and knowledge spillovers through forward and backward linkages in the host economies.[1] Realising the potential of receiving huge FDI inflows, South Asian countries have resorted to market reforms to attract FDI in the last couple of decades.

Most of the South Asian economies were closed economies until the late 1970s and early 1980s. However, a shift in economic policy began in South Asia in the 1980s when Bangladesh and Sri Lanka started reforming their economies to create more space for the domestic private sector and external competition. However, the real changes in South Asia occurred in the 1990s when even India was swept along by the changes in economic policy through liberalisation and integration with

[1] ADB (2007), South Asia Economic Report: FDI in South Asia.

P. Sahoo et al., *Foreign Direct Investment in South Asia*,
DOI 10.1007/978-81-322-1536-3_3, © Springer India 2014

the rest of the world. The important policy change with respect to India included adopting an FDI policy environment conducive to foreign investment. Initially, FDI was allowed in a restrictive way on mutually advantageous terms with the majority of stake held by domestic firms but things have progressively opened up with time (Sahoo 2006).

Subsequently, FDI flows to South Asian countries have been increasing in recent years. Though India is the most dominant destination of FDI in South Asia, Sri Lanka has the highest FDI intensity. Despite its relatively slow growth in FDI inflows, South Asia has witnessed much greater expansion in its share in global and Asian FDI stocks due to sharp rise in India's share. Further, in order to expand the growth of inward FDI, South Asia will have to capture the greater part of Inter-Asian FDI flows especially from China and ASEAN as well to be able to promote inter-SAARC FDI inflows (Mehta 2007). In SAARC, FDI from outside is more important than intra-regional investment in most countries (the only exception is Nepal, where Indian investments dominate).

South Asian countries have not only reformed their economies but have been aggressively negotiating and signing RTAs and investment treaties to attract FDI. India has bilateral tax treaties with 58 countries, Bangladesh with 20 countries, Sri Lanka with 39 countries, Pakistan with 23 countries, and Nepal with 3 countries. In case of agreements of double taxation avoidance, India has such agreements with 65 countries, Bangladesh with 20 countries, Sri Lanka 52 countries, Pakistan 52 countries, and Nepal with 3 countries.

According to World Investment Report 2011, FDI to South Asia declined to $32 billion, reflecting a 31 % slide in inflows to India and a 14 % drop in investment to Pakistan, the two largest recipients of FDI in the subcontinent. In India, the setback in attracting FDI was partly due to macroeconomic concerns, such as a high current account deficit and inflation, as well as to delays in the approval of large FDI projects. These factors are hindering the Indian government's efforts to boost investment, including the planned $1.5 trillion investment in infrastructure between 2007 and 2017. In contrast, inflows to Bangladesh have increased by nearly 30 % to $913 million; the country is becoming a major low-cost production location in South Asia.

Institutional reforms and incentive policies in South Asia to promote FDI are not unique for each host country. The most common are partial or complete exemption from corporate taxes and import duties. These policies and reforms are typically the result of formal legislation, which apply to all foreign corporations with few restrictions. These restrictions vary considerably across South Asian countries. In many cases, they require multinationals to establish production facilities in the host country in specified line of activities, such as export processing zone (EPZs), and to export output-embodying inputs imported duty-free. Direct subsidies and other types of concessions are often negotiated between multinational firms and host governments on a case-by-case basis.

Overall, there has been a complete turnaround in FDI policy, from closed to an open-door policy, in South Asian countries over time. Robust economic growth with impressive showing of the services sector and exports, the region's large domestic markets, and positive perception of foreign investors has induced FDI inflows into the region. However, the level of FDI inflow into South Asia is still low compared to other Asian regions and emerging market economies beyond Asia. This is considered the result of poor business climate, poor infrastructure, restrictive labour policy and labour unrest, political uncertainties and civil conflicts, weak regulatory systems, and rampant corruption. However, the fact that region has unlimited potential is evident. If the South Asian region works towards achieving macroeconomic and political stability, institutes proper regulatory and policy frameworks for foreign investment, promotes infrastructure development, facilitates the development of small and medium enterprises, enhances skill of the labour force with proper education and training, and facilitates greater regional cooperation in terms of promotion of trade and investment, it will not only help the region attract more FDI but also help the region sustain its current momentum of economic growth. In this chapter, an attempt has been made to briefly review the FDI policies of the five South Asian countries and present future prospects of FDI into South Asia. A summary of FDI policy frameworks in South Asia is presented in Table 3.A.1.

3.2 FDI Policy Framework in India

3.2.1 Evolution of FDI Policy in India

The FDI environment in India has undergone a sea change since the inception of economic reforms in 1991. The positive changes can be particularly attributed to the evolving policy framework. The government now acts as a 'facilitator' of private investment by creating an enabling environment. It bridges the gaps in critical infrastructure to encourage investment and acts as a 'partner' to the private sector in 'public–private partnerships' (PPP). There is a widely accepted view that FDI flows to India would accelerate over time given the positive medium to longer-term prospects for the economy. Forbes puts India at 77th place—ahead of China at 90th place—in its 2010 list of the best countries for business. Equally, the UN Conference on Trade and Development report *World Investment Prospects Survey* 2010–2012 and the AT Kearney FDI Confidence Index 2012 rate India as the second most promising country for investment and business. China is ranked first and Brazil third after India. However, India's recent progress on FDI has come with some amount of difficulty. India has had a fluctuating policy towards attracting FDI since 1948. Its initial favourable attitude to foreign investment was followed by a more restrictive phase and then, an effort to attract foreign investment in a more aggressive and welcoming manner. Overall, Indian policies towards foreign investment have been markedly gradualist.

The evolution of FDI in India has four phases. Phase one between 1948 and 1969 comprised a careful reception of foreign investment with a view to speedy industrialisation of the country. India ensured that regulation, ownership, and effective control remained in its hand. Objective was to create locational advantage with import substitution. The second five-year plan emphasised on establishment of heavy industry, and in the third five-year plan, government issued a list of industries in 1961 taking into account gap in capacity in relation to plan targets where foreign investment was welcomed. This included some industries that were earlier reserved for PSUs like drugs, aluminium, heavy electrical equipment, fertiliser, and synthetics. The response to the creation of localisation advantages led to jump in the share of manufacturing in the FDI stock to over 40 % from 20 % at the time of independence. In the course of this phase, the locational, ownership, and international advantage were considered necessary to make a transition to second phase.

In second phase 1969–1991, certain capabilities for process and product adaptation were built in the country and infant industry protection was put in place to protect domestic skills and capabilities from competition. Outflow because of remittance of dividend, profit, royalties, and technical fee abroad because of serving of FDI and technology imports from the earlier period had grown sharply and had become a significant proportion of the foreign exchange account of the country. All these factors forced the government to impose restrictions on the process of foreign collaboration approvals and adopted a more restrictive attitude towards FDI (Kidron 1965; Kumar 1987). Thus, a new agency FIB (Foreign Investment Board) was established in 1968 to deal with all cases involving foreign investment or collaboration up to 40 % foreign equity and above, and this was to be further screened by a cabinet committee. There were more liberal FDI policies towards technology transfer whereas the renewals of foreign collaboration were more restricted.

At the same time, FERA (Foreign Exchange Regulation Act) was enforced which required the foreign companies operating in India to register themselves as Indian companies with up to 40 % foreign equity. The 40 % was the maximum limit to dilute the foreign equity for Indian companies; but for the companies in high technology, tea plantation, export manufacturing, or high-priority companies, there was some relaxation (Kumar 1987, 1995; Sahoo 2006, 2012). FDI stock rise between 1974 and 1980 was only Rs. 163 million. The increase in overall FDI however marked the reorganisation that took place in the pattern of FDI in the country during the period. One striking trend was liquidation of FDI stock in non-manufacturing sector largely due to takeover by government in certain activities like general insurance companies in 1971 and takeover of the petroleum sector between 1974 and 1976. On the other hand, virtually all fresh inflows were directed to manufacturing sector. Within manufacturing sector, new inflows were directed to technology-intensive sectors such as electrical goods, machinery and machine tools, and chemical and allied products (in particular, chemicals and medicines and pharmaceuticals). The rise in importance of technology-intensive products in the FDI stock was at the expense of traditional consumer goods industries such as food and beverages, textile products, and other chemical products (Desai 1984; Kumar 1987, 1995).

In the late 1970s, the oil shock led to slowdown in manufacturing exports. A highly protected local market and growing dominance of multinational corporations in marketing ensured that Indian goods suffered from technological obsolescence and inferior quality of product. The government took steps in this regard by making policies liberal for import of technology and capital goods, reducing import restriction and tariffs, and encouraging the multinational corporations to set up export-oriented units in India (Desai 1984; Dasgupta and Siddharthan 1985; Kumar 1987, 1995). These steps were displayed in the policies taken in the 1980s (Kumar 1995). For instance, the policy statements of 1980 and 1982 spelled out liberal policies towards industrial licensing rule, a host of incentives, and exemption from foreign equity restrictions under FERA to 100 % export-oriented units. It was decided to set up four more EPZ in addition to the two existing ones, namely, those at Kendal (set up in 1965) and at Santa Cruz (set up in 1972) to attract MNEs to set up export-oriented units. The trade policies in this period gradually liberalised the imports of raw material and capital goods by gradually expanding the list of items in the Open General License (OGL). Between 1984 and 1985, 150 items and 200 types of capital goods were added to OGL list. Tariffs on imports of capital goods were also slashed. Imports of designs and drawings and capital goods were permitted under a liberalised Technical Development Fund Scheme.

Approach towards foreign licensing collaboration was made less restrictive. Tax rates on royalties were reduced from 40 to 30 % in 1986. A degree of flexibility was introduced in the policy concerning foreign equity participation, and exceptions from the general ceiling of 40 % on foreign equity were allowed on the merits of individual investment proposals. There were liberalised procedures for outward remittance of royalty, technical fee, and dividend. A 'fast channel' was set up in 1988 for expediting clearances of FDI proposals from major investing countries, namely, Japan, Germany, USA, and UK. Thus in the 1980s, important changes in the policy regimes existing in the country were fastened to enhance international competition of Indian companies. Increasing emphasis on international competitiveness made Indian enterprises to undertake strategic asset-seeking type of investments in trading and other services in industrialised countries (Dasgupta and Siddharthan 1985; Kumar 1987, 1995).

Thus, in the pre-liberalisation period, India followed a cautious and selective approach while formulating FDI policy in view of the dominance of 'import substitution policy of industrialisation'. With the objective of becoming 'self-reliant', there was a dual nature of policy intention—FDI through foreign collaboration was welcomed in the areas of high technology and high priorities to build national capacity and discouraged in low technology areas to protect and nurture domestic industries. The FDI policy prior to 1991 was characterised by de-licensing of some of the industrial rules and promotion of Indian manufacturing exports as well as emphasising on modernisation of industries through liberalised imports of capital goods and technology. This was supported by trade liberalisation measures in the form of tariff reduction and shifting of large number of items from import licensing to OGL.

Third phase, i.e. between 1991 and 2000, coincides with the inception of economic reforms by the Government of India. A positive and friendly FDI policy was a part of the government reform's agenda. During the period 1990–1992, there was severe balance of payment crisis, political uncertainty, and increase in India's external debt. As a result, credit rating agencies lowered India's rating in both long-term and short-term borrowing; India had difficulty in borrowing from the international market; and there was outflow of foreign currency deposits kept in India by non-resident Indians (NRIs). Rise in prices of petroleum due to the Gulf war led to virtual stoppage of remittance from Indian workers in the Gulf. India was on the verge of default in respect of external payment liability. Therefore, to tide over the crisis, India adapted a programme of macroeconomic stabilisation and structural adjustment supported by the IMF and World Bank. The industrial approval system in all industries was abolished except in 18 strategic or environmentally sensitive industries. In 34 high-priority industries, FDI up to 51 % was approved automatically if certain norms are satisfied. Trading companies engaged primarily in export activities were also allowed up to 51 % foreign equity. To attract FDI in the energy sector, 100 % foreign equity was permitted in the power generation. A new package for 100 % export-oriented projects and companies in EPZs was announced. The Foreign Investment Promotion Board (FIPB) was set up and authorised to provide a single window clearance by the Prime Minister's office to invite and felicitate investment in India by international companies. Existing companies were also allowed to raise foreign equity levels to 51 % for proposed expansion in priority industries. India became a signatory to the Convention of the Multilateral Investment Guarantee Agency (MIGA) (MIGA promotes FDI into developing countries by ensuring investors against political risk) (Reserve Bank of India (RBI) 2012).

During this phase, the Foreign Exchange Regulation Act of 1973 was amended and restrictions placed on foreign companies by the FERA were lifted. These relaxations and reforms of policies had a positive impact resulting in active courting of foreign investors at the highest levels. Rupee was first converted on trade and finally on current account. In March 1997, exchange earners, other than exporters, were also brought under the fast track route. A series of measures to encourage the software industry in India to expand capacity, reduce costs, improve quality, and invest abroad were put in place. As part of the reform process preceding the introduction of Foreign Exchange Management Act (FEMA), the neutrality condition attached to the Overseas Direct Investment was done away with in 1999. The scope for outward FDI, however, expanded significantly after the introduction of the FEMA in June 2000.

Fourth phase between 2000 until date is characterised by liberalised framework under FEMA and reflected in the increasing globalisation of the Indian economy. In the year 2000, a paradigm shift occurred, where except for a negative list, all the remaining activities were placed under the automatic route.[2] FDI under the

[2] Investment proposals falling under the automatic route and matters related to FEMA are dealt with by RBI, while the government handles investment through approval route and issues that are related to FDI policy per se through its three institutions, namely, the Foreign Investment Promotion Board (FIPB), the Secretariat of Industrial Assistance (SIA), and the Foreign Investment Implementation Authority (FIIA).

automatic route does not require any prior approval by either the government or the RBI. Under approval route, approvals of composite proposals involving foreign investment/foreign technical collaboration are also granted on the recommendations of the FIPB. The easing of the FDI policy has been quite regular. The dividend-balancing condition was removed (Press Note 7 of 2000). Caps were gradually raised in a number of sectors/activities. The non-banking financial companies (NBFC Sector) were placed on the automatic route. The insurance and defence sectors were opened up to a cap of 26 %. The cap for telecom services was increased from 49 to 74 %. FDI was allowed up to 51 % in single brand retail. In 2002, the per annum upper limit for automatic approval was raised to US$100 million. Such upper limit was, however, discontinued when the automatic route for outward FDI was further liberalised in March 2003 to enable Indian parties to invest to the extent of 100 % of their net worth. Since then the limit of outward FDI has gradually increased to 400 %.[3]

The year 2010 saw the continuation of the rationalisation process. All existing regulations on FDI were consolidated into a single document for ease of reference. Downstream investment through internal accruals was specifically permitted. Circular 1 of 2011 allowed the issue of shares against noncash considerations (in respect of import of capital goods/machinery/equipment and preoperative/pre-incorporation expenses) and also provided flexibility in fixing pricing of convertible instruments through a formula, rather than upfront fixation. The requirement of government approval for establishment of new joint ventures in the 'same field' was also done away with. As a result, non-resident companies were allowed to have 100 % owned subsidiaries in India. Government has since allowed FDI, in limited liability partnerships. Figure 3.1 shows the evolution of FDI policy in India.

Some of the FDI-related reforms in India have remained long pending. In fact, this has led to loss of investor's confidence and decline in FDI inflows into India in recent years.

However, the Government of India resumed reforms to attract FDI from the late 2012 onwards. The reforms like revision of fuel prices, allowing 51 % FDI in multi-brand retailing, allowing international airlines to invest in domestic airlines, hiking FDI equity from 49 to 75 % in broadcasting services, and disinvestment of four public sector undertakings are welcome steps in attracting more FDI.

The clearance of 51 % FDI in multi-brand retailing in September 2012, which was approved by the Cabinet in November 2011 after 2 years of deliberation but suspended due to the ensuing political furore, is a big step and will change the way

[3] The ceiling of 400 % of net worth, however, is not applicable for (a) investments made out of balances held in the Exchange Earners' Foreign Currency (EEFC) account of the Indian party or out of funds raised abroad through ADRs/GDRs and (b) Indian companies engaged in the energy and natural resources sectors, such as oil, gas, coal, and mineral ores, though they would require prior approval of the Reserve Bank of India (Khan 2012).

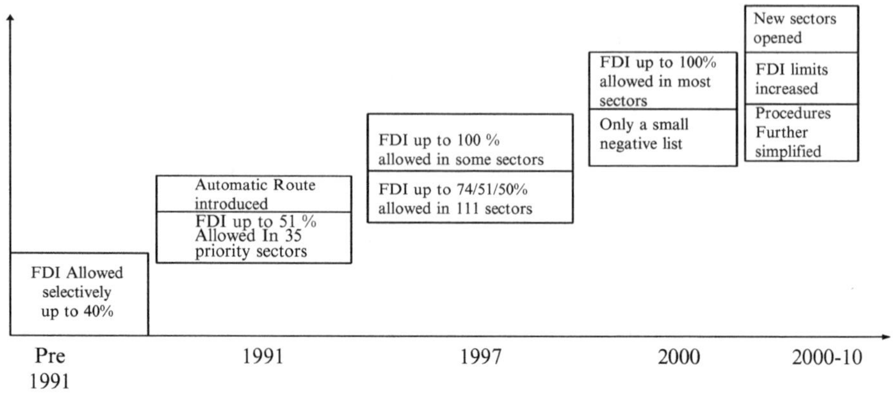

Fig. 3.1 Evolution of FDI policy in India

business is conducted in India.[4] There are many economic advantages, particularly for consumers and producers. The scale economies and assured supply chains of organised multi-brand retailing would offer better varieties of products at lower and stable prices to consumers. Further, big retailers would buy products directly from famers and producers, cutting middlemen and making way for better price realisation since competition would increase manyfold offering alternative opportunities to producers. The provision of 50 % FDI fund going to back-end infrastructure such as storage, logistics, and better extension services would substantially reduce wastage and trade and transaction costs. All these would go a long way in reducing volatility in supply and thereby prices, particularly for perishables. The provision of 30 % sourcing from SMEs in India would help them to expand capacity, improve quality, and be exposed to international supply chains.[5]

Another reform measure announced in 2012 is allowing foreign airlines to invest up to 49 % in the civil aviation sector. FDI would be very useful in the civil aviation sector which is short of capital and on the verge of collapse. Any FDI inflow into the sector would improve connectivity, affected by crisis in two of its largest airlines, Kingfisher and Air India, but boost technology upgradation and management

[4] The policy comes with a few riders keeping in mind the interests of 'mom-n-pop' (*Kirana* store), improving supply chains and getting Indian SMEs to adopt to the latest technologies. The riders are that FDI in multi-brand retail is to be allowed in 51 cities with population of more than one million, 30 % of total procurement is to be made from Indian SMEs, investment of 50 % of total FDI fund in back-end infrastructure, and veto power is to be given to states to allow foreign multi-brand retailers.

[5] However, there is no free lunch and FDI supported by big retailing will affect impact on *Kirana* shops, as they lack the financial muscle to stand up to the challenge in terms of variety, quality, packaging, offers, etc. It is most likely that unorganised retailing would have comparatively slow growth. However, with proper financial support, unorganised small retailers may evolve over time adding more to product varieties that carry out their store renovation and innovative customer catering such as home delivery and credit sales to survive in the market. In fact, it would make them competitive.

practices. Along with multi-brand retailing and civil aviation, hiking FDI equity from 49 to 75 % in broadcasting services, the disinvestment of four PSUs and a hike in diesel prices announced 2 days back strongly signals the governments' intention in pushing big-bang reforms to attract FDI into India.

However, India's regulatory policies in terms of procedural delays, complex rules, and regulations related to land acquisition, legal requirements, and environmental obligations might have played a role in holding the investors back from investing into India in recent years. The uncertainty created by the actions taken by policymakers might have led to unfriendly business environment in India.

3.2.2 State-Level Reforms: Success Stories

Since India is a federal system and states have their own responsibilities and control over many subjects that affect investment, it is essential to carry out reforms at the state level and to improve coordination between the centre and states to implement reforms. Over the years, many states have launched initiatives to simplify procedures, reduce delays in approval, and facilitate the implementation of projects to promote FDI. Though many states compete to attract FDI, a few states such as Gujarat, Andhra Pradesh, Maharashtra, Karnataka, and Tamil Nadu have succeeded in attracting most of the FDI (more than 70 % of total FDI inflows into India). Major reforms undertaken by these major FDI recipient states are as follows (Sahoo 2012).

- The industrial policy of these states has always been very proactive for sustainable industrial development. The competitive politics of development forced these state governments to make proactive market reforms.
- These state governments have taken initiatives to review their labour laws and procedures and to amend certain provisions to make them more flexible and investor friendly.[6]
- These states have enacted laws and created autonomous bodies for single window and fast track clearances for investors within a particular time frame.
- In order to attract foreign investment in general and in SEZs in particular, these states offer incentives in the form of exemptions of tax and duties.
- These state governments are working on a priority basis to provide quality infrastructure, keeping international standards as the benchmark.
- These states are proactive in providing land for industrial use at reasonable and competitive prices without excessive administrative and procedural complications.
- These state government industrial policies are forward-looking and are reviewed regularly to emphasise strategic and emerging sectors such as information

[6] Gujarat state has transferred various state labour laws to the Development Commissioner in order to achieve flexible labour laws in SEZs.

technology, pharmaceuticals, biotechnology, electronics, telecommunications, engineering, automobiles, and nanotechnology. These states also design appropriate policy and facilitate development of industrial parks and estates for specific traditional sectors where they have a comparative advantage.[7]

3.2.3 *Major Institutional Reforms to Promote FDI*

The most important reform in FDI policy during post-reform period is setting up institutions with well-defined objectives to bring down unnecessary delays from processing to implementation of FDI projects. The major objectives of these institutions have been to coordinate among stakeholders, review policy reforms,[8] and resolve issues related to investment, which would reduce time taken from approval to implementation. Major institutions are:

3.2.3.1 Foreign Investment Promotion Board (FIPB)

The FIPB under the Ministry of Finance is the nodal, single window agency for all matters relating to FDI whose objective is to promote FDI into India by (1) undertaking investment promotion activities, (2) purposeful negotiation/discussion with potential investors, (3) early clearance of proposals, and (4) reviewing policy and putting in place appropriate institutional arrangements, transparent rules, and procedures for investment promotion and approvals. The FIPB has been mandated to give its approval within 30 days for fast approvals of FDI projects. Further, the Foreign Investment Promotion Council (FIPC) was set up in 1996 under FIPB to identify the projects where foreign investment is required. FIPC, whose members are from industry and commerce, has a target-oriented approach to identify potential sectors and projects that need FDI and identify countries to mobilise FDI.

3.2.3.2 Secretariat for Industrial Assistance (SIA)

The SIA, Ministry of Commerce and Industry, provides a single window service for entrepreneurial assistance, investor facilitation, receiving and processing all applications, assisting entrepreneurs and investors in setting up projects (including liaison with other organisations and state governments), and in monitoring the

[7] For example, Gujarat facilitates the creation of apparel parks, gem and jewellery parks, R&D institutions, and centres of excellence.

[8] Dee (2009) emphasises on autonomous and independent institutions to review policies for identifying better policy options and assisting policy coordination within government for effective structural reforms.

implementation of projects.[9] The Entrepreneurial Assistance (EA) unit under SIA delivers the important function of attending enquiries of investors and arranging meeting between investors and concerned government administrative departments. There is another cell called Investment Promotion and Infrastructure Development (IP&ID) which disseminates and coordinates information industry-wise and facilitates investment, particularly in infrastructure sectors.

3.2.3.3 Foreign Investment Implementation Authority (FIIA)

FIIA was set up in 1999 to facilitate implementation of approved investment. It provides a proactive one stop after service care to foreign investors by helping them obtain necessary approvals, sort out operational problems, review policy framework, and meet with various government agencies to find solution to their problems. FIIA entertains complains about implementation bottlenecks and make recommendations to government administration, both centre and states, for speedy implementations. For fast track approval from different administrative agencies, FIIA sets up Fast Track Committee (FCA) involving important representatives of various ministries and government agencies to give approval and permission within a time framework. Project Monitoring Wing (PMW), established in 1998 within IP&ID and working under FIIA since 2001, coordinates with central and state government ministries and departments for monitoring approved projects.

3.2.4 Foreign Investment Policy and Routes for Investment Inflows

Foreign investment is permitted in virtually every sector, except those of strategic concern[10] and foreign companies are permitted to set up 100 % subsidiaries in India. No prior approval from exchange control authority, RBI, is required, except for certain specified activities. Under current policy, FDI can come into India in two ways.[11]

3.2.4.1 Automatic Route

Under this route, the investors are only required to notify the regional office concerned of RBI within 30 days of receipt of inward remittances and file the required documents with that office within 30 days of issue of shares to foreign

[9] See http://dipp.gov.in for day-to-day updates on issues related to foreign investment.

[10] Such as defence (opened up recently to a limited extent), rail transport, and prohibited sectors such as (1) retail trading (except for single brand product retailing), (2) atomic energy, (3) lotteries, and (4) gambling and betting

[11] For more FDI policy in India, see Sahoo and Nataraj (2008).

investors. The FDIs under automatic approval and government approval are regulated by the Foreign Exchange Management Act 1999 (FEMA) [see Chapter 6] vide Reserve Bank's Notification FEMA. 20/2000-RB [see Chapter 6] dated 3 May 2000 as amended from time to time. Under the approval route, the proposals are considered in a time-bound and transparent manner by the FIPB. Approvals of composite proposals involving foreign investment/foreign technical collaboration are also granted on the recommendations of the FIPB.

3.2.4.2 Automatic Route for New Companies

Investment in public sector units as also for EOU/EPZ/EHTP/STP units would also qualify for the automatic route. Investment under the automatic route shall continue to be governed by the notified sectoral policy and equity caps and RBI will ensure compliance of the same. The National Industrial Classification (NIC) 1987 shall remain applicable for description of activities and classification for all matters relating to FDI/NRI investment.

3.2.4.3 Automatic Route for Existing Companies

Besides new companies, automatic route for FDI/NRI investment is also available to the existing companies proposing to induct foreign equity. For existing companies with an expansion programme, the additional requirements are that (1) the increase in equity level must result from the expansion of the equity base of the existing company without the acquisition of existing shares by NRI/foreign investors, (2) the money to be remitted should be in foreign currency, and (3) proposed expansion programme should be in the sector(s) under automatic route. Otherwise, the proposal would need government approval through the FIPB. For this, the proposal must be supported by a board resolution of the existing Indian company.

For existing companies without an expansion programme, the additional requirements for eligibility for automatic approval are (1) that they are engaged in the industries under automatic route, (2) the increase in equity level must be from expansion of the equity base, and (3) the foreign equity must be in foreign currency. The automatic route for FDI and/or technology collaboration would not be available to those who have or had any previous joint venture or technology transfer/trademark agreement in the same or allied field in India.[12] Equity participation by international

[12] In this context, Press Note 18 (1998 series) was a provision by which foreign companies entering into a JV with an Indian company needed to get a "no objection" from their Indian partner before they set up another JV with a new partner or even a 100 % owned company in the country. The provision was misused by Indian promoters who arm-twisted their foreign partners even if their own JVs were languishing or defunct. The provision was seen as a severe disincentive by foreign companies to align with Indian partners with majority stake in the JV and was an impediment to FDI inflow. Under Press Note 1, foreign firms will not need permission from Indian partners before setting up a business in a related field. They will, however, need permission if setting up a business in the same field as their Indian JV.

financial institutions such as ADB, IFC, CDC, and DEG in domestic companies is permitted through automatic route subject to SEBI/RBI regulations and sector-specific cap on FDI.

3.2.4.4 Prior Government Approval Route (for Both Foreign Investment and Foreign Technical Collaboration)

In those limited sectors requiring prior government approval, proposals are considered in a time-bound and transparent manner by FIPB. For all activities that are not covered under the automatic route, government approval through the FIPB is necessary.

3.2.5 Taxation Policy in India

India is moving towards reforming its tax policies and systems to facilitate globalisation of economic activities. The corporate tax rate for foreign companies is 40 %. The net tax rate is far lower than this because of various deductions and exemptions[13] available under the tax laws. Tax holidays are available in special economic zones set up to make industry globally competitive. Infrastructure sector projects enjoy special tax treatment/holidays. A user-friendly tax administration is being introduced with round-the-clock electronic filing of customs documents from 31 March 2004.

Since the onset of liberalisation in the country, tax structure of the country is also being rationalised keeping in view the national priorities and practices followed in other countries. Foreign nationals working in India are generally taxed only on their Indian income. Income received from sources outside India is not taxable unless it is received in India. The Indian tax laws provide for exemption of tax on certain kinds of income earned for services rendered in India. Further, foreign nationals have the option of being taxed under the tax treaties that India may have signed with their country of residence. India has entered into Double Taxation Avoidance Agreements

[13] Following tax exemptions are available in different sectors: Deduction of 100 % of the profit from business of Development or operation and maintenance of ports, air ports, roads, highways, bridges, rail systems inland waterways, inland ports, water supply projects, water treatment systems, irrigation projects, sanitation and sewage projects, solid waste management systems; Generation, distribution and transmission of power; Development, operation and maintenance of an Industrial Park or SEZ; By undertakings set up in certain notified areas or in certain thrust sector industries in the North-eastern states and Sikkim; By undertakings set up in certain notified areas or in certain thrust sector industries in Uttaranchal & Himachal Pradesh; Derived from export of articles or software by undertakings in FTZ/EHTP/STP; Derived from export of articles or software by undertakings in SEZ; Derived from export of articles or software by 100 % EOU and; An offshore banking unit situated in a SEZ from business activities with units located in the SEZ.

(DTAA) with 65 countries including countries like USA, UK, Japan, Germany, and Mauritius. In case of countries with which India has DTAA, the tax rates are determined by such agreements and are indicated for some countries as under:

3.2.6 Repatriation of Investment Capital and Profits Earned in India

All foreign investments are freely repatriable except for cases where NRIs choose to invest specifically under non-repatriable schemes. Non-residents can sell shares on the stock exchange and repatriate sale proceeds if they hold a tax clearance certificate issued by authorities in charge of income tax. Profits, dividends, etc. (which are remittances classified as current account transactions) can be freely repatriated. There are relaxations for acquiring immovable properties for both non-residents and NRIs.[14]

3.2.7 Labour and Employment Laws

Under the Constitution of India, labour is a subject in the concurrent list where both the central and state governments are competent to enact legislation subject to certain matters being reserved for the centre. Some of the important labour acts, which are applicable for carrying out business in India, are Employees' Provident Fund and Miscellaneous Provisions Act 1952, Employees' State Insurance Act 1948, Workmen's Compensation Act 1923, Maternity Benefit Act 1961, Payment of Gratuity Act 1972, Factories Act 1948, Dock Workers (Safety, Health & Welfare) Act 1986, Mines Act 1972, Minimum Wages Act Payment of Bonus Act 1965, and Contract Labour [Regulation & Abolition] Act 1970.

3.2.8 Policy Regarding Intellectual Property Rights

India is a signatory to the agreement concluding the Uruguay Round of GATT negotiations and establishing the World Trade Organization (WTO). This agreement contains an agreement on Trade Related Aspects of Intellectual Property Rights (TRIPS), which lays down minimum standards for the protection and

[14] A person resident outside India, who has been permitted by RBI to establish business in India, has general permission to acquire immovable property in India, which is necessary for the activity. A non-resident Indian (NRI) can acquire by way of purchase any immovable property in India other than agricultural/plantation/farmhouse.

enforcement of intellectual property rights. To protect intellectual property rights and geographical indications, the law on trademarks and the geographical indications of goods has been passed in 1999. India is a signatory to the agreement concluding the Uruguay Round of GATT negotiations and establishing the WTO. This agreement, inter alia, contains an agreement on Trade Related Aspects of Intellectual Property Rights (TRIPS), which came into force from 1 January 1995. It lays down minimum standards for protection and enforcement of intellectual property rights in member countries, which are required to promote effective and adequate protection of intellectual property rights with a view to reducing distortions and impediments to international trade. The obligations under the TRIPS Agreement relate to provision of minimum standards of protection within the member country's legal systems and practices.

As regards the status of various intellectual property laws in India and standards in respect of various areas of intellectual property, a law on trademarks has been passed by Parliament and notified in the gazette on 30 December 1999. This law repeals and replaces the earlier Trade & Merchandise Act 1958. A new law for the protection of geographical indications, namely, the Geographical Indications of Goods (Registration and the Protection) Act 1999, has also been passed by the Parliament and notified on 30 December 1999. A law called the Designs Act 2000 relating to industrial designs, which repeals and replaces the earlier Designs Act 1911, has also been passed by Parliament in its Budget Session 2000. The Act has been brought into force from 11 May 2001. A bill on patents to amend the Patents Act 1970 was passed by Parliament on 14 May 2002

3.2.9 *Policy Regarding Acquisition of Immovable Property*

A person resident outside India, who has been permitted by RBI to establish a branch, or office, or place of business in India (excluding a liaison office), has general permission of RBI to acquire immovable property in India, which is necessary for, or incidental to, the activity. However, in such cases a declaration, in prescribed form (IPI), is required to be filed with the Reserve Bank, within 90 days of the acquisition of immovable property. Foreign nationals of non-Indian origin who have acquired immovable property in India with the specific approval of the RBI cannot transfer such property without prior permission from the RBI. An Indian citizen resident outside India (NRI) can acquire by way of purchase any immovable property in India other than agricultural/plantation/farmhouse. He may transfer any immovable property other than agricultural or plantation property or farmhouse to a person resident outside India who is a citizen of India or to a person of Indian origin resident outside India or a person resident in India.

3.2.10 Incentives for Foreign Investment

The increasing mobility of international firms and the gradual elimination of barriers to global capital flows have stimulated competition among governments to attract FDI, often through tax incentives (World Bank). As more and more governments have tried to attract multinational companies and enhance the associated technology spillovers, fiscal incentives have become a global phenomenon—from tax holidays and import duty exemptions to investment allowances and accelerated depreciation.[15] India has a number of special economic zones (SEZ), and there are incentives given in India's SEZ and development zones[16]: The SEZ zones are considered as foreign territory in all that concerns taxes and customs. Companies in the SEZ are eligible for a total exemption from tax for the first 5 years and a 50 % exemption from the tax due for the next 5 years.

- Entrepreneurs who supply infrastructure resources in the SEZ are eligible for a 10-year exemption from tax.
- Industrial concerns—export-oriented undertakings (EOU), located in FTZ, Software Technology Parks (STP), or in Hardware Technology Parks if the total production is intended for export—are entitled to an exemption from taxes for 10 years as well as to an exemption from import taxes.
- Companies carrying scientific research and other activities specified by law are also eligible for 5–10 years tax holiday of 30–100 %.
- Industries located in North East India or the state of Sikkim are entitled to 10-year tax exemption for activities performed during 1 April 2007–1 April 2017.

3.2.11 Restrictions on FDI and Rationale

FDI Restrictions in Indian Sectors have been imposed in a number of sectors such as atomic energy, chit fund business, and retail and lottery business. FDI Restrictions in Indian Sectors have been imposed by the Government of India in order to protect the interests of the domestic industries. However, the several policy initiatives taken by the Government of India in the 1990s helped to transform the country from a restrictive regime with regard to FDI to a liberal one. As in 2012, FDI in India is encouraged in almost all the sectors of the country's economy under

[15] http://rru.worldbank.org/documents/publicpolicyjournal/253Moris-020603.pdf

[16] http://www.worldwide-tax.com/india/ind_invest.asp

the automatic route and approval route. At the same time, the government has restricted FDI in a few sectors. The various sectors having restrictions of FDI are:

(a) Atomic energy
(b) Betting and gambling
(c) Chit fund business
(d) Plantation or agricultural activities
(e) Real estate business
(f) Business in transferable development rights
(g) Lottery business
(h) Retail trading
(i) Railway transport
(j) Mining of chrome, zinc, gold, diamonds, copper, iron, gypsum, manganese, and sulphur
(k) Ammunition and arms

3.3 FDI Policy in Bangladesh

3.3.1 Evolution of FDI Policy in Bangladesh

In the late 1980s and 1990s, Bangladesh announced a series of measures and liberalised its FDI policy framework. In recent years, Bangladesh has significantly improved its investment and regulatory environment, including the liberalisation of the industrial policy, abolition of performance requirements, and allowance of full foreign-owned joint ventures. Since 1996, new sectors have been opened up for foreign investment, including the telecommunications sector.

FDI is encouraged in all industrial activities in Bangladesh excluding those on the list of reserved industries such as production of arms and ammunitions, forest plantation and mechanised extraction within the bounds of a reserved forest, production of nuclear energy, and printing and minting fresh currency notes. The same policy includes industries in which foreign investment is explicitly discouraged: banking, insurance, and other financial institutions. Nonetheless, foreign investors enjoy the same incentives as domestic entrepreneurs in respect of tax holidays, accelerated depreciation allowances, concessional duties on imported capital machinery, and other measures, as contained in the Industrial Policy 1999 and 2005. The establishment of convertibility of the taka for current account transactions, in April 1994, has facilitated foreign investment, by eliminating the requirement to obtain prior approval from the Bangladesh Bank on current account transactions.

The capital market also remains open for portfolio investment. The policy framework for foreign investment in Bangladesh is based on the Foreign Private Investment (Promotion and Protection) Act 1980. It provides for non-discriminatory treatment between local and foreign investments and protection of foreign investment for expropriation by the state and ensures repatriation of profits and proceeds from sales of shares. Additionally, there is no limitation pertaining to equity participation by a foreign investor. Investments can be undertaken independently or through joint ventures with the local, private, or public sector. All foreign investments must be registered with one of the three sponsoring agencies: the Bangladesh EPZs Authority (BEPZA), the Bangladesh Small and Cottage Industries Corporation (BSCIC), or the Board of Investment for all other private investment.

A World Bank study concluded in 2005 suggested that Bangladesh has experienced a more stable form of capital inflow, with FDI making up about 85–90 % of total capital flows. Both FDI and private debt inflows in Bangladesh have largely financed imports of machinery and equipment—a sign that Bangladesh is only in the preliminary phase of FDI flows. In 2009–2010 (February), there were 89 new foreign and joint venture investment projects registered under the Board of Investment, Bangladesh, amounting to $590 million. The projects were mainly in the services, engineering, clothing, and agricultural sectors. The country encourages foreign investment in export-oriented industries and in high-technology products that either substitute imports or add to exports. Foreign investments may be undertaken either independently or through joint ventures, with either the local, private, or public sector. The government has liberalised its industrial and investment policies in recent years by reducing bureaucratic control over private investment and opening up many areas. Bangladesh allows entry of foreign investment into all sectors other than the five reserved sectors, which are reserved only for public investment and even domestic private investment is not allowed in these.[17]

The legal policy allows 100 % equity participation by foreign investors, provides for fair and equitable protection against nationalisation or expropriation by the state, provides full indemnification in the event of financial loss due to civil unrest, and ensures repatriation of invested capital, dividends, and the proceeds from the sale of shares. Repatriable dividends, if invested, are treated as new investments. For bringing in new investments, government approval is not needed. Foreign firms and companies may also raise loans locally and they do not require the permission of the central bank for remittance of profit, technical assistance fees, and royalties.

3.3.2 FDI Institutions in Bangladesh

All foreign investments must be registered with one of the three sponsoring agencies: the BEPZA, the BSCIC, or the Board of Investment for all other private investment. Registration with the sponsoring agency provides with a 'one-stop' service for infrastructure and institutional support services including pre-investment counselling;

[17] http://www.bangladesh-bank.org/

electricity, gas, water, and sewage connection; and telecommunication facilities. The BEPZA and BSCIC are also responsible for allocating industrial plots, entitlement to import items on the restricted list, approving payments of royalties, technical know-how or technical assistance fees, and appointing and remunerating foreign personnel.

3.3.3 Intellectual Property Rights and Investment Protection

The government recognises the importance of intellectual property rights for attracting FDI and is making efforts to update its legislation and improve enforcement. The country has been a member of the World Intellectual Property Organization (WIPO) since 1985 and signed the Paris Convention on Intellectual Property in 1991. The Foreign Private Investment (Promotion and Protection) Act of 1980 guarantees protection against expropriation. If a foreign investor becomes subject to a legal measure that has the effect of expropriation, adequate compensation will be paid to the investor and it will be freely repatriable. Similarly, adequate protection is available for intellectual property rights, such as patents, designs, trademarks, and copyrights.

3.3.4 Labour Laws

Workers are entitled to elect collective bargaining agents (CBAs) to negotiate their demands with management. A trade union may be formed if 30 % of employees support it. All trade unions need to be registered. There are 47 labour laws covering matters such as wages, industrial disputes, and working conditions. Foreign nationals can be employed as long as their number does not exceed 15 % of the total number of employees. Overall, Bangladesh has taken considerable steps to reform and liberalise all its economic policies including FDI. With low labour costs and almost no restrictions on the entry and exit of foreign investors, Bangladesh is on the track towards becoming an attractive destination for FDI in the South Asian region.

3.3.5 Investment Incentives in Bangladesh

One of the major aspects of FDI policy in Bangladesh is incentives for foreign investors.[18] Some of the major incentives are tax exemptions for power generation, import duty exemptions for export processing, an exemption of import duties for export-oriented industries, and tax holidays for different industries. Double taxation

[18] http://www.bizbangladesh.com/investment_incentives.php

can be avoided by foreign investors based on bilateral agreements. Facilities for the full repatriation of invested capital, profit, and dividend exist. There are also tariff concessions given to FDI forms to set up business. An import duty, at the rate of 5 % ad valorem, is payable on capital machinery and spares imported for initial installation.[19] For 100 % export-oriented industries, no import duty is charged in the case of capital machinery and spares. Duties and taxes on the import of goods that are produced locally are higher than those applicable to imports of raw materials for the production of such goods.

3.3.5.1 Tax Holiday and Benefits

Tax holiday facilities are available for 5 or 7 years depending on location of the industrial enterprise. Tax holiday facilities are provided in accordance with the existing laws. The period of tax holiday is calculated from the month of commencement of commercial production. Tax holiday certificate is issued by NBR for the total period within 90 days of submission of application. This facility can be availed of by industries set up within 30 June 2000. Capital gains from the transfer of shares of public limited companies listed with a stock exchange are tax-exempt. In computing capital gain, deductions are made from the full value or sales proceeds or the fair market price (whatever is higher) of the capital assets. Dividend income which is received by shareholders (other than companies) is tax-exempt. However, this benefit is not available to shareholders of private limited companies. Royalties and technical know-how fees received by any foreign collaborator, firm, company, or expert are also tax-exempt. Bangladesh has replaced the sales and excise tax by the more modern value-added tax (VAT). The VAT is imposed at a flat rate of 15 %. Excise duties do exist on a few items and a turnover tax may be imposed on small-scale activities that cannot be taxed through the VAT. Salaries of foreign technicians are exempt for a period of 3 years from the date of their arrival in Bangladesh provided their salaries are for services stipulated under a contract approved by the National Board of Revenue.

3.3.5.2 Accelerated Depreciation

Industrial undertakings not enjoying tax holiday will enjoy accelerated depreciation allowance. Such allowance is available at the rate of 100 % of the cost of the machinery or plant if the industrial undertaking is set up in the areas falling within the cities of Dhaka, Narayanganj, Chittagong, and Khulna and areas within a radius of 10 miles from the municipal limits of those cities. If the industrial undertaking is set up elsewhere in the country, accelerated depreciation is allowed at the rate of 80 % in the first year and 20 % in the second year.

[19] The value of spare parts should not, however, exceed 10 % of the total C&F value of the machinery.

3.3.5.3 Incentives to Non-resident Bangladeshis (NRBs) and Export-Oriented Industries

Investment of NRBs will be treated at par with FDI. Special incentives are provided to encourage NRBs to invest in the country. NRBs will enjoy facilities similar to those of foreign investors. Moreover, they can buy newly issued shares/debentures of Bangladeshi companies. A quota of 10 % has been fixed for NRBs in primary public shares. Furthermore, they can maintain foreign currency deposits in the Non-resident Foreign Currency Deposit (NFCD) account.

Export-oriented industrialisation is one of the major objectives of the Industrial Policy 1999. Export-oriented industries are given priority and public policy support is ensured in this respect. The following incentives and facilities are provided:

1. Duty-free import of capital machinery and spare parts up to 10 % of the value of such capital machinery will continue.
2. Existing facilities for bonded warehouse and back-to-back letter of credit to continue.
3. The entire export earnings from handicrafts and cottage industries will be exempted from income tax. For all other industries, income tax rebate on export earnings will be given at 50 %.
4. The facility for importing raw materials, which are included in the banned/ restricted list, but required in the manufacture of exportable commodities, will continue.
5. Hundred per cent export-oriented industry outside EPZ will be allowed to sell 20 % of their products in the domestic market on payment of applicable duties and taxes.

Bangladesh is located virtually as a land bridge between the emerging markets of South Asia and the fast-growing markets of South East Asia and the ASEAN countries. It is a potential entry point for servicing the region covering Nepal, Bhutan, and the seven North East Indian states and for the resource-rich northern Myanmar. Bangladesh being a low-income populous country, there is a great scope for tapping the underdeveloped markets in the country. As economic growth has begun to pick up in significant measure because of opening up of its economy, the middle class and its purchasing power are beginning to grow. Bangladesh has potential for foreign investment in areas such as oil, gas, mineral exploration/ production/distribution, electric power generation/distribution, telecommunication network, service expansion, pharmaceutical production plants, agro-based investments, and textile machinery/equipment. Overall, Bangladesh has been promoting FDI for several decades now with one of the most liberal investment policy and incentive regimes in South Asia. Its investment friendly climate offers generous and attractive packages for incentives for foreign investors like 100 % ownership and tax and duty exemptions.

3.4 FDI Policy in Pakistan

FDI has played a small but important role in Pakistan's economic development. The share of FDI to GDP has been less than 1 % in most years. Nevertheless, FDI was crucial for the success of import substitution and infant industry policies in the formative years after independence in 1947, through joint ventures or licensing, franchising, and distribution arrangements between start-up Pakistan firms and foreign companies.

3.4.1 Evolution of FDI Policy and FDI Policy Framework in Pakistan

Pakistan's large domestic market and policy environment are generally attractive to foreign direct investment, but terrorist violence and natural disasters are keeping investors at bay. Pakistan was the tenth largest recipient of inward FDI (IFDI) in Asia during 2006–2008. Pakistan has also been successful in attracting investment from other developing countries. There are several joint ventures with foreign companies. Though the policy regime is investor friendly, inward FDI flows are erratic and relatively low due to internal difficulties such as governance and terrorism. Retaining the confidence of both foreign and domestic investors is vital.

Pakistan was an agricultural economy in 1947 and the private sector was the main vehicle for industrial investment during the 1950s and 1960s and the involvement of the public sector was restricted to three out of 27 basic industries. Therefore, from the beginning the private sector had a key role to play in Pakistan's development. It was also set that in the event of private capital not forthcoming for the development of any particular industry of national importance, the public sector might set up a limited number of standard units. Pakistan's investment regime was as open as any other developing country, and the country had an investment incentive structure more generous than most. Pakistan signed its first bilateral investment treaty with Germany in 1959. By the late 1960s, the economy was largely dominated by the private sector in important areas like banking, insurance, certain basic industries, and international trade in major commodities. The services sector was reserved for local investors. Foreign investment was not allowed in the field of banking, insurance, and commerce (Khan and Kim 1999).

On 1 January 1972, the Government of Pakistan issued an Economic Reforms Order taking over the management of ten major categories of industries, seven commercial banks, development of financial institutions, and insurance companies. In 1975, there was another round of nationalisation of small-sized agro-processing units. The sudden shift towards nationalisation of private sector industrial units shattered private investors' confidence. At the same time, there was also acceleration in the direct investment by the public sector in new industries ranging from the basic manufacture of steel to the production of garments and breads. The status of the public sector as a catalyst and gap filler in the 1950s and 1960s changed to that of repository of the 'commanding heights' of the economy (see Khan and Kim 1999). All foreign investment was, however, exempted from the purview of nationalisation.

The early 1970s was the era of nationalisation, which was a feature of the entire South Asian region, including India and Sri Lanka. Although foreign enterprises were exempted, new inflows to the country collapsed.[20] A fresh round of liberalisation measures were introduced only from the mid-1970s onwards. An adequate legal framework for foreign investment was provided through the Foreign Private Investment Act (Promotion and Protection Act) 1976. The Act also guaranteed the remittance of profit and capital and the appreciation of agreements on the avoidance of double taxation (Sahoo 2006). However, Pakistan began to actually open up its economy and liberalise its FDI policies towards the end of the 1980s. A new industrial policy package was introduced in 1989 recognising the role and importance of the private sector, and a number of regulatory measures were taken to improve the business environment in general and attract FDI in particular (Khan and Kim 1999). The Board of Investment (BOI) was set up in October 1990, attached to the PM's secretariat, to help generate opportunities for FDI and provide investment services. BOI is a 'one window facility' which helps the establishment of new industries. To facilitate foreign investment, Pakistan has signed bilateral agreements on the promotion and protection of investment with 46 countries (Khan and Kim 1999; Sahoo 2006).

By the mid-1990s, restrictions to entry, ownership, admission, and repatriation had been relaxed and eliminated. Investor guarantees, property protections, and national treatment were stipulated in Pakistan's constitution and relevant laws were enforced. Several incentives were given to foreign investors, which included a variety of credit facilities, concessional customs duties, tax holidays, a favourable visa policy, and special investment zones. It is easier to do business in Pakistan as compared to other countries in the South Asian region.[21] The privatisation programme and incentive packages have not been without controversy. In November 1997, the Government of Pakistan announced the New Investment Policy that included major policy initiatives to attract FDI, which had earlier been restricted to the manufacturing sector. It was now opened up to sectors like services and agriculture, which constitute three-fourths of GNP. The main objective of the new policy is to enhance the level of foreign investment in the field of industrial base expansion, infrastructure and software development, electronics, engineering, agri-food, value-added textile items, tourism, and construction industries. Foreign investment on a repatriable basis is also allowed in agriculture, services, infrastructure, and social sectors, subject to the following

[20] Direct investment fell from US$ 70 million in 1972 to 0 in 1973 and turned negative (to –US$ 6 million) in 1974. It did not recover until 1981.

[21] It takes less time and costs to start a business in Pakistan than in India or any other country in the subcontinent. Pakistan also scores high investor protection. See World Bank's Doing Business 2012.

conditions: (a) the basis for joint venture is (60:40), (b) foreign equity to be at least $1 million, (c) foreign companies registered in Pakistan allowed to invest, and (d) for social sector and infrastructure projects, the joint venture requirement is waived (100 % foreign equity may be allowed) (Sahoo 2006). The privatisation process received a setback in 2006 when the Supreme Court, citing irregularities, annulled the divestment of Pakistan Steel Mills.

3.4.2 FDI Policy Framework

Foreign investors are allowed to hold up to 100 % equity of industrial projects without any permission from the government except in certain fields of activity such as (1) arms and ammunition; (2) high explosives; (3) radioactive substances; (4) security printing, currency, and mint; and (5) alcoholic beverages and liquors. A BOI, attached to the Prime Minister's Secretariat, was established to attract FDI. A 'one window' facility was established to overcome difficulties in setting up new industries.

Foreign investment at 100 % equity on a repatriable basis is allowed in the service, infrastructure, and social and agricultural sectors subject to certain conditions including registration of company with the Security and Exchange Commission of Pakistan (SECP) and intimation to the State Bank of Pakistan. Foreign equity of 100 % is allowed in the service sector, infrastructure projects, and social sector projects on a repatriable basis. FDI is also actively encouraged in tourism, housing and construction, information technology, etc.

The new industrial policy package announced in 1997 opened up virtually all Pakistan's industrial sectors to foreign investment. The requirement for government approval of foreign investment was removed with the exception of few industries. In all industrial sectors, other than those indicated above, foreign equity participation of up to 100 % was allowed and foreign investors were allowed to purchase equity in existing industrial companies on a repatriable basis. There was also no requirement of having local partners. Foreign investment was, however, excluded from agricultural land, forestry, irrigation, and real estate including land, housing, and commercial activities (UNCTAD 1994).

All the investors, whether domestic or foreign, were required to obtain No Objection Certificate (NOC) from the relevant provincial government for location of the project. Thus, the physical location of the investment was effectively controlled by the provincial government, which was considered a major bottleneck in speedy industrialisation. At present, an NOC is only required if foreign investment is envisaged in the areas which are in the negative list of the relevant provincial government. According to the authorities, only a few areas are on the negative list of provincial governments. The foreign investors in the past were not free to negotiate the terms and conditions of payment of royalty and technical fee suited to the requirements of foreign collaborators for transferring technology. Later this restriction was removed and the investors were allowed to negotiate the

Table 3.1 Foreign investment policies in Pakistan

Policy regime	Remarks
Restricted sectors	Arms and ammunition High explosives Radioactive substances Security printing currency and mint New units of alcohol manufacturing except industrial alcohol are banned
100 % equity	Yes, for all sectors
Incentives	Incentives are industry specific but have local content requirement
Restrictions on royalty or technology transfer payments	No
Performance requirements	No (only for eligibility of incentives)
EPZ incentives	Yes, complete exemption of taxation from federal, provincial, and municipal bodies
Automatic approval	Yes
National treatment	Yes
MIGA signatory	Yes
Tax holidays	No, only custom duty and sales tax exemption

Source: Sahoo (2006) and BOI Pakistan (www.Pakboi.gov.pk)

terms of conditions as suited to them as well as acceptable to the multinationals wishing to transfer the requisite technology.

Foreign investment is fully protected through the Foreign Investment Act 1976, Protection of Economic Reforms Act 1992, and Foreign Currency Accounts Protection Act 2001. Table 3.1 highlights the liberal investment policies in Pakistan.

3.4.3 Investment Policy for FDI in Different Sectors

3.4.3.1 Investment Policy of Pakistan for Manufacturing and Industrial Sector

Foreign investors are allowed to hold 100 % equity in industrial projects without permission of the government. No government sanction is required for setting up any industry, in terms of field of activity, location, and size, except for the sectors mentioned in Table 3.1. There is no restriction on payment of royalty or technical fees for the manufacturing sector. However, such agreements shall be registered with the State Bank of Pakistan. The payments of royalties and technical service fees to foreign companies will be taxed at 15 %. However, reduced rates under treaties with different countries remain applicable. Foreign investors are allowed to hold 100 % equity of non-manufacturing projects on repatriation basis subject to the terms and conditions.

3.4.3.2 Investment in Different Sectors in Pakistan (Service Sector, Infrastructure, Social Sector, Tourism Sector, Information Technology Sector, and Housing and Construction)

FDI in a service sector is allowed in any activity subject to obtaining permission, NOC, or licence from the concerned agency/agencies and fulfilling the requirements of the respective sectoral policy. Foreign investors may hold 100 % equity allowed on repatriation basis and the minimum amount of foreign equity investment in the project shall be 0.15 million dollars. FDI in an infrastructure sector is allowed for infrastructure projects, which may include development of an industrial zone(s). Foreign investors may hold 100 % equity allowed on repatriation basis and the minimum amount of foreign equity investment in the project shall be 0.30 million dollars. FDI in the social sector is allowed in the following fields: education, technical/vocational training, human resource development (HRD), hospitals, and medical and diagnostic services.

Foreign investors may hold 100 % equity allowed on repatriation basis and the minimum amount of foreign equity investment in the project shall be 0.30 million dollars.

Tourism sector is treated as an industry by virtue of Ministry of Industries and Production Circular *No. 1-129/99-INV-IV* dated 2 August 1999. In lieu of *SRO No. 455(I)/2004* dated 12 June 2004, any plant, machinery, or equipment, which is not manufactured locally and is used for tourism, hotels, or tourism-related projects, is importable at custom duty of 5 % and zero-rated sales tax. Housing and Construction sector is also treated as an industry by virtue of Finance Division Notification No. 10 (10)/IF-II/98 dated 7 April 1999 and 4 June 1999. In lieu of *SRO No. 455(I)/2004* dated 12 June 2004, any plant, machinery, or equipment, which is not manufactured locally and is used for housing and construction-related projects, is importable at custom duty of 5 % and zero-rated sales tax. Local, as well as foreign, companies involved in real estate projects will not market these projects unless the title of the property has been transferred in the name of a company incorporated in Pakistan and 'Commencement of Business' certificate has been issued by the SECP.

3.4.3.3 Investment in Information Technology Sector in Pakistan

Computer Software and Information Technology is also treated as an industry by virtue of government notification *No. 3 (2)/97-INV-IV* dated 5 March 1997. In lieu of *SRO 457(I)/2004* dated 12 June 2004, any plant, machinery, or equipment of IT, which is not manufactured locally and as certified through CBR by the facilitation Committee of BOI from time to time, is importable at custom duty of 5 % and zero-rated sales tax.

3.4.4 Taxation Policy and Investment Incentives in Pakistan

Since 1997, attractive tariff and tax incentives have been given to foreign investors. Remittances of royalties, technical and franchise fees, capital, profits, and dividends are allowed. Further, foreign investment is fully protected through the Foreign Investment (Promotion and Protection) Act 1976, Protection of Economic Reforms Act 1992, and Foreign Currency Accounts (Protection) Ordinance 2001.

In the manufacturing sector, the customs duty on imported raw materials used in producing for exports is 0 %, while a customs duty of 5 % is charged on imports of plants, machinery, and equipment not manufactured locally. The import of raw materials, subcomponents, components for the manufacture of plants for sugar, cement, power, chemical, fertilisers, oil and gas, etc. is free. In all these cases, the sales tax is zero. The corporate tax rate is around 35 %. The Government of Pakistan has signed agreements for the avoidance of double taxation with 52 countries including developed countries.

The full repatriation of capital, capital gains, dividends, and profits is allowed. A facility for contracting foreign private loans (which does not involve any guarantee by the government) is available to all foreign investors who make investments in sectors open to foreign investment, for the cost of plant and machinery required for setting up the project. There are no restrictions on the payment of royalties or technical service fees for the manufacturing sector. The payment of royalties and technical service fees to foreign companies is taxed at 15 %. However, concessions under different treaties with different countries apply.

3.4.4.1 Investment Incentives for Foreign Investment in Pakistan

Pakistan has the most liberal investment policy in the South Asian region. New incentives[22] and further liberalisation measures include almost all economic sectors are open for foreign investors; foreign equity up to 100 % allowed; no government permissions required and only terms and conditions apply; attractive incentives package such as 0–5 % customs duty on import of machinery, no sales tax on import of machinery, and no withholding tax on import of machinery; remittance of capital, profits, royalty, technical, and franchise fee allowed; equal treatment towards local and foreign investors; network of EPZs/industrial estates; and import of raw material for export manufacturing zero rated.

3.4.4.2 Policy Framework for Establishment of Economic Zones in Pakistan

Full exemption of custom duties and taxes strictly on import of capital equipment including plants, machinery, and equipment. Corporate income tax holiday for a

[22] http://www.fauji.org.pk/webforms/InvestmentClimatePak.aspx?Id=111&Id2=126

period of 5 years existing initial depreciation/allowance of 50 % shall be reconsidered to be enhanced to 100 %. Federal government/agencies are to provide gas, electricity, and other utilities at the zero point of the economic zones.

3.4.5 *Repatriation of Investment Capital and Profits Earned in Pakistan and Expatriate Facilitation*

Foreign nationals, e.g., investors, executives, and expatriate employees, having 'FBR's Pass Booklet' are allowed duty-free import of food stuff and other consumable items equivalent to US$1,000 per year per person in Pakistan. However, import exceeding the above duty-free limit of US$1,000 will be allowed on payment of normal import duties. Various communities of foreign investors and their employees are allowed to establish exclusive clubs with recreational facilities. One airport entry pass for protocol purpose will be issued to foreign and local investors/companies, provided the equity investment is at least US$10 million. ID and BOI extend a courtesy service covering reception in Pakistan, hotel bookings, accommodation, transport bookings, and assisting with the business itinerary, for foreign investors visiting Pakistan. Improvements have been made pertaining to the procedures for work visas, business visas, and opening of branch/liaison office by foreign companies. No compulsion for a limited company to offer shares to the public irrespective of the size of capital or total value of assets.

3.4.5.1 Labour and Employment Laws

One major drawback to FDI in Pakistan is its labour laws, which are overprotective and complicated, discouraging job creation, inhibiting business expansion, and thereby discouraging much-needed productive investment. Labour disputes are common, creating problems for management, and productivity losses have acted as an impediment to foreign investment.

The Pakistan government has taken several proactive measures to ease the foreign investment environment in the country. FDI has been encouraged in all sectors of the economy. The economy has overcome government instability in the past and recovered relatively quickly after the 2005 earthquake. However, FDI continues to elude Pakistan for several reasons. These include institutional weakness, corruption, ineffective legal environment, political uncertainty, and unsustainable diplomatic relations of Pakistan with major international powers. Further, terrorist violence and natural disasters are keeping investors at bay.

3.5 FDI Policy in Sri Lanka

3.5.1 Evolution of FDI Policy in Sri Lanka

Sri Lanka's economic policy regime can be mapped into four distinct phases (Athukorala 2004). They are (1) 1948–1959, open, non-interventionist, and free market policies; (2) 1960–1977, import substitution industrialisation policies; (3) 1977–1990, export-oriented liberalisation policies; and (4) 1990 onwards, second wave of comprehensive liberalisation which includes among other things privatisation programmes, tariff cuts and reforms in tariff structures, easing exchange rate controls on current account transactions, and most importantly several important changes to the foreign investment policy framework in line with the increased outward orientation of the economy.

Foreign investment policies continued to remain extremely liberal until the mid-1960s permitting many MNEs to set up affiliates within Sri Lanka to undertake the domestic production of items previously supplied from their overseas production centres. By the mid-1960s, Sri Lanka evolved dualistic foreign investment policies, characterised by restrictions on import substitution projects, and favoured treatment of export-oriented projects. Tax concessions for export-oriented foreign ventures relaxed foreign exchange restrictions on the remittance of dividends; interest and profit origination in such ventures was introduced by the five-year plan 1972–1977. However, these measures in favour of EOFDI were affected in an overall and significant anti-export bias throughout this period. This anti-export bias was created by cumulative impact of stringent trade controls, high export taxes and the overvalued exchange rate, stringent performance requirement, and bureaucratic red tape in operation. Facing a dismal economic outcome of this inward-looking policy, Sri Lanka started extensive economic liberalisation policies in 1977. This started with:

1. Replacing quantitative restrictions on imports with tariffs and revising tariff structure to bring uniformity
2. Reducing restrictions on foreign investment with new incentive for export-oriented foreign investment under attractive free trade zone scheme
3. Financial sector reforms
4. Adjusting interest rates to levels above the rate of inflation
5. Opening the banking sector to foreign banks
6. Freeing credit markets to determine interest rates
7. Limits on the public sector participation in the economy
8. A programme for privatisation of public enterprises
9. Exchange rate realignment
10. Incentives for non-traditional exports

The reform process lost momentum in the early 1980s and a second wave of liberalisation was implemented in early 1990s. This emphasised on further privatisation programme, tariff cuts, simplification of the tariff structure, removing exchange controls on current account transactions, and outward orientation of the economy.

Sri Lanka pioneered South Asia's economic liberalisation over three decades ago. Liberalising many areas of the economy, the government embraced strategies and policies that were more than conducive for international investment. In line with the government's policy, efforts were intensified to attract investments to target sectors in which Sri Lanka had strong foundation for growth as well as areas where it is nationally important to develop. By offering incentives to induce high-value investment to priority sectors, the BOI promotes diversification of Sri Lanka's industry and services with special focus on advanced technology and value addition. The government has made necessary amendments to the tax system of the country to ensure that the overall tax regime for all sectors is less complex and at a lower rate across the economy.

However, there are some exclusions and limitations as per policy. Under exchange control powers, businesses are wholly or partially reserved for national investors, such as coastal fishing and money lending. Sri Lanka being among the first countries in South Asia to liberalise its economy has certainly improved its business climate; by today's standards, they do not create a liberal investment framework for all investors.

The telecommunications, power, and energy sector attracted most of FDI inflows. Achieving political stability through the end of the conflict, FDI inflows are expected to be realised with the initiation of infrastructure development especially in the Northern and Eastern provinces. More importantly, FDI inflows to manufacturing sector would bring spillover effect to other industries leading to sustainable FDI inflows in the long run. Sri Lanka is a founder member of the MIGA. According to the Index of Economic Freedom 2011, the country has been ranked 107 of 179 countries and 19th of the 41 countries in the Asian Pacific Region.[23] Sri Lanka has been rated as one of the most improved countries in the world in economic freedom as per the 2011 rankings.

3.5.2 Policy Framework and Institutions in Sri Lanka

3.5.2.1 Entry and Establishment of FDI

FDI is permitted in most sectors but like most of its neighbouring South Asian economies such as India, Sri Lanka has a long negative list of sectors where FDI is barred completely or where foreign investors may only take a minority stake in an enterprise. However, a comparative study among Asian countries shows that Sri Lanka's list of restricted activities is relatively small. However, there are a few areas totally reserved for Sri Lankans, such as money lending, pawnbroking, retail trade investment, providing personal services other than for the export of tourism sectors, coastal fishing, and education of students and award of local educational

[23] Index of Economic Freedom measures the pro-business policy environment of a country.

degrees. However, there are regulated areas such as the growing and processing of primary commodities, mining, timber-based industries, and education, where foreign investment is restricted to 40 % and approval by the BOI is required. In a few cases, FDI entry and incentives are subject to performance requirements.[24]

Foreign investment is mainly encouraged in enterprises that make extensive use of foreign capital or technology, in export-oriented industries, and in infrastructure projects. In many sectors, automatic approval is given for equity participation up to 100 %. For restricted sectors such as telecommunication, education, mass transportation, and mining, permits are required from other government agencies for more than 49 % equity participation. There are no exchange controls on current account transactions and no barriers to the remittance of corporate profits and dividends for foreign enterprises.

3.5.3 FDI Institution

As a part of the FDI policy, Greater Colombo Economic Commission was set up in 1978 with wide-ranging powers to facilitate FDI in the fully export-oriented ventures. The immediate goal for the country was to generate FDI, exports, foreign exchange, and employment. The commission was authorised to set up EPZs. In 1992, all FDI promotion activities were placed under the commission and rechristened BOI. The incentive scheme under EPZs includes:

1. Complete foreign ownership of investment projects
2. A tax holiday for up to 10 years with complete tax exemption for remuneration of foreign personnel employed, royalties, and dividend of shareholders during that period
3. Duty exemption for import of inputs and assistance with custom clearance
4. Industrial services at subsidised rates
5. Unlimited access to foreign currency credit at interest rates prevailing in world financial markets
6. Access to foreign financing through FCBUs and other incentives.

The BOI is many organisations in one: an EPZ and industrial park owner, developer, and manager; a facilities developer; an FDI regulator and promoter; an investment facilitator; a regulator with respect to building, town planning, and environmental permits for its clients; a customs authority for its clients; and a fiscal incentives administrator. The BOI is empowered to grant special concessions to companies satisfying specific eligibility criteria, which was designed to meet strategic economic objectives of the government.

[24] The general condition is that the manufacturing enterprises have to export 80 % of output while the service sector has to export 70 % of its output.

But the BOI has been weak in two areas that are visible in its investment performance record. First, it has not been a strong attractor of FDI but has rather facilitated those investors who expressed interest in Sri Lanka on their own initiative or that of local business partners. Second, it has not helped to improve the regulatory, tax, and operating conditions of small- to medium-scale Sri Lankan investors.

The most important feature of FDI policy measure in Sri Lanka was the establishment of the BOI (formerly Greater Colombo Economic Commission) in 1978, with wide powers of tax relief and administrative discretion in all matters related to FDI. It is structured to function as the central facilitation point for investors and empowered to enter into agreements with investors providing tax holidays, tax concessions, and exemptions from custom duty and exchange control laws. Overall, the BOI of Sri Lanka provides all services for foreign investors including approval of projects, grant of licences, and tax incentives.

The major operational implication is that the BOI of Sri Lanka need not screen all proposed FDI. Only proposed joint ventures on the negative list would require approval. In principle, resources devoted to this function could be reduced. BOI responsibilities would also include coordinating and related policy matters, such as adding activities to or removing them from the negative list. It is difficult to pinpoint the reduction in staffing that could be entailed, as the Investment Department of the BOI considers applications for incentives and FDI approval jointly. Almost all foreign investors will seek incentives. Moreover, the Investment Department deals with both domestic and foreign investors and joint ventures.

The following transparent investment laws aim to foster FDI:

(a) Total foreign ownership is permitted across almost all areas of the economy.
(b) No restrictions on repatriation of earnings, fees, capital, and on Foreign Exchange Reserves transactions relating to current account payments.
(c) Safety of foreign investment is guaranteed by the constitution.
(d) Existence of a transparent and sophisticated legal and regulatory framework. Covering all prerequisite business law enactments.
(e) Bilateral investment protection agreements with 27 countries and DTAA with 38 countries.

3.5.4 Treatment and Protection of FDI,[25] Repatriation of Profits, and Intellectual Property Law

Sri Lanka does not set out principles of foreign investor treatment and protection in its national law. However, it has a network of Bilateral Investment Treaties with almost 24 countries. The repatriation of capital and profits is guaranteed. In

[25] Investment Policy Review of Sri Lanka (UNCTAD 2003)

practice, there is ready access to foreign exchange and the prospect of the nearly full abolition of exchange controls. The Bilateral Treaties guarantee investor protection against nationalisation, expropriation, or restrictions that amount to constructive expropriation, except for a public purpose, and in such an event, they guarantee 'prompt, adequate, and effective compensation' based on the market value of expropriated property before the expropriation was effected or such an eventuality became public knowledge. The affected investor also has the right to judicial review. Repatriation of investment capital and profits earned in Sri Lanka is guaranteed, but in a weak format—transfers are subject to exigencies of foreign exchange.

Though the country allows repatriation of profits up to 100 %, practices preferential tax rates, and is liberal in such respects, there is a list of economic activities that are not completely open to foreign investment. The restrictions/regulations to foreign investment in the economy are given in Table 4.5. The country is very active in the bilateral and regional trading and investment agreements, having built an extensive network of investment agreements with almost all investing home countries. It has BIPPAs with China (1986), India (1997–1998), and Pakistan (1997) and avoidance of double taxation agreements with India (1982), China (2003), Pakistan (1981), and Nepal (1999) in the South Asian region. Being an island country and with FTAs with both India and Pakistan, Sri Lanka also enjoys the status of a regional hub. According to the BOI of the country, there are nine EPZs/parks and two industrial parks in the country.

Sri Lanka's intellectual property law is WTO compliant, under the trade-related intellectual property rights agreement. Both process and product patents are recognised, and the patent period complies with international standards. Copyright protection is available, and the period of protection conforms to international standards.

3.5.5 Labour Laws and Regulations

Labour policies in Sri Lanka are extremely restrictive and pose impediments to foreign investors and investment in the country. Most of the laws favour the employee, and in case of retrenchment, the decisions and the compensation package are largely in favour of the employee. Further, like other South Asian countries such as India, Sri Lanka has industrially active and politically influential trade unions. Another serious restrictive labour law in Sri Lanka is the Termination of Employment of Workmen (special provisions) Act (TEWA) of 1971, which restricts employers from dismissing employees except for serious disciplinary infractions.

3.5.6 Investment Incentives in Sri Lanka

The Sri Lankan government offers a wide range of incentives[26] for investors. These incentives are available to both foreign and domestic investors without preference, provided the investment is undertaken through a company incorporated in Sri Lanka. Incentives offered fall under two classes or 'regimes' and the investor may be eligible for inducements provided by either of these regimes. Following the example of its counterparts such as India, Sri Lanka provides a range of tax incentives to foreign investors including breaks on taxes on corporate profits and dividends, VAT, and import and excise duties. Sri Lanka has also signed a wide net of double taxation treaties.[27] Some of the fiscal incentives include an initial tax holiday of 5 years followed by a long-term concessionary rate, varying from 15 to 20 % depending on the industry, import duty exemptions on capital equipment in some industries, and zero duties in raw materials in the export of manufactured goods.

Following the example of its counterparts such as India, Sri Lanka provides a range of tax incentives to foreign investors including breaks on taxes on corporate profits and dividends, VAT, and import and excise duties. Sri Lanka has also signed a wide net of double taxation treaties. Some of the fiscal incentives include an initial tax holiday of 5 years followed by a long-term concessionary rate, varying from 15 to 20 % depending on the industry, import duty exemptions on capital equipment in some industries, and zero duties in raw materials in the export of manufactured goods.

3.5.6.1 BOI Incentives Under Section 17 of the BOI Law

Regulations have been framed under Section 17 of the BOI Law to 'grant specific incentives to new and existing enterprises satisfying specific eligibility criteria'. These incentives usually entail a combination of exemptions covering income tax, customs duty, and foreign exchange controls, which are conferred on an eligible company by way of signing an agreement with the BOI. It should be noted that exemptions from the Goods and Services Tax (GST) Act, National Security Levy Act, and Excise (Special Provisions) Act cannot be conferred on a company by virtue of signing a BOI Agreement. Exemptions or concessions if applicable under these statutes are available to all companies regardless of whether they have signed a BOI Agreement.

Foreign investment entry to operate under the normal laws is granted under Section 16 of the BOI Act, which entitles the enterprise to repatriate profits and

[26] http://www.buildsrilanka.com/boi/boi-InvestIncen_GenPol.htm

[27] By the end of 2001, there were 30 DTTs in force and another seven pending. They cover all the principal FDI home countries.

dividends attributable to foreign shareholders. Since specific rights and privileges outside the Inland Revenue, Customs Ordinance, and Exchange Control Laws are not granted to companies approved under Section 16, the signing of a BOI Agreement is not necessary. Note that export-oriented companies operating under the normal laws are eligible to borrow in foreign currency under new guidelines issued by the central bank. FDI entry requires prior approval only where it impinges on a limited 'negative list' of restricted activities in Sri Lanka.

3.5.7 Taxation Policy in Sri Lanka

Principal taxes that affect business in Sri Lanka are taxes on corporate profits and dividends, VAT, and import and excise duties. In the standard direct tax regime, profits are taxed at 30 %, with reasonably rapid depreciation allowances and loss carryforward of 6 years. VAT was introduced in 2002. Rates are two-tier—10 % on essentials and 20 % on non-essentials. Exports are zero rated. However, the effective implementation of VAT has been delayed owing to a challenge as to whether the composition of VAT on retail and wholesale trade is consistent with the sales tax prerogatives of Provincial Councils of the country.

The current approach to tax design is characterised by an uncompetitive standard fiscal regime that is relieved by a patchwork of discriminatory and bureaucratic incentives. An alternative approach would be to reform the standard regime so that it is attractive for most investors but has the flexibility to provide special regimes on a sector or activity basis where warranted to ensure international competitiveness.

3.5.8 Pending FDI Reforms

A few reforms would attract more FDI to Sri Lanka. These include reforming the standard tax regime, consider cutting the headline profit tax rate to 15 % and retain key elements of the corporate tax regime, including rapid rates of depreciation allowance and 10 % tax on dividends. Special measures could be developed to attract talented diaspora members such as improved tax treatment of offshore-sourced passive income, neutral tax treatment of offshore pension arrangements, income tax concessions for gains from exercise of stock options, and measures to cushion the impact of low personal relief threshold on very high earners. Fiscal stability certificates should no longer be required for new investments except in the case of major projects, especially those requiring substantial debt financing.

Dispute settlement should be (a) impartial and speedy, (b) no undue regulatory impositions on labour costs, and (c) the feasibility to hire and fire employees as commercial needs dictate. The Industrial Disputes Act includes comprehensive machinery for resolving industrial disputes. However, decisions are slow and many employers feel that the system and its administration favour the interests of employees. Other areas such as competition regulation and intellectual property rights are a concern. Even though they are based on international conventions, enforcement is a different matter.

While Sri Lanka welcomes foreign investment, there are restrictions that limit its potential. Sri Lanka prohibits the sale of public and private land to foreigners despite the fact that there is no basis in law for this prohibition. Any investment with over 25 % foreign equity will be treated as foreign investment for the purpose of these measures. The government has also proposed to impose a tax in the amount of 100 % of the lease value when state land is leased to foreign investors. The tax for the entire lease periods would be due at the time the lease is signed, unless the investors pay the entire lease in a foreign currency. Besides challenges such as limited employment, complexity of legal framework, and poor infrastructure (electricity, roads, water, medical services, telecommunications) have led to poor FDI inflow in the country.

At the problems end, resolution of the labour severance issue ought to be the top priority. Rationalisation of taxes is required to provide competitive arrangements for all investors. The scope of restrictions on FDI entry should continue to be reviewed, as they may no longer be compatible with Sri Lanka's objectives.

3.6 FDI Policy in Nepal

3.6.1 Evolution of FDI Policy in Nepal

Nepal has adopted an open and liberal policy to welcome foreign investors. The industrial policy and the foreign investment and Technology Act 1981 initially paved the way towards inward FDI throughout the Nepalese economy. Private sector was encouraged and the government would act merely as a mediator providing infrastructure and productive environment for investment. A clear-cut policy towards foreign investment was introduced in Nepal in the 1980s, with the enactment of the Investment and Industrial Enterprise Act of 1987. In its pursuit of outward-oriented policies, Nepal began to encourage private foreign investment in every industrial sector (medium and large scale), while limitations were set on the level of foreign equity holdings. In the case of medium-sized industries, foreign equity of 50 % was allowed.

In large industries exporting more than 90 % of their total production, foreign equity was allowed up to 100 %. In other large industries, the maximum was set at 80 % foreign equity. New projects by foreign investors required the formal approval of the Foreign Investment Promotion Division of the Ministry of Industry. In a step to further liberalise its foreign investment policy, Nepal announced a new set of incentives through the 1987 Act, under which the full remittance of dividends for investments in convertible currency was allowed. The repatriation of capital was made possible and foreign workers were allowed to be brought in when nationals were not available. A five-year tax holiday on profits was allowed, and this was later extended to 10 years. Importers were allowed to import their inputs duty-free, through either a duty drawback or bonded warehouse facility. FDI flows to Nepal have historically been very low. In the 1990s, there was significant improvement. Low FDI inflow probably reflects the uncertainty caused by frequent changes of government and the insecurity created by the Maoist insurgency. It also did not help to be a landlocked country in a slow-growth region. FDI is expected to grow sharply since the insurgency problem has been solved.

After becoming a WTO member in 2004, Nepal has been pursuing further opening up and liberalisation policies on the FDI. Nepal is also a member of the South Asian Preferential Trade Arrangement (SAPTA) and the Bay of Bengal Initiative for Multi-Scrotal Technical and Economic Cooperation-Free Trade Area (BIMST-ECFTA). New initiatives on FDI have been taken with the aim of enhancing sustained growth and reducing poverty.

3.6.2 Policy Framework, Incentives, and Licensing in Nepal

Policy Framework: Most sectors have been opened up to foreign investors, allowing 100 % equity or joint ventures with Nepalese investors.[28] The sectors that have been opened up to foreign investment are manufacturing, energy-based industries, tourism, mineral resource-based industries, and agro-based industries and services. However, there are a few industries where investment is prohibited, including national security, cottage (i.e., craft) industries, personal services of a kind that would normally be performed by self-employed people, and real estate. FDI is also not permitted in the retail business; travel agencies; cigarette, tobacco, and alcohol production other than for export; and a range of small tourist-related activities, including tourist lodging. Nepal encourages foreign investment as joint venture operations with Nepalese investors or as 100 % foreign-owned enterprises. Foreign investment is permitted up to 100 % equity shareholding in medium- and large-scale industries. In cottage and small industries, permission may be granted to use foreign technology in the form of investment. Foreign investment is welcome in Nepal in practically every sector of economic activity with the exception of the following: (1) defence industries which produce items like military armament, ammunition, or explosive materials and (2) cigarettes and bidi.

---

[28] Since Nepal is a small country with a unique ecosystem, the government is sensitive to the environmental impact of industries. Projects must go through environmental impact assessments and initial environmental examinations.

3.6.2.1 Criteria for Approval

In the granting of approval for foreign investment involving new investment, modernisation, diversification, or expansion, the projects will be assessed taking into account the following criteria:

- Priority will be granted to investments in industry prescribed by HMG (His Majesty's Government)
- Financial and technical viability
- Contribution to employment generation
- Foreign exchange earnings or savings
- Competitiveness of products in international markets
- Appropriateness of technology
- Terms and conditions of investment and technology transfer
- Participation of Nepalese nationals in investment and management

3.6.2.2 Investment Environment

The Industrial Policy and Industrial Enterprise Act of 1987 by the Government of Nepal opened up the economy to FDI. But the country is still not an active participant in the FDI flows in the region or in the world. This Act provided for FDI into the country with the exception of environment and defence-related industries. Nepal undertook other liberalisation measures such as permitting full remittances of profits and tax holidays. The Foreign Investment and Technology Transfer Act of 1992 further allowed 100 % foreign ownership in all industries except in defence, cigarettes, bidis, and alcohol (Athukorala and Sharma 2006, UNCTAD). Compared to other LDCs, Nepal is an open economy open to foreign investment, though recent changes in laws regarding foreign investment have abolished tax holidays.

3.6.2.3 Investment Incentives

The Government of Nepal provides several incentives to industries that are set up for export purposes. They include an income tax exemption on export income, exemption on foreign investor's interest income earned abroad, and a relaxation of taxes on specific industries.

3.6.2.4 Foreign Exchange Regulation

Nepal maintains a formal foreign exchange control regime that requires the surrender of foreign currency export proceeds. The foreign investment law provisions cover convertibility only for capital[29] and dividend repatriation and foreign debt service.

[29] Although this appears to be contradicted by the central bank, which explicitly states that it does not guarantee convertibility on the capital account

3.6.2.5 Labour Law

The labour law is highly restrictive from an investor standpoint. By modern commercial standards, it impedes business flexibility in many instances. There are protective labour laws relating to retrenchment, wages, promotion, etc.

3.6.3 Intellectual Property Protection

Nepal recently became a member of the WTO and therefore is still in the process of making its intellectual property rights (TRIPS) WTO compliant. Only process patents are protected and not product patents. Though all trademarks are registered with the department of industries, it is believed that infringements of trademarks are quite common, as is the case with copyrights.

It is said that Nepal has the maximum potential to attract foreign investment among the low-income countries in the region. It is considered a friendly country that offers market potential, flourishing local entrepreneurial culture in both small and large business, etc. The only drawback of late has been political instability. If Nepal can overcome that, it will be able to grow fast with the help of FDI.

Nepal cannot be far from the benefits of FDI. So Nepal has placed top priority for the attraction of FDI and its development by adopting different polices and rules at the national and international level to promote foreign investment and technology transfer for making the economy viable, dynamic, and competitive through the maximum mobilisation of the capital, human, and other natural resources.

3.6.4 Foreign Investment Incentives and Facilities in Nepal

Foreign investors are eligible to receive the following incentives and facilities[30]:

- Income received from exports is free from income tax.
- Income tax is exempt for a period of 5 years from the date of commercial production in the case of production-oriented industry (other than cigarettes, bidi, and alcohol), energy-based industry, agro-industry, forestry industry (other than saw mills and catechu), and mineral exploration industry.
- National priority industries are exempt from income tax for a period of 7 years.
- Specified industries, as, for example, tourism, service, and construction industries, are eligible for exemption from income tax for a period of 5 years on the recommendation of the Industrial Promotion Board and upon publication in the Nepal Gazette.

[30] http://www.catmando.com/gov/industry/fipd/fipd10.htm

- Industries are entitled to a reduction in tax rate on each income tax slab by 5 percentage points.
- Industries established in remote, underdeveloped, and less developed areas, other than cigarette, bidi, and alcohol industries, are entitled to an additional tax exemption of 50, 20, and 10 % and in respect of excise duty, 25, 15, and 10 %, respectively.
- Industries are entitled to deduct one-third of the value of the fixed asset investment as depreciation allowed under income tax law.
- Industries established as public limited companies with a minimum of 15 % of shares distributed to more than 100 persons are entitled to a 5 % reduction in corporate income tax.
- Industries in operation which diversify production through reinvestments or expand installed capacity by 25 % or more or modernise technology or develop ancillary industries either in the same industries or in other industries are entitled to set off 40 % of the value of the new fixed investment in computing taxable income. Such definitions may be made in 1 year or in instalments within a maximum period of 3 years.
- Industries, which invest in modern plant, machinery, and equipment, which control environmental pollution are entitled to deduct 50 % of the investment so made as deductible expenses in computing taxable income.
- Preoperating expenses incurred in connection with skill development and training will be allowed to be capitalised.
- Ten per cent of the gross profit is allowed as a deduction against net income because of expenses connected with technology or product development and skill enhancement.
- Dividends declared from investments made in industry are exempt from income tax.
- Five per cent of the gross income would be allowed as a deduction in computing net income on account of donation made for the improvement of schools, colleges, universities, private hospitals, religious places, and other social welfare activities.
- Five per cent of the gross income is allowed as a deduction in computing net income as expenses on account of expenditure incurred on advertisements for the promotion of products or services and for miscellaneous expenses.
- Industries (other than cigarette, bidi, alcohol, saw mill, and catechu) using 90 % or more domestic raw materials in production shall be entitled to 2 years tax exemption in addition to the tax exemption provided for production-oriented, energy-based, forest-based, and mineral exploration industries. This concession shall not apply to industries specified as national priority industries.
- Industries that provide direct employment to 1,000 persons or more shall be entitled to an additional 2-year exemption from income tax.
- Interest income earned by a non-resident on a foreign loan will be taxed at a concessionary rate of 15 %. Similarly royalties and technical and management fees earned by a non-resident person will be taxed at 15 %.

- No premium, customs duty, excise, sales tax, or local tax will be imposed on raw materials to be used by industries established in the EPZs or by any industry permitted to operate bonded warehouse facilities that export 100 % of their products.
- Export-oriented industries receiving duty drawback facilities under the Industrial Enterprises Act and industries manufacturing intermediate goods to be used for the production of exportable commodities will be refunded the amount of premium, customs duty, excise, and sales tax paid on the raw materials used to produce such intermediate goods, as well as the excise and sales tax paid on such intermediate goods on the basis of the actual volume of the export of the commodities manufactured by using them. For this purpose, transferable tax credit system will be used.
- Priority will be given to arrange infrastructure required for the establishment of industries.
- Industries will be given priority for government land and land in industrial districts for the establishment of industries.

Nepal's political environment is still volatile. However, Nepal has attempted to create a peaceful environment for investors in the last few years. FDI has always been a key priority for Nepal Government. The FDI policy revised in 1992 has proved the relevance of FDI to Nepal. Moreover, FDI has created several employment opportunities to the Nepalese economy. However, prior to the 1990s, Nepal's failure to attract FDI was mainly because of insurgency, lack of infrastructure facilities, unskilled workforce, landlocked economy, and political instability. But Nepal's business environment is getting better and, to attract investors, the Government of Nepal had declared the year 2012 as 'Nepal Investment Year'.

3.7 Conclusion

South Asian region led by India is of the most attractive destinations of FDI in the world. Despite their problems, the South Asian countries have undertaken several measures in the last two decades to ease the norms and procedures for FDI in South Asia. The countries have not only undertaken major reform measures but the governments in these countries have acted as facilitators and promoted FDI, realising that it is an important determinant of growth and employment in the country. The effort of the South Asian countries in transforming their FDI polices is reflected in the actual increase of inflows to the region.

Countries in the region face different challenges, such as political risks and obstacles to FDI, which need to be tackled to build an attractive investment climate, the report says. Nevertheless, recent developments have highlighted new opportunities. For example, the political relationship between India and Pakistan, the two major economies on the subcontinent, has been moving towards greater engagement. Nepal Government declared 2012 the Year of Investment in Nepal. However, the countries in the region have continued to attract FDI fighting all odds.

FDI growth seems to be keeping its momentum in 2012. As economic growth in India has slowed, however, concerns have risen about short-term prospects for FDI inflows to South Asia as per the World Investment Report 2012. The global economic situation has created further uncertainties. Whether countries in the region can overcome old challenges and grasp new opportunities will depend to a large extent on governments' efforts to further open up their economies and deepen regional economic integration. The entire region has opted for a liberal FDI regime with emphasis on single window clearance, speedy clearances, encouraging private sector and PPP, and several incentives to foreign investors including tax sops, setting up of SEZ, investment promotion zones, and BOIs to keep up the pace of FDI inflows. Hence, it is evident that South Asia will remain an important and sought-after destination for FDI in the Asian region.

Appendix

Table 3.A.1 Foreign investment policies of South Asia

	India	Pakistan	Nepal	Sri Lanka	Bangladesh
Restricted sectors	1. Arms and ammunitions 2. Defence aircrafts and warships 3. Atomic energy 4. Railways	1. Arms and ammunitions 2. High explosives 3. Radioactive substances 4. Security printing, currency, and mint 5. New units of alcohol manufacturing except industrial alcohol is banned	1. Cottage industries 2. Personal business services 3. Arms and ammunitions 4. Consultative services	1. Nonbank money lending 2. Pawnbroking 3. Retail trade with a capital investment of less than $1 million	1. Arms and ammunitions 2. Production of nuclear energy 3. Security printing and minting 4. Forestry in reserved forest areas 5. Railways
100 % equity	For certain sectors, sectoral caps exist	Yes, for all sectors	Yes, except restricted sectors	Yes, except a few sectors such as telecom, education, mass, transportation, and mining	Yes
Incentives	Yes, central government gives for R&D measures. State governments give a wide variety of incentives	Incentives are industry specific but has local content requirement	Yes, with export requirement and local content requirement	Yes, with export requirement and minimum investment	Yes. It varies depending upon the location of industries
Restrictions in royalty or technology transfer payments	No, but certain minimum conditions to be met such as lump sum payments not exceeding US$2 million	No	No	No	No. The condition is that it should not exceed 6 % of previous year's sales
Performance requirements	Yes, specific rules for automobile sectors	No (only for eligibility of incentives)	No (only for eligibility of incentives)	No (only for eligibility of incentives)	No

(continued)

Table 3.A.1 (continued)

	India	Pakistan	Nepal	Sri Lanka	Bangladesh
EPZ incentives	Yes	Yes, complete exemption of taxation from federal, provincial, and municipal bodies	No	No. Industrial processing zones for better land allocation	Yes
Automatic approval	Yes, by RBI	Yes	No. Approval is given by Industrial Promotion Board (IBP)	Yes, by BOI	Yes, by BOI and BEPZ authority
National treatment	Yes	Yes	Contract terms are given precedence over Nepali law in investments valued at more than Nepali rupees 500 million	Yes	Yes
MIGA signatory	Yes	Yes	Yes	Yes	Yes
Tax holidays	Yes	No, only customs duty and sales tax exemption	Income earned from exports is free from income tax	Yes	Yes

Source: Author's compilation

References

ADB (2007) Drivers and limitations, Global development network series. South Asia economic report. ADB, Manila

Ashfaque H. Khan and Yun-Hwan Kim (1999) "Foreign Direct Investment In Pakistan: Policy Issues And Operational Implications" EDRC REPORT SERIES NO. 66, Asian development Bank, Manilla

Athukorala P (2004) Post-crisis export performance in Thailand. ASEAN Econ Bull 211:19–36

Athukorala PC, Sharma K (2006) Foreign investment in a least developed country: the Nepalese experience. Transnatl Corp 15(2):125–146

Dasgupta A, Siddharthan NS (1985) Industrial distribution of Indian exports and joint ventures abroad. Dev Chang 16:159–174

Dee P (2009) Institutions for economic reforms in Asia. Routledge, New York

Desai AV (1984) India's technological capability: an analysis of its achievements and limits. Res Policy 13(5):303–310

Khan HR (2012) Outward Indian FDI – recent trends & emerging issues. Address delivered by Shri. HR Khan, Deputy Governor, Reserve Bank of India at the Bombay Chamber of Commerce & Industry, Mumbai on March 2

Khan AH, Kim Y-H (1999) Foreign direct investment in Pakistan: policy issues and operational implications. EDRC report series no. 66. Asian Development Bank, Manila

Kidron M (1965) Foreign investment in India. Oxford University, London, 368pp

Kumar N (1987) Foreign direct investments and technology transfers among developing countries. In: Panchamukhi VR et al (eds) The third world and the world economic system. Radiant, New Delhi, pp 139–165

Kumar N (1995) Foreign direct investment, technology transfer and exports of developing countries: trends and policy implications, UNIDO document no. ID/WG.542/6(SPEC.). UNIDO, Vienna

Mehta S (2007) Inwards FDI to South Asia: identifying the driver. SAARC J Hum Res Develop 46–64

Reserve Bank of India (RBI) (2012) Master circular on foreign investment in India, Mumbai, July

Sahoo P (2006) FDI in south Asia: trends, policy, impact and determinants, vol 56, Asian development bank institute discussion paper series. Asian Development Bank Institute, Tokyo

Sahoo P (2012) Foreign direct investment in India: unfinished agenda. In: Philippa D (ed) Economic reform processes in South Asia: toward policy efficiency. Routledge, New York, pp 109–136

Sahoo P, Nataraj G (2008) FDI in south Asia: policy trends and perspectives. Gitam J Manag 1(1):35–77

UNCTAD (1994) World investment report. UNCTAD, Geneva

UNCTAD (2003) World investment report. United Nations Conference on Trade and Development, Geneva

Chapter 4
Foreign Direct Investment Inflows into South Asia

4.1 Introduction

In the recent past, the development of endogenous growth theory has invited the attention of academicians and policymakers. This growth theory has motivated the researchers to explore new avenues of economic growth. In this endeavour, various factors such as human capital, financial development, international trade, and foreign investment—along with the primitive inputs, i.e. labour and capital—have emerged as the key factors of difference in growth across countries. It is well documented in the literature that FDI plays a vital role in determining the economic growth through capital accumulation, investment efficiency, and technology upgradation. A conducive business environment is one of the key prerequisites for attracting FDI into a region. But in providing this attractive and safe business environment, the South Asian region faces two major challenges: weak integration processes at the regional level and political risks and obstacles at the country level, such as instability in Afghanistan, security concerns in Nepal and Pakistan, and macroeconomic as well as political issues in India. At the country level, high political risks and obstacles have been an important deterrent of FDI inflows. However, recent developments have highlighted new opportunities. For instance, the political relationship between India and Pakistan, the two major economies on the subcontinent, has been moving towards greater cooperation, with Pakistan granting India most favoured nation (MFN) status in November 2011 and India recently announcing that it will allow FDI from Pakistan (UNCTAD 2012).

Progress in regional economic integration (with the South Asian Association for Regional Cooperation as the key architect) has been slow. Trade barriers between neighbouring countries in the region are among the highest in the world. South Asia is perhaps one of the least integrated developing regions: intra-regional trade accounts for about 2 % of total GDP, compared with more than 20 % in East Asia. In addition, investment issues have not yet been included in the regional integration process. As a result, the region has not been able to realise its potential

P. Sahoo et al., *Foreign Direct Investment in South Asia*,
DOI 10.1007/978-81-322-1536-3_4, © Springer India 2014

for attracting FDI inflows, especially in promoting intra-regional FDI flows. In 2011, intra-regional greenfield investment accounted for merely 3 % of the regional total, compared with 27 % in East and Southeast Asia.

Nevertheless, high economic growth in major economies in the subregion has created a momentum for regional integration in recent years, and South Asian countries have increasingly realised that regional integration can help them improve the climate for investment and business. The inclusion of an investment agenda in the regional integration process and, in particular, the creation of a regional investment area can play an important role in this regard. The region's main obstacle in attracting FDI is its poor business climate (UNCTAD 2011a, 2012). This chapter considers the influential role of FDI and details its status in South Asian countries, including total inflow and outflow, major investment sources, and top sectors receiving FDI and intra-regional trade and investment.

4.2 Global FDI and FDI Inflows into South Asia

Global FDI inflows in 2010 reached an estimated $1,244 billion—a marginal increase from the 2009 level of $1,185 billion. However, there was an uneven pattern between regions and also between subregions (UNCTAD 2011a). FDI flows to developed countries have typically been much higher than flows to developing countries. As a result, until very recently, the global trend largely mirrored trends in the developed world.

A major break from this pattern took place in 2004, when FDI flows to developed countries declined, whereas global flows increased, spurred by the surge in FDI to developing countries (Table 4.1). FDI flows to developed countries gradually declined from $1,227 billion in 2000 to $619 billion in 2005 and increased thereafter to $1,306 billion in 2007. Since then, FDI flows to developed countries declined continuously due to the global economic crisis in 2007–2008. In fact, this is in line with the overall decline in FDI flows to the world. On the contrary, along with the shift in trade to developing economies, there has been a consistent increase in FDI inflows to the developing world, with most of the growth being concentrated in Asia and Latin and Central America. Now, developing and developed countries have almost equal shares.

FDI flows to developing countries were fairly stable in the 1980s. The 1990s witnessed a gradual rise in FDI, largely brought about by the dramatic changes in the policy structures of the 'Asian Tigers', which had begun to embark on programmes of structural liberalisation and open-market reform, aimed at ushering in a phase of export-led growth. Another contributing factor may have been the recovery of the Latin American economies, which had begun to emerge from the debt crisis of the 1980s. FDI inflows in absolute value to South Asia have increased continually and particularly since 2000. FDI inflows attracted by South Asia have steadily grown from $5.5 billion to $52 billion over 2000–2008 before declining to $32 billion in 2010 under the shadow of the crisis (Table 4.1). The growth of FDI

Table 4.1 FDI inflows into selected countries (1990–2010) (billions of US$)

Host region/ economy	1990–1995 (annual avg.)	2000	2005	2006	2007	2008	2009	2010
World	225.3	1,491.9	982.6	1,461.8	1,971.0	1,744.1	1,185.0	1,244.0
Developed economies	145.0	1,227.5	619.1	977.8	1,306.8	965.1	602.8	601.9
Developing countries	59.6	240.2	332.3	429.4	573.0	658.0	510.5	573.5
Asia	47.3	133.7	215.8	283.4	339.2	375.6	307.5	357.8
Southeast Asia	34.6	57.3	40.7	56.7	75.4	46.9	37.9	79.4
South Asia	1.8	5.6	14.4	27.8	34.3	51.9	42.5	31.9
India	0.7	2.3	7.6	20.3	25.3	42.5	36.4	24.6
Bangladesh	0.6	0.6	0.8	0.8	0.7	1.1	0.7	0.9
Sri Lanka	0.1	0.2	0.3	0.5	0.6	0.8	0.4	0.5
Pakistan	0.4	0.3	2.2	4.3	5.6	5.4	2.3	2.0
Nepal	0.1	–	0.0	0.0	0.0	0.0	0.0	0.0
PRC	19.3	40.7	72.4	72.7	83.4	108.3	95.0	105.7
Republic of Korea	1.0	9.2	7.1	4.9	2.6	8.4	7.5	6.8
Malaysia	4.6	3.7	4.1	6.1	8.6	7.2	1.4	9.1
Singapore	5.7	5.4	15.4	29.3	37.0	8.6	15.2	38.6
Indonesia	2.1	−4.5	8.3	4.9	6.9	9.3	4.8	13.3
Thailand	1.9	2.8	8.1	9.5	11.4	8.4	4.9	5.8
Argentina	3.5	11.1	5.2	5.5	6.4	9.7	4.0	6.3
Brazil	20.0	32.7	15.1	18.8	34.6	45.1	25.9	48.4

Source: World Investment Reports, Various Issues

inflows to the region has accelerated since 2005 to an annual average rate of 25 %, with the bulk of the inflows going to the larger South Asian countries, namely, India and Pakistan, which accounted for 84 % of total FDI inflows to the region in 2010. Stable economic situation and a more open FDI climate encouraged inflows to India, resulting in an increase in FDI inflows to South Asia.

Global FDI inflows as ratio of GDP increased from 0.6 % during 1980–1990 to above 1.7 % in the period 1991–2000 and further to 2.7 % during the last half of the 2000s. Comparison of FDI inflows as ratio of GDP across region indicates that all the regions have experienced increased FDI inflows as ratio of GDP over 1980–2010. However, the South Asian region has a lower FDI ratio than the world average and all other regions in all periods—despite having received higher FDI in last decade all periods. FDI inflows as ratio of GDP for South Asia increased from 0.08 % during 1980–1990 to above 0.5 % in the period 1991–2000 and further to 2.3 % during the last half of the 2000s. Developing Africa and America stand first and second in terms of ratio of FDI inflows to GDP during the last half of the 2000s (Fig. 4.1).

FDI stock as a ratio of GDP across various regions also provides similar picture. Global FDI stock as a ratio of GDP increased from 17 % during 1980–1990 to above 25 % in the period 1991–2000 and further to 54 % during the last half of

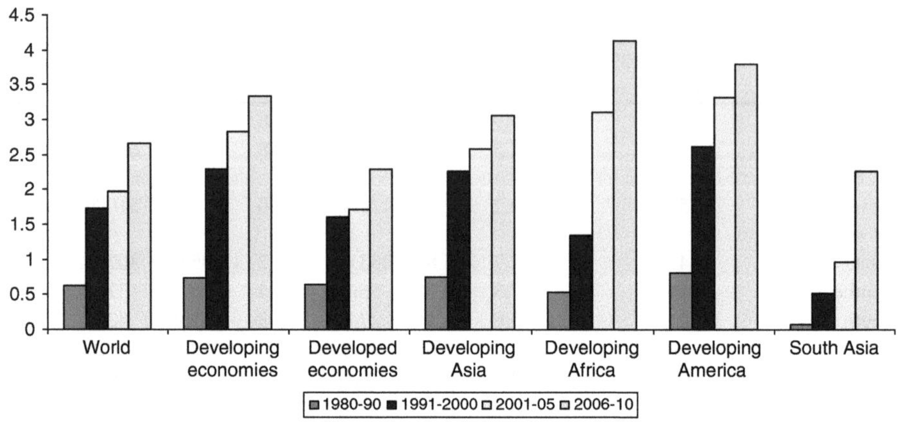

Fig. 4.1 FDI inflows as ratio of GDP: across regions (Source: UNCTAD 2011a, b)

2000s. FDI stock as ratio of GDP for South Asia also increased over time. FDI stock as ratio of GDP for South Asia increased from 2.14 % during 1980–1990 to above 4.7 % in the period 1991–2000 and further to above 28 % during the period 2006–2010. The global stock of FDI as a ratio of GDP has been increasing, but the South Asian region's stock is lower than of any other region for all periods considered above and even lower than developing Africa. This shows that South Asia has immense scope for attracting high FDI inflows (Fig. 4.2).

To put South Asia in a global and regional comparative perspective, we look at the trends in its shares. Comparative FDI share in global FDI inflows for different regions is presented in Fig. 4.3. As observed from Table 4.3, the shares of developed economies have increased since the early 1980s until the beginning of the 1990s. Thereafter, the shares of developed economies have declined from the peak of the 1980s, and recently, the shares of developed economies have been hovering around the 50 % mark.

On the other hand, the share of developing countries declined in the 1980s, but increased in the 1990s, and has been close to 50 % recently. FDI inflows to developed and developing countries are converging over time (Fig. 4.3), and faster than in the 1980s.

Importantly, FDI flows to the developing Asian and Latin American economies have increased substantially over the years with wide fluctuations. However, as a whole, Asian economies are the most favourable destination for world FDI (20.5 % during the last half of the 2000s against 10.3 % for developing Latin America). In contrast, the share of Africa and South Asia remained low, although FDI has increased since the early 1990s. Nevertheless, in comparison, South Asia's share of FDI in Asia as a whole is seen to be far below that of East Asia's. However, South Asia's relative position as a destination for FDI among other Asian developing countries has been improving continually since the early 2000s.

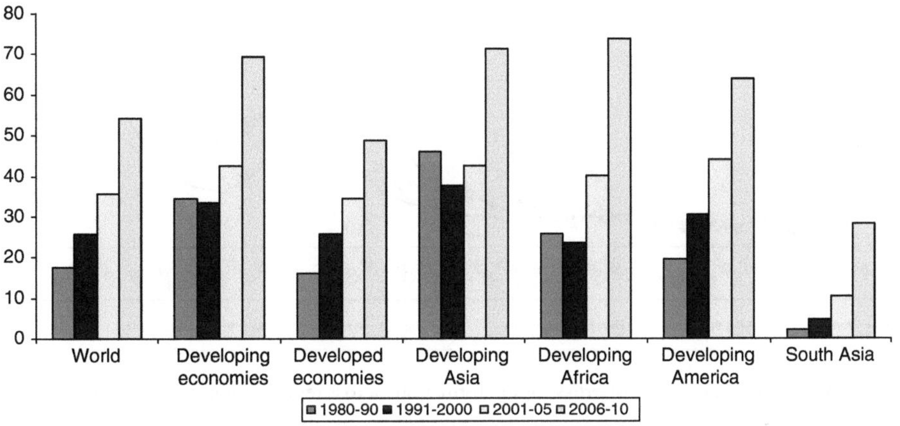

Fig. 4.2 FDI stocks as ratio of GDP: across regions (Source: UNCTAD 2011a, b)

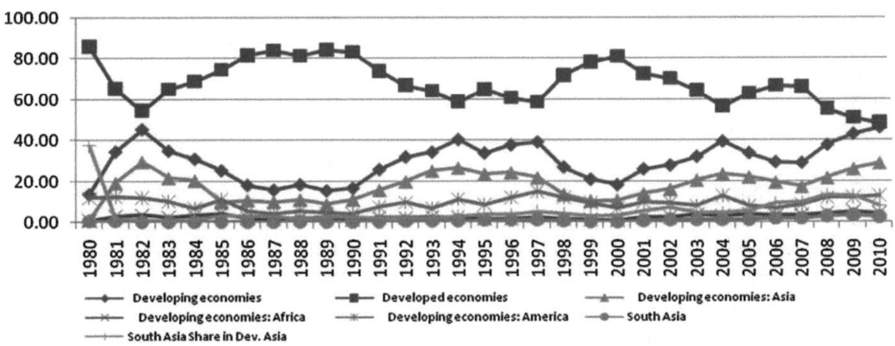

Fig. 4.3 Share of various regions in total FDI inflows (Source: World Investment Report, various issues)

We look at the pattern of the share of FDI inflows in gross capital formation to examine the relative importance of FDI in the productive capacities of different economies. Figure 4.4 presents FDI inflows as ratio of gross capital formation for different regions. It suggests that the relative importance of FDI as a source of capital investment is much smaller for South Asian countries than for developing countries. However, South Asia has caught up in recent years with other developing countries, including Asian developing countries. The proportion of FDI in gross capital formation in South Asia has steadily increased, especially since the early 1990s, and stood at around 7 % during 2006–2010. Notwithstanding the recent increase in FDI proportion in capital formation, the South Asian region's average is still below the average of all the regions including the world.

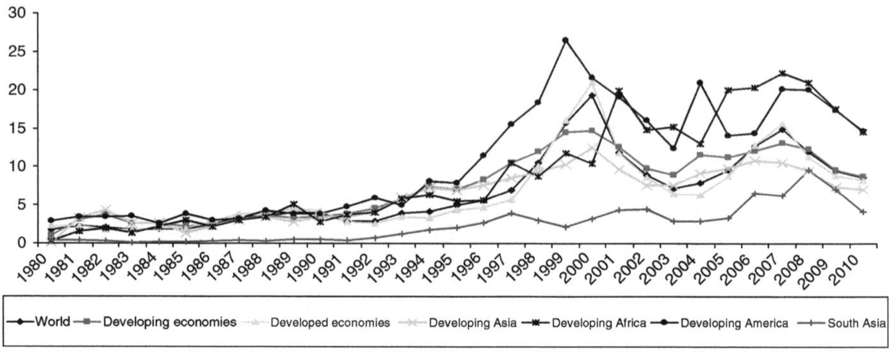

Fig. 4.4 FDI inflows as ratio of gross capital formation: across regions (Source: World Investment Report, various issues)

Table 4.2 South–South FDI flows ($billions)

Years	World outward FDI	South–South FDI flows	South–South FDI (% of world total)	Growth rate (%)
1990	241	12	5	−14
1995	363	27	7	10
2000	1,233	35	3	−6
2001	753	41	5	16
2002	537	30	6	−26
2003	566	39	7	29
2004	920	77	8	96
2005	893	88	10	15
2006	1,411	145	10	64
2007	2,267	180	8	25
2008	1,928	187	10	4
2009	1,100	149	14	−20

Source: UNCTAD (2010b)

4.2.1 South–South FDI Flows

During the 1990s and 2000s, developing countries have emerged as major sources of foreign investment. As Table 4.2 indicates, South–South FDI has been growing rapidly—around 20 % per annum over the period 1990–2009—and now accounts for around 14 % of total FDI flows. Annual South–South FDI flows have increased significantly from around $12 billion in 1990, peaking at $187 billion in 2008, before falling to $149 billion in 2009—due mainly to the global financial crisis (UNCTAD 2010b). Asia also dominates South–South FDI flows, although not very prominently. With the sharp decline of OFDI flows from developed countries since the global crisis of 2007–2008, the importance of investment from other developing countries (South–South FDI) has increased and accounted for an estimated 34 % in 2010 compared to 25 % in 2007 World Bank (2011).

Usually, developing country OFDI seeks efficiency, resources, and markets. It also seeks to build a global presence and buy brand names, technology, processes, management know-how, and marketing and distribution networks (UNCTAD 2007; World Bank 2011). Econometric investigations establish a statistically significant relationship between bilateral cross-border investment by emerging market firms in countries with strong growth potential, sound institutions, and strong trade links. Moreover, the analysis confirms the hypothesis that emerging market companies tend to expand abroad to exploit growth opportunities absent in their home economies or to escape an unfavourable economic climate (World Bank 2011).

In terms of modes of entry, South–South FDI inflows are dominated by greenfield investment, whereas South–North FDI is dominated by mergers and acquisitions (M&A). Greenfield investments accounted for 72 % of emerging market firms' investment in other emerging markets during 2003–2009 and accounted for the majority of South–South FDI flows even during the height of the expansion (World Bank 2011). In contrast, emerging market firms' investment in advanced economies occurs mainly through M&A transactions—85 % of all such investments occurred over 2003–2009 (World Bank 2011).

The major beneficiaries of rapid growth of South–South FDI flows have been the low-income countries, particularly sub-Saharan Africa. For example, low-income countries have received $93 billion in FDI from emerging markets since 1997. In 2010 alone, FDI flows to low-income countries amounted to $13.3 billion (World Bank 2011). China, India, UAE, Malaysia, and South Africa are major sources of South–South FDI into low-income countries. In addition, investments from the Gulf Cooperation Council (GCC) countries in African LDCs have recently increased significantly. For example, flows of FDI from developing nations hit a record $300 billion in 2008. South–South FDI flows peaked at 187 billion in 2008, representing 14 % of the total global flow, up from 12 billion in 1990 (5 % of the total global flows). For example, China's outward FDI stood at $59 billion in 2010 (4.7 % of global outward FDI), up from $0.8 billion in 1990 (0.34 %). On the other hand, India sent $13.1 billion in 2010 (0.9 %), nearly 500-fold that in 1990 (UNCTAD 2011a). Similarly, sector-wise South–South FDI flows indicate that FDI was predominantly centred on metal and mining, oil and gas, and telecommunications sectors. However, mining companies played a larger role within North–South acquisitions than within South–South acquisitions.

4.3 FDI Inflows to South Asian Countries

South Asian countries have been making consistent efforts to attract more FDI by liberalising their FDI policy frameworks to compete with other countries in the region. However, given the wars and ethnic strife in most countries, the region is nowhere close to Southeast Asia. India has attracted the maximum FDI in South Asia. While India's share of FDI to developing countries has been, and still is, significantly lower than that of the major Latin American and East Asian economies, it receives the maximum FDI in South Asia.

India is the largest not only in terms of economic size but also in terms of recipients of maximum FDI inflows in the subregion. FDI inflows to India have increased from $7.6 billion in 2005 to $20.3 billion in 2006 and more than doubled in 2008 to $42.5 billion, before declining to $24.6 billion in 2010. Pakistan has also attracted growing magnitudes of FDI inflows rising from $0.3 billion in 2000 to $5.6 billion in 2007 (Table 4.1). However, in 2010 FDI inflow declined more than half of its level of 2008 to $2.0 billion, with the growing internal security concerns and lower economic growth.

Bangladesh is the third largest recipient of FDI inflows in the region. FDI inflows to Bangladesh increased from $0.6 billion in 2000 to $0.8 billion in 2005 and further to $0.9 billion in 2010.

FDI inflows to Sri Lanka stagnated at around $0.2 billion over 2001–2005 and increased remarkably to $0.8 billion over 2006–2008, reflecting much improvement in confidence in the country's growth potential with the easing of security concerns. However, FDI inflow declined to $0.4 billion during 2009 and $0.5 billion in 2010.

Nepal is a landlocked country in South Asia and receives the least amount of FDI due to continual political unrest. However, FDI inflows have increased substantially in recent years compared to the 1990s or early 2000s, due partly to the liberalisation of the region's policy regimes since the early 1990s (Kumar 2010). Increases in FDI inflows in South Asia were also associated with a manifold increase in investment by national investors. There is great complementarity and linkages between foreign and national investment (Agrawal 2000). The rapid growth in FDI inflows to South Asia is due mainly to its sustained high growth rates (Mehta 2007). More importantly, the region has been pursuing open economic policies in recent years, which improved economic efficiency of capital and labour and became an advantage (Kumar and Singh 2009).

In the past three decades, India bagged the lion's share of FDI in South Asia, particularly since 1994; it captured nearly 80 % on average from 2000 to 2010. Pakistan is the second largest recipient of FDI inflows to South Asia; however, its share has been declining in recent times (Fig. 4.5).

On the other hand, Bangladesh has demonstrated a better position over Sri Lanka in bagging FDI from the last half of the 1990s, although, in general, the trend declined for both economies over 2003–2010. For instance, Bangladesh received 0.8 % of FDI in South Asia on an average in the 1980s, which increased to 6 % in the 1990s and to 4.2 % in the 2000s. On the other hand, Pakistan bagged 38.8 % of FDI in South Asia on average in the 1980s, which declined to 26 % in the 1990s and further to 11.8 % in the 2000s. In contrast, India's share increased from 38.9 % in 1980s to 57 % in the 1990s and further to 80 % during the 2000s. Nepal booked the lowest percentage of FDI in South Asian economies. In the same year, Nepal experienced a negative FDI share (Fig. 4.5). This indicates that India has been a favoured destination for FDI, particularly during the 2000s, due to higher economic

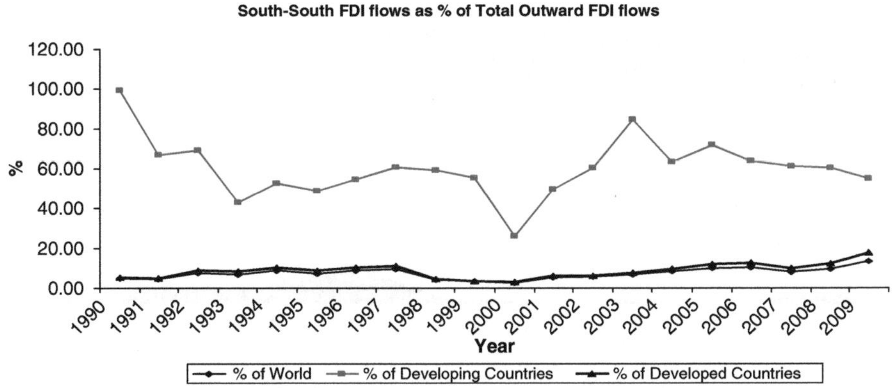

Fig. 4.5 South–South FDI flows as percentage of world total outflows (Source: World Investment Report, various issues)

growth and a number of vital reforms in important sectors such as finance and services. On the other hand, both Pakistan and Nepal demonstrate mixed results in capturing FDI in the South Asian economies over the last three decades.

It is argued that the evaluation of performance of any economic variable does not convey a meaningful result unless it is normalised by GDP or capital formation. To get a better picture, a cross-county comparison of FDI inflows and FDI stock as a ratio of GDP is presented in Figs. 4.6 and 4.7 for selected developing countries. Figure 4.6 indicates that South Asian countries have attracted less FDI than Asian, African, or Latin American countries. Asian developing countries such as China, Malaysia, and Thailand have far better FDI–GDP ratio. For example, FDI inflows as ratio of GDP for China increased from 0.5 % in 1980–1990 to 3.9 % during 1991–2000 but declined to 2.8 % during 2000s. During 1980s and 1990s, Malaysia had the highest FDI ratio of other countries. However, during the 2000s, Indonesia had the highest FDI–GDP ratio.

Figure 4.6 depicts that none of the South Asian economies bagged FDI to the value of even 1 % of their GDP during the 1980s or 1990s. During the 1980s, Pakistan captured the highest average FDI over GDP (0.26 %) followed by Sri Lanka and India. Poor FDI performance of South Asian countries was related to their government's inward policies in the 1980s that restricted liberalisation of foreign trade. During the 1990s, Pakistan dominated the inward FDI of South Asia in terms of FDI as a percentage of GDP, followed by Sri Lanka and Bangladesh. India occupied the fourth position during that time. However, the picture changed slightly during the 2000s. Although Pakistan still dominates FDI inflows in the 2000s (1.91 % of GDP) followed by India (1.63 % of GDP) and Bangladesh (0.97 % of GDP), the gap between India and Pakistan has narrowed. Both Pakistan and India are somehow comparable to South Africa in terms of FDI–GDP ratio. Pakistan and India have done better than any other South Asian country (Fig. 4.6).

Malaysia had the best ratio of FDI stock to GDP in the 1980s, 1990s, and 2000s, but Thailand and South Africa are catching up now, largely because these countries

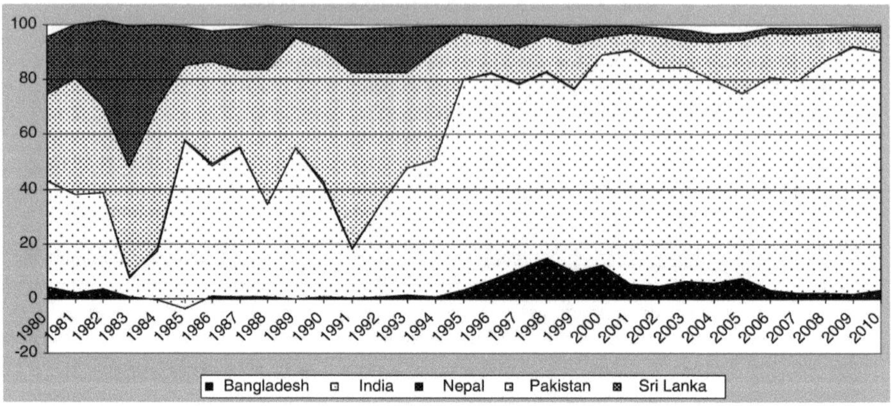

Fig. 4.6 Country FDI share in South Asia (Source: World Investment Report, various issues)

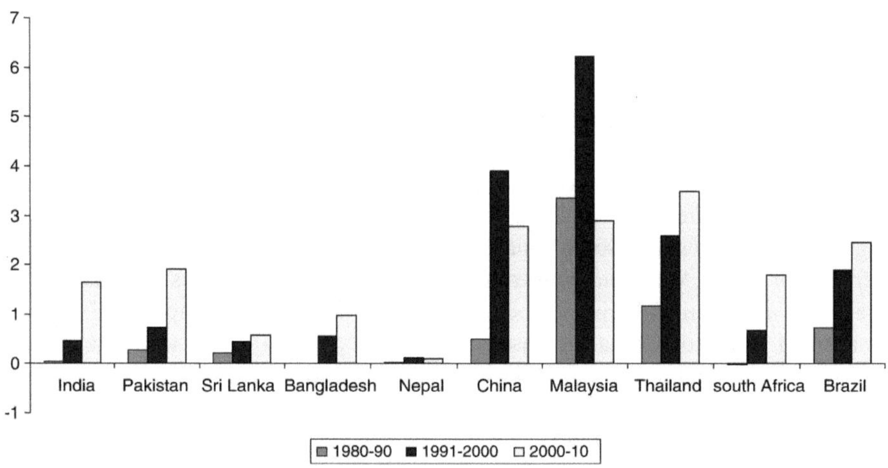

Fig. 4.7 FDI inflows as ratio of GDP: across countries (Source: World Investment Report, various issues)

followed a liberal FDI policy. South Asian countries' position compared to other developing countries indicates that all the South Asian countries have performed badly. Among South Asian countries, Pakistan and Sri Lanka are better positioned than India and Bangladesh (Fig. 4.7).

Figure 4.8 presents FDI as a percentage of gross capital formation (GCF) over 1980–1990, 1991–2000, and 2001–2010 for selected developing countries. Malaysia dominates on this metric as in FDI inflows and stock over GDP in all three periods (except Brazil during 2000s), closely followed by Thailand and Brazil. FDI did not play major role in capital formation in all South Asian countries except Pakistan. However, FDI capital formation is increasing for all countries over time except Nepal.

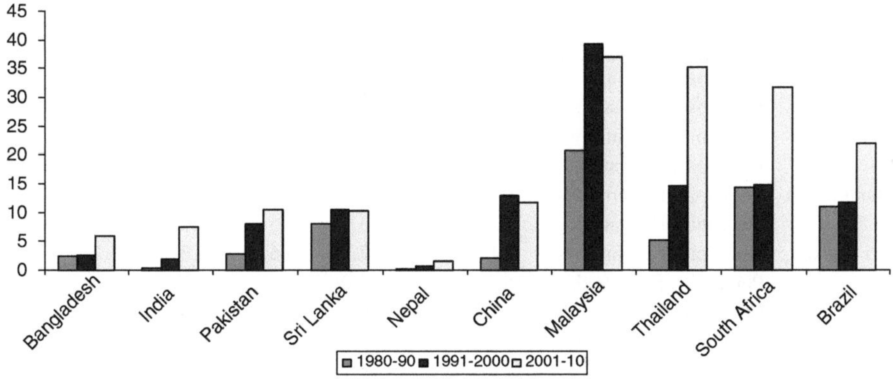

Fig. 4.8 FDI stocks as ratio of GDP: across countries (Source: World Investment Report, various issues)

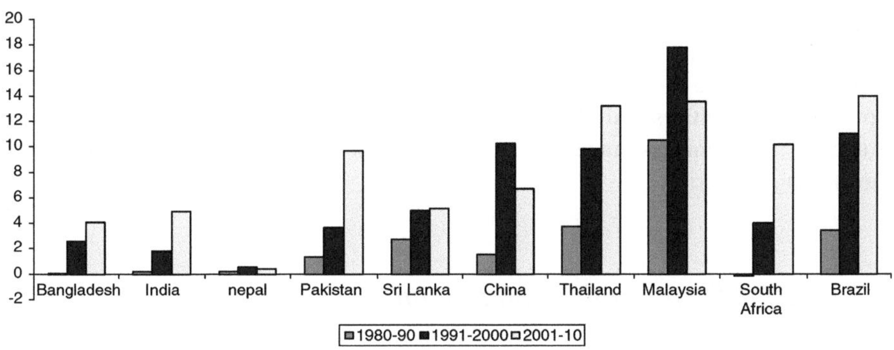

Fig. 4.9 FDI inflows as ratio of gross fixed capital formation: across countries (Source: World Investment Report, various issues)

Among South Asian countries, Sri Lanka is seen to maintain the leadership position during the 1980s (2.75 %) and 1990s (5 %) followed by Pakistan (1.32 and 3.67 %, respectively). However, during the 2000s, Pakistan gained the leading position (9.66 %), and Sri Lanka (5.17 %) and India (4.93 %) occupied the second and the third positions, respectively. In terms of FDI over capital formation, Bangladesh improved its position from fourth in the 1980s to third in the 1990s and before slipping to fourth in the 2000s. For Nepal, FDI as a ratio of capital formation remains negligible over three decades (Fig. 4.9).

In addition to this, along with the world average, we present FDI inflow and FDI stock per capita in US$ terms for South Asian countries, all of which are well below the world average in both FDI inflow and FDI stock per capita (Table 4.3), although their per capita FDI inflows and stock have increased over three decades (except Nepal). Sri Lanka has the best per capita FDI inflows in the subregion, followed by Pakistan and India. India has overtaken Pakistan in per capita terms only recently.

Table 4.3 Trends in FDI per capita inflows to South Asian countries ($)

Country	Indicators	1980	1985	1990	1995	2000	2005	2010
India	Per capita FDI inflows	0.1	0.1	0.3	2.3	3.4	6.7	20.2
	Per capita FDI, stock	0.8	1.2	2.4	7.2	18.7	45.0	188.0
Pakistan	Per capita FDI inflows	0.8	0.6	2.5	3.9	2.1	13.9	11.6
	Per capita FDI, stock	11.6	15.8	23.5	56.6	61.8	80.1	149.0
Bangladesh	Per capita FDI inflows	0.1	−0.1	0.0	0.8	4.5	6.0	6.1
	Per capita FDI, stock	6.9	6.6	5.9	6.5	20.6	29.7	46.9
Sri Lanka	Per capita FDI inflows	2.8	1.5	2.5	3.6	9.2	13.7	22.9
	Per capita FDI, stock	18.3	37.4	45.0	80.0	92.1	134.0	267.0
Nepal	Per capita FDI inflows	0.0	0.0	0.3	0.0	0.0	0.1	1.3
	Per capita FDI, stock	0.1	0.2	0.4	0.8	3.8	5.4	8.4
World	Per capita FDI, stock	12.1	11.5	39.1	59.8	229.0	151.0	180.0
	Per capita FDI inflows	156.9	203.0	393.0	592.0	1,216.0	2,101.0	2,775.0

Source: UNCTAD, Database

Nepal had the lowest per capita FDI and had negative or zero per capita FDI in some years. Therefore, we find that FDI inflow has increased over time to South Asian countries, as in the case of other developing countries. The large difference between South Asian countries and other developing countries is decreasing over time, but South Asian countries have to make a serious effort to catch up with other developing countries.

4.3.1 FDI Performance and Potential

The UNCTAD's *Inward FDI Performance Index*, which measures the amount of FDI that countries receive relative to the size of their economy (GDP), shows a change in the ranking of host countries, which reflects a shift in terms of FDI performance towards developing and transition economies from developed countries. The index for developed countries as a group is below unity, and their ranking has fallen since the global economic crisis of 2007–2008. In contrast, developing countries increased their performance index in the period 2005–2010, and they all have indices above unity (UNCTAD 2011a).

The rise of FDI to developing countries also varies across countries within a region. Tables 4.4 and 4.5 present the Inward FDI Performance Index[1] and FDI

[1] The UNCTAD FDI inward performance index is a measure of the extent to which a host country receives inward FDI relative to its economic size. It is calculated as the ratio of the country's share in global FDI inflows to its share in global GDP. A value greater than 1 indicates that the country/region receives more FDI than its relative economic size, a value below 1 that it receives less.

Table 4.4 Inward FDI Performance Index for South Asia and selected developing countries

Economy	1990	1995	2000	2005	2008	2009	2010
India	96	95	115	120	80	67	97
Bangladesh	105	107	103	109	117	120	114
Sri Lanka	70	103	109	117	109	116	113
Pakistan	66	93	122	92	74	100	110
Nepal	91	123	134	135	136	134	134
PRC	57	17	62	70	97	83	86
Singapore	1	1	6	12	61	20	9
Thailand	14	72	78	48	84	84	83

Source: UNCTAD (2011a, b)

Table 4.5 Inward FDI Potential Index for South Asia and selected developing countries

Economy	1990	1995	2000	2005	2008	2009
India	86	97	92	84	86	79
Bangladesh	107	116	108	115	119	114
Sri Lanka	102	93	106	122	117	110
Pakistan	91	111	131	125	126	121
Nepal	110	130	133	138	140	139
PRC	42	49	44	34	30	27
Singapore	9	3	2	2	2	3
Thailand	40	45	52	64	63	56

Source: UNCTAD (2011a, b)

Note: FDI potential and performance indices refer to the 3-year moving averages using data for the three previous years including the year in question. The ranking includes 140 countries. Change of potential and performance: 'minus' denotes improving ranking

Potential Index[2] for South Asia and a few other countries in the region. Most South Asian countries, along with PRC and Thailand, have managed to increase their inward FDI performance and FDI Potential Index consistently over the years. In fact, countries like Pakistan and Bangladesh have fared better than large economies such as India, although the potential of larger economies is higher. However, India's FDI Performance Index has increased significantly in 2008 and 2009 and taken a slight dip in 2010 which may be due to delays in FDI reform measures as a result of a halt in major economic reforms. India has not been able to liberalise its FDI policy framework to the extent that some of its neighbours, like

[2] The UNCTAD FDI Potential Index to compare the relative potentials of different countries attracting FDI inflows is based on major economic variables: (1) market attractiveness, which explains market size (GDP purchasing power parity) and growth potential (real GDP growth rate); (2) availability of low-cost labour and skills, which includes unit of labour cost (hourly compensation and labour productivity) and size of manufacturing workforce (existing skill base); (3) presence of natural resources—resource exploitation (value of fuels and ores exports) and agricultural potential (availability of arable land); and (4) enabling infrastructure, which includes all kinds transport infrastructure and energy infrastructure such as consumption, and telecom infrastructure telephone lines/100 inhabitants-mobile cellular subscriptions/100 inhabitants and fixed broadband internet subscriber/1,000 inhabitants) (page no 30, UNCTAD 2012).

Table 4.6 Component-wise FDI inflows to South Asia (in million $)

	Types of component	1990	1995	2000	2005	2010
India	Equity capital	NA	2,144	2,400	5,975	20,304
	Reinvested earnings	NA	0	1,350	2,760	9,424
	Other capital	NA	0	279	226	652
	Total FDI	NA	2,144	4,029	8,961	30,380
Pakistan	Equity capital	4,014	11,867	6,301	51,747	NA
	Reinvested earnings	1,508	3,384	8,941	13,600	NA
	Other capital	490	1,647	326	281	NA
	Total foreign assets	6,012	16,898	15,588	65,628	NA
Bangladesh	Equity capital	NA	NA	350	425	232
	Reinvested earnings	NA	NA	77	247	380
	Other capital	NA	NA	150	172	124
	Total FDI	NA	NA	578	845	792

Note: Data before the year 1996 is not available

Bangladesh and Sri Lanka, have accomplished in recent years. Though the sectoral caps on insurance and retail have increased, there is a policy paralysis on various other fronts. However, India's potential inward index has been improving over the years.

Similarly, the FDI Performance Index indicates that India has done better in recent years than other South Asian countries, whose performance and potential rankings have declined. For instance, Bangladesh ranked 103 among a set of 140 countries in the FDI Performance Index and 102 in the FDI Potential Index in 1990. In 2010, Bangladesh ranked 114 in both the FDI Performance and potential index, although can improve its ranking in both. Thus, most countries in the region have the potential to improve their FDI performance rankings. The potential index covers much of the benefits accruing due to the potentialities of skilled manpower, improved infrastructure facility, and growing demand in the system. The performance index considers existing foreign resource utilisation and efficiency while understanding the importance of scale economies. An economy may perform in alignment with its potentials subject to its other macroeconomic fundamentals.

4.3.2 *Component-Wise FDI Inflows to South Asia (in Million $)*

Component-wise FDI can be divided into three components: equity capital, reinvested earnings, and other capital. However, data is not available in this format for all South Asian countries except for Bangladesh, India, and Pakistan. Table 4.6 provides FDI inflows by components for Bangladesh, India, and Pakistan. It explains that equity capital constitutes the major component of FDI for all three countries. Reinvested earnings are the second largest component in FDI inflows, and other capital is the third largest component. The continuous rise in reinvested earnings in these three countries indicates improved economic performance and increased profits of foreign affiliates. Besides the above two components, intercompany loans or other capital is found to play an important role in FDI inflows in Bangladesh than in Pakistan or in India.

4.4 Country-Wise FDI Inflows to South Asia: Composition, Pattern, and Distribution

Having analysed FDI inflows to South Asia, an attempt has been made to trace the FDI source countries and sector-wise FDI inflows to each of the South Asian countries over two decades. This analysis is important for two reasons. First, it reflects FDI policies of a host country in promoting certain preferred sectors, and second, it shows the preference of foreign investors to a particular country and the sectors of their interest. Although sector-wise FDI data is not uniformly available, a major effort has been made to ensure meaningful comparison across countries. This section is devoted to the sectoral distribution of FDI in South Asia. Sector-wise FDI distribution indicates that the services sector attracts more FDI than the manufacturing and primary sector both globally and in South Asia.

4.4.1 India

For better policymaking, it is important to know the source economies of FDI and their relative share in total FDI inflows of a country. Keeping this in mind, country-wise FDI inflows to India are provided in Table 4.7. Mauritius was the top source of FDI inflow into India over 2000–2010 and the source of over 40 % of the total FDI inflow into India since the financial year (FY) 2005–2006. Two reasons for the huge inflows could be that most business persons in Mauritius are of Indian origin and India's double taxation treaty with Mauritius, which facilitates tax-free inflows into India. Singapore and the USA have emerged as the second and the third largest investors into India, followed by Japan and the other developed countries like the UK, the Netherlands, Cyprus, Germany, Singapore, and France, which are India's major trading partners. Nearly one-quarter of India's exports go to the EU and the other quarter to North America; these two regions are the largest investors in India. In sum, FDI inflows in India are seen to have been heavily reliant on a single economy—Mauritius. Besides, the top 10 economies are found to have shared approximately more than 80 % of the total FDI into India since 2005–2006. In terms of the share of developing and developed countries in total FDI, developing countries (54 %) have a higher share than developed countries (46 %) during 2000–2010. However, between August 1991 and March 2000, developed countries had a higher share (64 %) than developing countries (36 %).

Table 4.7 India: FDI share of top ten countries (% share)

Countries	August 1991–2000	2005–2006	2006–2007	2008–2009	2009–2010	2010–2011	2000–2010
Mauritius	10.6	46.3	40.5	41.1	40.2	36.0	42.0
Singapore	2.0	5.0	0.8	12.6	9.2	8.8	9.0
USA	21.9	9.1	3.7	6.6	7.5	6.0	7.0
UK	7.5	4.8	4.1	3.2	2.5	3.9	5.0
Netherlands	2.2	1.4	11.9	3.2	3.5	6.2	4.0
Japan	4.3	3.8	5.4	1.5	4.6	8.0	4.0
Cyprus	0.0	1.3	0.7	4.7	6.3	4.7	4.0
Germany	3.8	5.5	0.5	2.3	2.4	1.0	2.0
France	2.4	0.3	0.4	1.7	1.2	3.8	2.0
UAE	0.3	0.9	1.7	0.9	2.4	1.8	1.0
Developed countries	64.0	42.0	45.0	43.0	42.0	52.0	46.0
Developing countries	36.0	58.0	55.0	57.0	58.0	48.0	54.0
Total	100	100	100	100	100	100	100

Source: SIA news Letter, various issues

Given the fact that India is the largest recipient of FDI in South Asia, we take up sectoral distribution of FDI of India first. The distribution of FDI by different sectors and their respective shares for India are presented in Table 4.8. Between August 1991 and March 2005, the electronics equipment industry attracted the maximum FDI, followed by telecommunications, transportation, and the services sector; together, these attracted 38 % of the FDI in India. The power, chemicals, and food processing industries also contributed significantly. The rough estimation of sector-wise FDI indicates that the services sector attracted higher FDI, followed by manufacturing and primary sector.

Similarly, during 2000–2010, the financial and nonfinancial services sector in India received the lion's share of FDI, followed by telecommunications, computer software and hardware, and housing and real estate. In the past 3 years (FY 2008–2009 to 2010–2011), the services sector alone bagged 22, 16, and 17 % of the total FDI in India, respectively, and was the top recipient. During the same time, the share of FDI for the telecommunications sector declined marginally from 9 % in 2008–2009 to 8 % in 2010–2011. Two new sectors—housing and real estate and construction activities—entered the top five. The share of FDI for housing and real estate sector increased from 3 % in 2006–2007 to 11 % in 2009–2010 and thereafter declined to 6 % in 2010–2011. Likewise, the distribution of FDI in the construction sector increased from 6 % in 2006–2007 to 11 % in FY 2009–2010. However, the share of this sector declined to 5 % in 2010–2011. The other important sectors for FDI in the recent period have been metallurgical, automobiles, power, and petroleum and natural gas. A rough estimation of sector-wise FDI indicates that the services sector attracted the most FDI in recent times, followed by the manufacturing and primary sector. FDI inflows into different sectors in India have made a dramatic shift in the recent decade, from transportation, electrical equipment, fuels, food processing, and drug and pharmaceutical sectors to services, telecommunications, housing and real estate, construction, computer software and hardware, automobiles, telecommunications, and power sectors.

The services sector has attracted significant foreign investment. This may be due to low-cost wages along with the wide demand–supply gap in financial services particularly in banking, insurance, and telecommunications. Also, over the years, India has enhanced its potential in knowledge process outsourcing, financial analysis, and business processing. All these factors coupled with the removal of the cap on FDI in services have added to the growth momentum of the sector. At present, Indian services sector has recorded a phenomenal growth and continuously seeking the foreign attention.

4.4.2 Pakistan

FDI inflows to Pakistan by major economies are presented in Table 4.9. It is evident that the USA is the largest investor in Pakistan in all the periods. The UK and the UAE have emerged as the second and third largest investors in Pakistan since

Table 4.8 Major sector-wise distribution of FDI in India (% share in total FDI)

Sectors	August 1991–2005	Sectors	2006–2007	2008–2009	2009–2010	2010–2011	2000–2010
Electrical equipments	14.13	Services sector	29.7	22.6	16.2	17.0	21.0
Telecommunications	8.66	Telecommunications	3.0	9.3	9.8	8.6	8.0
Transportation industry	8.17	Computer software and hardware	16.6	5.7	3.4	4.0	8.0
Services sector	7.94	Housing and real estate	3.0	10.4	11.4	6.3	8.0
Fuels (power + oil refinery)	6.63	Construction activities	6.3	7.3	11.0	5.7	7.0
Chemicals	5.51	Automobile industry	1.8	4.2	4.8	6.7	5.0
Food processing industries	3.03	Power	1.0	3.3	4.9	6.5	4.0
Drugs and pharmaceuticals	2.59	Metallurgical industries	1.1	3.5	1.6	5.7	3.0
Cement and gypsum products	1.92	Petroleum and natural gas	0.6	1.3	1.0	2.9	2.0
Metallurgical industries	1.68	Chemicals	0.9	2.4	1.4	2.1	2.0

Source: SIA newsletter, various issues

Table 4.9 Pakistan: FDI share of major countries (%)

Countries	1990–1991	1995–1996	2000–2001	2005–2006	2007–2008	2008–2009	2009–2010	2010–2011
USA	52.8	29.3	28.8	14.7	17.8	24.2	23.4	22.2
UK	13.7	29.0	28.1	6.9	16.8	8.5	7.1	13.2
UAE	3.7	4.8	1.6	40.4	13.0	10.8	4.8	11.0
Japan	10.6	7.5	2.8	1.6	1.3	2.4	2.0	1.2
Hong Kong	1.3	3.1	1.1	0.7	14.5	6.2	4.2	0.4
Switzerland	–	–	1.1	4.9	3.4	3.1	6.1	7.7
Saudi Arabia	0.4	2.5	17.6	7.9	2.0	0.8	−2.4	−6.0
Germany	5.1	2.6	4.8	0.8	1.6	1.2	2.1	2.4
Malaysia	–	–	–	–	–	12.1	5.7	0.7
Norway	–	–	0.5	7.2	0.5	5.1	2.7	−3.0
China	–	–	–	0.1	13.8	0.3	–	–
Developed countries	88.0	81.0	72.0	52.0	67.0	58.0	57.0	62.0
Developing countries	11.0	19.0	28.0	46.0	33.0	42.0	43.0	38.0
Total	100	100	100	100	100	100	100	100

Source: *Handbook of Statistics on Pakistan Economy* 2010

1990–1991. The share of the USA declined from 52.8 % of the total inflows in 1990–1991 to only 15 % in 2005–2006, but again increased to 22 % in 2010–2011. These three economies (the USA, the UK, and the UAE), together contributed 70 % of FDI in Pakistan in 1990–1991, which declined to 63 % in 1995–1996, and further to 46 % in 2010–2011, albeit with considerable fluctuations. Besides these three economies, Switzerland, Germany, Japan, Saudi Arabia, and Hong Kong have been major investors in Pakistan over the past two decades. Besides these countries, other countries such as Malaysia, Norway, and China have emerged as important contributors of FDI to Pakistan in recent years.

In terms of the share of developing and developed countries in total FDI, developed countries have contributed higher FDI than developing countries during the entire period under consideration, except in 2005–2006, when a larger contribution from the UAE brought the shares of developing and developed countries closer. Indeed, the role of developing and transition economies as sources of FDI is increasing with time. Notably, the share of both developed and developing countries has been fluctuating quite considerably over time. Therefore, based on the share of top countries, FDI inflows to Pakistan have become more diversified in recent times.

4.4.2.1 Sector-Wise Distribution of FDI in Pakistan

Table 4.10 provides the distribution of FDI by major sectors in Pakistan. The agricultural sector attracted the least FDI during 2001–2011. The manufacturing sector attracted the second highest amount of FDI. In the manufacturing sector, the chemicals and oil and gas sectors have emerged as attractive due to the Pakistan government's liberal policy. In comparison to the manufacturing sector, FDI inflows to services sector attracted the highest amount of FDI in Pakistan. However, in recent years, the share of services declined quite dramatically due to significant slowdown in FDI to communication and financial business sector. The communication and financial business sectors attracted the most FDI—the communication sector received 31 % of the FDI inflow into Pakistan on average between 2000–2001 and 2009–2010.

Similarly, the financial business sector attracted around 19 % of the total inflow during the same period. Therefore, like India, the majority of FDI in Pakistan flows to the services sector, followed by the manufacturing sector. Overall, the sectoral decomposition of FDI in Pakistan shows high concentration in a few sectors such as oil and gas, communications, and financial business. The existing literature mentions the liberalisation and privatisation of the financial sector as the main factor of the massive inflow of foreign capital. For oil and gas exploration, Pakistan has the fifth largest reservoir of coal. At the same time, it is highlighted that the power sector of Pakistan has great potential for investment (Khan 2011). Industrial sector got advantage because foreign investors were allowed to hold 100 % of the equity in industrial project on a repatriable basis, without any prior approval during early 1990s (Khan and Khan 2011).

Table 4.10 Sector-wise distribution of FDI in Pakistan (% share in total FDI)

	2000–2001	2005–2006	2006–2007	2007–2008	2008–2009	2009–2010	2010–2011
Agriculture	0.1	0.1	–	0.2	0.1	0.1	0.1
Manufacturing	66.0	30.3	13.3	15.1	26.3	47.1	59.2
Chemical	8.1	3.3	0.9	1.5	2.0	5.3	5.1
Oil and gas exploration	26.3	12.7	10.6	11.7	20.8	34.4	33.6
Services	0.2	58.7	62.2	69.1	50.6	20.9	34.9
Communication	25.3	33.9	37.0	30.1	24.2	13.5	13.2
Finance business	8.6	17.6	18.1	34.5	19.0	7.6	7.4

Source: *Handbook of Statistics on Pakistan Economy* 2010

Table 4.11 FDI inflows to Sri Lanka by major countries (%)

Countries	1978–1995	2005	2006	2007	2008	2009	2010
South Korea	32.7	1.7	1.7	1.5	1.1	0.3	0.5
Australia	15	1.1	0.7	0.6	0.9	1.0	1.6
Hong Kong	11.9	5.4	7.7	4.9	8.4	4.4	5.5
Japan	11.6	1.4	6.4	6.6	1.9	3.2	2.6
Germany	7	0.7	0.9	0.6	0.4	0.6	–
Singapore	6.4	10.7	4.9	2.8	2.3	3.6	8.2
India	1.2	6.2	4.5	5.9	14.2	7.75	21.3
Malaysia	0.2	32.4	27.3	40.4	17.0	27.3	14.0
USA	1.1	4.6	5.9	3.6	6.4	3.6	2.8
UK	1.4	9.3	6.7	13.1	9.8	6.8	12.0
Sweden	2.1	3.5	8.3	4.3	4.2	3.2	2.3
Developed countries	53.0	51.0	39.0	34.0	40.0	49.0	53.0
Developing countries	47.0	49.0	61.0	66.0	60.0	51.0	47.0
Total	100	100	100	100		100	100

Source: For 1978–1995 data Athukorala (1997); the data from 1996 to 2003 is not available, and for other years, data is from Board of Investment (BOI), Sri Lanka

4.4.3 Sri Lanka

The major country-wise contribution of FDI to Sri Lanka is presented in Table 4.11 over 1978–2010. As far as the country-wise share of FDI to Sri Lanka is concerned, the table indicates that South Korea was the largest provider of FDI (32.7 %) during the period of 1978–1995. Other major contributors were Australia (15.0 %), Hong Kong (11.9 %), Japan (11.6 %), and Singapore (6.4 %.) In the recent period, however, Malaysia has taken leadership along with India. Besides these countries, the UK, Singapore, Hong Kong, and the USA have become the major FDI suppliers in Sri Lanka. For instance, in 2009, Malaysia alone contributed 27.3 % of FDI in Sri Lanka, although its share dropped to 14 % in 2010. Similarly, India contributed 8 % of FDI in 2009, which increased to 21.3 % in 2010. It is to be noted that India's contribution to Sri Lanka's FDI was only 1.2 % during the period of 1978–1995.

Apart from these economies, Sweden, Hong Kong, and South Korea were other major contributors of FDI in Sri Lanka since the year 2005. The combined contribution of India, Malaysia, and the UK is more than 47 % of total FDI in Sri Lanka in 2010. Therefore, based on share of top countries, FDI inflows to Sri Lanka have become more diversified in recent times. In addition to this, Table 4.11 indicates that developing countries have dominated FDI inflows to Sri Lanka.

4.4.3.1 Major Sector-Wise Distribution of FDI in Sri Lanka

The sectoral decomposition of FDI inflows in Sri Lanka is presented in Table 4.12 over 2000–2010. Table 4.12 reveals that FDI has been concentrated in infrastructure and manufacturing sectors. The share of manufacturing sector peaked in 2005,

Table 4.12 Major sector-wise distribution of FDI in Sri Lanka (% share)

	2000	2005	2006	2007	2008	2009	2010
Agriculture	–	0.2	0.1	0.1	0.3	0.6	1.2
Manufacturing	18.3	47.1	38.9	23.7	21.3	27.3	30.9
Textiles, apparel, leather	10.3	16.5	17.1	8.5	8.1	8.5	7.3
Infrastructure	51.2	49.1	54.5	71.7	74.3	63.3	59.2
Telecommunication	12.4	38.9	43.6	55.0	62.2	49.2	39.7
Power generation	4.1	5.5	1.3	12.6	9.9	11.2	11.3
Services	17.1	42.6	50	59.6	66.3	57.9	48.3

Source: BOI, Sri Lanka

but it reduced to just 30.9 % in 2010. Within the manufacturing sector, textiles, apparel, and leather attracted highest amount of FDI. They have shared 17 % of the FDI in Sri Lanka in 2005, although the same dropped to 7.3 % in 2010 with considerable fluctuations over time. The largest FDI share has gone to the infrastructure sector in recent times.

For example, 49.1 % of total FDI in 2005 was in infrastructure; this share went up to 74.3 % in 2008 but declined to 59 % in 2010. Within the infrastructure sector, the telecommunications sector received the bulk of the FDI. The share of this sector went up from 12.4 % in 2000 to 38.9 % in 2005 and further to 62 % in 2008. Thereafter, the share of telecommunication sector declined to 39.7 % in 2010. The share of services sector including telecommunications shows similar trend. For example, the share of services sector increased from 17 % in 2000 to 42.6 % in 2005 and further to above 66 % in 2008. Another important sector that attracted significant amounts of FDI is power generation. Overall, the sectoral decomposition of FDI in Sri Lanka is found to be concentrated on the services/infrastructure sector over 1999–2009. The share of the agricultural sector remained very low during 2000–2010.

4.4.4 Bangladesh

Country-wise contribution of FDI inflows to Bangladesh is presented in Table 4.13 over the period 1996–2010. The UK was the highest contributor of FDI in the 1990s and early 2000s. However, its share has been declining since then. Importantly, Australia was the second largest FDI provider in Bangladesh only in 1996–1998 but has lost its position since then. Now, FDI from Australia is negligible. The USA became the largest investor in Bangladesh only in 2005–2006; its share has declined to less than 4 % in recent times. Besides the UK and the USA, Egypt has become one of the major contributors of FDI during the 2000s. Japan and South Korea contributed higher amount of FDI in Bangladesh during the last half of the 1990s than in the 2000s. On the other hand, Malaysia, Hong Kong, Norway, Japan, and the UAE, which contributed little FDI to Bangladesh during the last half of the 1990s, have become more prominent in the 2000s. Interestingly, the share of the

Table 4.13 FDI inflows to Bangladesh by major countries (%)

Countries	1996–1997	2000–2001	2005–2006	2006–2007	2007–2008	2008–2009	2009–2010
UK	37.9	29.0	10.5	15.7	19.4	11.0	7.2
Australia	23.2	0.0	–	–	–	–	0.9
Egypt	–	–	9.0	15.6	17.1	32.1	2.1
Japan	11.1	3.1	3.0	3.6	3.5	6.1	2.4
South Korea	12.3	6.1	6.7	3.7	4.7	4.2	5.1
USA	6.0	3.6	25.1	20.3	7.1	3.7	3.8
Hong Kong	2.0	4.8	5.8	7.8	5.4	4.9	7.9
Malaysia	0.0	1.4	3.5	5.7	0.2	8.2	4.4
Denmark	1.0	10.4	2.2	1.2	0.9	0.4	0.8
Norway	–	0.3	7.2	10.4	0.8	6.2	6.1
UAE	–	–	13.5	7.8	17.4	7.3	3.6
Netherlands	0.2	31.8	1.9	2.3	2.8	4.1	5.3
Developed countries	83.0	87.0	60.0	65.0	49.0	41.0	75.0
Developing countries	17.0	13.0	40.0	35.0	51.0	59.0	25.0
Total	100	100	100	100	100	100	100

Source: Bangladesh Bank 2010

Netherlands, which contributed the maximum amount of FDI in 2000, dropped recently to 5 %. Finally, developed countries have contributed higher amounts consistently, but the share of developing countries has been increasing since 2005–2006 except the year 2009–2010.

As far as the country-wise share of FDI to Bangladesh is concerned, the UK invested the most (37 %). Other major contributors were Australia (23 %), Hong Kong (7.9 %), and Japan (6.9 %). Besides these countries, the UK, Hong Kong, and the USA have become the major FDI suppliers in Bangladesh. For instance, in 2009, Malaysia alone contributed 8.2 % of FDI in Bangladesh, although its share has reduced to 4.4 % in 2010. Apart from these economies, Hong Kong and South Korea were other major contributors of FDI in Bangladesh since the year 2005. The share of Norway, U.K. and Hong Kong are 6.1%, 7.2% and 7.9% respectively. Therefore, based on the share of top countries, FDI inflows to Bangladesh have become more diversified in recent times.

The sectoral FDI distribution of Bangladesh is presented in Table 4.14. Sectoral distribution of FDI from Bangladesh is available from 1996 to 1997. The manufacturing sector attracted a higher percentage of FDI in the late 1990s and early 2000s. However, the share of this sector has declined in recent times. For example, the share of the manufacturing sector increased from 66 % in 1996–1997 to 88 % in 2005–2006 and declined thereafter to 34 % in 2009–2010. In the manufacturing sector, power, gas and petroleum, and textile and weaving captured a higher share of FDI during 1996–2009. On the other hand, the services sector attracted a very meagre amount of FDI in the initial years. However, the share of the services sector has surpassed the manufacturing sector since 2005–2006. Within the services sector, the communication sector has contributed significant part of the capital inflows. The increased privatisation efforts by government telecom sector are one of the fastest-growing sectors in the Bangladesh economy (Rahman 2012). It is also highlighted that the FDI flow to export processing zones (EPZs) was able to demonstrate high growth, in recent years most likely because of assured power and utility facilities and better infrastructure (CPD 2010). Like India and Pakistan, agricultural sector attracted lowest FDI in Bangladesh. In fact, agricultural sector share has never been above 32 % in any year except the year 2000–2001.

4.4.5 Nepal

Finally, the share of key source economies (in percentage) in total FDI inflows in Nepal over the period 1990–1991 to 2010–2011 is presented in Table 4.15. It is important to note that India is the largest supplier of FDI and remained so over 1990–2010. In the export-oriented garment industry, Indian firms set up production facilities in Nepal to circumvent quota restrictions imposed under the Multi-Fibre Arrangement (MFA) on garment exports from India. Another major inducement for Indian investors has been the opportunities for profit making created by Nepal's low tariffs (Athukorala and Sharma 2006). The country had signed Bilateral Investment

Table 4.14 Major sector-wise distribution of FDI in Bangladesh (% share)

	1996–1997	2000–2001	2005–2006	2006–2007	2007–2008	2008–2009	2009–2010
Agriculture	0.1	2.8	0.2	0.2	1.1	1.3	1.2
Manufacturing	66.6	88.2	45.0	47.7	37.3	19.2	25.5
Power, gas and petroleum	29.8	55.6	28.0	29.0	20.5	5.0	8.1
Textile and weaving	12.2	19.8	9.8	13.3	12.1	13.6	17.3
Services	33.0	7.8	55.0	51.7	59.4	74.0	72.6
Trade and commerce	32.2	6.3	19.0	13.1	21.6	12.7	16.3
Transport and communication	0.4	1.0	36.2	38.4	37.8	60.3	56.3

Source: Bangladesh Bank 2010

Table 4.15 FDI inflows to Nepal by major countries (%)

Countries	1990–1991	1995–1996	2000–2001	2005–2006	2007–2008	2008–2009	2009–2010	2010–2011
India	48.3	63.0	56.1	37.8	40.3	35.1	43.9	47.6
China	0.5	6.4	13.4	10.9	18.2	11.6	7.9	10.4
USA	20.4	0.7	5.6	15.7	1.4	0.3	0.6	7.3
UAE	–	–	–	1.1	–	10.2	4.3	–
Norway	1.6	4.9	–	0.3	–	–	–	1.7
Japan	5.7	3.6	3.0	3.7	1.0	0.2	0.2	1.7
S. Korea	2.5	0.2	3.2	3.5	1.5	1.0	1.9	6.3
UK	–	0.8	0.3	3.0	2.7	0.4	0.2	2.3
Canada	–	0.4	2.1	2.2	0.7	34.7	15.4	3.2
Singapore	–	2.1	1.3	1.3	9.2	0.2	0.1	2.2
Developed countries	45.0	26.0	23.0	44.0	38.0	25.0	23.0	28.0
Developing countries	55.0	74.0	77.0	56.0	62.0	75.0	78.0	71.0
Total	100	100	100	100	100	100	100	100

Source: Department of Industry, GON

Table 4.16 Major sector-wise distribution of FDI in Nepal (% share)

	1990	1995	2000	2005	2007	2008	2009	2010
Agriculture	0.0	1.2	0.3	1.4	1.0	4.1	–	3.6
Manufacturing	98.1	31.4	58.5	35.0	12.7	18.9	7.9	61.4
Services	1.7	19.0	28.3	57.0	15.9	32.0	27.5	30.8
Tourism	1.5	16.6	17.3	6.0	7.6	12.2	16.2	11.7

Source: Department of Industry, GON

Promotion and Protection Agreement (BIPA) and Double Taxation Avoidance Agreement (DTAA) agreements with India in 2011 (Poudel 2012). After India, the USA was the second largest investor in Nepal in 1990–1991, and its share has fluctuated widely and now stands at 7.3 % in 2010. Furthermore, it is evident from Table 4.10 that China has become the second largest important contributor of FDI to Nepal. FDI share of China increased from a meagre 0.5 % in 1990–1991 to 13.4 % in 2000–2001 and further to the peak of 18.2 % in 2007–2008. Apart from these economies, Canada, South Korea, the UK, Norway, Singapore, Japan, and the UAE have become important contributors of FDI to Nepal. In fact, FDI inflow from Canada was the second highest during 2008 and 2009. Japan was the third largest investor in 1990–1991, and its share has been declining since then. Overall, we find that the top 10 economies in Nepal captured almost 84 % of the total FDI over the period 1990–1991 to 2010–2011, where the major contribution has come from India. More importantly, the contribution of developing countries has remained higher than developed countries over the period 1990–2010.

4.4.5.1 Distribution of FDI by Major Sectors

Table 4.16 provides the distribution of FDI by major sectors in Nepal in percentage terms over 1990–2010. Based on availability of data, we classified total FDI in Nepal into four major sectors, namely, agriculture, manufacturing, services, and tourism. As observed from Table 4.16, the manufacturing sector captured the major share of the FDI in Nepal followed by the services and agricultural sector. The share of agricultural sector increased from 1.2 % in 1995 to 4.1 % in 2008 and then declined to 3.6 % in 2010. On the one hand, the share of manufacturing sector declined from 98 % in 1990–1991 to 59 % in 2000 and further to 19 % in 2008 before bouncing back to above 60 % in 2010. In contrast, the share of FDI in the tourism sector dropped significantly in the 2000s in comparison to the 1990s. On the other hand, the services sector received less FDI during the first half of the 1990s, but it increased significantly in the period of 1995–1996 to 2005–2006, with a few exceptions. As a whole, similar to other South Asian economies, the sectoral decomposition of FDI in Nepal is found highly concentrated in a few sectors, namely, manufacturing, service, tourism, and energy, of course with a considerable volatility over time. Tourism has been the important sector for Nepal in terms of FDI as Nepal is considered one of the leading tourist destinations.

The above discussion of country-wise inflows of FDI to South Asian economies indicates that there is no common source of FDI for all countries. For instance, the UK, the USA, and Egypt have become the major FDI source economies for Bangladesh, whereas Mauritius, the USA, and Japan have become the key players for India. On the other hand, FDI inflows into Pakistan have been dominated by the USA, the UK, and the UAE. In the case of Nepal, leadership role has gone to India, China, and the USA. Finally, India, Malaysia, and the UK have contributed the major part of FDI to Sri Lanka. The reason for this wide variation in the source economies of FDI inflows relates to political and economic relationship of each country with the source economies. For example, it has been highlighted that higher FDI from Mauritius to India is due to the double taxation avoidance treaty signed by India in 1986. On the other hand, higher FDI inflows from the USA to Pakistan are mainly due to their long-standing political and economic relation between these two countries since the early 1950s. More importantly, Nepal is a landlocked county and shares a large boundary with India. Besides, India is the largest trading partner of Nepal. This has major implication for FDI inflows to Nepal and that is why India is the largest contributor FDI to Nepal.

In the case of Bangladesh, both the UK and the USA are major contributors of FDI due to the biased foreign policy followed by Bangladesh over time. However, in recent times, because of improvement in the political and economic relationship, FDI flows from India to Bangladesh have increased. On the other hand, Sri Lanka also received investment mostly from India followed by Pakistan, the USA, and China. This has been reflected in country-wise FDI inflows in recent times. Therefore, we find that India has become one of the important contributors of FDI in Nepal, Sri Lanka, and Bangladesh since the last few years.

Second, FDI flows to Bangladesh and Pakistan are more diversified compared to other countries. Further, there are considerable fluctuations in receiving FDI inflows from a single economy in this region. For example, Mauritius alone accounts for approximately 36 % of FDI in India in recent times, whereas Hong Kong accounts for only 7.9 % of FDI in Bangladesh. Further, India accounts for nearly 21 % of inflows into Sri Lanka in 2010. Similarly, 48 % of the FDI inflows into Nepal came in from India. However, USA was the largest investor in Pakistan accounting for nearly 21.2 % of the total inflows into Pakistan.

Third, there are considerable differences among South Asian countries in terms of FDI share for developed and developing countries. For example, developing countries have contributed more FDI to India, Nepal, and Sri Lanka. On the other hand, developed countries have contributed to the major share of FDI in Pakistan and Bangladesh.

The sector-wise analysis of FDI inflow in South Asia indicates some broad patterns. First, agricultural sector received least amount of FDI in all five South Asian countries. However, manufacturing sector share varies across all the South Asian countries. Initially, it was the manufacturing sector that attracted highest share of FDI in all the South Asian countries. However, the share of manufacturing sector fluctuated quite considerably in all the countries in the region. For instance, in Bangladesh, the manufacturing sector received the maximum share of FDI

(88 %) in the late 1990s and early 2000s, but its share declined below services sector in recent times. Same is the case of Pakistan, Sri Lanka, and Nepal. On the other hand, in the case of India, it is the services sector that dominated total FDI inflows over the period 1991–2010. Further, within the manufacturing sector, there is widespread country-wise variation. For instance, in the case of Bangladesh, petroleum and gas dominated the manufacturing sector, whereas in India, automobile, power, and chemicals have dominated the manufacturing sector. In the case of Pakistan, oil and natural gas and chemicals constitute majority of the manufacturing sector. In Sri Lanka, textiles, apparel, and leather attracted highest amount of FDI.

Third, South Asian economies vary in decomposing FDI into other sectors, too. For instance, the trade and commerce and construction sectors have become other attractive sectors for FDI in Bangladesh in recent times, whereas in the case of India, it is computer software and hardware and telecommunication, and it is construction, transport, and chemicals for Pakistan. On the other hand, Nepal has developed an interest in promoting services, tourism, and energy sectors as other important areas for FDI, whereas Sri Lanka has shown interest in the textile, wearing apparel, and leather sectors.

To conclude, the sectoral decomposition of FDI in South Asian economies shows heterogeneity, although they have liberalised FDI policies significantly since the beginning of 1990s. Sectoral decomposition of FDI is in line with global-level decomposition of FDI. According to UNCTAD (2011a), services sector at the global level attracted highest amount of FDI followed by manufacturing and agricultural sector.

4.5 Intra-regional Trade and FDI in South Asia

Although South Asian countries share a common cultural, historical past, and physical proximity, they are not economically integrated due to mutual distrust, political antagonism, and bitter memory of the partition. However, like other regions, South Asian countries founded the forum called South Asian Association for Regional Cooperation (SAARC) in 1985 for collective self-reliance in the region. However, SAARC remained a political forum and hardly engaged in economic areas of cooperation. Even the South Asian Free Trade Agreement (SAFTA) has failed to make any impact.

Focusing our attention on the South Asian region, we first look at bilateral arrangements between South Asian countries. In this age of growing regionalism and seeking mutual benefits, countries are looking to form alliances for trade and investment. Developing countries like India and other South Asian countries are no different and trying for bilateral/regional agreements in recent years.

Table 4.17 Bilateral investment facilitation treaties among South Asian countries

	India	China	Pakistan	Bangladesh	Sri Lanka	Nepal
India	1	BIPA 2007	DTT	DTT, BIPA 2009	BIPA 1997, DTT	DTT 1987
Pakistan			1	BIT 1995, DTT	BIPA 1997, DTT	
Bangladesh				1	DTT	
Sri Lanka					1	DTT 1999
Nepal						1

Source: UNCTAD publications, BOI Sri Lanka, BOI Pakistan, Ministry of Finance India, & news reports

Table 4.17 shows the ties among the South Asian countries, especially with two important neighbours of India. On 9 February 2009, India and Bangladesh signed a Bilateral Investment Protection Agreement (BIPA). Moreover, talks are also on between India and Nepal for a BIPA.[3]

4.5.1 *Indian Investment in Pakistan*

The investment regime in Pakistan has been liberal particularly since 1997 when the government of Pakistan announced the new investment policy that included major policy initiatives to attract FDI, which had earlier been restricted to the manufacturing sector. India on the other hand due to the political mistrust with Pakistan has missed out on the opportunity of investing in that country. The basis of the mutual ban on investments between the two countries is purely political in nature, and it is likely to continue till the Kashmir issue is fully resolved. Though Pakistan has a liberal investment policy and India is losing out on this because of the bilateral political conflict, China is using it to its utmost advantage.

4.5.2 *Indian Investment in Bangladesh*

Bangladesh and India have had an agreement for the avoidance of double taxation on income and capital since 1991.[4] Till 2007, Bangladesh was in the negative list according to the Indian FEMA (Foreign Exchange Management Act) and was therefore banned from direct investment in India. Though Bangladesh did not ban Indian investments, there was mutual mistrust partly because of the Indian ban and the Indian complaint about Bangladesh not welcoming Indian investment. However, the Indian ban was removed for Bangladesh by the end of 2007, and FDI has

[3] http://finmin.nic.in/the_ministry/dept_eco_affairs/dea.html

[4] http://www.unctad.org/sections/dite_pcbb/docs/dtt_Bangladesh.PDF

now been allowed through the Foreign Investment Promotion Board (FIPB) route.[5] This has been done in expectation of mutual openness and to ease Indian investment in major deals in Bangladesh such as the proposed Tata ($3 billion) project. In February 2009, a Bilateral Investment Promotion and Protection Agreement was signed between India and Bangladesh to promote and protect bilateral investments between these two countries.

The Tata deal, which was proposed to be about $3 billion, however, did not work through. The proposed deal between Essar Group India and four steel companies from Bangladesh (S Alam, PHP, KDS, and Abul Khair) for a joint venture steel plant in Chittagong was also an important one which seems to have failed. The Indian government also regularly transfers assistance to Bangladesh in the form of grant, loans, and transport assistance. In the period 1999–2000 and 2008–2009, the total amount of grant support from India has been about $0.4 million. In the same period, loans have totalled about $0.6 million, and transport assistance grant has been around $0.05 million.[6] However, Indian aid, grants-in-aid and soft loans are substantially lower compared to China's assistance.

4.5.3 Indian Investment in Sri Lanka

India and Sri Lanka BIPA (1997) ensures bilateral encouragement and provision of favourable conditions for investments; fair, equable, national, and MFN treatment; non-discriminatory guarantee against expropriation; no less favourable compensation against losses; and free transfer of returns and investments and the right of subrogation. The agreement also includes provisions for dispute settlement and entry of personnel of the other party.

India is one of the top investors in Sri Lanka. The Annual Report of the Central Bank of Sri Lanka quotes India as being the second largest source of FDI ($126 million) after Malaysia in 2008. Some of the major Indian investing firms in Sri Lanka are Indian Oil Corporation, Taj Hotels, L&T, Ambujas, Tatas, CEAT, and Ashok Leyland.[7] The Trincomalee thermal power plant is an important project between the two countries. According to the BOI of Sri Lanka, the sectors that have attracted Indian investments in bulk are steel, cement, rubber products, tourism, computer software, IT training, and other professional services.

A FICCI study has found that investment flows between India and Sri Lanka had increased significantly during 1996–2002 due to the signing of the Free Trade Agreement between the two countries.[8] The Free trade Agreement (FTA) provided an opportunity for Indian investors to set up units in Sri Lanka and import raw

[5] http://rbidocs.rbi.org.in/rdocs/notification/PDFs/85338.pdf

[6] Source: Annual Budgets, GOI, Expenditure volumes of various years

[7] http://meaindia.nic.in/foreignrelation/srilanka.pdf

[8] http://www.ficci.com/press/404/UNDER.doc

materials from India at zero duty and then to export finished goods to India duty free again. Such arrangements have boosted FDI from India into Sri Lanka. Table 4.18 shows according to the report, the total cumulative FDI from India into Sri Lanka was only $62 million from April 1996 to March 2002 which shot up to $312 million by 2008 as a result of the FTA (Table 4.18). India has also been a regular source of grants and financial loans to Sri Lanka. Between 1999–2000 and 2008–2009, India dispersed about $1.5 million in financial loans and another $0.4 million in grants to the country.[9] Regarding FDI from Sri Lanka into India, the amount and the share in the total FDI inflows are negligible though FDI flows have received a boost since the FTA (Table 4.19).

4.5.4 India–Nepal

Nepal has a double taxation avoidance agreement with India since 1987, and a BIPA is under negotiation stage between the two countries. Indian investments in Nepal have been growing over the years (Table 4.20). According to the Indian Embassy in Nepal, most Indian investment ventures in Nepal are in the services and manufacturing sectors such as banking and insurance services and in tourism. Important Indian players in Nepal are Dabur, ITC, Hindustan Lever Limited, CONCOR, SBI, PNB, LIC, Oriental Insurance, Asian Paints, and Colgate-Palmolive. Nepal has steadily received a stream of grant from the Indian government. Table 4.20 shows that about $1.8 million of Indian grant was given to Nepal between 1999–2000 and 2008–2009.[10] Table 4.20 demonstrates there was a gradual increase in FDI during 2002–2008 but particularly huge investment in 2007–2008.

4.6 Global and South Asia FDI Outflows

At the global level, FDI outflows increased during 1990–2010. In the recent years, outflows increased from $1,170 billion in 2009 to $1,323 billion in 2010, indicating annual growth of 13 % (Table 4.21). The share of developed economies remained higher compared to developing countries, although FDI outflows from developing and transition economies also increased strongly by 21 %. They now account for 29 % of global FDI outflows (UNCTAD 2011b). FDI outflows from Asia have also risen significantly in the recent years. Outward FDI from developing and transition economies reached $388 billion in 2010, a 21 % increase over 2009 (UNCTAD 2010b). The share of developing countries in global outflows increased to 29 % from 16 % in 2007, the year prior to the financial crisis.

[9] Source: Annual Budgets, GOI, Expenditure volumes of various years.

[10] Source: Annual Budgets, GOI, Expenditure volumes of various years.

Table 4.18 FDI from India to Sri Lanka (approved)

FDI from India to Sri Lanka ($ million)	April 1996 to March 2002	2002–2003	2003–2004	2004–2005	2005–2006	2006–2007	2007–2008	April 8–August 8 2008–2009	Total
	61.6	6.6	44.5	10.0	17.4	8.3	6.9	157.0	312.3

Source: Ministry of Finance, India

Table 4.19 FDI inflows in India ($million)

	1991–1999	2000	2001	2002	2003	2004	2005	2006	2007	2008
Total FDI inflows	62,944	8,242	5,695	2,292	1,297	3,753	4,360	11,119	19,155	33,028
FDI from Sri Lanka	4.9	1.7	1.0	0.2	0.8	0.4	0.4	3.0	1.3	5.3
Share of Sri Lanka (%)	0.01	0.02	0.02	0.01	0.07	0.01	0.01	0.03	0.01	0.02

Source: SIA Newsletters, DIPP
Note: Approval data up to 2003 in Rs million. Converted using RBI exchange rates

Table 4.20 Indian investments in Nepal

	Cumulative up to 2002/2003	2003/2004	2004/2005	2005/2006	2006/2007	2007/2008	Cumulative up to 2007/2008
Indian investment (US$million)	101.5	23.1	16.2	22.1	28.2	70.7	293.4
Growth (%)	7.6	236	−31.2	34	30.8	122.5	31.7
No. of industries	280	10	15	31	28	37	401

Source: Indian Embassy in Nepal http://www.south-asia.com/Embassy-India/indneprel.htm#2

Table 4.21 FDI outflows into selected countries (1990–2010) ($billions)

Host region/economy	1990–1995[a]	2000	2005	2006	2007	2008	2009	2010
World	255.6	1,232.0	882.0	1,405.0	2,174.0	1,910.0	1,170.0	1,323.0
Developed economies	213.0	1,094.0	745.0	1,154.0	1,829.0	1,541.0	850.0	935.0
Developing countries	31.7	134.0	122.0	226.0	294.0	308.0	270.0	327.0
Asia	51.0	117.0	134.0	217.0	303.0	353.0	295.0	308.0
Southeast Asia	–	11.7	18.1	28.7	55.4	25.1	33.8	42.2
South Asia	0.0	0.5	3.5	14.8	17.7	19.9	16.4	15.1
India	0.2	1.3	3.0	14.3	17.2	19.4	15.9	14.6
Bangladesh	0.0	0.0	0.0	0.0	0.0	0.0	0.0	0.0
Sri Lanka	0.0	0.0	0.0	0.0	0.1	0.1	0.0	0.0
Pakistan	–	0.0	0.1	0.1	0.1	0.0	0.1	0.0
Nepal	–	–	–	–	–	–	–	–
PRC	2.7	0.9	12.2	21.2	22.5	52.1	56.5	68.0
Hong Kong	15.0	59.3	27.1	44.9	6180.0	50.6	63.9	76.1
Republic of Korea	2.0	4.2	6.4	11.2	19.8	20.3	17.2	19.2
Malaysia	1.2	2.0	3.1	6.0	11.3	15.0	7.9	13.3
Singapore	3.1	5.9	11.2	18.8	32.7	−0.3	18.5	19.7
Indonesia	1.2	0.2	3.0	2.7	4.6	5.9	2.2	2.7
Thailand	0.4	0.0	0.5	1.0	3.0	4.0	4.1	5.1
Argentina			1.3	2.4	1.5	1.4	0.7	1.0
Brazil	0.7	2.2	2.5	28.2	7.1	20.5	−10.1	11.5

Source: World Investment Reports, Various Issues
Note: [a]Annual average

4.6.1 FDI Outflows from South Asia

FDI outflows from South Asia have surged in the recent years. In 2011, outflows from the region rose by 12 % to $15 billion, after a decline of 3 years. The decline in outflows may be attributed to sluggish demand in the developed world due to global economic shocks. As similar to inflows, India holds a strong dominant position in total outflows from the region. The outflows from India recorded an increase from $13.2 billion in 2010 to $14.8 billion in 2011. However, Indian TNCs became less active in acquiring overseas assets. The amount of total cross-border M&A purchases decreased significantly in all three sectors: from $5.2 billion to $111 million in the primary sector, from $2.5 billion to $1.5 billion in manufacturing, and from $19.0 billion to $4.5 billion in services. The drop was compensated largely by a rise in overseas greenfield projects, particularly in extractive industries, metal and metal products, and business services (UNCTAD 2012). The increase in outflows can be linked with an improvement in the global economy and the outcome of more cautionary policies adopted by the global leaders though the world economy is yet to recover completely from the two economic crises, namely, financial crisis and sovereign debt crisis. The greater outflows from India may be the result of a complex structure of tax laws, delay in clearing projects, and land acquisition issues.

Besides developed countries, investors from developing countries from South, East, and Southeast Asia and Latin America were the major drivers for the strong growth in FDI outflows in recent times. Outflows from the largest FDI sources Hong Kong and China increased by more than $10 billion each, reaching historical highs of $76 billion and $68 billion in 2010 compared to 2009, respectively. Other developing countries such as Indonesia, Thailand, Malaysia, South Korea, and Brazil have experienced significant amount of FDI outflows during the period 2005–2010 (Table 4.21).

In addition to this, India has also emerged as one of the important sources of FDI flows among developing countries and in South Asia. For instance, FDI flows from South Asia increased from a meagre $4 million on average during 1991–1995 to above $3.5 billion in 2005 and further to $15 billion in 2010. The share of India in South Asia increased from 85 % in 2005 to above 97 % in 2010. Besides India, Sri Lanka and Pakistan also experienced significant amount of FDI outflows during the same period (Tables 4.21 and 4.22). In terms of per capita FDI flows from India, it increased from less than a dollar in 1990 to above $2.6 and further to $12 in 2010. Similarly, in terms of GCF, it increased from 0.11 % in 1995 to 1.03 % in 2005 and further to 2.44 % in 2010. FDI flows from India as percentage of GCF is a significant proportion compared to the level of FDI inflows (around 5 % during 2001–2010). Hence, it can be stated that FDI flows now represent a two-way street unlike in the 1990s when the region would only serve as the host to FDI inflows.

In the literature it is found that FDI flows from developing countries are both market seeking and resource seeking (Cheung and Qian 2008). Other factors responsible for FDI flows from developing countries are high costs of production

Table 4.22 FDI outflows from South Asia

Country	Indicators	1980	1985	1990	1995	2000	2005	2010
India	Total FDI Outflows (million$)	4.0	3.0	6.0	119.0	514.0	2,985.0	14,626.0
	% of GDP	0.0	0.0	0.0	0.0	0.1	0.3	0.9
	% of GCF	0.0	0.0	0.0	0.1	0.5	1.0	2.4
	Per Capita FDI Outflows (in $)	0.0	0.0	0.0	0.1	0.5	2.6	12.0
Pakistan	Total FDI Outflows (million$)	0.0	25.0	2.0	0.0	11.0	45.0	46.0
	% of GDP	0.0	0.1	0.0	0.0	0.0	0.0	0.0
	% of GCF	0.0	0.3	0.0	0.0	0.1	0.2	0.2
	Per Capita FDI Outflows (in $)	0.0	0.3	0.0	0.0	0.1	0.3	0.3
Sri Lanka	Total FDI Outflows (million$)	0.0	1.3	0.8	5.6	2.0	38.0	45.0
	% of GDP	0.0	0.0	0.0	0.0	0.0	0.2	0.1
	% of GCF	0.0	0.1	0.1	0.2	0.1	0.8	0.4
	Per Capita FDI Outflows (in $)	0.0	0.1	0.0	0.3	0.1	1.9	2.2
Bangladesh	Total FDI Outflows (million$)	0.0	0.0	0.5	1.7	2.0	3.3	15.4
	% of GDP	0.0	0.0	0.0	0.0	0.0	0.0	0.0
	% of GCF	0.0	0.0	0.0	0.0	0.0	0.0	0.1
	Per Capita FDI Outflows (in $)	0.0	0.0	0.0	0.0	0.0	0.0	0.1

Source: UNCTAD, database

and inadequate infrastructure in domestic markets (UNCTAD 2006), local business conditions (Andreff 2003), bad domestic investment climate and high inflation (Svetlicic et al. 1994), and high economic growth in transitional economies (Andreff 2002). Moreover, government policies in connection with taxation and stability (Andreff 2002, 2003), institutional support, guidance, and incentives (Svetlicic 2007; Wee 2007) have appeared key factors for affecting foreign investment decisions of domestic firms. In South Asia's outflows, India has contributed remarkably. The reasons for significant FDI outflows are explicit as the performance of India in doing business as per the global competitiveness report has been poor. The doing business index is a good representation of economic and institutional environment of an economy.

4.6.2 FDI Outflows from India and Its Reasons

The aim of globalisation often begins with transfer of technology, financial instruments, skilled and unskilled labour, and output to the other nations. It targets to reduce the cost of production and extracting the full advantage through scale economies. Consequently, countries have significantly improved their own competitiveness in the world market and started to produce more specialised products.

There has been a tremendous increase in the outward FDI by India over the last few years. In 2008, India was the 7th largest OFDI investors among emerging Asian nations and 21st globally. With the OFDI being just a mere $0.2 billion in 1990, India has come a long way and increased its investment to over $79 billion by the year 2010 (UNCTAD data). A lot of these investments are due to the easing of trade policy norms by India. According to the UNCTAD 2006 by the United Nations Conference on Trade and Development, the main reasons Indian companies are engaged in outward FDI are, firstly, market-related factors as increased number of companies are in search of the perfect market for their product. The IT sector, more predominantly, finds a budding market overseas. Secondly, specialisation is another important factor. More companies have recognised and related to their roles in a global economy as opposed to a domestic one; hence, specialisation from abroad can be used to improve the company's business strategy. Thirdly, there has been an increased awareness on the positive effects of encouraging FDI leading to more liberal trade policies. Therefore, the governments of the targeted countries are supportive towards inward FDI because it adds to the growth of their economy. In addition to this, major factors encouraging Indian companies to invest abroad is the fact that they will get such a huge global market to portray their products, there are huge cash reserves, and there are large foreign exchange reserves. Also, there is a larger distribution network comprising of foreign companies, technology spillovers providing access to foreign technologies, knowledge spillovers promising a better management strategy and learning outcome. Moreover, FDI assures a better use of natural resources by environment protection clauses. Lastly, brand names are a strategic asset for marketing and promotion. What started with the setup of a textile factory in Ethiopia by the Aditya Birla Group and an assembly plant for sewing machines in Sri Lanka by the Shriram Group soon spread, and India has been investing abroad greatly now. Even though it can still invest more according to its GDP, it has come a long way. The largest investments of Indian outward FDI are Tata Steel's purchase of the English company Corus in 2007, Hindalco's acquisition of the Canadian aluminium giant Novelis in 2007, the procurement of Jaguar and Land Rover in the UK by Tata Motors in 2008, and the acquisition of the South African company MTN by Bharti Airtel India in 2009.

Prior to the 1990s, Indian OFDI was more concentrated towards the developing countries and mostly the developing regions of Asia and Africa. Also, all outward investment was more country and sector specific due to reasons such as a lack of profitable market elsewhere and stringent trade policies. After 2000, however, there had been a tremendous liberalisation in trade policies which included reduction in restriction on imports, privatisation, and full conversion of currency on balance of payments, deregulation of exchange rate, and reforms in the exchange rate policy. All these measures made stringent laws no longer a probing issue. Hence, the Indian firms have increased their share on OFDI to developed countries while making their investment more broad based and manufacturing sector oriented (Rajan 2009).

Table 4.23 Top ten country-wise overseas investments by Indian companies ($billion)

Country	2008–2009	2009–2010	2010–2011	2011–2012	Total
Singapore	4.06	4.20	3.99	1.86	14.11
Mauritius	2.08	2.15	5.08	2.27	11.57
Netherlands	2.79	1.53	1.52	0.70	6.54
USA	1.02	0.87	1.21	0.87	3.97
UAE	0.63	0.64	0.86	0.38	2.51
British Virgin Islands	0.00	0.75	0.28	0.52	1.55
UK	0.35	0.34	0.40	0.44	1.53
Cayman Islands	0.00	0.04	0.44	0.14	0.62
Hong Kong	0.00	0.00	0.16	0.31	0.46
Switzerland	0.00	0.00	0.25	0.16	0.41
Other countries	7.65	3.19	2.65	1.23	14.71
Total	18.58	1.371	16.84	8.86	

Source: UNCTAD (2012)

There was rapid internationalisation of the Indian MNCs investing abroad due to increased technological and knowledge spillover effects, as a result of which the OFDI shifted from developing countries to developed countries.

Even though Indian OFDI shifted to developed countries, its share of FDI to developing countries has also been growing at a rapid pace, proving that the shift in OFDI to developed countries is not at the cost of investing in developing countries. Between 1990–1999 and 2000–2007, Indian OFDI in developing countries increased manifold by more than five times from US$1.9 billion to around US $8.8 billion. For 2002–2008, the data suggests that developed countries like the UK and the USA have surprisingly small shares of India's approved OFDI at around 6 % each as compared to countries like Singapore, the Netherlands, and Mauritius and other offshore financial centres which account for 22, 15, and 25 % of OFDI, respectively (UNCESCAP). This data proves that over 50 % of India's approved OFDI is towards the financial centres. In the recent years, the pattern of FDI outflows for India has remained same (Table 4.23).

Indian OFDI flows into Africa grew rapidly during the period 2000–2007 as compared to the past. Initially, in the 1970s, the entry of Indian companies was mostly limited to Nigeria, Kenya, and Uganda. Now, the number has risen significantly, and Indian companies invest in 28 African countries. Mauritius attracts most of Indian OFDI in Africa and until 2007 accounted for 73 % of the total investment in the continent. After Mauritius, Sudan is the host country that attracts a major part of Indian OFDI. India has been investing in Sudan more recently, since 2003, and it already accounts for 12 % of Indian OFDI in Africa. India has recently started investing heavily in Libya. Nigeria, Senegal, and Liberia have centres of Indian OFDI, but these are not very prominent. Kenya is an important destination for OFDI since 1970 as well. Here, OFDI was majorly in pharmaceuticals, followed by other machinery and equipment, chemicals, textiles and wearing apparel, and paper and paper products (UNCTAD). Earlier, investment in Africa was mainly centred on the manufacturing sector, but the trends have changed since 1990, and the primary and

Table 4.24 Major sector-wise overseas investments by Indian companies

Years	2008–2009	2009–2010	2010–2011	2011–2012	Total
(Billion US$)					
Manufacturing	10.18	5.35	5.04	2.74	23.31
Financial insurance, real estate business, and business services	3.55	4.41	6.53	2.53	17.03
Wholesale and retail trade, restaurants, and hotels	1.17	1.13	1.89	1.00	5.19
Agriculture and allied activities	2.38	0.95	1.21	0.41	4.94
Transport, communication, and storage services	0.31	0.38	0.82	1.34	2.85
Construction	0.35	0.36	0.38	0.37	1.46
Community, social, and personal services	0.39	0.18	0.70	0.18	1.45
Electricity, gas, and water	0.14	0.84	0.10	0.04	1.19
Miscellaneous	0.12	0.11	0.10	0.51	0.18
Total	18.58	13.71	16.84	8.73	57.86

Source: UNCTAD (2012)

services sector play a crucial role in Indian OFDI in Africa. Despite this, manufacturing sector still accounts for maximum OFDI. The manufacturing sector comprises of chemicals, rubber and plastics, transport equipment basic metal and products, and machinery and equipment. The manufacturing sector is followed by the services sector which comprises software and IT, financial services, insurance, transportation, film, and entertainment (UNCTAD 2012). Indian investors perceive manufacturing sector as one of the import options for strengthening its competitiveness (Table 4.24).

India has been investing heavily in Latin America and the Caribbean recently. Bermuda attracts maximum (around 45 %) OFDI, followed by Cuba, Trinidad and Tobago, St Vincent, and Bahamas. Indian OFDI plays a major role in Brazil, South America. Argentina, Paraguay, and Venezuela are also centres of OFDI in South America. Generally, Central American countries are not an attractive destination for Indian OFDI, but Mexico has attracted a tremendous amount of Indian investment. Mexico is a preferred destination for OFDI because it provides a huge global market because of the NAFTA agreement that forms the Free Trade Area between Mexico, the USA, and Canada.

Also, it provides labour at low cost which proves beneficial. In May 2003, a 10-year bilateral trade agreement was signed between Mexico and India, so OFDI is expected to increase further. Mexico mainly attracts investments in the pharmaceutical sector. In Latin America, as a whole, more than half of the investment is in the services sector, followed by the primary sector and then the manufacturing sector. Software and telecommunication are the two most important services in the services sector and account for 30 and 18 % of the total OFDI in Latin America, respectively (UNCTAD 2012).

Ever since 1961, Indian multinationals have been investing in the Asia and Oceania region, and this is governed by the geographical and cultural proximity of India to the region which promotes trade and investment. In the region, Southeast Asia has been the largest host to Indian investments. Singapore, with 35 % of Indian OFDI in Southeast Asia, is the most attractive destination for Indian OFDI as it has very well-structured telecommunication facilities and infrastructure to facilitate trade (UNCTAD 2012). Singapore has liberal foreign investment policies and also allows preferential access to the ten members of ASEAN market and hosts 13 other countries as a destination for FDI, thereby making it a favourable location for Indian investment abroad. Indonesia, Thailand, and Malaysia are also destinations that prove attractive for Indian ODFI. Coming to West Asia, India invests heavily in the UAE and Oman. East Asia is the third largest OFDI target for India in the region. Hong Kong has received maximum OFDI followed by mainland China. Hong Kong has a port and is a great destination for investment due to the global market present there. Lastly, South Asia is the fourth most important centre for Indian OFDI and is concentrated mainly in Sri Lanka and Nepal. The India–Sri Lanka FTA was formed in 2000, and since then OFDI to Sri Lanka has increased greatly. Nepal is a good choice for new ventures taken up by Indian investors as it has lower risks and still provides an international market.

The Indian firms started investing in the region around 1961, so from 1961 to 1969, all the investments were made in the manufacturing sector. From 1970, the Indian services sector started engaging in OFDI in Asia, and it outpaced the investment in manufacturing sector by 2000. For Asia, the data for overall sectoral distribution shows that most of the OFDI was made in the manufacturing sector with 57.5 %, followed by the services sector with 32 %, and then the remaining 10 % was invested in the primary sector (UNCTAD 2012). Within the manufacturing sector, chemicals received the largest amount of investment of $547 million (UNCTAD 2012). Pharmaceuticals, transport equipment, computer and electronics, electrical machines, food and beverages, metal and metal products, and precious gems and jewellery are other important sectors that receive a significant amount of investment. A total of $1,586 million was invested in Asia by Indian companies in the services sector. In this sector, India invested the maximum amount in software services. Film and entertainment, telecommunication, and construction and engineering are other important sectors being invested in by India in the region. The primary sector comprises investment mainly in the oil and gas sector.

India started investing in Southeast Europe and the CIS subregion from the late 1970s. The investment in the region has been a little erratic as in the 1980s there were just a few cases of Indian OFDI in the region, and while the trend started picking up in the 1990s, it declined briefly in the period 1999–2001 and picked up pace again from 2002. Russia is the most attractive destination for OFDI as it accounts for a tremendous 81 % of the total investment in the Southeast Europe and CIS region. Kazakhstan is the second most attractive host for Indian investment in the region. In this region, due to its abundant and rich reserves of oil, Indian OFDI has been concentrated mainly in the primary sector comprising oil and gas. A total of $1,073 million, 77 % of the total investment in the region, has been invested in accessing gas and oil resources mainly from Russia and Kyrgyzstan (UNCTAD 2012). The manufacturing and services sector account for 12 % each of the OFDI share in the region. The manufacturing sector includes mainly the three sectors of pharmaceuticals, food and beverages, and chemicals, while in the services sector, maximum investment occurs in construction and engineering.

Looking at Indian OFDI as a whole, we can look at data revealed by the RBI until 2011 and see the sectoral distribution of OFDI that followed. According to the RBI, the overall sector pattern of outward FDI during 2006–2007 to 2010–2011 shows that it has been mainly invested in services and manufacturing sector. During January–March 2010, 33 % of the amount of outward FDI was in manufacturing, followed by financial insurance, real estate and business services, and then by wholesale and retail trade and restaurants and hotels. Within the manufacturing sector, investment has mainly been in the manufacture of drugs, medicines, and allied products; refined petroleum products; textile articles; and of steam engines and turbines. Areas such as data processing, software development, and computer consultancy services; architectural and engineering; and other technical consultancy activities were dealt with in the services sector. Lastly, the wholesale and retail trade and restaurants and hotels comprised trade in electronic equipment and accessories and such gadgets. The sector-wise outflows by India clearly suggest that India is concentrating on sectors where country has greater competitiveness. It seems that India is exploring the very best option to exploit the resources for enhancing its strength further in the world market.

To sum up, it is clear that India has increased its FDI and spread itself diversely since the 1960s, but according to the rate of growth of its GDP, it should be investing more in other countries in the form of FDI. Looking at the regions it has invested in the most, Singapore and Mauritius are the countries that have received maximum Indian OFDI. India had been increasing its share of investment in developed countries, but there is a need to continue to increase it further. Mostly, India had been investing in the manufacturing sector but the investment in the services sector is increasing steadily and has proven to be very beneficial for Indian investors. India has come a long way but still has a long way to go in terms of OFDI.

UNCTAD (2006) lists the ‘home country drivers of outward FDI’ as market conditions, trade conditions, costs of production, local business conditions, and home government policies. Mostly, developing countries have small markets which make firms hesitant on expanding further. Therefore, firms explore market opportunities abroad by analysing whether to export or invest in these markets. Mostly, all firms in developing countries start with exports and then proceed to invest in a foreign land. Wells (1983) stated that in countries like Bangladesh, Pakistan, Nepal, and Sri Lanka, exports precede 85 % of all the cases of outward FDI. Initially, by exporting into foreign markets, the firms gain knowledge about these markets and the policies and regulations that are being followed in the host countries. This helps them learn new technical know-how of refining their business and company strategies. Also, there is a fierce competition faced by local firms in the home market by foreign competitors; hence, firms from developing countries want to expand their business abroad. Rising labour costs in countries are other factors for expanding operations in another country.

4.6.3 FDI Outflows from Bangladesh

Bangladesh is considered a developing country and has shown a GDP growth of over 5 % during the last few years. Despite this, it has not been indulging in outward FDI too much, except in the form of exports. According to UNCTAD data, the FDI outflows from Bangladesh are below $0.1 billion. Bangladesh does not have an extensive outward FDI industry and mainly engages in export of ready-made garments, which is responsible for around 80 % of the country's export revenue. Three-fourths of the working population is engaged in the garment industry. A few other sectors such as ceramics, pharmaceuticals, software development, and seafood are growing and contributing to the growth of Bangladesh's economy. The textile industry of the country contributes to the maximum economic growth in the country with investment mainly in the USA and the EU.

The following chart shows historical data on FDI outflows as a percentage of GDP in Bangladesh from 1990 to 2011. Bangladesh has signed many bilateral treaties with other countries. These treaties help facilitate OFDI and exports from Bangladesh to these countries in addition to strengthening political ties. Bangladesh has opened an NGO named BRAC in Afghanistan as an attempt for reconstruction in microfinance. In the Middle East, Bangladesh is seeking to increase economic ties with Saudi Arabia by investing in ceramics, leather, and pharmaceutical products. Coming to Southeast Asia, Bangladesh investment in Indonesia is increasing significantly for pharmaceuticals as Indonesia has recently signed a deal with a pharmaceutical company called Eskayef Bangladesh Ltd. to export its goods to their country. Bangladesh has been investing in Malaysia; even though trade and investment are in Malaysia's favour, there are projects like the Dhaka–Chittagong highway worth $1.2 billion which is to be completed and many power generation and port development projects in the way. Japan happens to be the country's 11th largest export market, and imports from Bangladesh comprise 26 % of the total exports from LDCs, second to imports from Cambodia. Imports comprise leather goods, ready-made garments, and shrimp. By 2004, Japan had become Bangladesh's fourth largest source of OFDI, behind the USA, the UK, and Malaysia.

Bangladesh investment in Africa has been growing as well. Bangladeshi investment in Egypt mostly takes place, agro-processing, pharmaceuticals, science, technology, and tourism. Also, a lot of Bangladeshi students are pursuing higher education in Egypt, which amounts to foreign investment in the form of education. Similarly, Bangladesh had invested in Sudan in the pharmaceutical industry and in the field of higher education as more students are going to Sudan to study ahead.

A total of approximately 48 % of the total products being exported from Bangladesh are for Europe, and the products majorly comprise jute and raw materials. Also, France receives around 6 % of total Bangladesh exports. Germany is a major importer of Bangladeshi products as well. These imports mainly comprise machinery, pharmaceuticals, and chemical and electrical goods. The UK,

Table 4.25 FDI flows from Bangladesh

Bangladesh	2006	2007	2008	2009	2010	2011
Outward FDI flows (*millions of dollars*)	3.60	21.00	9.30	29.30	15.40	9.20
FDI stocks (*millions of dollars*)	105.00	112.00	80.00	119.00	100.00	107.00

Source: World Bank

similarly, receives a great proportion of investment from Bangladesh in the form of exports. Bangladesh exports its raw materials such as jute, textiles, and clothing to New Zealand (Table 4.25).

Overpopulation, poor infrastructure, corruption, political instability, and a slow implementation of economic reforms are considered to be Bangladesh's biggest hindrances to sustainable development and increasing their outward FDI in order to be a stronger economy. Also, Bangladesh needs to focus and improve its logistics in terms of trade in garments and clothing as they cater mainly to the European market and their garments are yet to reach the standards preferred by the market there. Retailers like Zara, H&M, and many other companies prefer to export garments from Bangladesh, but the quality needs to improve if Bangladeshi companies want to open their markets and engage in outward FDI.

4.6.4 FDI Outflows from Pakistan

Pakistan has been increasing exports and OFDI to several countries across the globe by maintaining peace treaties and special status in a few bilateral treaties. Pakistan encourages in OFDI to mainly the UK, the USA, Singapore, Malaysia, the UAE, Saudi Arabia, and Qatar.

There are 6,000 Pakistani companies operating in the UAE. For example, Netsol is a Pakistani software company, Fosh Tech is another such company dealing in electronic field in Singapore, and many banks such as HBL invest in countries across the world. Pakistan is planning to invest and expand its textile industry in Bangladesh due to the long-standing energy crisis which coupled with security crisis, and political unrest has taken a toll on the industry. Also, Bangladesh is a favourable location to invest in as it has free export access to seven countries including Canada, Australia, the USA, and the EU. Availability of cheap labour is an added advantage.

Pakistan is known to be the first country in the world to have a Bilateral Investment Promotion and Protection Agreement with Federal Republic of Germany in 1959. Since then, Pakistan has 47 such agreements with countries across the globe, including Azerbaijan, Iran, Kazakhstan, Kyrgyz Republic, Tajikistan, Turkey, Turkmenistan, and Uzbekistan (Fig. 4.10 and Table 4.26).

The FDI: net outflows as a percentage of GDP in Pakistan was last reported at 0.03 in 2010, 0.04 in 2009, and 0.03 in 2008, according to the World Bank

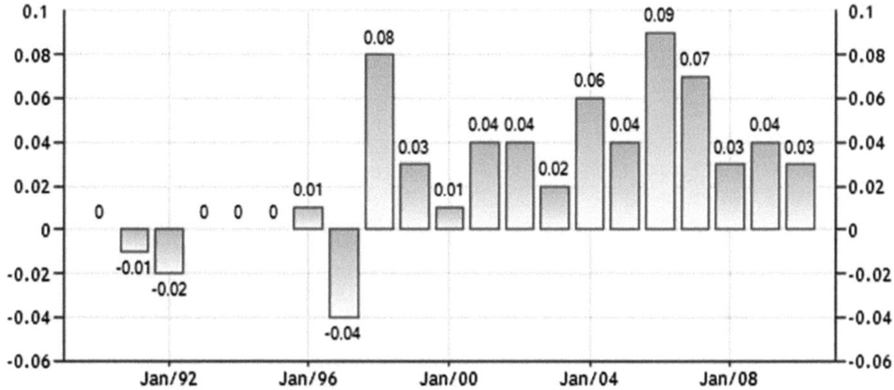

Fig. 4.10 FDI outflows from Pakistan (1990–2011; % of GDP)

Table 4.26 FDI flows from Pakistan

Pakistan	2006	2007	2008	2009	2010	2011
Outward FDI flows (*millions of dollars*)	109.00	98.00	49.00	71.00	47.00	62.00
FDI stocks (*millions of dollars*)	1,010.00	1,249.00	1,960.00	1,851.00	1,361.60	1,432.03

Source: World Bank

Pakistan's economy has suffered in the past from decades of internal political disputes, a fast-growing population, mixed levels of foreign investment, and a costly, ongoing confrontation with neighbouring India. However, IMF-approved government policies and a significant amount of FDI have been put in place. This has helped renew access to global markets and has generated substantial macroeconomic recovery for the country during the last decade. If efforts be put to engage in more bilateral agreements and to make peaceful relations with more countries, Pakistan will soon start participating more actively in outward FDI and in promoting economic growth of the country.

4.6.5 FDI Outflows in Sri Lanka

Sri Lanka is a developing economy off the southern coast of India. In spite of years of civil war, the country has recorded strong growth rates in recent years and promises high growth in the years to come. The main sectors of the Sri Lanka's economy are tourism, tea export, apparel, and textile and rice production. Remittances also constitute an important part of country's revenue.

There exists trade between Sri Lanka and many developed countries of the world as the country is very well known for its tea, apparels, clothing, and textiles. For example, the two-way trade between Australia and Sri Lanka in 2008–2009 was

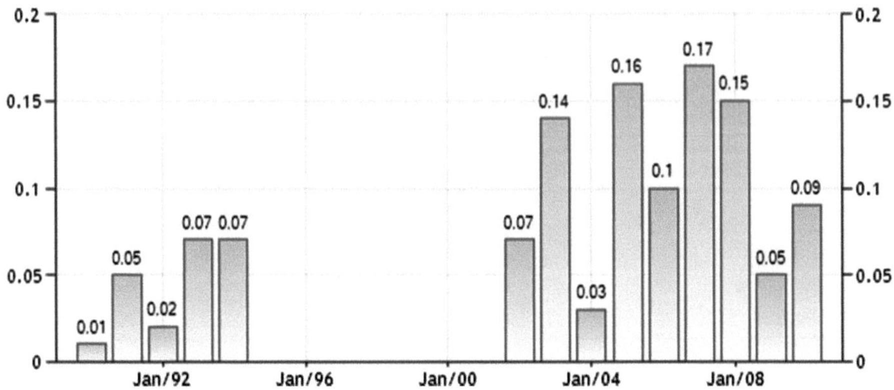

Fig. 4.11 Net flow of OFDI from Sri Lanka (%GDP)

Table 4.27 FDI flows from Sri Lanka

Sri Lanka	2006	2007	2008	2009	2010	2011
Outward FDI flows (*millions of dollars*)	29.00	55.00	61.70	20.00	45.67	50.00
FDI stocks (*millions of dollars*)	197.79	252.79	314.49	334.49	380.15	430.15

Source: World Bank

valued at $329 million per annum. Sri Lanka mainly exported tea and other food products, as well as textiles, clothing, and articles of iron and steel. Also, education continues to play a significant role in the investment as Australia happens to be the leading provider of tertiary education services to Sri Lankan nationals. The number of Sri Lankans studying in Australia has been increasing continuously. Also, Sri Lanka exports mainly tea, along with textiles, rubber, and ceramics to New Zealand, and exports were recorded at NZ$37 million annually in December 2008 (Fig. 4.11).

The FDI net outflows as a percentage of GDP in Sri Lanka was last reported at 0.09 in 2010, 0.05 in 2009, and 0.15 in 2008 (World Bank Report 2011) (Table 4.27).

In Sri Lanka, there may be some unreported outward investment (especially after giving the approval by the Controller of Exchange which allows many companies to invest abroad) due to the delay in reporting the actual transaction. Further reinvestments of retained earnings are not captured under the outward FDI or in FDI abroad. Also, the coverage of the outward FDI is not adequate. At present while providing data statistics, only the FDI of BOI companies are taken into account. This is due to the fact that currently only the flows of FDI for the purpose of compiling balance of payments (BOP) are considered. BOI captures all the FDI flows since its establishment in 1978. However, the reinvested earnings of companies qualified as FDI, which were incorporated prior to 1978, are not captured as FDI. These companies are non-BOI and unlisted companies. Therefore, according to the present methodology, the FDI flows are understated in the BOP statistics. However, the difficulty in identifying those companies could be overcome by conducting a screening survey for the first time before conducting a comprehensive survey (Central Bank of Sri Lanka 2009).

In due time, Sri Lanka will start investing and opening up more companies and investing abroad as its economy is still in the process of opening up to the outside world, and it needs to gain expertise in more products other than tea, which is their main exports. Sri Lanka will face fierce competition in the field of garments and clothing, and they need to better their technique in order to invest abroad and succeed.

4.6.6 FDI Outflows from Nepal

Germany maintains the biggest export market for Nepalese products, but export of Nepalese products to Germany has been declining since 1999. The decline in the export of woollen carpets has been the main reason for decrease in overall export to Germany handicraft, silver jewellery, woollen and pashmina goods, Nepalese paper and paper products, tea, medicinal herbs and essential oils, ready-made garments, spices, honey, etc. which are some other products that Nepal exports to Germany. Some joint venture companies have started export of micro- transformers and high-value garments and knitwear to the German market. Nepal exports clothing, floor covering, carpet, cotton dress, paintings, and pastels to Australia and imports refined petroleum and vegetables. There is growing volume of trade with Australia which occurs in trade deficit to Nepal. Japan happens to be one of the important trading partners of Nepal. Nepal exports pashmina products, ready-made garments, woollen goods, carpets, handicrafts, handmade paper products, leather goods, and silverware and jewellery. Nepal trades in similar products with Indonesia, Malaysia, Vietnam, India, Thailand, New Zealand, and South Africa.

Nepal mainly engages in exports; there is no information or data on the outward FDI by Nepal as yet. There are many countries investing heavily in the development in Nepal, and in a few years' time, Nepal would have gained competitive advantage to engage in outward FDI and do well considering the prominence of its handicrafts and textiles market abroad.

4.7 Summary and Conclusion

The South Asian region has always been a challenging region, and the analysis of FDI inflows into South Asia is not only interesting but also helps in understanding the reasons behind 'why FDI continues to elude South Asian region'. Even though all the economies of the region have gone in for extensive liberalisation of their FDI policies and made the environment for foreign investors congenial to do business, as compared to other emerging economies like Brazil and Mexico, the South Asian region attracts far lesser FDI. However, in the recent years, the region has become more attractive, and despite the recession in the global economy and the eurozone area, all the economies of the region have managed to increase their FDI inflows. This is largely attributable to the improved economic climate in the region. A close analysis of FDI in the region shows that equity capital comprises the major component of FDI for South Asian countries. Reinvested earnings are the second largest component in FDI inflows, and other capital is the third largest component. The continuous rise in reinvested earnings in India, Sri Lanka, and Bangladesh countries indicates improved economic performance and increased profits of foreign affiliates. The chapter has not only analysed the trends in FDI inflows into the region but also detailed the sectoral distribution of FDI in the region along with the sources of FDI into the region. At the global level, sector-wise FDI distribution indicates that services sector attracts higher amount of FDI as compared to manufacturing and primary sector. This has been the trend in the South Asian region as well. Given the fact, India, the dominant country in the region, missed the manufacturing revolution and directly graduated to the services sector; it was a foregone conclusion that FDI would naturally flock to the services sector. Moreover, the sector-wise analysis of FDI inflow in South Asia also indicates that agricultural sector received least amount of FDI in all five South Asian countries.

Similarly, country-wise inflows of FDI to South Asian economies indicate that there is no common source of FDI for all countries. For instance, the UK, the USA, and Egypt have become the major FDI source economies for Bangladesh, whereas Mauritius, the USA, and Japan have become the key players for India. On the other hand, FDI inflows into Pakistan have been dominated by the USA, the UK, and the UAE. In the case of Nepal, leadership role has gone to India, China, and the USA. Finally, India, Malaysia, and the UK have contributed major part of FDI to Sri Lanka. The reason for this wide variation in the source economies of FDI inflows relates to political and economic relationship of each country with the source economies. For example, it has been highlighted that higher FDI from Mauritius to India is due to double taxation avoidance treaty signed by India in 1986. On the other hand, higher FDI inflows from the USA to Pakistan are mainly due to their long-standing political and economic relation between these two countries since early 1950s. More importantly, Nepal is a landlocked county and shares a large boundary with India. Besides, India is the largest trading partner of Nepal. This has major implication for FDI inflows to Nepal and that is why India is the largest contributor FDI to Nepal.

In the case of Bangladesh, both the UK and USA are major contributors of FDI due to biased foreign policy followed by Bangladesh over time. However, in recent times, the political and economic relationship between India and Bangladesh has improved a lot and is reflected in FDI flows from India to Bangladesh. On the other hand, Sri Lanka also received investment mostly from India followed by Pakistan, the USA, and China. This has been reflected in country-wise FDI inflows in recent times. Therefore, we find that India has become one of the important contributors of FDI in Nepal, Sri Lanka, and Bangladesh since the last few years.

Second, in terms of diversification, FDI flows to Bangladesh and Pakistan are more diversified compared to India, Sri Lanka, and Nepal. Further, there are considerable fluctuations in receiving FDI inflows from a single economy in this region. For example, Mauritius alone accounts for approximately 36 % of FDI in India in recent times, whereas Hong Kong accounts for only 7.9 % of FDI in Bangladesh, and India bags approximately 21 % of Sri Lanka's FDI in 2010. On the other hand, approximately 48 % of the FDI in Nepal was captured by India, whereas the USA bagged 21.2 % for Pakistan in 2010–2011. Third, in terms of FDI share from developed and developing countries, there are considerable differences among South Asian countries. For example, developing countries have contributed more FDI to India, Nepal, and Sri Lanka. On the other hand, developed countries have contributed to the major share of FDI in Pakistan and Bangladesh.

It appears that the South Asian region is gradually moving towards becoming a world-class investment destination. All the governments in the region realise that FDI is good debt and have taken various measures to decrease red tapism, reduce procedural delays, simplify the tax structure for investors, and increase the equity caps to nearly 100 % in all the sectors to welcome FDI into the region. Single window clearance is the norm in the region. If the South Asian region further liberalises its FDI policy and undertakes domestic reforms and increases intra-regional trade, it will better project itself as an attractive destination for FDI and enhance the development of the region.

FDI outflows from South Asia have surged in the recent years. In 2011, outflows from the region rose by 12 % to $15 billion, after a decline of continuous 3 years. As similar to inflows, India holds a strong dominant position in total outflows from the region. The recent phenomenon in the developing countries has been the outflow of FDI. Outflows from India, the region's dominant source of FDI, increased to $14.8 billion. Though cross-border M&As slid across all three sectors—extractive industries, manufacturing and services—the drop was compensated largely by a rise in overseas greenfield projects, particularly in extractive industries, metal and metal products, and business services.

References

Agrawal P (2000) Economic impact of foreign direct investment in South Asia. Indira Gandhi Institute of Development Research, Mumbai

Andreff W (2002) The new multinational corporations from transition countries. Econ Syst 26:371–379

Andreff W (2003) The newly emerging TNCs from economies in transition: a comparison with third world outward FDI. Transnatl Corp 12:73–118

Athukorala P (1997) Foreign direct investment and manufacturing for exports. In: Laxman WD (ed) Dilemmas of development fifty years of economic change in SriLanka. Sri Lanka Association of Economists, Colombo, pp 386–422

Athukorala PC, Sharma K (2006) Foreign investment in a least developed country: the Nepalese experience. Transnatl Corp 15(2):125–146

Bilateral Investment Promotion and Protection Agreements (BIPA) (2007) Ministry of finance. Government of India. http://www.finmin.nic.in/bipa/Sri%20Lanka.pdf
Cheung YW, Qian XW (2008) The empirics of China's outward direct investment. In: Presented at Cesifo conference on Macro, Money and International Finance, Munich, 14–15 March 2008
Central Bank of Sri Lanka (2009) Annual report, Central Bank of Sri Lanka, Colombo
Center of Policy Dialogue (CPD) (2010) State of the Bangladesh Economy in FY 2009–10. Center of Policy Dialogue, Dhaka
http://finmin.nic.in/bipa/bipa_index.asp
http://finmin.nic.in/bipa/Sri%20Lanka.pdf
www.ficci.com/spdocument/20182/StatusPaperIndiaSriLanka.pdf
Khan MA (2011) Foreign direct investment in Pakistan: the role of international political relations, TMD working paper Series. Oxford University Press, Oxford
Khan MA, Khan RSA (2011) Foreign direct investment and economic growth in Pakistan: sectoral analysis, Working papers no.67. Pakistan Institute of Development Economics, Islamabad
Kumar N (2010) Capital flows and development: lessons from South Asian experiences, MPDD working papers. Macroeconomic Policy and Development Division, UNESCAP, Bank Kong
Kumar R, Singh M (2009) India's role in South Asia trade and investment integration, ADB working paper series on regional economic integration. Asian Development Bank, Manila
Mehta S (2007) Inwards FDI to South Asia: identifying the driver. SAARC J Hum Res Develop 3: 46–64
Poudel BS (2012) Promoting foreign investment in Nepal: prospects and challenges. Available at SSRN: http://ssrn.com/abstract=2128969 or http://dx.doi.org/10.2139/ssrn.2128969
Rahman A (2012) Foreign direct investment in Bangladesh, prospects and challenges, and its impact on economy. Asian Institute of Technology, Pathum Thani
Rajan RS (2009) Outward foreign direct investment from India: trends, determinants and implications, Institute of South Asian studies working paper no.66. National University of Singapore, Singapore
Svetlicic M (2007) Outward foreign direct investment by enterprises from Slovenia. Transnatl Corp 16:55–87
Svetličič M, Rojec M, Lebar S (1994) Internationalisation strategies of Slovenian firms: the German market case. In: Obloj K (ed) High speed competition in a New Europe, proceedings of the 20th conference of EIBA, Warsaw
UNCTAD (2006) World investment report – FDI from developing and transition economies: implications for development. United Nations Conference on Trade and Development, Geneva
UNCTAD (2007) World investment report. United Nations, New York
UNCTAD (2010a) World investment report. United Nations, New York
UNCTAD (2010b) Strengthening productive capacities: a south-south agenda. United Nations Conference on Trade and Development, Geneva
UNCTAD (2011a) World investment report. United Nations, New York
UNCTAD (2011b) World investment report 2011, Non_equity modes of international production and development. United Nations Conference on Trade and Development, Geneva
UNCTAD (2012) World investment report 2012, towards a generation of investment policies. United Nations Conference on Trade and Development, Geneva
Wee K (2007) Outward foreign direct investment by enterprises from Thailand. Transnatl Corp 16:89–116
World Bank (2011) Global development horizons 2011. World Bank, Washington, DC

Chapter 5
FDI in China: A Comparative Perspective with India

5.1 Introduction

The rise of the two giant Asian economies—China and India—has created a remarkable effect on the world economy. Along with Russia and Brazil, China and India are considered the engines of world growth. Until the late 1970s, China and India used to have very low-income levels and were purely agrarian-based economies not receiving much FDI. Both had inward-oriented trade and investment regimes, central planning, and lacklustre export sectors. Today, China stands on a higher plane than India in terms of economy. India's per capita income is USD 440 and China's per capita income is USD 990. The population residing below the poverty line in China is 3 %, whereas in India, the population below poverty line is 30–40 %. Many of the emerging economies like China and ASEAN countries have been able to perform better than South Asia and India in attracting FDI inflows. Therefore, an attempt is being made in this chapter to understand China's FDI policy with the objective of drawing some useful lessons for South Asia in general and India in particular.

A shift to market reforms in the late 1970s in China and during early 1990s in India saw their rise as huge global exporters. The two countries make up over one-third of the world's population and about one-tenth of its exports. Their exports increasingly comprise of sophisticated manufactures and services, rather than simple labour-intensive exports. Rapid trade-led growth has lifted hundreds of millions out of poverty in both economies. And the giants' exports and growth have rebounded faster than many others following the global financial crisis. Together accounting for 2.5 billion people, China and India today are engines of growth in the midst of rapid economic transformation in the global economy. As recently as 1991, China and India stood at similar levels of economic development. However, the two nations have approached the development challenge in very different ways. China has pursued a manufacturing-led growth strategy, whereas India has chosen a more service-based development model. Moreover, according to the UNCTAD (2003), FDI has largely helped drive China's economic growth. For

P. Sahoo et al., *Foreign Direct Investment in South Asia*,
DOI 10.1007/978-81-322-1536-3_5, © Springer India 2014

instance, in 1989 foreign-affiliated accounted for less than 9 % of total Chinese exports, but by 2002 they provided half. About two-thirds of the FDI flows to China went to the manufacturing sector in China in 2001 (Wei 2006). In India, on the contrary, FDI has been much less important in driving economic growth except in the IT sector. Sharma (2003) found that foreign investment appears to have statistically no significant impact on export performance. FDI in Indian manufacturing has been and remains domestic market seeking. In the above backdrop, this chapter attempts to elucidate the FDI policy reforms in China with the objective of drawing a few useful policy lessons for South Asia and India. FDI has eluded South Asia for several decades now despite the fact that the region has made consistent efforts to improve the environment for foreign investors by liberalising their FDI policy. Therefore, it is important to study in detail and understand the factors, reasons, or policies that made China a success story in receiving huge amount of FDI compared to South Asia.

5.2 Macroeconomic Picture of China and India

India and China are the two fastest-growing economies in the world. They have a substantial influence on world trade and politics and are a part of all major groupings including the G33 and G20. However, there is a major difference in the way that the two countries launched their economic reform programme. It is said that in the year 1973–1974 when China undertook its reform programme, there was no underlying crisis in its economy. In fact, the reforms in China were largely strategy based and not crisis driven as compared to India where the reforms were crisis driven. In the year 1990, India did not have sufficient foreign exchange reserves to last even 3 weeks of imports. It had double digits of inflation and was carrying a huge debt burden. Therefore, the government of India was left with no option but to go in for a major reform programme comprising of both short- and long-term measures and structural adjustment programme comprising of privatisation and globalisation and opening up the economy to the outside world. The reforms in India are hence said to be crisis driven. Since China started its reform programme much earlier than India, it had a lead start in all development parameters and dislodged Japan to become the second largest economy in the world after the USA. In fact, the two economies of India and China are not comparable, and India can only emulate some of the effective policies followed by China to enhance its growth and development. India experienced high growth during the first phase of its reforms from 1991 to 2001 and post 2001; India has been slow in implementing the second-generation reforms. Table 5.1 gives a complete macro picture of both the economies with respect to various indicators.

Table 5.1 is indicative of the fact that both the economies have done exceedingly well on all the parameters but are not comparable to each other. China has consistently performed well and has remained one of the fastest-growing economies in the world exhibiting high growth rates of nearly 11 % during

Table 5.1 India–China macro view

	China						India					
	1980–1990	1991–2001	2002–2008	2009	2010	2011	1980–1990	1991–2001	2002–2008	2009	2010	2011
Average GDP figure (billion US$ at 2000 constant price)	307	875	1,986	2,940	3,246	3,541	211	381	666	888	973	1,040
GDP growth	9.2	10.25	11	9.2	10.4	9.1	5.7	5.5	7.4	8.2	9.5	6.7
Per capita growth rate	7.65	9.21	10.36	8.65	9.87	8.59	3.35	3.58	5.8	6.7	8	5.4
Agricultural growth rate	5.54	3.72	4.43	4.2	4.3	4.5	4.4	3.1	2.5	1	7	2.76
Industry sector growth rate	10	13.1	12	9.9	12.4	9.9	6.1	5.3	8.6	8.4	7.2	3.4
Manufacturing growth rate	9.6	12.5	11.8	12.41	9	9	5.7	5.7	8.5	9.7	7.6	2.5
Services sector growth rate	12.6	10.9	11.8	9.5	9.34	9.06	6.2	7.4	9.2	10.4	9.35	8.9
GDCF (% of GDP)	36	38.7	41.9	48.2	47.7	46.8	20.9	24.2	32.5	36.6	35.1	35.5
Exports (% of GDP)	12.2	20.5	34	26.7	29.5	29.3	5.9	10.5	18.7	20.1	22.7	24.6
Total trade (% of GDP)	24.6	38.9	62.8	49	55	56	13.7	21.8	40	45.6	49.7	54.5
Total trade (% of world trade)	1.43	2.84	6.55	8.75	9.7	10	0.58	0.64	1.12	1.7	1.86	2.06
Forex reserve	7.5	7.4	13.5	24.2	21.4		5.1	5.4	10	9.8	7.8	7.4
Current a/c balance (% of GDP)	0.04	1.51	6.08	5.23	5.15	–	−1.6	−1	−0.36	−1.9	−3.07	
Fiscal deficit % GDP	−1.7	−2.4	−1.2	−3.1	−2.3	−1.25	−8.7	−8.0	−7.3	−9.8	−9.2	−8.6
Government expenditure (% of GDP)	14.5	15	14.2	13.4	13.4	12.7	11.3	11.8	11	12	11.9	11.7
Total revenue (% of GDP)	6.7	5.6	10.6	11.9	12.1		12.5	12	12.5	12.25	11.4	

Source: WDI (2012)

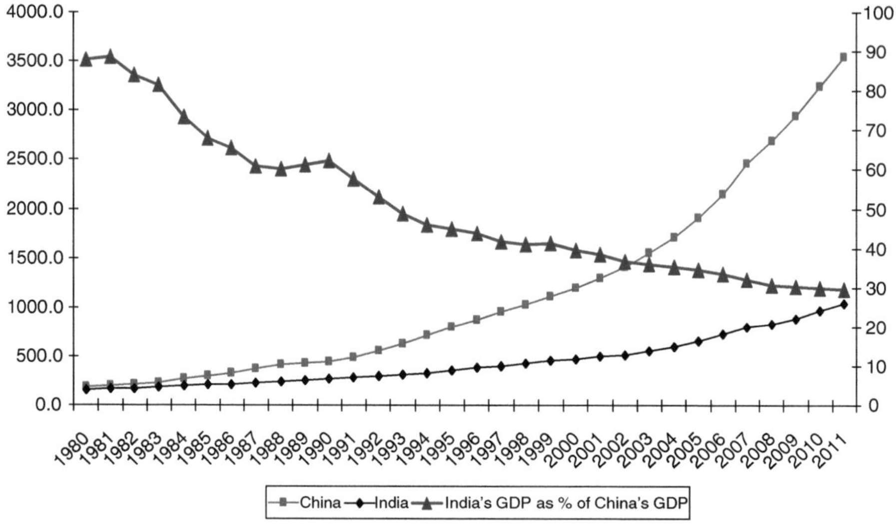

Fig. 5.1 GDP of China and India (in US$ billion, 2000 price) (Source: WDI 2012)

2002–2008. India too has done well during its reform period; however, the growth rates in India lag behind that of China showing an average rate of growth of 7.4 % during 2002–2008. However, the gap between size of China and India's GDP is getting bigger and bigger (see Fig. 5.1). The same is the case with per capita income growth in both the countries. One of the striking features of China's growth story has been the rapid growth of its industrial and manufacturing sector. On the contrary, India has missed the manufacturing bus and directly moved on to being a services sector-driven economy. China's manufacturing growth is one of the prime reasons for attracting FDI into the country. China is able to provide ample supply of low-cost, productive manpower to attract FDI and provide the basis for a comparative advantage in low-technology and labour-intensive exports. China's labour productivity is higher than India's, and this advantage underlies the PRC's entry into labour-intensive manufactures (World Economic Forum 2010). Meanwhile, the roots of India's relative success in information technology (IT) and business process outsourcing lie in other factors, including its exposure to English and a long period of British colonial rule; the establishment of Indian Institutes of Technology that provide a base for world-class IT professionals and engineers; close links with a Diaspora of professionals and business people who provided relevant contacts, information, and capital; and falling telecommunications costs that made it profitable to outsource services (Yusuf et al. 2007; Kowalski 2010).

Further, in 1978, China and India were at similar low levels of openness—both had exports- and imports-to-GDP at 12.2 and 5.9 %, respectively, reflecting a history of restrictive trade regimes and state control. While analysing the contribution of exports to GDP for China, there was a positive and a continuous increase

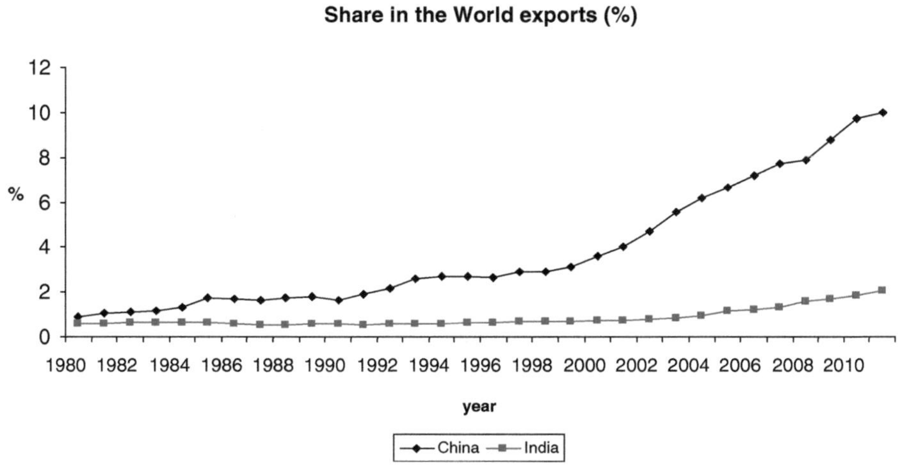

Fig. 5.2 Share of India's and China's exports in world exports

until the year 2008 and thereafter a slight decline. In case of India, there was a continuous and steady rise in exports as a percentage of GDP. Irrespective of the global meltdown, the Indian economy was able to maintain its share of trade in GDP as 45.6 % in 2009 compared to an average of 40 % during 2002–2008 as shown in Fig. 5.1. Moreover, China's GDP has expanded faster than India's since the 1970s. The GDP growth rate after trade liberalisation in China (1980–1990) reached 9.2 %, whereas in India the post liberalisation (1991 onwards) during the same period average growth rate stood at 5.5 %. Overseeing the trend, we could say that the trade–GDP ratios understate the growth rate of China. By 2011, China occupied 10 % share in world's trade compared to India at 2.06 % (see Figs. 5.2 and 5.3), which reflect higher integration of China economy compared to India in terms of share in the world exports and trade openness. China is also doing better in terms of exports as percentage of GDP (Fig. 5.4).

Most importantly, the giants' trade was relatively resilient in the wake of the global financial crisis. However, there was a sharp rebound in exports of goods and services, which rose to $1.7 trillion in the PRC and $326 billion in India. Interestingly, these levels were in excess of precrisis levels in both countries, underscoring the importance of large dynamic domestic markets, competitive export capabilities, and the growing importance of South–South trade cooperation (Wignaraja and Lazaro 2010).

All the top MNCs in the world have been flocking to China to do business. The reason being China is ranked high in all the doing business indicators. In fact, according to the global competitiveness report 2011 and doing business by World Bank, China is ranked 26 in the overall index of doing business as compared to India's rank of 56 in 2011. Though it takes less number of days to start a business in India as compared to China, the number of days to enforce a commercial contract is

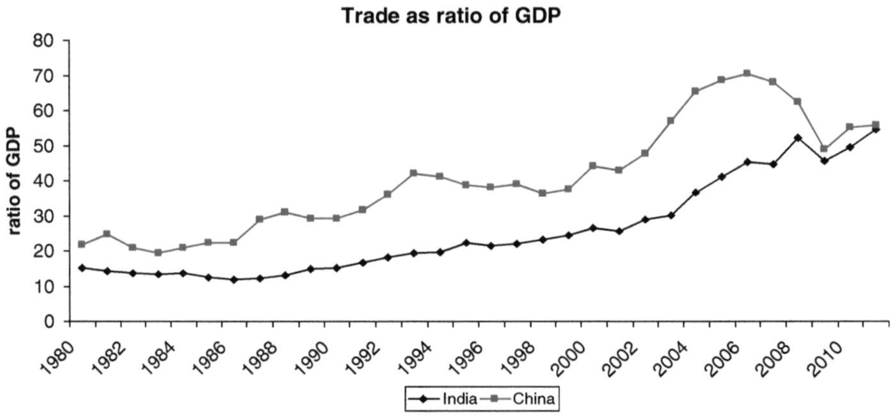

Fig. 5.3 Trade openness of India and China

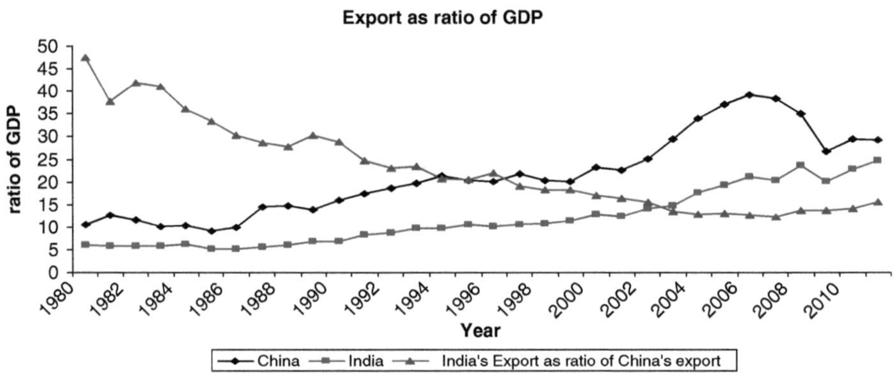

Fig. 5.4 Exports as percentage of GDP

exceedingly high in the case of India vis-à-vis China (406 days in China and 1,420 days in India). Moreover, due to poor infrastructure in India, the trade and transaction costs in India are much higher as compared to China leading to high cost of doing business in India (see Table 5.2).

There is a plethora of literature showing the link between infrastructure and economic growth across the world. It is opined that infrastructure has a strong positive impact on economic growth (see Sahoo and Dash 2012; Sahoo et al. 2012). China leads India in all infrastructure indicators as is evident from Table 5.3 below. The growth story of China is largely attributable to its infrastructure sector (see Table 5.7 and 5.8 for other important indicators related to governance index and human capital where in China has consistently performed well as compared to India).

Table 5.2 Doing business indicators

	China					India				
	2000	2006	2008	2010	2011	2000	2006	2008	2010	2011
Overall index rank	39	54	30	13	26	57	42	50	51	56
Institution	50	80	56	35	48	49	34	53	58	69
infrastructure	57	60	47	16	44	68	62	72	86	89
Macroeconomy	6	6	11	21	10	45	88	109	73	105
Business sophistication	45	65	43	13	37	37	25	27	44	43
Innovation	39	46	28	7	29	37	26	32	39	48
	2005	2006	2008	2010	2011	2005	2006	2008	2010	2011
Nos. of days to start a business	41	48	35	37	38	89	71	33	30	29
Nos. of days to enforce commercial contract	241	241	406	406	406	425	425	1,420	1,420	1,420
Nos. of procedures to enforce contract	25	25	35	34	34	40	40	46	46	46
Cost of exports (US$ per container)			390	500	500			820	945	1,055
Cost of imports (US$ per container)			430	545	545			910	960	1,025
Hourly compensation costs of manufacturing (US$)	0.57[a]	0.81	1.36			0.53[a]	0.64	0.77		

Source: Global Competitiveness report and doing business by World Bank
[a]Figures for the year 2002

Table 5.3 Infrastructure indicators

	China				India			
	1990	2000	2005	2010	1990	2000	2005	2010
Electric power consumption (KW per capita)	511	993	1,783	2,774	268	387	456	590
Energy use (kg of oil equivalent)	760	867	1,301	1,793	362	434	471	580
Paved roads (% of total roads)			41	57	47	48	47	51
Total rail route (in 1000 km)	53.3	58.6	62.2	66.2	62.3	62.7	63.4	63.9
Air freight trans. (milli.ton for km)	818	3,900	7,579	1,744	663	548	7,775	1,720
Air pass. transport (1,000 pop)	14.6	49	105	200	12.4	16.4	24.5	53.4
Internet users (1,000 pop)	0	1.8	8.5	34.3	0	0.53	2.39	7.5
Total telephones (per 1,000 persons)	0.6	18.1	57	86	0.58	3.42	12.3	64.3
Labour force participation (% of total population working)	79	77	75	74	61	59.5	61	55.6

Source: WDI (2012)

5.3 A Comparative Outlook of the Trends in FDI Flows

China offered investment opportunities to the foreign players much before India did and thereby attracted raging FDI inflows. Further, a few researchers opine that 'China's remarkable structural transformation to the production of manufactures for export which began in the late 1970s was largely unforeseen. Its performance has created the largest growth surprise ever experienced by the world economy' (Winters and Yusuf 2007, p. 1) and project that the two giants will both be among the world's largest trading economies within a couple of decades (Winters and Yusuf 2007). It has been widely recognised that success of China's manufacturing exports is mainly because of participation of foreign firms and foreign investment.

It is further said that China was swifter with the launch of an open-door policy towards FDI in 1978, while India did not adopt a major reform package until 1991 (Lardy 2003; Kowalski 2010). Henceforth, in volume terms, FDI in China exceeds that in India many-fold. Even after 10 years of economic reforms, India lagged much behind China in 2001, acquiring only 7.25 % of the FDI dollars that its neighbour received. With the annual FDI inflows of over $46 billion of China compared with a trivial amount of $3.4 billion into India in 2001, it is virtually a settled fact that India trails significantly behind China in attracting FDI in spite of its undying competitive efforts in the market for FDI inflows.

Thirdly, China evolved a comprehensive FDI policy that enabled it to attract record inflows of export-oriented FDI into manufacturing and to technologically upgrade it over time. This comprehensive FDI policy included the deregulation of entry rules, as

Table 5.4 FDI inflows comparison—India and China

	China				India			
	FDI flows (in million US$)	% of GDP	% GFCF	% of total FDI to developing countries	FDI flows (in million US$)	% of GDP	% of GFCF	% of FDI to developing countries
1981	265	0.09	0.33	1.10	91.9	0.04	0.22	0.38
1991	4,366	1.02	3.82	10.9	75	0.1	0.10	0.18
2001	46,878	3.6	10.3	21.6	5,478	1.1	4.7	2.5
2002	52,743	3.6	10.0	30.4	5,630	1.1	4.6	3.2
2003	53,505	3.2	8.3	28.1	4,321	0.7	2.8	2.3
2004	60,630	3.1	7.7	20.8	5,778	0.8	2.7	2.0
2005	72,406	3.2	8.0	22.1	7,622	0.9	2.9	2.3
2006	72,715	2.6	6.6	17.0	20,328	2.1	6.6	4.8
2007	83,521	2.4	6.1	14.5	25,506	2.1	6.2	4.4
2008	108,312	2.4	5.9	16.7	43,406	3.4	10.1	6.7
2009	95,000	1.9	4.1	18.3	35,596	2.6	8.1	6.9
2010	114,734	2.0	4.3	18.6	24,159	1.4	4.5	3.9
2011	123,985	1.8		18.1	31,554	1.6		4.6

Source: WIR (2011)

well as the introduction of active policies such as incentives, infrastructure, and technology support. All this led to freer trade and markets were pivotal to the giants' export success and complemented in nurturing domestic capabilities and other advanced areas that may not have developed in their absence (Amsden 2001). Another significant difference in attracting FDI inflows in both the countries has been their geographical location. China continues to receive a large chunk of its inflows from its neighbours like Hong Kong and Taiwan, whereas India's neighbours in South Asia—Sri Lanka, Nepal, Pakistan, and Bangladesh—are all economies in turmoil experiencing internal problems and not in a position to invest in India. In fact, India has been largely dependent on the developed world for its FDI inflows.

Moreover, majority of the foreign investors prefer China over India, more so in recent years for investment opportunities as China has a bigger market size than India and offers easy accessibility to export markets, government incentives, developed infrastructure, cost-effectiveness, and macroeconomic climate. India on the other hand has skilled and efficient manpower, talented management system, rule of law, transparent system of work, cultural affinity, and regulatory environment, but due to poor implementation of the policy, procedural hassles, and red tapism, investors avoid India.

Table 5.4 shows the FDI inflows in the two countries during 1981 to 2011. It is evident from the table below that there is no comparison between the two countries with respect to FDI inflows. China has consistently managed to get increased inflows that stood at nearly $123 billion in 2011 as opposed to India's $31 billion in 2011. China gets nearly 18 % of the total inflows to developing countries compared to India's 4.6 %. FDI as a ratio of GDP is an indicator of the attractiveness of an economy to draw FDI. A country with a ratio of FDI to GDP that is greater than unity is reckoned to have received more FDI than that implied by the

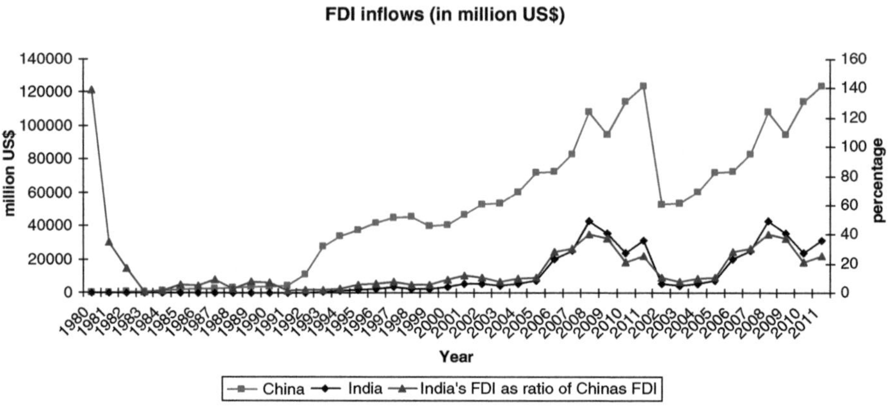

Fig. 5.5 FDI inflows to India and China

Table 5.5 FDI inflows comparison—India and China

	China		India	
	FDI Potential Index Rank	FDI Performance Index Rank	FDI Potential Index Rank	FDI Performance Index Rank
1990	42	57	86	96
1995	49	17	97	95
2000	48	62	92	115
2005	34	70	84	120
2006	33	91	83	100
2007	32	104	85	112
2008	30	97	86	80
2009	27	83	79	67
2010		86		97

Source: WIR (2011)

size of its economy. It indicates that the country may have a comparative advantage in production or better growth prospects reflecting larger market size for the foreign firm. On the other hand, a country that has the ratio value of less than one may be more protectionist and technologically backward, or may possess a political and social regime that is not conducive for investments. The yawning gap between China and India in attracting the non-debt-creating FDI flows has indeed been a matter of significant policy concern for India, because in the process India is supposed to be losing a lot of markets and a lot of capital investment to China. Figure 5.5 shows the difference between FDI inflows to China and India in US dollar millions. However, India's FDI as percentage of FDI flows to China has improved in recent years, particularly 2000 onwards (Fig. 5.5).

The two countries are also not comparable with respect to FDI Potential Index rank and FDI Performance Index rank. India is ranked much below China in the FDI performance index rank (see Table 5.5). India has the potential to perform better and improved both its potential and performance index rankings in the last few years.

The sources and the sectors from which FDI inflows enter the two countries are more or less similar with a few differences. In the case of China, its neighbouring countries Hong Kong and Taiwan are its top source of FDI inflows; in the case of India, it happens to be Mauritius because of the double taxation treaty operational between India and Mauritius. In fact, USA is one of the top investors in India, and a large chunk of US investment into India is routed through Mauritius, and US companies have a good presence in the Indian market. Other countries investing in both China and India include Japan and Singapore. The only difference being that China also gets huge inflows form Virgin Islands and Cayman Islands, which is not the case with India. Among the top ten sectors attracting FDI inflows in both the countries, manufacturing tops the chart in the case of China and Services sector in the case of India. Real estate and construction are common to both the countries. The coastal areas/provinces in China receive the maximum FDI, whereas in the case of India, the advanced states like Maharashtra, Delhi, Karnataka, and Gujarat continue to get maximum inflows leading to skewed distribution of FDI across states in India. In fact, the same could be said of China with most of the FDI concentrated in the coastal areas and the hinterland not developing as much as the coastal areas (see Table 5.6 for details). Undoubtedly, China has been successful in attracting large-scale FDI not only in Asia but also tops the list among the leading emerging economies in the world including the economies in South and Latin America. In sum, the geographical proximity to a developed economy automatically creates a spillover effects on it neighbours. China's strategic location has a shared history with its neighbours. Its location is helping to attract export-oriented manufacturing FDI from Hong Kong, the Republic of Korea, and other ASEAN nations. China continues to be the top destination for FDI in the world. Hence, the FDI policy followed by China can help other economies especially South Asia to draw some useful policy lessons from the Chinese experience and use it to further FDI in the South Asian region.

5.4 FDI Accounting in China and India

As per the IMF definition,[1] direct investment enterprises are those in which the foreign direct investor owns an amount of shares or voting power that allows him/her to participate effectively in the management of the enterprise or in its control. However, IMF does not define the concept of lasting interest in terms of a specific period. The IMF threshold is 10 % ownership of the ordinary shares or voting power or the equivalent for unincorporated enterprises. The above-mentioned definition of FDI includes as many as 12 different elements, namely, equity capital, reinvested earnings of foreign companies, intercompany debt

[1] According to the IMF, FDI is the category of international investment that reflects the objective of a resident entity in one economy ('direct investor' or parent enterprise) obtaining a 'lasting interest' and control in an enterprise resident in another economy ('direct investment enterprise'). The two criteria incorporated in the notion of 'lasting interest' are the existence of a long-term relationship between the direct investor and the enterprise and the significant degree of influence that gives the direct investor an effective voice in the management of the enterprise.

Table 5.6 Sources of FDI, top FDI recipients, and regional distribution of FDI inflows to India and China

China						India					
Top ten countries	% of FDI (as of 2010)	Top ten sectors (as of 2010)	% of total inflows	Top FDI receiving provinces (2006–2008)	% of total inflows	Top ten countries (2000–2011)	% of FDI	Top ten sectors	% of total inflows	Top FDI receiving provinces	% Top FDI receiving provinces
Hong Kong	41.8	Manufacturing	58.3	Jiangsu	17.1	Mauritius	42	Services sector	21	Maharashtra	35
Virgin Islands	10.1	Real estate	15.4	Guangdong	13.5	Singapore	10	Computer hardware and software	8	Delhi	20
Japan	6.6	Lease and business services	4.96	Shandong	7.8	USA	7	Telecommunication	8	Karnataka	6
USA	5.9	Wholesale retailing	3.83	Zhejiang	7.8	UK	5	Real estate	7	Tamil Nadu	6
Taiwan	4.7	Finance	2.74	Liaoning	7.1	Netherlands	4	Construction	7	Gujarat	5
ROK	4.3	Transport	2.59	Fujian	6.7	Japan	4	Automobile	5	Andhra Pradesh	5
Singapore	4.23	Construction	1.85	Shanghai	6.6	Cyprus	4	Power	5	West Bengal	1
Cayman Islands	1.95	Research	1.67	Tianjin	4.4	Germany	2	Metallurgical	3	Punjab	1
Germany	1.55	Gas and water	1.42	Beijing	4.2	France	2	Petroleum and Gas	2	Goa	1
UK	1.54	Computer	1.2	Sichuan	2.7	UAE	1	Chemicals	2	Madhya Pradesh	0.5

Source: http://www.fdi.gov.cn/pub/FDI_EN/default.htm and SIA news letter, India transactions including short-term and long-term loans, overseas commercial borrowings (financial leasing, trade credits, grants, bonds), noncash acquisition of equity, investment made by foreign venture capital investors, earnings data of indirectly held FDI enterprises, control premium, and noncompetition fee. FDI, defined in accordance with IMF guidelines, can take the form of greenfield investment in a new establishment or merger and acquisition of an existing local enterprise. The IMF definition of FDI is based on source of capital funds from the point of view of the subsidiary in the host country, but not on the use of funds. The IMF definition has been accepted by most countries and also by UNCTAD for reporting FDI data, yet there are also considerable intercountry variations in defining and measuring FDI, since every country does not follow IMF guidelines

5.4.1 Chinese FDI Accounting

China adheres to the IMF standard of FDI computing. China includes all the components of IMF in its definition of FDI. It also classifies imported equipment as FDI. China's FDI numbers also include a substantial amount of roundtripping. The reinvested earnings and other capital together accounted for about 30 % of total FDI inflows during 1997 and about 46 % of total FDI inflows during 2000 in China.

5.4.2 Roundtripping

Roundtripping can take many forms such as under-invoicing exports, over-invoicing imports, and overseas affiliates of Chinese companies borrowing funds or raising capital in the stock market and reinvesting them in China. Evidence that 'roundtripping' takes place may be found in the 'errors and omissions' of the balance of payments, whose movements were highly correlated with those of FDI inflows. Other evidence may be found in China's FDI outflows, especially to Hong Kong, which rose sharply in 1992 at the same time that Hong Kong capital inflows to China increased.

The estimated magnitude of 'round tripping', however, varied significantly. The most recent estimate is from the World Bank (UNCTAD 2003). They estimated about 20–30 % of FDI in China was due to roundtripping, based primarily on China's capital flight as reflected by the errors and omissions. It has to be noted that even after adjusting for roundtripping, China is still far ahead of India in FDI. In 2003, China's FDI was 39.6 billion of which 25 % was roundtripping; this was still nearly ten times that in India, with the latter figure already being adjusted.

5.4.3 Indian FDI Accounting

The analysis by Pfeffermann (1997) has highlighted the lacunae in India's system of computing FDI, which does not tally with the global standards of the IMF. As per the existing definition in India, FDI statistics in India are monitored and published by two official sources: (a) RBI and (b) SIA in the Ministry of Commerce and Industry. In comparison to the international standard, the FDI statistics in India appear to be limited because it includes only one component—foreign equity capital reported on the basis of issue/transfer of equity or preference shares to foreign direct investors. The FDI accounting procedure in India also omits noncash acquisition of equity, investment made by foreign venture capital investors, earnings data of indirectly held FDI enterprises, control premium, noncompetition fee, etc. as per IMF definition, which are normally included in other country statistics.

As for the support of the argument that FDI estimates for China are inflated, Bransletter and Freenstra (2002) provided an interesting view that what is seen as China story may not be so accurate. Beginning in 2005, the Chinese Ministry of Commerce revised estimates of China's net FDI stock that reduced its size by half. This massive reduction indicates that previously reported figures were very inflated. Bransletter and Freenstra (2002) find that share of fixed asset investment performed by FIE grew from 0 % in mid-1990s to less than 10 % in mid-2000s. Foreign-invested enterprises accounted for less than 5 % of urban employment in China in the middle of the current decade. Foreign-invested enterprises account for relatively little investment, or employment generation in contemporary China and American investment is but a minor component of that small contribution. Dooley et al. (2003, 2004) argue that Asian developing countries exhibit inefficient allocation of domestic saving which results in export of capital to USA, and this capital is reinvested in Asian developing countries including China through MNCs in the form of FDIs.

5.5 Evolution of FDI Policy in China

Within three decades of reform and opening up, China has become a top destination of FDI. The United Nations Conference of Trade and Development released a report on 23 October 2012, stating that China replaced the USA as the world's top destination for FDI by attracting US$59.1 billion in the first 6 months of 2012. China's biggest attraction to global investment is its huge market and low-cost production.

The post-1978 reforms marked the beginning of a gradual, highly coordinated transition process in China, which continued over the next three decades. The initial focus of these reforms was promotion of exports by attracting FDI. Therefore, FIEs enjoyed a preferential treatment when compared to domestic enterprises. In fact, FIEs were entitled to markedly different treatment depending on the region and industry, and this differential treatment was outlined by policies. China designated certain parts of the country as special economic areas, and each was governed by different policies (Guoqiang 2005). The FDI in China was encouraged for the purpose of:

- Transforming traditional agriculture, developing modern agriculture, and promoting the industrialisation of agriculture
- Producing transportation infrastructure, energy sources, raw materials, and other basic industries
- Tapping into cutting-edge, technology-oriented industries such as electronic information, bioengineering, new materials and aviation and aerospace, as well as establishing local R&D centres

- Encouraging foreign businesses to utilise advanced and applicable techniques to transform traditional industries as well as upgrade their equipment and facilities
- Using raw and renewable resources comprehensively
- Encouraging export-oriented FDI projects (Guoqiang 2005)

In the 1970s and 1980s, government policies were characterised by forming new regulations to permit joint ventures using foreign capital and setting up SEZs and open cities. In July 1979, law on joint ventures using Chinese and foreign investment was adopted which gave foreign investment a legal status in China. In 1983, four SEZs were set up in Shenzhen, Zhuhai, Shantou, and Xiamen. The law of 1979 further liberalised the domestic market and simplified the business environment for foreign joint ventures. In 1984, concept of SEZs was extended to another 14 coastal cities and Hainan Island. Twelve of the fourteen cities were designated technology promotion zones in 1985 to accelerate the transfer of technology. In sum, establishment of SEZ has played a major role in drawing FDI into China. In 1978, FDIs were permitted only in SEZs along the coastal areas. During 1980–1990, the Chinese government authorised municipalities to establish SEZs based on their geographical location, industrial condition, and human capital. There were 222 state-level economic zones and 1,346 municipal-level economic zones by 1994, and China began to see consistent investment in the provinces.

Since the late 1970s, China has gradually opened its economy to the outside world in six stages: (1) establishment of SEZ, (2) further opening of coastal cities, (3) further expansion of already open coastal region, (4) development and opening up of Pundong new area in Shanghai, (5) opening up nationwide, and (6) accession to WTO. Additionally tax benefits were offered to export-oriented joint ventures and those employing advanced technology. The government attempted to guarantee further the autonomy of joint ventures from external bureaucratic interference to eliminate many unfair, local costs and to provide alternative way for joint venture to balance foreign exchange.

The importance of the 1986 provision is that it provides incentive for FDI rather than merely permitting it. China's proactive policies towards FDI resulted in increasing inflow of foreign capital in the late 1980s and in particular early 1990s. From the mid-1990s, while maintaining favourable environment for foreign business, government policies began to focus more on linking FDI promotion to domestic industrial objective. FDI project which could take advantages of the rich natural resources and relatively low labour cost in the central and northwest region was to be vigorously encouraged.

China's FDI system dramatically changed during the period of 2006–2008. In 2008, China reversed its prior tax policy concerning FDI. Under the old policy, foreign investors were taxed at a lower rate than domestic investors. Investors in specific regions such as Pundong were provided with various tax exemptions. All this was eliminated in the new income tax code, which mandates a neutral FDI investment framework: no incentives based on nationality or region. Incentives are instead provided for specific encouraged business activities. A limited exception to this policy is provided that allows for tax benefits for investment in the central and western regions. FDI through M&A is strongly discouraged and direct foreign investment in real estate is prohibited. FDI policy changed from export-led growth to quality investment supporting domestic-led growth.

5.5.1 Investment Policies

The introduction of foreign investment by China obtained great success as it successfully provided all its investors with excellent environment for investment, production, and operation. The environment of Chinese macroeconomy improved day by day, and the utilisation of foreign investment obtained significant achievements during the tenth five-year plan. China has enforced two policies called Develop China's West at Full Blast and Strategy of Reviving Rusty Industrial bases to encourage FDI into its western and northeast regions (Guoqiang 2005).

Capital- and technology-intensive industries attracted much more foreign investment; a number of large foreign investment projects were launched during the tenth five-year plan after years of preparation. Foreign-invested corporations set up good examples in introducing and applying advanced technology, management, and concept; pushing market and global oriented development of China's economy and enterprises; and successfully nurturing some industries with international competitiveness in the fields of electronic and information, integrated circuits, light industry and textile, electric appliance, and general machinery products.

During this period, the foreign preferential loans actually utilised throughout China totalling $20.7 billion, which supported 150 key projects including projects like trunk line highways in Sichuan and other provinces, several trunk line railways, the coal-bed gas project, pollution treatment along the basins of the Huaihe River, the projects of agricultural comprehensive development etc. Emphasis was laid on specific regions like central and western, which gained more than 70 % of preferential loans when the foreign preferential loans were being arranged. International commercial loans (except loans granted by foreign-invested enterprises) worth $25.8 billion have been borrowed in China, which mainly supported projects on energy and traffic urgently needed in the national economic development as well as some industrial projects with short construction period, good economic returns, and ability to generate foreign exchange earnings through export such as the hydropower station.

Capacities of managing foreign debts were further enhanced, and the foreign debt scale is in step with the level of the national economic development and the situation of the international balance of payment. The regulations and policies on foreign capital utilisation have been improved constantly, and the management level has been advanced gradually.

Among all the elements of investment introduced by China, the *soft environmental element* is most important one, especially the market-based degree and policies of foreign investments including construction of law systems and establishment and implementation of policies and encouraging measures for foreign investment. Chinese government continues to perfect the environment for investment in the future.[4]

Further, an important change in China's FDI has been that the Chinese government's less motivation to attract large quantities of FDI. It is far more interested in improving the quality of FDI. The latest catalogue for Guiding Foreign

Investment industries continues the trend of encouraging FDI in 'Green' subsectors, adjusting the incentive—mix to current industrial needs. In fact, the Chinese government is trying to move away from attracting labour-intensive, low-technology investment and towards more efficient, more productive and less polluting investment.

5.5.2 China's Bilateral Investment Treaties

In this age of growing regionalism seeking mutual benefits and partnership, countries seek to form trade and investment alliances. This trend encompasses developing countries also. The WIR 2007 states that for the first time, there are now three developing countries among the top ten signatories of BITs (bilateral investment treaties) worldwide, and one among them is China.

5.5.3 Manufacturing Policy

Since the reform and opening up, China's manufacturing industry has enjoyed very fast development and forms the pillar industry of the national economy of China. The manufacturing industry serves as the dominant sector for economic growth and basis for economic transformation. The upgradation of its manufacturing industry has enabled China to primarily establish the status as a 'big country of manufacturing' and laid the sound foundation for China to transform itself as a 'strong country of manufacturing'. More than 80 % of FDI in China is in greenfield investments, and most FDI is in the manufacturing industry (Guoqiang 2005). These incentives were implemented through the following steps:

- Easing of regulations especially the ones, which govern the entry and operation of foreign enterprises. For example, the Sino-Foreign Equity Joint Venture Law of 1979 for encouraging the formation of joint ventures between foreign and the local investors, technology transfers to local partners, and domestic sourcing of inputs.
- Providing efficient, cost-competitive infrastructure for export processing commencing with four SEZs along China's southern coast, so as to allow foreign producers to operate with good infrastructure and minimum hindrances.
- Introducing a complex system of tax incentives (including a 15 % corporate tax rate).
- Formalising a duty drawback system in order to ensure duty-free access to all imported raw materials and components for export processing.
- Providing liberal labour laws in SEZs to ensure continuous availability of skill labour at lower wages.
- With the liberalisation of the system of export licensing and quotas, only 8 % of exports were subject to export licensing and quotas by the year 1999 in comparison to 66 % in 1991.

In respect of utilisation of foreign capital, the manufacturing industry always stayed in a dominant position. In 2008, there were 11,568 foreign capital projects in the manufacturing industry, accounting for 42.04 % of the total foreign capital projects. The major task of China at the new stage in the new century was to achieve industrialisation[5]. Under the background of significant development of global scientific and technical revolution and the spreading of informatisation, China has abandoned the road of traditional industrialisation and has taken to the new path of industrialisation driven by informatisation. The new industrialisation features high content of science and technology, good economic benefits, low-energy consumption and environmental pollution, and full playing of the advantage of human resources. The former four features are requirements to adapt to global scientific and technical progresses and sustainable economic development. The main tasks of China is to adjust the industrial structure in future and take a new path of industrialisation, enhance independent innovation abilities, encourage and support the development of advanced production capacities and restrict and abandon backward production capabilities with the reform and opening up and scientific and technical progress as the drive, avoid blind investment and low-level repeated construction, and promote the optimal upgrading of industrial structure. Pursuit of development mode focusing on conservation, environmental protection, and safety will be the main development direction of China's manufacturing industry[6].

5.5.4 FDI Institution: Beijing Investment Promotion Bureau

Beijing Investment Promotion Bureau is a bureau-level public service unit responsible for the professional service of investment promotion directly under People's Government of Beijing Municipality. The organisation and setup of Beijing Investment Promotion Bureau is an important measure adopted by the municipal government for optimising development environment, transferring governmental functions, and constructing service-oriented government. Beijing Investment Promotion Bureau aims at 'emancipating the mind, keeping pace with the times, developing and making progress unceasingly, and credible service', devotes to the marketing and propagation of Beijing's economic image, wholeheartedly provides complete professional services for Chinese and foreign investors, and sets up a bridge between the government and enterprises.

5.5.5 Investment Channels in China

Investment channel is integrated over investment info and promotion networks in 31 provinces, cities, and autonomous region across China. It offers investor both at home and abroad nationwide easy access to investment-related info. It also works to strength horizontal connections between investments and promotes agencies across China with the aim of maximising the use and sharing of information.

However, China continues to experience rising wages and production costs, so the widespread offshoring of low-cost manufacturing to that country has been slowing down and divestments are occurring in the coastal areas. Meanwhile, structural transformation is shifting FDI inflows towards high-technology sectors and services. For instance, FDI in real estate alone accounted for more than 20 % of total inflows to China in 2010, and the share was almost 50 % in early 2011. Mirroring similar arrangements in some developed countries, China established a joint ministerial committee in 2011 to review the national security implications of certain foreign acquisitions (WIR 2011).

5.5.6 Overseas Investment from China

In China many companies are the sources of overseas investments including government-owned giant enterprises, whereas in India it is almost always the private giants. In order to understand Chinese investments in South Asia in comparison with Indian investments in the region, we need to understand the motives of Chinese overseas investment in general. In terms of buying out companies and M&A activity, WIR 2007[2] reports that from China the largest and most active buyers are in the oil and gas industry. For example, China National Petroleum Corporation acquired PetroKazakhstan for $4.1 billion in 2005, and Sinopec bought the Russian–UK JV Udmurtneft for $3.5 billion in 2006. The main motive for Indian companies investing overseas appears to have been to gain access to new technologies and competencies and to build stronger positions in global markets. In 2006–2007, the Indian Tata Group acquired the Corus Group (UK/Netherlands)—in the steel industry—for about $12 billion (though the deal was not recorded in 2006, as the payment was not completed). However, WIR 2007 also states that both India and China have relatively greater overseas investments in energy and extractive industries than do the other investing countries of Southeast Asia. So these two growing giants are scrambling to gain access to oil and raw materials in the world. Further, Chinese efforts in this direction are more eager and older than India's. This belief is supported at least in the South Asian region by the hints provided by Chinese investments (discussed as below). This idea is also strengthened by the views of other research done on Chinese overseas investments. A paper by the Eurasia group[3] states clearly that around the early 1990s Chinese efforts to secure energy resources overseas grew as it became a net importer of oil, and after the September 11th attack contributing to a sense of risk in the world. This concern rose to the top of China's foreign policy priorities.

China is actively pursuing overseas investments. It is in the process of establishing the first group of eight overseas economic and trade cooperation

[2] World Investment Report 2007.

[3] 'China's overseas investments in oil and gas production' prepared by the Eurasia group for the US-China Economic and Security Review Commission, 16 October 2006.

zones in the following countries: in Nigeria, Mauritius and Zambia in Africa, in Mongolia, Pakistan and Thailand in Asia, and in Kazakhstan and the Russian federation in Southeast Europe and the CIS (WIR 2007). For example, the zone in Pakistan is a joint venture between Haier (China) and Ruba group (Pakistan).[4] It is understood that Chinese investments in South Asia are just an extension of its international policy. According to China's Ministry of Commerce, 50 similar zones will be established over the next few years, facilitating more FDI from China into other developing and transition economies. China also established in 2007 a government investment company the China Investment Corporation to manage a $200 billion fund drawn from the country's huge foreign currency reserves. Although the investment strategy and policy of this company has not yet been clarified, it is expected to invest in foreign companies, partly through direct investment. The country has also abolished quotas on the purchase of forex for overseas investments and has strengthened its support for overseas investments by Chinese enterprises.

5.6 Political Economy of FDI Policy: Autocracy vs. Democracy

5.6.1 Political Economy of Chinese

The Chinese government decentralised approval authority of FDI from the central government to local governments and signed a number of agreements with the USA that committed itself to increase market access and strengthen intellectual property rights protection (Lardy 1994). In the meantime, the number of BITs also increased dramatically in this period. As a result, a huge volume of FDI flowed into China. And the reform adopted by the ruling elite in China after the collapse of the Soviet Union even convinced many foreign observers that the Chinese Communist Party had indeed found a formula to survive the worldwide political instability among the communist regimes (Miles 1997). Overall, it is clear that China's further openness towards FDI starting in the early 1990s was largely driven by the political unrest and instability in the communist world. It is true that there was an intense political struggle over ideology and economic policy among the elite, but Deng finally won out and pushed FDI liberalisation to a new stage.

[4] http://english.mofcom.gov.cn/aarticle/counselorsreport/asiareport/200806/20080605612598.html

5.7 Major Reasons for Discrepancy Between FDI Performances in China and South Asia

Economic structure, liberalisation and preferential policies, and cultural and legal environment played an important role for attracting FDI. In economic structure, market size, abundant supply of cheap labour, infrastructure, and scale effect are the major determinants of FDI. FDI was attracted by the enormous market potential that China had to offer and at the same time contributed to GDP growth through various channels. It appears that market size was more important as a determinant of FDI from Europe and USA than for FDI from Hong Kong SAR and Taiwan province of China, as the latter trend was more export oriented. In contrast, many European and American MNCs have set up factories in China with the aim to produce for the domestic market. Mixed low wage costs appear to have played a significant role in attracting FDI to China. Some analysts suggested that low wage cost have especially been an important factor in attracting export-oriented FDI from Hong Kong SAR and Taiwan province of China as a response to rising wage cost in their own and other economies in the region. This contributed to China's rapid emergence as an important global competitor in labour-intensive manufacturing. The devolution of investment decision to local government, particular in open economic zones (OEZ), allowed them to upgrade infrastructure in an effort to attract FDI. In addition, economies of scale make it more efficient for foreign multinationals to locate in the same area, which allow them to share information and facilities, such as school and health facilities for expatriate workers.

In the initial stage of the reform process, China was not evidently better placed to attract much FDI like India which had many similar characteristics like China. Both were at a lower-income level, closed economies and agriculture were and largely are the mainstay of both the economies, and both did not receive much FDI. This scenario has changed dramatically since the implementation of economic reforms and open-door policy in both the economies. While India's GDP per capita more than doubled between 1978 and 2000, China's GDP per capita quadrupled. India remains a closed economy, while China has become more integrated into the closed economy.

China's increasing openness to the outside world can be seen in the rapid growth of its foreign trade. Export and import as a share of GDP rose from negligible amount to nearly 25 %. The average tariff rate in China fell from well over 50 % in the early 1980s to about 15 % now, less than half of that in India. Equally important is that China exempts many goods entirely from import duties and because a significant share of imports of goods subject to high tariffs are imported illegally, actual tariff collection as a per cent of the total value of imports has been much lower.

While India's GDP per capita stood more than doubled between 1978 and 2000, China's GDP per capita quadrupled. India remains a closed economy while China has become more integrated into the closed economy. China increasing openness to the outside world can be seen in the rapid growth of its foreign trade. Export and import as a share of GDP rose from negligible amount to nearly 25 %. The average tariff rate in China fell from well over 50 % in the early 1980s to about 15 % now, less than half of that in India.

5.7.1 Manufacturing vs. Services

China and India have each pursued distinctive styles of reforms as they shifted to outward-oriented, market-based economies after long periods of inward-oriented, centrally planned policies. Both differed in their processes of implementing gradual approach to reforms, which include timing, speed, stages, and specific measures adopted. Accordingly, differences in trade and investment policies have influenced China's rise as a massive global exporter of manufactures and India's expansion into high-skill service exports alongside manufactures.

5.7.2 SEZ in China

In 1978, with the starting of reform process, China announced the establishment of SEZ. By 1980, four SEZs were installed—Shenzhen, Zhuhai, Shantou, and Xiamen. The experiment of SEZs was extended in 1984, when the government announced that the open policy was to be extended to large areas inside the country as well as 14 coastal cities. One year later, in 1985, the open policy was further extended which resulted in the creation of three OEZs: Pearl River Delta, Southern Fujian Delta, and Yangtze River Delta. These OEZs, similar to the SEZs, have been equipped with incentives to promote export production and inflow of foreign capital. Originally, the SEZs were intended to serve as a place for testing new reforms of enterprise management, finance, and labour matters, whereas this experiment was meant to be extended to larger parts of the country if proved successful. The main goal of the SEZs was to promote FDI by giving incentives such as lower taxes, lower tariffs, and less restrictions regarding labour market and government control. The SEZs were created to serve the transfer of high-technology industries, acquisition of modern technology and management expertise, creation of employment, earning of foreign exchange through promotion of exports, promotion of economic development and regional development, creation of economic links with developed countries (e.g. with Hong Kong or Taiwan), experiment of new economic reform with market forces, and setting up of a link between the economic hinterland and overseas. To achieve these goals, SEZs were assured autonomy from the central planning by the Communist party, as well as simplified administration. This seems a puzzling environment, since the government thus created a 'market environment in the zones, while maintaining intensive control mechanisms for the rest of the economy' (Ota 2003). However, the industries within SEZs were not meant to interfere with the existing domestic industry, since the emphasis within SEZs was placed on export.

In short, the factors that might explain China's huge success in attracting FDI are many. One of these is the early success of the SEZs, but this success alone does not explain the continuing surge of FDI that has flowed to China during the 1990s and the first years of the twenty-first century. Thus, those nations that wish to learn from the Chinese experience should view this experience holistically and not to draw

Table 5.7 Governance index

	China				India			
	1996	2000	2005	2010	1996	2000	2005	2010
Control of corruption rank	43.4	50.2	31.7	32.5	39.5	45.9	42.4	35.9
Rule of law	39.2	35.4	40.4	44.5	61.7	60.3	56.9	54.9
Regulatory effectiveness	48.5	36.3	50.5	45	37.7	51	47.1	39.2
Government effectiveness	45.4	52.7	49.8	59.8	53.7	52.2	54.1	55
Political stability	38.9	31.7	29.3	24.1	17.8	18.3	18.8	10.8
Voice and accountability	12	11.5	7.2	5.2	62	57.2	62	59.2

Source: World Bank governance index

Table 5.8 Indicators relating to human capital

	China				India			
	1980	1990	2000	2010	1980	1990	2000	2010
Health and education expenditure % of GDP	5.8	6.5	7.5	8.8	6.8	7.6	8.7	8.8
literacy ratio	65.5	77.8	90.9	94	40.8	48.2	61	75
Average Life expectancy	67	69.5	71.2	73.3	55.3	58.4	61.6	65.1
Infant mortality rate	49.8	38.3	27.3	15.8	101.7	81.4	62.7	48.2
School enrolment ratio primary	113.7	128.9	114.6	111	83.6	93	93.8	116
School enrolment ratio secondary	51.5	38.5	62.1	81.2	29.1	38	45.3	63.2

Source: WDI (2011)

unwarrantedly optimistic conclusions from the SEZs themselves. EPZs such as the SEZs might indeed achieve catalytic effects in nations other than China, but only if other elements are put into place.

5.7.3 Governance and Human Capital

It is believed that better governance and better human capital are factors responsible for attracting FDI into the economy. Table 5.7 shows governance index and human capital of China and India. It can be observed China fares better in all indicators of governance except rule of law and voice and accountability. Based on an Economic Freedom Index survey held in 2003, Wei (2005) observed that China scores better than India only in macro management and low taxes. But India scores better than China in degree of government intervention, treatment of foreign investment, and respect for property rights. From the indicators relating to human capital, it can be seen that though China and India spend same amount on health and education in terms of share of GDP, in outcome indicators like literacy ratio and life expectancy, India lags behind China (Table 5.8). Does it show ineffectiveness of implementation process in India? Does this indicate that we have to admit, though grudgingly, that despite all the hoopla and outcry about human rights and authoritarian policies of China, businesses prefer China as it gives them a stable environment in near term? Does India's democracy and rule of law fail it in attracting FDI? Wei (2005) points out that China has 'more business oriented' and more FDI friendly policies than India. According to UNCTAD (2002, 2003) on average, it takes about 10 permits in India compared to 6 in China and 90 days in India relative to 30 days in China to start a new business. It takes 43 clearances at the central government level and 57 at the state government level when it came to a foreign-invested power plant. This can be easily said for other industries.

5.8 Policy Lessons for South Asia from China's FDI Success

The growth in China's economy since the implementation of government reforms in the late 1970s has surpassed even the most optimistic predictions by economists. Much of this economic success can be attributed to very aggressive policies encouraging FDI. Data provided by the IMF shows that China's total FDI in 1985 was $2.3 billion. The 2010 estimate exceeds $150 billion of FDI (IMF statistics).

In the late 1970s and early 1980s, China began to open its borders to foreign investors as part of the country's larger economic reform agenda. One of the first regulatory reforms established the authority for the creation of special economic development zones. Legislation was enacted to allow joint ventures between Chinese firms and foreign companies wanting to conduct business in China.

In 1985, China expanded its FDI regulations to permit the development of technology parks. In an attempt to attract foreign companies to transfer technology to Chinese firms, the Chinese government implemented a series of laws that provided preferential tax treatment to foreign companies investing in technology-intensive industries. In 1987, wholly owned foreign firms were permitted to conduct business in China.

Throughout the 1990s and into the twenty-first century, FDI continued to grow. The Chinese government was quite deliberate in providing industry-specific incentives for these investments. The emphasis was placed on technology transfer, export development, and infrastructure applications (Fung et al. 2002). In 2002, the IMF published a policy paper that concluded that China's success in attracting FDI helps to explain why other countries in the region have followed China's lead. Specifically, the study identifies six characteristics that correlate with increased levels of FDI. These are the development and implementation of government policies that promote private investment, the capacity to export to North American and European markets, a strong postsecondary research and development capability, a reliable and affordable supply of labour, high-quality infrastructure especially in transportation, and highly developed technological capacity. In fact, the success of China in attracting FDI is unparalleled and one of the major reasons contributing to its growth story.

The FDI policies followed by China have had a spillover effect throughout Southeast Asia, and many of the countries have emulated the Chinese example. Therefore, South Asia too can learn much from the Chinese experience and formulate polices suited to project South Asia as an attractive destination of FDI.

For instance, India shares with China many of the structural factors that have been important determinants of FDI—market size, abundant labour, and a large Indian diaspora. So a priori, there seems to be no reason why India cannot become an attractive destination for FDI if it so chooses. However, there is a difference in how political choices are made in these two countries. In China, the political leadership imposed a vision for the path of growth and development of the country. In India, reaching a political consensus on any major policy issues is an uphill task. Further, in China a great deal of autonomy in economic decisions was given to the localities—it allowed a market-based economy to develop alongside a centrally planned system. Although this decentralisation created problem, it also gave local authorities strong incentives to grow and develop their economies. This could be emulated by India in particular and South Asia in general.

In South Asia, particularly in India, post-1991 reforms, a large chunk of FDI has moved into the services sector. This is because the investment climate in the manufacturing sector is relatively unattractive. Apparently, South Asia and India have also missed out on the era of relocation of manufacturing facilities from the East Asian Tiger Economies. However, given the rapid growth in the South Asian region, it still stands a fair chance of attracting decent and high-quality FDI inflows into the region if it revives agriculture, manufacturing, and domestic sectors. China has followed a comprehensive approach to FDI comprising of a series of measures including creation of world-class infrastructure and supply of cheap labour, power, SEZs, flexible labour laws, preferential treatment, and single window clearance to FDI in contrast to the piecemeal and compartmentalised approach to FDI by South Asia.

Moreover, accession to WTO in 2001 broadened China's 'opening up' policies and led to continued FDI flow towards the economy. Today, China is a major importer of raw materials, manufacturer of basic goods, and exporter of consumer goods. The Chinese government itself plays a significant role in economy in general and FDIs in particular. The government gives huge tax deductions to the companies when they enter domestic market. They encourage MNCs to enter the domestic market with advanced technologies, and this way the country's economy gains access to newer technology more quickly. The Chinese government has worked extensively to better the investment environment, which has a huge appeal to the world. According to UNCTAD, 'China is experiencing structural adjustments in their FDI flows, including the relocation of labour-intensive and low end market-oriented FDI to neighbouring countries'.

Undoubtedly, FDI has played a significant role in rebuilding the manufacturing sector in China. Learning from China, the South Asian region needs to draw the right lessons from China and concentrate on improving the domestic economic environment through second-generation reforms, invest in infrastructure, focus on privatisation, reduce corruption, and improve policy implementation to attract FDI into the region.

In conclusion, it can be said that while it is natural that China and India will be compared to each other, they do not easily lend themselves for comparison. Reason for it is multifarious starting from different cultural more to political system. Except huge population, little else is similar. Indicators/numbers will not reflect it correctly. Policy aim and ease of its implementation are two key elements that separate these two giants. China due to its centralised political system can move ahead with reforms with speed and ease which is difficult to replicate in decentralised structure of India. Nonetheless, we have a lot to learn from China example and modify it to suit our need.

References

Amsden AH (2001) The rise of the rest: challenges to the west from late industrialising economies. Oxford University Press, New York

Bransletter LG, Feenstra RC (2002) Trade and foreign direct investment in China: a political economy approach. J Int Econ 58(2):335–358

Dooley MP, Folkerts-Landau D, Garber P (2003) An essay on the revived Bretton Woods system, NBER working paper no. 9971. National Bureau of Economic Research, Cambridge, MA

Dooley MP, Folkerts-Landau D, Garber P (2004) Direct investment, rising real wages and the absorption of excess labour in the periphery, NBER working paper no. 10626. National Bureau of Economic Research, Cambridge, MA

Fung KC, Iizaka H, Tong S (2002) Foreign trade of China, HIEBS working paper no. 1048, Hong Kong

Guoqiang L (2005) China's policies on FDI: review and evaluation. In: Moran TH, Graham EM, Blomstrom M (eds) Does foreign direct investment promote development. PIIE Publication, Washington, DC

Kowalski P (2010) China and India: a tale of two trade integration approaches. ICRIER, New Delhi

Lardy NR (1994) China in the world economy. Institute for International Economics, Washington, DC

Lardy NR (2003) Trade liberalization and its role in Chinese economic growth. In: International Monetary Fund and National Council of applied economic research conference, A tale of two giants: India's and China's experience with reform and growth, New Delhi

Miles J (1997) The legacy of Tiananmen: China in disarray. University of Michigan Press, Michigan

Ota Tatsuyuki (2003) The role of special economic zones in China's economic development as compared with Asian export processing zones: 1979–1995. Asia in Extenso, March 2003

Pfeffermann G (1997) Prospects for increasing FDI in low income countries. In: Iqbal Z, Kanbur R (eds) External finance for low income countries. IMF, Washington, DC, pp 194–206

Sahoo P, Dash RK (2012) Economic growth in South Asia: role of infrastructure. J Int Trade Econ Dev 21(2):217–252

Sahoo P, Das R, Nataraj G (2012) China's growth story: role of physical and social infrastructure. J Econ Dev 37(1):1–23

Sharma K (2003) Factors determining India's export performance. J Asian Econ 14:435–446

UNCTAD (2002, 2003) World investment report, annual. UN Publications, Geneva

UNCTAD (2011) World investment report 2011, Non_equity modes of international production and development. United Nations Conference on Trade and Development, Geneva

Wei W (2005) China and India: any difference in their FDI performances? J Asian Econ 16 (4):719–736

Wen Hui Wei (2006) China and India: any difference in their FDI performance? J Asian Econ 16(4):719–736

Wignaraja G, Lazaro D (2010) North–South vs. South–South Asian FTAs: trends, compatibilities, and ways forward, UNU-CRIS working papers W-2010/3. United Nations University Comparative Regional Integration Studies, Bruges

Winters LA, Yusuf S (2007) Introduction: dancing with giants. In: Winters LA, Yusuf S (eds) Dancing with giants: China, India and the global economy. World Bank, Washington, DC, pp 1–34

World Bank (2011) World development indicator, 2011. World Bank, Washington, DC

World Development Indicators (2011) The World Bank, Washington, DC

World Development Indicators (2012) The World Bank, Washington, DC

World Economic Forum (2010) Global competitiveness report 2010–11, Geneva

World Investment Report (2007) United Nations conference on trade and development, Geneva

World Investment Report (2011) United Nations conference on trade and development, Geneva

Yusuf S, Nabeshima K, Perkings DH (2007) China and India Reshape Global Industrial Geography. In book edited by Alan Winters and Shahid Yusuf titled "China, India and the Global Economy" co-published by IBRD/WB and IPS, Singapore, USA

Chapter 6
Determinants of FDI in South Asia

6.1 Introduction

Foreign direct investment (FDI) is an important source of development financing, particularly for developing and less developed economies, as it contributes to productivity gains by bringing in new investment, better technology, and management expertise and by opening up export markets. Given the economic benefits of FDI, South Asian countries, namely, India, Pakistan, Bangladesh, and Sri Lanka, have implemented wide-ranging reforms—encompassing deregulation, privatisation, and globalisation—to attract FDI. South Asian policymakers realise that credible efforts for sustainable growth must involve an upgrading of technology and scale of production and linkages to an increasingly integrated globalised production system, chiefly through the participation of multinational corporations (MNCs). Private capital, which was long seen with concern and suspicion before the 1980s, is now regarded as a source of investment and economic growth in South Asia. Consequently, FDI inflow to South Asia has increased since the early 1990s and more so since 2002. The FDI environment underwent a sea change in South Asian countries during the 1990s and more so in recent years. Although FDI inflow to South Asian countries has increased, it is still low.

FDI flowing into any country depends upon the rate of return on investment and the certainties and uncertainties surrounding those returns. The expectations of private investors in a host country are guided by several economic, institutional, regulatory, and infrastructure-related factors.[1] Before making an investment, investors look at certain major economic policy issues, particularly relating to trade, labour, governance, and the availability of physical and social infrastructure. However, some of the fundamental determinants of FDI, such as geographical

[1] These can be called as pull factors. However, there are push factors, which are equally important for FDI inflow into developing countries such as recession in developed economies and low international interest rates. The emphasis of the present study is to examine the pull factors responsible for FDI inflows into South Asian countries.

P. Sahoo et al., *Foreign Direct Investment in South Asia*,
DOI 10.1007/978-81-322-1536-3_6, © Springer India 2014

location, resource endowment, and size of the market, are largely outside the control of national policy (UNCTAD 2003). Nevertheless, national economic policies can facilitate and help create a conducive investment environment so that FDI inflows become consistent with the economic potential. Sound macroeconomic fundamentals—along with other factors such as high and sustained growth, macroeconomic stability, and world-class infrastructure—and proreform policies influence the decision of investors in a host country.

6.2 Theories of FDI

There are well-established theories explaining why FDI takes place and what the potential determining factors could be, including the market perfection hypothesis (MacDougall 1960), imperfection hypothesis (Hymer 1976), internalisation theory (Rugman 1986), eclectic approach (Dunning 1977), and new trade theories. However, there is not a single universally applicable theory of FDI. It differs in terms of factors and variables, which originate different theories and make them stand.

6.2.1 The Market Perfection Hypothesis

Until the 1950s, FDI was entirely explained within the traditional theory of international capital movements. This hypothesis explains that FDI is a result of capital flowing from countries with low rates of returns (capital-abundant countries) to high rates of return (capital-scarce countries) and expecting a marginal return with the marginal cost of capital. The exogenous growth theory explains that the marginal productivity of capital would fall once capital stock per capita increases after some level. Therefore, the countries with lower capital stock per capita will earn a greater rate of return that leads to movement of capital from richer countries to poorer nations.

Two early theoretical contributions in this line are Mundell (1957) and MacDougall (1960). Therefore, according to this hypothesis, FDI was motivated by higher profitability in foreign markets enjoying growth and lower labour costs and exchange risks. Agarwal (1980) explains that most empirical studies based on this approach failed to provide strong supporting evidence. Trends in the FDI flows over four decades indicate that developed countries received a larger share of FDI, which are capital abundant (WIR 2012). Furthermore, only a small number of developing countries receive significant amount of FDI inflows in the last decades, e.g. China accounts for nearly one-quarter of the total, and a few economies in Asia and Latin America account for the rest, whereas flows going to Africa are nearly negligible (WIR 2012). Therefore, capital does not go to high-return locations, i.e. developing countries with low capital endowments as predicted by this hypothesis.

6.2.2 *Imperfect Competition Approaches*

The earlier theories lacked the information on market failures. Hymer (1976) was the first analyst to recognise that investment abroad involves high costs and risks inherent to the drawbacks faced by multinationals because they are foreign. These include the cost of acquiring information due to cultural and language differences and the cost of less favourable treatment by the governments of host countries. The multinationals will thus have to have ownership advantages (e.g. innovative products, management skills, and patents) to offset the disadvantages (Dunning 1993). Two main types of market imperfections are relevant. One arises from MNEs' advantages with respect to firms with no foreign operations (due to access to raw materials, economies of scale, intangible assets such as trade names, patents, and superior management), and the other is due to transaction costs (such as information and negotiation costs, arising from recourse to the market). The internalisation theory explains that 'FDI arises from efforts by firms to replace market transaction with internal transactions' (Buckley and Casson 1976). When market risk and uncertainty are high, transaction costs are high, and internalisation of operations (FDI) is preferred.

A different approach to FDI was developed by Vernon (1966): the product cycle theory. Vernon developed this theory to explain various types of FDI made by US companies in Western Europe after the Second World War in the manufacturing industry. Vernon (1966) claims that a product goes through four stages: innovation, growth, maturity, and decline. According to this approach, in first stage, the product appears as an innovation, which is sold locally in the same country where it is produced (the USA). This is to facilitate satisfying local demand while having efficient coordination between research, development, and production units. In the second stage, the product is exported (to Western Europe). In third stage, competitors to this product arise in Europe. If conditions are favourable, the firm will establish foreign subsidiaries there to face increased competition. It may also establish subsidiaries in less developed countries to have access to cheaper labour costs to enhance its competitiveness.

6.2.3 *An Eclectic Approach*

Dunning (1977) developed the eclectic theory. He introduces this theory integrating the industrial organisation theory, the internalisation theory, and the location theory. These three conditions constitute the basis of the eclectic or OLI paradigm, where OLI stands for 'ownership, location, and internalisation'. Ownership means the sort of advantages that MNEs should have in the same line of what has just been explained when talking about Hymer's contribution (includes the right to technology, monopoly power, and size, access to raw materials, and access to cheap finance). Location gives the idea that for a MNE to establish a new plant in a foreign country, the host country must have some locational advantages compared to the MNE's home country. These advantages may be cheaper factors of production, better access to natural resources, a bigger market, and special tax regimes (Dunning and Lundan 2008). Finally, the internalisation idea had also been noted by Buckley and Casson (1976), who dealt with transaction costs. It may be more beneficial for a firm to exploit its ownership advantages within its subsidiaries than to sell or license them to other independent firms.

6.2.4 Vertical FDI vs. Horizontal FDI

A new literature on FDIs has been developed by integrating modern industrial organisation into trade theories. Within this approach, some studies concentrate on the analysis of horizontal MNEs or FDI (Markusen and Venables 1998), whereas others do the same on the vertical side of the phenomenon (Helpman 1984; Helpman and Krugman 1985). In the case of vertical FDI, firms separate geographically their different stages of the value-added chain.[2] Helpman (1984) introduced vertical MNEs in a model with monopolistic competition and differentiated products, where he formalise the logic of the fragmentation of production. In his model, the incentive for vertical FDI to arise stems from factor price differences across countries. Helpman showed that by splitting production processes with different input requirements, MNEs can exploit cross-country differences in factor prices by shifting activities to the cheapest locations.

On the other hand, in the models based on horizontal FDI, such as Brainard (1993), Markusen (1995), and Markusen and Venables (1998), foreign investment is alternative modality. The choice of multinational firms depends on the interaction between these key elements: the firm specific advantages (activities of research and development, managerial know-how, etc.), plant-level scale economies, and transport, geographical, and cultural distance costs. Horizontal FDI flows are increasing in countries similar in size as measured by GDP and factor endowments, i.e. the more similar in GDP and factor endowments two countries are, the more FDI will take place between them (Markusen and Venables 1998).

Thus, there are many reasons for FDI to take place. Recent years have seen more of efficiency-seeking FDI, which leads to the movement of capital from one place to other to restructure its existing investments to achieve an efficient allocation of international economic activity of the firms. This implies

1. International specialisation, whereby firms seek to benefit from differences in product and factor prices and to diversify risk

[2] Vertical FDI takes two forms: (1) backward vertical FDI, where an industry abroad provides inputs for a firm's domestic production process, and (2) forward vertical FDI, in which an industry abroad sells the outputs of a firm's domestic production processes.

2. Global sourcing, undertaken primarily by network-based MNCs with global sourcing operations by rationalising the global activities structure to save resources and improve efficiency
3. Seeking and securing natural resources, e.g. minerals, raw materials, or lower labour costs for the investing company

There is also market-seeking FDI to identify and exploit new markets for finished products. UNCTAD (1998, 2000) classifies a group of foreign investors who mainly invest in foreign countries to serve their domestic markets. These market-seeking foreign investors thus prefer to invest in countries that either have large domestic markets or are growing fast. In a few cases, FDI also moves to seek and secure natural resources and raw materials.

6.3 Brief Literature Review

Of late, there is a substantial literature explaining the determinants of FDI (Dunning 1993; Globerman and Shapiro 1999; Campos and Kinoshita 2002; Bevan and Estrin 2004). Athukorala (2009) asserts that there are several dimensions to the determinants of FDI, as MNCs decide to invest in foreign countries for many different reasons.

Overall, the determinants of FDI can be grouped into:

1. Economic conditions such as market size, growth prospect, rate of return, industrialisation, labour cost, physical infrastructure, and macroeconomic fundamentals
2. Host country policies such as the promotion of private ownership, trade policies/ FDI policy, legal framework, and governance

Except Agrawal (2000) and Sahoo (2006, 2012), no study focuses on infrastructure and reforms in South Asia. A few studies on developing countries include South Asian countries (such as Vadlamannati et al. 2009), and some studies are specific to South Asian countries (Shah and Ahmed 2003; Banga 2004). However, the present study is different and comprehensive, as mentioned in the introduction.

Using a panel of 69 countries, Ali et al. (2006) examine the role of institutions in determining FDI inflows during 1981 and 2005. They find that institutions are a robust predictor of overall FDI, and that the most significant institutional aspects are linked to property rights, the rule of law, and expropriation risk, especially in the services and manufacturing sectors.

Bartels (2009) examines the major determinants of FDI inflows to sub-Saharan countries. Using principal component analysis, the study finds that among other factors of FDI inflow are political economy, trade agreements, locational factors such as raw materials and local suppliers, and local demand factors. Mohamed and Sidiropoulos (2010) examine main determinants of FDI inflows to 12 MENA and 24 other countries over 1975–2006. Using, panel methodology (fixed and random), the study finds that the key determinants of FDI inflows in MENA countries are the size of the host economy, the government size, natural resources, and the institutional variables like corruption and investment profile.

Using sectoral FDI (primary, secondary, and tertiary), Walsh and Yu (2010) examine determinants of FDI inflows to for 27 emerging and developed market from 1985 to 2008. Using GMM system method, the study finds that macroeconomic determinants of FDI flows to secondary sector to both advanced and emerging economies are same. On the other hand, labour market flexibility and financial depth appear to matter far more for emerging economies than advanced ones. For tertiary FDI, macroeconomic conditions are more important for advanced economies than for emerging ones. The role of the qualitative and institutional factors is also found important. Liberalising labour markets and measures to increase financial deepening could attract more secondary FDI into emerging markets, though these effects are weaker among advanced economies. Mottaleb and Kalirajan (2010) examine determinants of FDI inflows to 68 developing countries belonging to Asia, Latin America, and Africa over 2005–2008. Out of 68 countries, 31 are low-income countries and 37 are lower-middle income countries. Using the random effect generalised least square estimation process, the study finds that besides GDP size and its growth rate, international trade, foreign aid, and a business-friendly environment are the most important and significant factors in determining FDI.

Khan and Nawaz (2010) examine the determinants of FDI inflows to Pakistan over 1970–2004. Among other factors, the study identifies GDP growth rate, volume of exports, human population, tariff on imports, and price index as major determinants of FDI inflows to Pakistan. From this brief review, we find that determinants of FDI vary from country to country, developed country to developing country, and sector to sector.

6.4 Potential Determinants of FDI

6.4.1 *Market Size*

The aim of FDI inflows to emerging countries is to tap the domestic market, and thus market size does matter for domestic market-oriented FDI. Market size is generally measured by GDP, per capita income, or size of the middle class. The size of the market or per capita income is an indicator of the sophistication and breadth of the domestic market. Thus, an economy with a large market size (along with other factors) should attract more FDI. Market size is important for FDI as it provides potential for local sales, greater profitability of local sales to export sales, and relatively diverse resources, which make local sourcing more feasible (Pfefferman and Madarassy 1992). Thus, a large market size provides more opportunities for sales and also profits to foreign firms and therefore attracts FDI (Noy and Vu 2007; Ramirez 2006; Chakrabarti 2001). However, studies by

Edwards (1990) and Asiedu (2002) show that there is no significant impact of growth or market size on FDI inflows. Further, Loree and Guisinger (1995) and Wei (2000) find that market size and growth impact differ under different conditions. In most of the empirical studies, real GDP or per capita GDP is considered (e.g. Armstrong 2009; Adhikary and Mengistu 2008).

6.4.2 Growth Prospects and Positive Country Conditions

Along with market size, the prospect of growth (generally measured by GDP growth rates) also has a positive influence on FDI inflows. Countries that have high and sustained growth rates receive more FDI flows than volatile economies. There are good numbers of studies showing the positive impact of per capita growth or growth prospect on FDI (Durham 2004 and Fan et al. 2007). Fan et al. (2007) document that higher economic growth rate is one of the major reasons for higher FDI inflows to China. The faster market increases in size, the more opportunities present for generating profits than the markets grow at a low rate or even not at all (Walsh and Yu 2010). To proxy market potential, a number of studies adopted the GDP per capita growth rate of a country (Al-Sadig 2009; Adhikary and Mengistu 2008). Following these empirical works, GDP per capita growth (GDPPCG) is taken as a measure of market potential and assumed that GDPPCG will be positively associated with inward FDI in South Asia.

6.4.3 Openness and Export Promotion

The key hypothesis from various theories is that gains from FDI are far higher in the export promotion (EP) regime than the import promotion regime. The theory proposes that import substitution (IS) regimes encourage FDI to enter in cases where the host country does not have advantages leading to extra profit and rent-seeking activities. However, in an EP regime, FDI uses low labour costs and available raw materials for export promotion, leading to overall output growth. Open to the global market through international trade can also provide scale economies similar to the countries with large domestic market to the foreign investors. Trade openness generally positively influences the export-oriented FDI inflow into an economy (UNCTAD 2009). Investors generally want big markets and like to invest in countries that have regional trade integration and also in countries where there are greater investment provisions in their trade agreements. In the empirical literature, various authors have uses various measures as proxies for trade openness. For instance, the World Bank (1993) and Yanikkaya (2003) adopt full trade measures of openness by using 'total trade volume as a percentage of GDP', while Sin and Leung (2001) and Moosa and Cardak (2006) use partial trade measures like 'export as a percentage of GDP'. In this study, we use export and import as ratio of GDP.

6.4.4 Labour Cost and Availability of Skilled Labour

Cheap labour is another important determinant of FDI inflow to developing countries. A high wage-adjusted productivity of labour attracts efficiency-seeking FDI both aiming to produce for the host economy as well as for export from host countries. Studies by Wheeler and Mody (1992) and Loree and Guisinger (1995) show a positive impact of labour cost on FDI inflow. Countries with a large supply of skilled human capital attract more FDI, particularly in sectors that are relatively intensive in the use of skilled labour. For example, the availability of numerous cheap labour in China replaced the positions of employees from Europe and United States for the big wage gap on the same job (Zhao and Zhu 2000). We use the nominal wage rate (*WAGE*) for manufacturing sector as a proxy for labour cost. We would generally expect a negative sign on the coefficient (e.g. countries with lower labour costs would attract more FDI). However, a positive relationship is also thought to be possible in the literature as wage rate could be regarded as a signal for the labour quality. Higher wage rate may indicate the higher skill labour that foreign investors seek (Zhao and Zhu 2000).

6.4.5 Infrastructure Facilities

The availability of quality infrastructure, particularly electricity, water, transportation, and telecommunications, is an important determinant of FDI. Infrastructure has a direct impact on cost of production, as good infrastructure increases effective utilisation of labour force and minimises cost of production (Wheeler and Mody 1992). On the other hand, Sachs et al. (2004) argue that the joint effect of poor infrastructure and low investment rate usually shrinks productivity of a firm, which deters FDI. Campos and Kinoshita (2003) have argued that good infrastructure is a necessary condition for foreign investors to operate successfully, regardless of the type of FDI. Therefore, when developing countries compete for FDI, the country that is best prepared to address infrastructure bottlenecks will secure a greater amount of FDI. The previous literature shows the positive impact of infrastructure facilities on FDI inflows (Zhang 2001; Asiedu 2002; Kok and Ersoy 2009). In empirical literature, there are a number of measures used for infrastructure condition of a country. For instance, Kok and Ersoy (2009) use per capita electric power consumption, whereas Banga (2003) uses the ratio of transport and communication over GDP, and Canning and Bennathan (2000) considered telecom density (the number of telephones per 100 people). Considering the availability of data, in this study, the construction of an infrastructure index has been attempted taking different infrastructure indicators.

6.4.6 Government Finance

Government finance is an important issue that affects FDI flows. A high fiscal deficit leads to more government liabilities and therefore more taxes and defaults on international debt. Therefore, fiscal stability is generally considered to be one of the indicators of macroeconomic stability. Hence, the smaller fiscal deficit is perceived to be conducive environment for robust private investment. In addition, empirical literature indicates that relatively large government expenditure tends to 'crowd out' private investment in an economy (Mkenda and Mkenda 2004). In this sense, one expects a negative relationship between government consumption expenditure and FDI inflows. We consider the fiscal deficit for government finance.

6.4.7 Human Capital

The availability of a cheap workforce, particularly an educated one, influences investment decisions and thus is one of the determinants of FDI inflow. Higher level of human capital is a good indicator of the availability of skilled workers, which can significantly boost the locational advantage of a country. Markusen (2001) and Rodríguez and Pallas (2008) find that human capital is the most important determinant of inward FDI. Borensztein et al. (1998), Noorbakhsh et al. (2001), and Asiedu (2002) found that the level of human capital is a significant determinant of the locational advantage of a host country and plays a key role in attracting FDI. Various authors have taken different proxy for human capital development. For example, Alsan et al. (2006) use life expectancy, whereas level of schooling is considered by Nonnemberg and Cardoso de Mendonça (2004). In this study, we use the gross secondary enrolment rate (*ENR*) as proxy for human capital development. Secondary school attainment of the host country represents accumulated stock of human capital, which is a measure of labour quality and indicative of the level of education and skills of the workers within a country. This variable is expected to be positively related to FDI inflows (Anyanwu 2012).

6.4.8 Exchange Rate

Exchange rate is considered as another important variable in affecting FDI inflows. A weaker real exchange rate might be expected to increase FDI as firms take advantage of relatively low prices in host markets to purchase facilities or, if production is re-exported, to increase home country profits on goods sent to a third market. For example, Ramirez (2006) argues that host country currency depreciation is likely to increase its exports, which in turn motivates foreign investment in export-oriented sectors. But on the other hand, a stronger real exchange rate (exchange rate appreciation) might be expected to strengthen the incentive of foreign companies to produce domestically: the exchange rate is in a sense a barrier to entry in the market that could lead to more horizontal FDI (Walsh and Yu 2010).

6.4.9 Institutions

Good quality institutional is likely another important determinant of FDI, particularly for developing countries as good governance is associated with higher economic growth, which may attract more FDI inflows. On the other hand, poor institutions that enable corruption tend to add to investment costs and reduce profits. Third, the high sunk cost of FDI makes investors highly sensitive to uncertainty, including the political uncertainty that arises from poor institutions (Walsh and Yu 2010). However, various studies have used different proxy for good institution, and empirical results are mixed. For example, Wheeler and Mody (1992) analyse firm-level US data and find the influence of regulatory framework, bureaucratic hurdles and red tape, judicial transparency, and the extent of corruption in the host country insignificant. However, Wei (2000) finds that corruption significantly adds to firm costs and impedes FDI inflows. On the other hand, Walsh and Yu (2010) use labour market flexibility, infrastructure quality, judicial independence, legal system efficiency, and financial depth as proxies for the institutional and qualitative. In this study, we use governance indicator provided by Heritage Foundation.

6.4.10 Financial Development

Financial development indicates the availability of credit for investment and growth. For example, Nasser and Gomez (2009) note that financial development is important in FDI decisions because it affects the cost structure of investment projects. Further, Kinda (2010) observes that financial development is an engine of economic growth, providing better business opportunities for customers and firms. In order to measure financial deepening, empirical literature outlines a number of measures such as the ratio of broad money to GDP (M2/GDP), the ratio of bank assets to GDP, liquid liabilities, domestic credit to the private sector, market capitalisation, and the ratio of the private investment to GDP (Beck 2002; King and Levine 1993; Levine et al. 2000). However, in this study, financial deepening is measured as the ratio of the domestic credit provided by the banking sector over GDP (DBC). It is expected that DBC will be positively associated with inward FDI. The financial development index (FIN) has been made by using principal component analysis which includes (1) bank branches per million people, (2) bank credit provided to domestic sector (per cent GDP), and (3) M2 by GDP ratio.

6.4.11 Rate of Return on Investment

The profitability of investment is one of the major determinants of investment. Thus, the rate of return on investment in a host economy influences the investment decision. Following previous studies (see Asiedu 2002), the log of inverse per capita GDP has been used as proxy for the rate of return on investment as capital-scarce countries generally have a higher rate of return on capital, implying low per capita GDP. This implies that the lower the GDP per capita, the higher the rate of return and thus FDI inflow. Alternatively, lending rate has also been considered to show the impact of lending rate on FDI inflows.

6.4.12 Regional Trade Agreements (RTAs)

The effect of RTAs on FDI can be divided into two parts: indirectly affects FDI flows through trade liberalisation process and directly affects FDI flows through investment liberalisation under the rules of the RTA (Worth 1998; Blomström et al. 1998; Blomström and Kokko 1997). While trade liberalisation can diminish inside regional tariffs and nontariff barriers to form a free trade area and an enlarged intra-regional market to attract more FDI inflows from outsiders, it can also reduce FDI to the region because of exports preference to FDI if external trade barriers are lowered as well. Thus, trade liberalisation can cause regional FDI inflows from outsiders to increase or decrease according to their trade strategies. Levy Yeyati et al. (2002) analyse the impact of RTAs on bilateral FDI stocks in a large sample of countries. Their findings indicate a significantly positive average impact of regional integration agreements on bilateral FDI. We use cumulative RTAs to capture the effect of trade agreements on FDI inflows.

6.4.13 Macro Stability Variables (MS)

Various macro indicators such as inflation rate, current account deficit and fiscal deficit considered as macro stability variables. For example, inflation rate is used as an indicator of macroeconomic instability (Buckley et al. 2007). A stable macro-economic environment promotes FDI by showing less investment risk. Similarly, higher government deficit crowds out private investment, thereby reducing FDI inflows. On the other hand, higher current account deficit increases higher fiscal deficit and exchange rate fluctuation, thereby reducing FDI inflows. Therefore, we expect the negative sign of this variable.

6.4.14 Policy Measures

The previous literature shows the impact of government policies including investment incentives on FDI inflows into a host country (Dunning 2002; Blomström and Kokko 2002; Schneider and Frey 1985; Grubert and Mutti 1991; Loree and Guisinger 1995; Taylor 2000; Kumar 2002). Though investment incentives are considered another determinant for FDI, the recent paper by Blomström and Kokko (2003) suggests that investment incentives alone are generally not an efficient way to increase national welfare. Policies to promote FDI take a variety of forms, but the most common are partial or complete exemptions from corporate taxes and import duties. Standard policies to attract FDI include tax holidays, import duty exemptions, and different kinds of direct subsidies. FDI inflows are also affected by corporate tax rate differentiation. Subsidising FDI helps multinational firms reduce production costs, improves incentives to create patents and trademarks, and enhances the relative attractiveness of locating production facilities in the country offering incentives and raising the economic benefits of FDI relative to exporting.

6.5 Data Sources, Model Specification, and Methodology

Annual data on GDP, growth rate of GDP, trade ratio, secondary enrolment ratio, current account deficit, labour force (ILO definition of the economically active population that includes both the employed and the unemployed), inflation rate, foreign debt, nominal exchange rate, banking sector credit to domestic sector, and government final expenditure are collected from World Development Indicators (2012). Data on fiscal deficit is collected from International Financial Statistics, IMF. Infrastructure variables considered in this study are air freight transport (million tons per km), electric power consumption (kwh per capita), rail density (per 1,000 population), energy use (kg of oil equivalent per capita), and total telephone lines (main line plus cellular phones) per 1,000 population which are taken from World development Indicators (various years). Data on FDI inflows are collected from UNCTAD. Data on nominal wage rate is collected from International Labour Organization. Data on governance indicator (proxied by index of economic freedom) is collected from the Heritage Foundation. Data on RTAs are collected from respective Ministry of Commerce and World Trade Organization.

6.5.1 Model Specification

Based on the above literature discussion, we specify the FDI function for South Asia as

$$\begin{aligned} \mathrm{FDIR}_t = \alpha + \beta_1 \mathrm{LGDP}_t + \beta_2 \mathrm{TR}_t + \beta_3 \mathrm{HUM}_t + \beta_4 \mathrm{RER}_t + \beta_5 \mathrm{WR}_t \\ + \beta_6 \mathrm{RTA}_t + \beta_7 \mathrm{INFRA}_t + \beta_8 \mathrm{MS}_t + \beta_9 \mathrm{FIN}_t + \beta_{10} \mathrm{FD}_t + u_t \end{aligned} \tag{6.1}$$

Similarly for panel analysis, our FDI function is

$$\begin{aligned}\mathrm{FDIR}_{it} = \alpha + \beta_1\mathrm{LGDP}_{it} + \beta_2\mathrm{TR}_{it} + \beta_3\mathrm{HUM}_{it} + \beta_4\mathrm{RER}_{it} + \beta_5\mathrm{WR}_{it} + \beta_6\mathrm{RTA}_{it} \\ + \beta_7\mathrm{INFRA}_{it} + \beta_8\mathrm{GOV}_{it} + \beta_9\mathrm{MS}_{it} + \beta_{10}\mathrm{FIN}_{it} + \beta_{11}\mathrm{FD}_{it} + u_{it}\end{aligned} \tag{6.2}$$

where *i* denotes countries, *t* denotes time, and L stands for log transformation. The variables are defined as:

FDIR = FDI inflows as ratio of GDP
GDP = real GDP (at US$ 2000 price)
TR = total trade as ratio of GDP
HUM = secondary enrolment ratio
RER = real exchange rate
WR = monthly manufactured wage rate (in US$)
RTA = cumulative value of regional trade agreements
INFRA = index of infrastructure stocks
GOV = governance indicator proxied by index of economic freedom
MS = macro stability variables such as inflation rate, current account deficit, and fiscal deficit
FIN = Financial Development Index
FD = fiscal deficit as ratio of GDP

6.5.2 *Methodology*

In this study, we use both time series and panel data analysis for getting robust estimation. Given that we have only 31 observations per country, autoregressive distributed lag (ARDL) technique is used. Two panel methods (GMM system and fully modified OLS (FMOLS)) are used to derive long-run determinants of FDI for South Asia. First, we conduct unit root and co-integration test before deriving long-run determinants of FDI by using appropriate methodology.

6.5.3 *Time Series Analysis*

6.5.3.1 ADF Unit Root Test

The first test in the empirical analysis is the examination of properties of variables by using ADF unit root test. The testing procedures of ADF are based on the null hypothesis that a unit root exists in the autoregressive representation of the series.

The augmented Dickey–Fuller or ADF test (see Dickey and Fuller 1981) is based on the following regression:

$$\Delta X_t = \alpha_0 + \alpha_1 t + \beta X_{t-1} + \sum_{j=1}^{k} \gamma_j \Delta X_{t-j} + \varepsilon_t \tag{6.3}$$

where Δ is the difference operator and ε_t is stationary random error. The null hypothesis is that X_t is non-stationary series, and it is rejected when β is significantly negative. The constant and the trend terms are retained only if significantly different from zero. The optimal number of lags, k, is determined by minimising the Akaike Information Criterion (AIC). The tests are done both with and without a time trend for five countries. The results are summarised in the Appendix tables (Tables 6.A.1, 6.A.2, 6.A.3, 6.A.4, 6.A.5, 6.A.6, 6.A.7).

It is seen that all FDI ratio (the dependent variables in various estimations) are integrated of order 1 {denoted, $I(1)$} except Sri Lanka, but the explanatory variables are a mixture of $I(0)$ and $I(1)$ variables. Variables such as fiscal deficit, growth of labour force, current account deficit, and inflation rate are level stationary or $I(0)$. All other variables are $I(1)$. Therefore, unit test results suggest that we have mixture of $I(0)$ and $I(1)$ variables.

6.5.3.2 ARDL Co-integration

Since we have mixture of $I(1)$ and $I(0)$ variables, co-integration procedures are applicable and can be used to examine the existence of a long-run relation between the variables, which is the second step in exploring the long-run determinants of FDI. We use autoregressive distributed lag (ARDL) method developed by Pesaran et al. (2001) to find out the long-run relationship among the relevant variables. *The Estimation Procedure Used—The ARDL Method*: For determining the long-run relationship, Pesaran and Pesaran (1997) have developed the ARDL method. This procedure is a good procedure to use for stationary variables as well as for a mixture of $I(0)$ and $I(1)$ variables. The existence of the long-run relationship is confirmed with the help of an F-test that tests that the coefficients of all explanatory variables are jointly different from zero. The usual critical values are applicable for the F-test when all variables are $I(0)$. However, different and higher critical values (provided in Pesaran and Shin 1998) are applicable when all or some of the variables are $I(1)$.

The augmented ADRL model can be written as follows:

$$\alpha(L)y_t = \mu_0 + \sum_{i=1}^{k} \beta_i(L)x_{it} + u_t \tag{6.4}$$

where $\alpha(L) = \alpha_0 + \alpha_1 L + \alpha_2 L^2 + \cdots + \alpha_t L^t$

and $\beta(L) = \beta_0 + \beta_1 L + \beta_2 L^2 + \cdots + \beta_t L^t$

where μ_0 is a constant, y_t is the dependent variable, and L is the lag operator such that $L^i x_t = x_{t-i}$. In the long-run equilibrium, $y_t = y_{t-1} = y_{t-2} = \cdots = y_0$ and $x_{it} = x_{it-1} = x_{it-2} = \cdots = x_{i0}$. Solving for y, we get the following long-run relation:

$$y = a + \sum_{i=1}^{k} b_i x_i + \gamma_t \tag{6.5}$$

where
$$a = \frac{\mu_0}{\alpha_0 + \alpha_1 + \cdots + \alpha_t}$$

$$b_i = \frac{\beta_{i0} + \beta_{i1} + \beta_{i2} + \cdots + \beta_{it}}{\alpha_0 + \alpha_1 + \alpha_2 + \cdots + \alpha_t}$$

$$\gamma_t = \frac{u_t}{\alpha_0 + \alpha_1 + \alpha_2 + \cdots + \alpha_n}$$

The error correction (EC) representation of the ARDL method can be written as follows:

$$\begin{aligned}\Delta y_t = \Delta\hat{\alpha}_0 - \sum_{j-2}^{p} \hat{\alpha}_j \Delta y_{t-j} + \sum_{i-1}^{k} \hat{\beta}_{i0}\, \Delta x_{it} - \sum_{i-1}^{k} \sum_{j-2}^{q} \beta_{i,\,t-j} \\ - \alpha(1,\, p)\mathrm{ECM}_{t-1} + \mu_t\end{aligned} \tag{6.6}$$

where $\mathrm{ECM}_t = y_t - \hat{\alpha} - \sum_{i-1}^{k} \hat{\beta}_{i0} \Delta x_{it}$

where Δ is the first difference operator, $\alpha_{j,\ t-j}$ and $\beta_{ij,\ t-j}$ are the coefficients estimated from Eq. (6.6), and $\alpha(1,p)$ measures the speed of adjustment. A two-step procedure is used in estimating the long-run relationship. In the first step, we investigate the existence of a long-run relationship predicted by theory among the variables in question. The short- and long-run parameters are estimated in the second stage if the long-run relationship is established in the first step.

Co-integration Results

The result of ARDL co-integration test is presented in Table 6.1. It is clear from Table 6.1 that there exists a long-run relationship among the variables when GDP is the dependent variable because its F-statistic exceeds the upper bound critical value (3.50) at the 5 % levels for all the countries. Given that we have only 31 observations, we have considered 2 lags and the lags are selected on the basis of AIC. Thus, the null of non-existence of stable long-run relationship is rejected. These results also warrant proceeding to the next stage of estimation.

Table 6.1 ARDL co-integration test (1980–2010)

Country	Dependent variable	*F*-stat	5 % critical value[a]	Result
India	FDIY	7.37[b]	3.50	Rejection of null of no co-integration
Pakistan	FDIY	9.38[b]	3.50	Rejection of null of no co-integration
Sri Lanka	FDIY	5.89[b]	3.50	Rejection of null of no co-integration
Bangladesh	FDIY	5.8[b]	3.50	Rejection of null of no co-integration
Nepal	FDIY	8.84[b]	3.50	Rejection of null of no co-integration

Note: The order of ARDL is selected on the basis of AIC
[a]Denotes upper bound critical values with seven independent variables
[b]Denotes rejection of null hypothesis of no co-integration in favour of co-integration

Long-Run Determinants of FDI

The empirical research evaluating the determinants of FDI always comes across the problem of endogeneity. For example, it has been discussed whether higher GDP, trade, and human capital development lead to higher FDI or higher FDI leads to higher GDP, trade, and human capital development. Given this reserve causality and possibility of more than one endogenous variable, we use ARDL methods to derive long-run determinants of FDI. The long-run relations obtained using ARDL procedures for five South Asian countries are shown in Table 6.2. Diagnostic test are checked to ensure that it is the best model and there is no misspecification bias in the model. The diagnostic tests include the test of serial autocorrelation (LM), heteroscedasticity (ARCH test), and omitted variables/functional form (Ramsey Reset).

India

In the case of India, column 2 of Table 6.2 shows that one of the most important variables is market size (LGDP) and significant at one per cent level of significance. The coefficient of real GDP is more than one. This is consistent with the fact that the horizontal FDI (i.e. FDI seeking a base to produce for the domestic market in the host country) is attracted to countries in which real income, and therefore domestic purchasing power, is relatively high. Previous studies such as Chakrabarti (2003) and Banga (2003) also found a positive significant relationship between FDI and market size. In terms of size, India is the largest country and attracts largest amount of FDI in South Asia. Similarly, in line with previous research, we also find a positive impact of openness on the FDI and the coefficient is more than one, indicating the fact that economies in which trade is important also receive relatively higher share of the FDI. As already known, the amount of FDI inflows to India increased significantly only after deep reforms were carried out in the early 1990s.

Table 6.2 Determinants of FDI in South Asia (1980–2010)

	India	Pakistan	Sri Lanka	Bangladesh	Nepal
Variables	Coefficients	Coefficients	Coefficients	Coefficients	Coefficients
Constant	268.4** (4.63)	−219.24* (−2.84)	−27.0** (−4.09)	−48.9*(−2.20)	9.93** (4.20)
LGDP	1.67** (2.39)	36.4* (2.85)	6.58** (3.94)	10.3* (2.04)	1.458* (2.80)
TR	0.12* (1.99)	0.11* (2.12)	0.02* (2.04)	−0.00 (−0.12)	0.05* (2.32)
HUM	0.01 (1.40)	–	–	–	0.02* (2..52)
Return	−3,621* (−2.19)	−13,515* (−2.77)	–	–	–
WR	0.04* (2.51)	−0.04* (−2.73)	−0.04* (−2.79)	−0.04* (−2.79)	0.16 (0.35)
RER	−0.03* (2.41)	−0.06** (−3.45)	−0.02* (−2.18)	−0.08* (−2.78)	−0.01* (−2.80)
INFRA	1.2 * (2.84)	0.43* (2.53)	0.45* (2.69)	0.37* (2.47)	0.02(1.35)
MS		−0.08** (−6.87)	−0.06*(−2.68)	−0.02*(−2.12)	−0.03* (−2.71)
TA	0.23** (2.64)	0.42* (2.77)	0.12** (2.62)	0.36** (3.22)	–
Model selection criteria (AIC)	(2,0,2,2,0,2,0,0)	(1,0,0,1,0,0,1,1)	(2,0,2,1,1,3,3)	(0,0,1,1,2,0,0)	(0,1,0,0,0,0,0)
Diagnostic test	ADJ. $R^2 = 0.91$, DW. Stat. = 1.8, LM = 0.8, ARCH = 1.7	ADJ. $R^2 = 0.92$, DW. Stat. = 2.2, LM = 2.3, ARCH = 1.3	ADJ. $R^2 = 0.75$, DW. Stat. = 2.2, LM = 2.1, ARCH = 0.66	ADJ. $R^2 = 0.83$, DW. Stat. = 2.1, LM = 1.19, ARCH = 1.8	ADJ. $R^2 = 0.74$, DW. stat. = 2.4, LM = 1.5, ARCH = 1.1
	Reset-0.68 (0.32)	Reset-0.67 (0.42)	Reset-2.1 (0.16)		Reset-2.1 (0.14)

Notes: ***, **, and * denote significance at 1, 5, and 10 level, respectively. Figures in the parentheses are *t*-ratio

This has been proved by the coefficient of openness. On the other hand, the impact of human capital is positive but insignificant. Stock of physical capital proxied by infrastructure index is found to be positively significant at 5 % level of significance. Therefore, improvement in infrastructure facilities attracts higher FDI inflows. This is consistent with the findings of Asiedu (2002) and Kok and Ersoy (2009). Therefore, further development of infrastructure will have positive impact on FDI inflows to India.

Real exchange rate is found to have negative impact on FDI inflows in India. This is expected as depreciation of rupee encourages higher FDI inflows. This is because a weaker real exchange rate might be expected to increase FDI as firms take advantage of relatively low prices in host markets to purchase facilities or, if production is re-exported, to increase home country profits on goods sent to a third market. Previous empirical studies also found negative impact of real exchange rate on FDI inflows (for instance, Ramirez 2006; Anyanwu 2012). Nominal manufacturing wage rate proxy for labour cost has positive impact on FDI. The positive relationship between wage rate and FDI for India indicates higher skill labours that foreign investors seek (Zhao and Zhu 2000). In addition, rate of return variable (inverse if per capital income) is negatively related to FDI inflows.

Finally, RTAs have positive and statistically significant impact on FDI inflows to India. Previous studies have also documented positive effect of RTA on FDI (Blomström and Kokko 1997; Baltagi et al. 2007). Some other variables such as inflation rate, foreign exchange reserve, fiscal deficit, growth of labour force, and foreign debt have been dropped as these variables are found insignificant. As we know, at the end of 2010, India had highest number of trade agreements in South Asia, and this has positive impact on FDI inflows.

Pakistan

In the case of Pakistan, real GDP, trade ratio, infrastructure stock, human capital, and RTAs have positive and significant impact on FDI flows. On the other hand, as expected variables such as real exchange rate, wage rate, and current account deficit have negative significant impact on FDI inflows. The coefficient of wage rate is negative, indicating cheap labour is another important determinant of FDI inflow to Pakistan. A high wage-adjusted productivity of labour attracts efficiency-seeking FDI both aiming to produce for the host economy as well as for export from host countries, particularly in textile sector in Pakistan. Other variables such as inflation rate, fiscal deficit, growth of labour force, financial development index, human capital, and foreign exchange reserve have been dropped as these variables are found insignificant for Pakistan.

Sri Lanka

In the case of Sri Lanka, real GDP and international trade affect FDI inflows positively, indicating size of the domestic economy is important variable. However, the size of GDP impact on FDI is much larger than trade impact. In addition to this, infrastructure facilities and trade agreements influence FDI inflows positively. Further, the coefficient of real exchange rate and current account deficit is negative and statistically significant. Sri Lanka had the history of highest current account deficit in South Asia, and this is detrimental to FDI inflows. Real exchange deprecation has positive impact on FDI inflows by increasing profit on goods sent to a third market. In addition, wage rate has native impact on FDI inflows, indicating higher labour cost affects FDI inflow adversely. Other variables such as human capital, inflation rate, fiscal deficit, growth of labour force, financial development index, and foreign exchange reserve are found insignificant and hence dropped from final estimation.

Bangladesh

For Bangladesh, the results suggest that in addition to GDP and infrastructure stock, RTAs have positive impact on FDI inflows. Openness does not have any significant impact on FDI. More importantly, current account deficit real exchange rate and wage rate have negative impact on FDI inflows. Like Pakistan and Sri Lanka, real exchange rate depreciation in Bangladesh increases competitiveness of textile exports where maximum FDI inflows. This increases profit of MNEs operating in this sector. Similarly, low wage rate in Bangladesh attracts higher amount of FDI to textile sector. On the other hand, higher instability in the form of higher current account deficit discourages FDI inflows. In terms of magnitude of impact, the size of the domestic economy has highest impact, and current account deficit has lowest impact on FDI inflows to Bangladesh.

Nepal

Finally, the results for Nepal indicate that GDP, human capital, and trade have significant positive impact on FDI inflows. In addition to this, other variables such as real exchange rate and current account deficit have expected sign with significant impact. However, nominal wage rate and infrastructure stocks have no significant impact on FDI. Trade agreement has no impact on FDI inflows as Nepal has least number of trade agreements in South Asia.

6.5.4 Panel Data Analysis

Like time series analysis, we also follow similar steps for panel data analysis. Panel data techniques have its advantages over the cross section and time series in using all the information available, which is not detectable in pure cross sections or in pure time series. It can also take heterogeneity of each cross-sectional unit explicitly into account by allowing for individual-specific effects (Davidson and MacKinnon 2004) and give 'more variability, less collinearity among variables, more degrees of freedom, and more efficiency' (Baltagi 2001). Furthermore, the repeated cross section of observations over time is better suited to study the dynamics of changes of variables like trade and finance.

6.5.4.1 Panel Unit Root Test

The first step in our analysis is to ascertain the stationary properties or unit root test of the relevant variables. It is well accepted that the commonly used time series unit root tests like Dickey–Fuller (DF), augmented Dickey–Fuller, and Phillips and Peron (PP) tests lack power in distinguishing the unit root null from stationary alternative, and that using panel data unit root tests is one way of increasing the power of unit root tests based on single time series (Maddala and Wu 1999). Over the period, multiple methods for unit root tests have been developed for panel data in the recent past and can be grouped as 'first-generation' tests (Maddala and Wu 1999; Levine et al. 2002; Im et al. 2003) based on the assumption of cross-sectional independence between panel units (except for common time effects) and 'second-generation' tests (Smith et al. 2004; Choi 2006; Pesaran 2007) allowing for cross-sectional dependence. In our analysis, we apply Pesaran (2007) methodology due to its advantages over other technique since it takes into account cross-sectional dependence.

Pesaran (2007) CIPS Unit Root Test

Let us consider the dynamic linear heterogeneous panel data model:

$$Y_{it} = (1 - \Phi)\ \lambda_i + \Phi_i Y_{i,t-1} + u_{it} \tag{6.7}$$

where u_{it} has the one common factor structure

$$u_{it} = \gamma_i f_t + e_{it} \tag{6.8}$$

in which $f_t \sim i{:}i{:}d{:}\ (0,\sigma^2{}_f)$ is the unobserved common effect, $\gamma_i \sim i{:}i{:}d{:}(0,\ \sigma^2{}_\gamma)$ the individual factor loading, and e_{it} the idiosyncratic component which can be $i{:}i{:}d{:}$ $(0,\ \sigma^2 i)$ or, more generally, a stationary autoregressive process. Rewriting (6.7) and (6.8) as

$$\Delta Y_{it} = \alpha_i + \beta_i Y_{i,t-1} + \gamma_i f_t + e_{it} \tag{6.9}$$

where $\alpha_i = (1 - \Phi)\ \lambda_i,\quad \beta_i = -(1 - \Phi)\quad \text{and}\quad \Delta Y_{it} = Y_{it} - Y_{i,t-1}$

Pesaran (2007) proposes to proxy the common factor f_t with the cross-sectional mean of Y_{it}, namely, $\overline{Y}_t = N^{-1}\sum_{i=1}^{N} Y_{it}$, and its lagged value(s) $\overline{Y}_{t-1},\ \overline{Y}_{t-2}, \ldots$. The test for the null of unit root regarding the unit i can now be based on the t-ratio of the

OLS estimate of β_i in the cross-sectionally augmented Dickey–Fuller (CADF) regression

$$\Delta Y_{it} = \alpha_i + \beta_i Y_{i,t-1} + c_i\ \overline{Y}_{t-1} + d_i\ \Delta\overline{Y}t + e_{it} \tag{6.10}$$

A natural test of the null H_0: $\beta_i = 0$ for all i, against the heterogeneous alternative $H_1 : \beta_1 < 0, \ldots, \beta_{N0} < 0, N_0 \leq N$ in the whole panel data set, is given by the average of the individual CADF statistics:

$$\text{CIPS}\ (N,\ T) = N^{-1}\sum_{i=1}^{N} ti\ (N,\ T) \tag{6.11}$$

The distribution of this test is non-standard, even asymptotically; 1, 5, and 10 % critical values are tabulated by the author for different combinations of N and T. In case of serial correlation of the individual-specific error terms, the testing procedure can be easily extended by adding a suitable number of lagged values of $\overline{Y}_{t-1}$ and ΔY_t in the CADF regression. The test has satisfactory power and size even for relatively small panels (Baltagi et al. 2007).

6.5.4.2 Panel Co-integration Test

Like panel unit root test, multiple panel co-integration test has been developed over the time and can be grouped as 'first-generation' co-integration tests (Maddala and Wu 1999; Pedroni 1999, 2004) based on the assumption of cross-sectional independence between panel units (except for common time effects) and 'second-generation' tests (Westerlund and Edgerton 2007; Westerlund (2007) ECM Test) allowing for cross-sectional dependence. We use Westerlund (2007) ECM test methodology due to its advantages over other techniques in their respective groups.

Westerlund (2007) ECM Co-integration Test

Westerlund (2007) co-integration test is a structural based test and considered as second-generation test. The four tests proposed by Westerlund (2007) assess co-integration properties in panel data by determining whether there exists EC for individual panel members or for the panel as a whole. The tests take no co-integration as the null hypothesis and are based on structural dynamics so that they do not impose any common factor restrictions. Consider the following EC model, where all variables in levels are assumed to be $I(1)$:

$$\Delta y_{it} = \delta' d_t + \alpha_i(y_{i,t-1} - \beta'_i x_{i,t-1})\sum_{j=1}^{pi}\gamma_{ij}\Delta y_{i,t-j} + \sum_{j=0}^{pi}\lambda_{ij}\Delta x_{i,\ t-j} + e_{it} \tag{6.12}$$

The parameter α_i measure the speed of adjustment, i.e. the speed at which the system returns to his equilibrium after a sudden shock in one of the model variables. As in Pedroni's test, there are two sets of statistics: two group statistics and two panel statistics. P_a *and* P_T are panel statistics which are based on pooling the information regarding the EC along the cross-sectional units. The panel statistics are given by

$$P_a = T\hat{\alpha} \quad \text{and} \quad P_T \frac{\hat{\alpha}}{\text{SE}(\hat{\alpha})}$$

The null and alternative hypothesis for the panel tests are H_0: $\alpha_i = 0$, H_1: $\alpha_i = \alpha < 0$ *for all i*. The rejection of null should therefore be taken as the rejection of no co-integration for the panel as a whole. G_α and G_T are group statistics which do exploit the information regarding the EC. The between group-mean tests can be calculated by: $G_T = \frac{1}{N}\sum_{i=1}^{N}\frac{\hat{\alpha}i}{\text{SE}(\hat{\alpha}i)}$ and $G_a = \frac{1}{N}\sum_{i=1}^{N}\frac{T\hat{\alpha}i}{\hat{\alpha}i}$

The null and alternative hypothesis for the group tests are $H_0 : \alpha i = 0$, $H_1 : \alpha_i < 0$ *for at least some i*. It means that the rejection of null indicates the presence of co-integration for at least one cross-sectional unit in the panel. As Westerlund (2007) demonstrates, the four tests could be adjusted to individual-specific short-run dynamics, including serially correlated error terms and non-strictly exogenous regressors, individual-specific intercept, and trend terms. Full details on the test construction and asymptotic distributions are found in Westerlund (2007). In sum, Westerlund's (2007) test has the advantage of greater power over the popular residual-based tests provided weak exogeneity condition is satisfied. In addition, the test allows for heterogeneity across the individual units of the panel. This model could also be generalised to account for cross-sectional dependence by simulating the finite sample distribution of each estimator via the bootstrap procedure.

Panel FMOLS

When we detect the existence of panel co-integration, Pedroni (2000) suggests fully modified ordinary least squares (FMOLS) to obtain the long-run co-integrating coefficients. In the presence of unit root variables, the effect of super consistency may not dominate the endogeneity effect of the regressors if ordinary least squares (OLS) is employed. Pedroni (2000) shows that OLS can be modified to enable inference in a co-integrated heterogeneous dynamic panel. In the FMOLS setting, non-parametric techniques are exploited to transform the residuals from the co-integration regression to get rid of nuisance parameters. Therefore, the problem of endogeneity of the regressors and serial correlation in the error term is avoided by using FMOLS.

6.5.4.3 Generalised Method of Moment

We also use generalised method of moment for estimating determinants. Generalised method of moment (GMM) proposed by Arellano and Bond (1991) is the commonly employed estimation procedure to estimate the parameters in a dynamic panel data model. In GMM-based estimation, first differenced transformed series are used to adjust the unobserved individual-specific heterogeneity in the series. But Blundell and Bond (1998) found that this has poor finite sample properties in terms of bias and precision, when the series are persistent and the instruments are weak predictors of the endogenous changes. Blundell and Bond (1998) proposed a systems-based approach to overcome these limitations in the dynamic panel data. This method uses extra moment conditions that rely on certain stationarity conditions of the initial observation. Consider following autoregressive (1) or AR (1) model:

$$y_{it} = \alpha y_{t-1} + \beta x_{it} + \eta_i + \nu_{it} \tag{6.13}$$

where y is the dependent variable, x is the explanatory variable, η is an unobservable country-specific effect, and ν is the error term. The number of countries is denoted by $i = 1,2,\ldots,N$ and the number of time periods is $t = 1,2,\ldots,T$. It is assumed that x_{it} is correlated with η_i and endogenous so to satisfy $E[x_{it}\nu_{is}] \neq 0$ for $i = 1,\ldots,T$ and $s \leq t$.

The two moment conditions for GMM system are:

$$E[x_{it-s\Delta}\nu_{it}] = 0 \text{ for } t = 3, \ldots, T, \quad i = 1, \ldots, N \text{ and } s \geq 2 \tag{6.14}$$

$$E[\Delta x_{it-s\Delta}\nu_{it}] = 0 \text{ for } t = 1, \ldots, T, \quad i = 1, \ldots, N \text{ and } s \geq 2 \tag{6.14}$$

To establish the validity of instrumental variables, specification tests are conducted. The first specification test is the Sargan test, of which the null is that there is no correlation between instruments and errors. The failure to reject the null of serial correlation of AR(1) can be viewed as evidence in favour of using valid instruments. The null hypothesis of the second test is that the errors are not serially correlated in a first differenced equation. If the null of no serial correlation of AR (2) model cannot be rejected, it can be viewed as evidence supporting the validity of instruments used.

Result Analysis

In the panel framework, we first conducted unit root test using Pesaran (2007) CIPS test. The CIPS unit root test for both 'constant' and 'constant and trend' specifications and allowing for the lag order to be at maximum equal to 3 ($p = 1\ 2, 3$) is presented in Table 6.A.6. It is clear that CIPS panel test does not reject the null of unit roots for the panel at level for all the variables except inflation rate, FDIY, foreign debt ratio,

Table 6.3 Westerlund (2007) EC model panel co-integration tests

	With trade	
Dependent variable LPI	Value	*p*-Value
Gt	−3.49a	0.03
Ga	−8.49	0.68
Pt	−5.68[a]	0.05
Pa	−10.67[a]	0.02

Notes: The Westerlund (2007) tests take no co-integration as the null. The test regression is fitted with constant and one lag and lead
[a]Denotes rejection of null of no co-integration at 5 % level

growth of labour force, and volatility of exchange rate. On the contrary, the differenced series are stationary leading us to conclude that a panel unit root is present in the level series. Hence, the CIPS test indicates that we have mixture of $I(0)$ and $I(1)$ variables.

Having established the non-stationarity of the series, we then proceed to test for the existence of a long-run relationship between real FDI and other relevant variables using EC panel co-integration test developed by Westerlund (2007). The results of Westerlund (2007) co-integration test with the asymptotic p-values based on 500 replications are presented in Table 6.3. When using the asymptotic p-values, except for $G_{a,}$ the no co-integration null is rejected in favour of existence of co-integration at 5 % level. This indicates that we have the evidence of co-integration for at least one panel as well as at for whole panel. Therefore, we find that the FDI and its determinants are co-integrated in line with the prediction of economic theory.

Long-Run Coefficients

The results of panel estimation for two different periods[3] (1980–2010 and 1995–2010) using two methods are presented in Tables 6.4 and 6.5. The GMM system passes all diagnosis test related to Sargan test of overidentifying restrictions and the Arellano–Bond test of first-order and second-order autocorrelation. The panel results more or less support the conclusions of time series proving robustness of the result. The market size (real GDP) and the trade openness seem to be strong determinants of the FDI inflows in South Asia. Thus, South Asian countries with large markets attract more FDI. Significant trade openness coefficient indicates that those economies in which trade is important also have relatively higher FDI. This is in line with the hypothesis that higher openness attracts higher FDI. South Asian countries have taken significant trade liberalisation since early 1990s, and this has been accompanied by higher FDI inflows during this period. Therefore,

[3]This is mainly due to the impact of governance indicator on FDI inflows, which is available from 1995.

Table 6.4 Determinants of FDI in South Asia (1980–2010)

	FMOLS	GMM
Variables	Coefficients	Coefficients
Constant		−1.55* (−1.96)
LGDP	0.82* (2.25)	0.39* (2.62)
TRADE	0.02** (3.43)	0.05** (2.34)
HUM	0.03** (3.45)	0.02* (2.86)
WR	0.01** (3.54)	0.01* (2.59)
RER	−0.02 (−0.36)	−0.01** (−5.30)
INFRA	1.03* (2.02)	0.14* (2.49)
CAD	−0.01* (−2.08)	−0.08**(−5.21)
TA	0.22** (3.20)	0.10** (3.12)
Arellano–Bond test for AR(1) in first differences		$z = -2.63$ $Pr > z = 0.00$
Arellano–Bond test for AR(2) in first differences		$z = -0.69$ $Pr > z = 0.77$
Sargan test of overid. restrictions:		$chi^2(53) = 138.22$, $Prob > chi^2 = 0.000$
Difference-in-Sargan tests of exogeneity of instrument subsets:		$chi^2(80) = 41.84$, $Pr > chi^2 = 0.11$
GMM instruments for levels Sargan test excluding group:		$chi^2(52) = 130.34$, $Pr > chi^2 = 0.03$

Notes: ***, **, and * denote significance at 1, 5, and 10 level, respectively. Figures in the parentheses are *t*-ratio

Table 6.5 Determinants of FDI in South Asia (1995–2010)

	FMOLS	GMM
Variables	Coefficients	Coefficients
Constant		−1.73** (−4.34)
LGDP	0.27** (3.01)	0.19* (2.02)
TR	0.08** (6.71)	0.02# (1.70)
GOV	0.04** (3.01)	0.04* (2.62)
TA	0.29** (3.26)	0.11** (4.38)
Infra	1.20* (2.02)	0.25** (3.34)
RER	−0.03# (−1.92)	
R^2		
Arellano–Bond test for AR(1) in first differences		$z = -1.90$, $Pr > z = 0.036$
Arellano–Bond test for AR(2) in first differences		$z = -1.28$, $Pr > z = 0.21$
Sargan test of overid. restrictions:		
Difference-in-Sargan tests of exogeneity of instrument subsets:		$chi^2(25) = 50.63$ $Pr > chi^2 = 0.09$
GMM instruments for levels		$chi^2(33) = 74.12$ $Pr > chi^2 = 0.04$

Notes: ***, **, and * denote significance at 1, 5, and 10 level, respectively. # Denotes significance level at 10% level. Figures in the parentheses are *t*-ratio

Table 6.6 ARDL Co-integration test (1980–2010)

Country	Dependent variable	*F*-stat	5 % critical value#	Result
China	FDI	6.58*	3.50	Rejection of null of no co-integration

* denotes rejection of null hypothesis at 5 % level and "#" denotes upper bound critical value

implementation of more liberal economic policies would certainly attract more foreign investments. The coefficient of human capital is positive as predicted by theory. Therefore, better human capital is relevant pull factor for foreign MNCs in developing countries. Like human capital development, another pull factor is infrastructure development (Khadaroo and Seetanah 2010; Calderon and Serven 2008). The coefficient of infrastructure stock is positive and significant in both GMM and FMOLS estimation. As Campos and Kinoshita (2003) have argued that good infrastructure is a necessary condition for foreign investors to operate successfully, regardless of the type of FDI and thus, good infrastructure facilities in South Asia are another important factor in attracting FDI. The coefficient of nominal wage rate is positive and significant (consistent with empirical literature). The coefficient of RTAs is positive and significant in all estimation procedure except FMOLS, indicating that trade liberalisation can diminish inside regional tariffs and nontariff barriers to form a free trade area and attract more FDI inflows from outsiders. The coefficient of real exchange rate is negative and significant. This is because exchange rate depreciation increases relative wealth of foreigner and reduces relative labour costs. Therefore, exchange rate depreciation relative US dollar increases FDI inflows to South Asian countries. Previous empirical studies also found negative impact of real exchange rate on FDI inflows (for instance, Ramirez 2006; Anyanwu 2012).

Finally, macroeconomic uncertainty variables such as current account deficit reduce FDI inflows as unstable macroeconomic environment reduces FDI by increasing investment risk. This is validated by the negative and significant coefficient of CAD. Most of the South Asian countries are running huge current account deficit in their external sector, and this has negative influence on FDI inflows.

The coefficient of financial development indicator (domestic credit by banking sector as ratio of GDP) is found to be negative. The negative significance of financial depth shows that greater financial development in South Asian countries leads to less FDI inflows, similar to the results of Anyanwu (2012) for African countries and Walsh and Yu (2010) for more advanced economies and in accordance with a priori expectations. However, the results are not given in Table 6.6.

The validity of the obtained results in GMM system depends on the statistical diagnostics; hence, we will start our interpretation with the model diagnostics. Compared to the OLS model, GMM system does not assume normality, and it allows for heteroscedasticity in the data. The GMM system approach assumes linearity and that the disturbance terms are not autocorrelated, or in other words that the applied instruments in the model are exogenous. The GMM estimator requires that there is first-order serial correlation AR(1) but that there is no second-order serial correlation AR(2) in the residuals. Our result supports the validity of the model specification. T*he Hansen test* of overidentifying restrictions does not reject the null at any conventional level of significance ($p = 0.11$); hence, it is an indication that the model has valid instrumentation. Further, our result also indicate that we do not have enough evidence to reject the null hypothesis of exogeneity of any GM instruments used, i.e. levels and differenced instruments, as well as the validity of standard IV instruments

In addition to this, we also present the estimated result for the period 1995–2010, since data on governance is available from 1995 onwards. In addition to trade and GDP, infrastructure stock and RTAs are found to have significant effect on FDI inflows during the period 1995–2010. More importantly, the results indicate that the government quality (proxied by index of economic freedom) is statistically significantly associated with higher FDI inflows to South Asia. Therefore, FDI inflows to the continent correlate positively with the prevalence of the rule of law, meaning that the quality of intuition matters for making FDI inflows go where they do in South Asia. Good quality institutional is likely another important determinant of FDI, particularly for developing countries as good governance is associated with higher economic growth, which may attract more FDI inflows (Wei 2000; Walsh and Yu 2010). The other variables are insignificant in attracting FDI to South Asia, hence dropped from final estimation.

6.6 Determinants of FDI: The Case of China

For assessing FDI determinants for China, we estimate Eq. (6.1). Like South Asian countries, we first started time series properties of variables by using ADF unit root test. The results are presented in Table 6.A.6. ADF unit root test for China indicates that trade openness, current account deficit, infrastructure index, government expenditure as ratio of GDP, FDI ratio, real exchange rate, and bank credit to domestic sector are $I(1)$ or, they are stationary at first difference. On the other hand, growth rate of GDP and human capital, real GDP, inflation rate, and fiscal deficit are stationary at level. Therefore, we have mixture of $I(1)$ and $I(0)$ variables. Hence, ARDL co-integration procedure is appropriate. The results of ARDL co-integration test are presented in Table 6.6. The result of ARDL co-integration test suggests that there exists long-run equilibrium relationship between FDI and its determinants as F-stat (6.58) exceeds the upper bound critical value (3.5) at the 5 % levels. Thus, the null of non-existence of stable long-run relationship is rejected in favour of co-integration.

Having seen that there exist long-run equilibrium relationship, we then proceed to the estimation of model (6.1) for China by using ARDL method. The long-run determinants of FDI for China are presented in Table 6.7. Maximum lag length used to derive long-run coefficients is 2 given that we have only 31 observations. Diagnostic test is checked to ensure that it is the best model

Table 6.7 Determinants of FDI in China (1980–2010)

	China
Variables	Coefficients
Constant	−100.34* (−2.63)
LGDP	21.95** (5.19)
TR	0.29** (4.46)
HUM	0.07* (2.06)
WR	0.08** (3.17)
INFRA	4.67 ** (3.84)
MS	0.08* (1.84)
TA	0.49*(2.84)
Model selection criteria (AIC)	(2,2,2,1,0,2,2,2)
Diagnostic test	ADJ. $R^2 = 0.93$, DW. Stat. = 1.9, LM = 1.2, ARCH = 0.7 Reset-1.68 (0.21)

Notes: ***, **, and * denote significance at 1, 5, and 10 % level, respectively. Figures in the parentheses are *t*-ratio

and there is no misspecification bias in the model. The diagnostic tests include the test of serial autocorrelation (LM), heteroscedasticity (ARCH test), and omitted variables/functional form (Ramsey Reset). The estimated long-run coefficients indicate that real GDP or size of the economy has highest impact on FDI inflows. The coefficient of real GDP is greater than one indicating one unit increase in real GDP will boost FDI inflows by more than one unit. China is now second largest economy after USA, and this remained one of the attractions for foreign investment. Infrastructure stock has second highest effect on FDI inflows to China. Like real GDP, the coefficient of infrastructure is greater than one indicating one unit increase in real GDP will boost FDI inflows by more than one unit. China's infrastructure investment is one of the highest (10 % of GDP), and results confirm the benefits of availability infrastructure for attracting higher amount of FDI. Availability of modern infrastructure therefore remained one of the attraction points for foreign investment to China. In addition to this, other important determinants of FDI are openness ratio, human capital, and cost of labour. All these variables have positive impact on FDI inflows. The results are in line with findings of Markusen (2001) and Rodríguez and Pallas (2008) that the availability of skilled workers can significantly boost the locational advantage of a country. The impact current account balance on FDI inflows is found positive and significant. This is because China has persistent current account surplus and this has positive impact of FDI inflows. The coefficient of trade agreement is found significant at 5 % level. Although China started trade agreements little later in 2002, it has ramped up number of trade agreements with other countries and trade blocks in recent years. By the end of 2010, China has total 15 trade agreements.

Other variables such as fiscal deficit, foreign exchange reserve, inflation rate, and financial development have no significant impact on FDI inflows to China.

6.7 Summary

In this chapter, we analyse major determinants of FDI inflows to South Asia by using both time series and panel methodology. First, time series properties of the variables are established by using ADF unit test. Then co-integration or long-run relationship between FDI and its determinants is established by using both ARDL co-integration test and Westerlund (2007) EC test. Long-run determinants of FDI are estimated by using both ARDL method and GMM system method. Overall, we find that the determinants of FDI for South Asia can be grouped under

- Economic conditions such as market size, rate of return, labour cost, human capital, physical infrastructure, and macroeconomic fundamentals such as current account balance
- Host country policies such as trade openness, exchange rate, and governance

Trade agreements (both bilateral and multilateral) are other very important determinants of FDI inflows to South Asia.

Appendix

Table 6.A.1 Unit root test for using ADF test (India)

Variables	At level with constant	Optimal lag	At level with constant and trend	Optimal lag	At first difference with constant	Optimal lag	Order of integration
LGDP	0.57	1	−2.20	2	−3.76*	0	*I*(1)
TR	−0.16	2	−2.55	3	−4.90*	1	*I*(1)
CAD	−1.57	1	−1.28	2	−3.41*	1	*I*(1)
FR	−1.40	1	−2.23	1	−3.70*	1	*I*(1)
HUM	−1.33	3	−3.36	2	−4.79*	1	*I*(1)
INFL	−3.13*	0					*I*(0)
FDIY	−1.33	1	−2.6	1	−3.78*	0	*I*(1)
FIN	−0.76	1	−1.81	3	−3.45*	2	*I*(1)
INFRA	0.76	3	−0.86	3	−3.75	1	*I*(1)
FD	−3.64*	3					*I*(0)
RER	−1.80	3	−0.18	2	−2.99*	0	*I*(1)
VRER	−4.55*	1					*I*(0)
GEXP	−3.49*	3					*I*(0)
GOV	−0.39	2	−2.38	2	−3.76*	1	*I*(1)
WR	−0.05	1	−0.15	2	−5.80	0	*I*(1)
ED	−1.66	1	−2.88	1	−3.92	0	*I*(1)
GCFR	−0.33	2	−1.01	2	−5.37	1	*I*(1)
GLF	−3.54*	1					*I*(0)
TA	3.61	2	1.57	2	−2.94	1	*I*(1)

* denotes rejection of null hypothesis of unit root at 5 % level

Table 6.A.2 Unit root test for using ADF test (Pakistan)

Variables	At level with constant	Optimal lag	At level with constant and trend	Optimal lag	At first difference with constant	Optimal lag	Order of integration
LGDP	−1.11	1	−2.25	1	−3.36*	0	*I*(1)
TR	−1.95	1	−2.03	3	−6.06*	0	*I*(1)
CAD	−3.17*	3					*I*(0)
FR	−1.40	1	−2.23	1	−3.70*	1	*I*(1)
HUM	−1.27	1	−1.54	1	−5.97*	0	*I*(1)
INFL	−1.22*	2	−1.78	3	−6.34*	0	*I*(1)
FDIY	−2.26	1	−3.2	1	−4.37*	2	*I*(1)
DBC	−0.76	1	−1.81	3	−3.45*	2	*I*(1)
INFRA	−0.07	1	1.88	2	−3.15*	1	*I*(1)
FD	−1.49	1	−2.10	1	−7.16	0	*I*(1)
RER	−1.65	2	−1.45	3	−3.34*	1	*I*(1)
VRER	−3.14*	0					*I*(0)
GEXP	−0.77	1	−2.72	2	−7.05*	0	*I*(1)
GOV	−3.01*	1					*I*(0)
WR	−2.81	3	−3.43	1	−5.01	1	*I*(1)
ED	−0.92	1	−1.86	1	−3.85	0	*I*(1)
GCFR	−4.62*	3					*I*(0)
GLF	−4.17*	0					*I*(0)
TA	0.65	1	−0.75	1	−3.44*	0	*I*(1)

* denotes rejection of null hypothesis of unit root at 5 % level

Table 6.A.3 Unit root test for using ADF test (Bangladesh)

Variables	At level with constant	Optimal lag	At level with constant and trend	Optimal lag	At first difference with constant	Optimal lag	Order of integration
LGDP	−1.90	3	0.13	1	−3.31*	0	*I*(1)
TR	−0.09	1	−3.24	3	−7.69*	0	*I*(1)
CAD	−1.66	3	−3.83*	1			*I*(0)
FR	−2.45	1	−2.42	1	−4.01*	1	*I*(1)
HUM	−2.02	1	−1.73	2	−4.08*	0	*I*(1)
INFL	−3.05*	0					*I*(0)
FDIR	−1.23	1	−3.13	3	−4.34*	1	*I*(1)
FIN	−0.76	1	−1.81	3	−3.45*	2	*I*(1)
INFRA	−0.07	1	1.88	2	−3.15*	1	*I*(1)
FD	−1.49	1	−2.10	1	−7.16*	0	*I*(1)
RER	−1.44	1	−4.53*	2			*I*(0)
VRER	−3.14*	0					*I*(0)
GEXP	−0.77	1	−2.72	2	−7.05*	0	*I*(1)
GOV	−2.61	1	−3.50	1	−4.48*	2	*I*(1)
WR	−1.52	3	−1.01	1	−6.05*	1	*I*(1)
ED	−0.62	3	−1.92	2	−3.81*	0	*I*(1)
GCFR	−0.21	1	−2.37	1	−4.35*	0	*I*(1)
GLF	−1.17	2	−2.29	1	−5.16*	1	*I*(0)
TA	0.26	3	−1.51	1	−3.09*	1	*I*(1)

* denotes rejection of null hypothesis of unit root at 5 % level

Table 6.A.4 Unit root test for using ADF test (Sri Lanka)

Variables	At level with constant	Optimal lag	At level with constant and trend	Optimal lag	At first difference with constant	Optimal lag	Order of integration
LGDP	1.43	1	−1.37	1	−4.05*	0	*I*(1)
TR	0.57	1	−0.24	1	−4.81	0	*I*(1)
CAD	−4.55	1					*I*(0)
FR	−1.56	1	−2.54	2	−5.65*	0	*I*(1)
HUM	0.86	1	−1.47	1	−3.58*	1	*I*(1)
INFL	−3.93*	1					*I*(0)
FDIY	−2.05	2	−3.92*	1			*I*(0)
DBC	−2.63	1	−2.82	1	=4.22	1	*I*(1)
INFRA	0.93	1	2.84	3	−3.21*	1	*I*(1)
FD	−3.51*	1					*I*(0)
RER	−1.22	2	−2.08	1	−4.42*	4	*I*(1)
VRER	3.28*	0					*I*(0)
GEXP	−0.64	1	−1.78	1	−4.37*	1	*I*(1)
GOV	0.14	1	−2.56	1	−4.88*	0	*I*(1)
WR	−1.41	2	−2.09	1	−3.82*	1	*I*(1)
ED	−0.43	1	−2.11	1	−5.37*	0	*I*(1)
GCFR	0.39	1	−2.41	2	−3.97*	0	*I*(1)
GLF	−4.44*	1					*I*(0)
TA	−0.40	1	−2.66	1	−3.11*	2	*I*(1)

* denotes rejection of null hypothesis of unit root at 5 % level

Table 6.A.5 Unit root test for using ADF test (Nepal)

Variables	At level with constant	Optimal lag	At level with constant and trend	Optimal lag	At first difference with constant	Optimal lag	Order of integration
LGDP	−2.35	2	−1.17	2	−5.35*	1	*I*(1)
TR	1.52	1	−1.15	1	−3.86*	0	*I*(1)
CAD	−1.36	1	−2.53	1	−4.72*	1	*I*(1)
FR	−1.72	1	−2.62	1	−3.44*	2	*I*(1)
HUM	−1.60	1	−3.46	2	−3.92*	0	*I*(1)
INFL	−3.20*	1					*I*(0)
FDIY	−2.64	2	−3.05	2	−3.67*	2	*I*(1)
DBC	0.67	1	−2.51	3	−3.46*	1	*I*(1)
INFRA	2.48	3	1.18	3	−3.29*	2	*I*(1)
FD	−2.11	1	−2.11	1	−4.96	0	*I*(1)
RER	−0.99	1	−1.16	3	−4.27*	0	*I*(1)
VRER	−5.07*	0					*I*(0)
GEXP	−2.57	2	−1.94	2	−3.63	1	*I*(1)
LGOV	−2.38	1	−2.73	1	−3.60*	2	*I*(1)
WR	0.56	1	−1.17	1	−3.46	1	*I*(1)
LED	−0.83	3	−0.14	3	−2.96*	0	*I*(1)
LGCFR	1.48	1	−1.04	2	−6.48*	0	*I*(1)
GLF	−1.88	1	−1.73	1	−4.24*	1	*I*(1)
TA	−0.39	1	−2.41	1	−3.45*	1	*I*(1)

* denotes rejection of null hypothesis of unit root at 5 % level

Table 6.A.6 Unit root test for using ADF test

Variables	At level with constant	Optimal lag	At level with constant and trend	Optimal lag	At first difference with constant	Optimal lag	Order of integration
LGDP	0.63	4	−4.49*	3			*I*(10)
TR	−0.92	1	−3.04	1	−3.81*	0	*I*(1)
CAD	−1.78	1	−2.80	1	−4.63*	1	*I*(1)
FR	−1.14	1	−2.14	2	−4.59*	0	*I*(1)
HUM	1.22	1	−5.47*	1			*I*(0)
INFL	−3.57*	1					*I*(0)
FDIY	−2.09	2	−1.82	1	−3.56*		*I*(1)
DBC	−2.63	1	−2.82	1	−4.22*	1	*I*(1)
INFRA	2.28	1	1.84	3	−4.15*	1	*I*(1)
FD	−4.01*	1					*I*(0)
RER	−2.62	0	−1.62	1	−5.22*	1	*I*(1)
GEXP	−0.24	1	−1.48	1	−3.87*	1	*I*(1)
WR	3.41	2	2.09	2	−3.89*	1	*I*(1)

* denotes rejection of null hypothesis of unit root at 5 % level

Table 6.A.7 Panel unit root test using Pesaran (2007)

	At level			
Variables	Constant	Constant and trend	First difference	Conclusion
LGDP	1.33	−1.51	−3.49**	*I*(1)
FDIY	−2.77*			*I*(0)
TRADE	−1.29	−1.43	−3.06**	*I*(1)
CAD	−2.66*			*I*(0)
FR	−2.01	−1.91	−2.86*	*I*(1)
ED	−2.45*			*I*(0)
HUM	−1.15	−2.21	−3.06**	*I*(1)
INFL	−3.42**			*I*(0)
FIN	−2.17	−2.66	−3.43**	*I*(1)
INFRA	−1.54	−1.88	−4.24**	*I*(1)
GLF	−2.60*			*I*(0)
RER	−1.20	−1. 98	−3.69**	*I*(1)
VER	−3.28**			*I*(0)
GEXP	−1.27	−2.66	−3.61**	*I*(1)
FD	−0.73	0.01	−5.86**	*I*(1)
WR	0.40	−1.48	−5.12**	*I*(1)
GOV	−1.00	−1.34	−2.53*	*I*(1)
TA	−0.52	−0.91	2.91**	*I*(1)
Return				

Notes: The null hypothesis is that the panel has a unit root. Critical values are tabulated by Pesaran (2007). In Table II (a–c), we report the ones for $T = 30$ and $N = 10$

'**' and '*' indicate significance of the test at 1 and 5 % level, respectively

References

Adhikary BK, Mengistu AA (2008) Factors influencing foreign direct investment (FDI) in "South" and "Southeast" economies. J World Invest Trade 9(5):27–437

Agarwal JP (1980) Determinants of foreign direct investment: a survey. Weltwirtschaftliches Archiv 116(4):739–773

Agrawal P (2000) Economic impact of foreign direct investment in South Asia. Indira Gandhi Institute of Development Research, Mumbai

Ali F, Fiess N, MacDonald R (2006) Do institutions matter for foreign direct investment? Open Econ Rev 21(2):201–219

Al-Sadig A (2009) The effects of corruption on FDI flows. Cato J 29(2):267–294

Alsan M, Bloom DE, Canning D (2006) The effect of population health on foreign direct investment inflows to low- and middle-income countries. World Dev 34(4):613–630

Anyanwu JC (2012) Why does foreign direct investment go where it goes? New evidence from African countries. Ann Econ Finance 13–2:433–470

Arellano M, Bond S (1991) Some tests of specification for panel data: Monte Carlo evidence and an application to employment equations. Rev Econ Stud 58:277–298

Armstrong SP (2009) The Japan–China economic relationship: distance, institutions and politics. PhD dissertation, Australian National University, Canberra

Asiedu E (2002) On the determinants of foreign direct investment to developing countries: is Africa different? World Dev 30(1):107–119

Athukorala P-C (2009) Trends and patters of foreign direct investment in Asia: a comparative perspective. Margin-J Appl Econ Res 3(4):365–408

Baltagi B (2001) Econometric analysis of panel data. Wiley, Chichester/New York

Baltagi BH, Egger P, Pfaffermayr M (2007) Estimating models of complex FDI: are there third-country effects? J Econom 140(1):260–281

Banga R (2003a) Impact of government policies and investment agreements on FDI inflows, Working paper, no. 116. Indian Council for Research on International Economic Relations, New Delhi

Banga R (2004) Impact of government policies and investment agreements on FDI inflows, working paper, no.116. Indian Council for Research in International Economic Relations, New Delhi

Bartels LM (2009) Economic inequality and political representation. In: Jacobs LR, King DS (eds) The unsustainable American state. Oxford University Press, Oxford/New York, pp 167–96

Beck T (2002) Financial development and international trade: is there a link? J Int Econ 57:107–131

Bevan AA, Estrin S (2004) The determinants of foreign direct investment into European transition economies. J Comp Econ 32:775–787

Blomström M, Kokko A (1997) Regional integration and foreign trade investment, NBER working paper, no. 6019. National Bureau of Economic Research, Cambridge, MA

Blomström M, Kokko A (2002) FDI and human capital: a research Agenda, OECD development centre working papers 195. OECD, Paris

Blomström M, Kokko A (2003) The economics of foreign direct investment incentives, NBER working paper, no. 9489. National Bureau of Economic Research, Cambridge, MA

Blomström M, Kokko A, Globerman S (1998) Regional economic integration and foreign direct investment: the North American experience, Working paper series in economics and finance, no.269. Stockholm School of Economics, Stockholm

Blundell R, Bond S (1998) Initial conditions and moment restrictions in dynamic panel data models. J Econom 87:115–143

Borensztein E, Gregorio JD, Lee JW (1998) How does foreign direct investment affect economic growth? J Int Econ 45:115–135

Brainard SL (1993) A simple theory of multinational corporations and trade with a trade-off between proximity and concentration, NBER working paper, no. 4269. National Bureau of Economic Research, Cambridge, MA

Buckley PJ, Casson M (1976) The future of the multinational enterprise, vol 1. Macmillan, London

Buckley P, Wang C, Clegg J (2007) The impact of foreign ownership, local ownership and industry characteristics on spillover benefits from foreign direct investment in China. Int Bus Rev 16:142–158

Calderon C, Serven L (2008) Infrastructure and economic development in Sub-Saharan Africa, Policy research working paper series 4712. The World Bank, Washington, DC

Campos N, Kinoshita Y (2002) Foreign direct investment as technology transferred: internalization theory. Bull Econ Res 38(2):101–118

Campos NF, Kinoshita Y (2003) Why does FDI where It goes? New evidence from transition economies, IMF working paper, no.228. International Monetary Fund, Washington, DC

Canning D, Bennathan E (2000) The social rate of return on infrastructure investments. World Bank research project, RPO 680–89, Washington, DC

Chakrabarti A (2001) The determinants of foreign direct investment: sensitivity analysis of cross-country regressions. Kyklos 54:89–114

Chakrabarti A (2003) A theory of the spatial distribution of foreign direct investment. Int Rev Econ Finance 12:149–169

Choi I (2006) Combination unit root tests for cross-sectionally correlated panels. In: Corbae D, Durlauf S, Hansen B (eds) Econometric theory and practice: frontiers of analysis and applied research, Essays in honor of Peter C. B. Phillips. Cambridge University Press, Cambridge/New York, pp 311–333

Davidson R, MacKinnon JG (2004) Econometric theory and methods. Oxford University Press, New York, pp 298–305

Dickey DA, Fuller WA (1981) Likelihood ratio statistics for autoregressive time series with a unit root. Econom J Econom Soc 49:1057–1072

Dunning JH (1977) Trade, location of economic activity and the MNE: a search for an eclectic approach. In: Ohlin B, Hesselborn PO, Wijkmon PM (eds) The international location of economic activity. Macmillan, London, pp 395–418

Dunning JH (1993) Multinational enterprises and the global economy. Addison Wesley, Wokingham/Reading

Dunning JH (2002) Determinants of foreign direct investment: globalization induced changes and the role of FDI policies. Paper presented at the annual bank conference on development economics in Europe, Oslo, Mimeo

Dunning JH, Lundan SM (2008) Multinational enterprises and the global economy. Edward Elgar, Cheltenham

Durham J (2004) Absorptive capacity and the effects of foreign direct investment and equity foreign portfolio investment of economic growth. Eur Econ Rev 48(2):285–306

Edwards S (1990) Capital flows, foreign direct investment, and debt-equity swaps in developing countries, NBER working paper, no. 3497. National Bureau of Economic Research, Cambridge, MA

Fan JPH, Morck R, Xu LC, Yeung BY (2007) Does "Good Government" draw foreign capital? Explaining China's exceptional foreign direct investment inflow, World Bank policy research working paper 4206. World Bank, Washington, DC

Globerman S, Shapiro D (1999) The impact of government policies on foreign direct investment: the Canadian experience. J Int Bus Stud 30(3):513–532

Grubert H, Mutti J (1991) Taxes, tariffs and transfer pricing in multinational corporate decision making. Rev Econ Stat 73(2):285–293

Helpman E (1984) A simple theory of international trade with multinational corporations. J Polit Econ 92:451–471

Helpman E, Krugman PR (1985) Market structure and foreign trade: increasing returns, imperfect competition, and the international economy. The MIT press, Cambridge, MA

Hymer S (1976) The international operations of national firms: a study of direct investment. MIT Press, Cambridge

Im K, Pesaran MH, Shin Y (2003) Testing for unit roots in heterogeneous panels. J Econom 115(1):53–74

Kinda T (2010) Investment climate and FDI in developing countries: firm-level evidence. World Dev 38(4):498–513

King RG, Levine R (1993) Finance and growth: Schumpeter might be right. Q J Econ 108(3):717–737

Khadaroo AJ, Seetanah B (2010) Transport infrastructure and foreign direct investment. J Int Dev 22:103–123

Khan RIA, Nawaz MA (2010) Economic determinants of FDI in Pakistan. J Econ 1(2):99–104

Kok R, Ersoy AB (2009) Analyses of FDI determinants in developing countries. Int J Soc Econ 36(1/2):105–123

Kumar N (2002) Globalisation and the quality of foreign direct investment. Oxford University Press, New Delhi

Levine R, Loayza N, Beck T (2000) Financial intermediation and growth: causality and causes. J Monet Econ 46:31–77

Levine B, Svoboda E, Hay JF, Winocur G, Moscovitch M (2002) Aging and autobiographical memory: dissociating episodic from semantic retrieval. Psychol Aging 17:677–689. doi:10.1037/0882-7974.17.4.677

Levy Yeyati E, Stein E, Daude C (2002) Regional integration and the location of FDI. Inter-American development bank seminar paper prepared for the IDB-IIC 43rd annual meeting, Looking beyond our borders: opportunities and challenges of the new regionalism, Fortaleza

Loree DW, Guisinger SE (1995) Policy and non-policy determinants of U.S. equity foreign direct investment. J Int Bus Stud 26:281–299

MacDougall GDA (1960) The benefits and costs of private investment from abroad: a theoretical approach. Econ Rec 36:13–35

Maddala G, Wu S (1999) A comparative study of unit root tests and a new simple test. Oxford Bull Econ Stat 61(1):631–652

Markusen JR (1995) The boundaries of multinational enterprises and the theory of international trade. J Econ Perspect 9(2):169–189

Markusen J (2001) Contracts, intellectual property rights, and multinational investment in developing countries. J Int Econ 53:189–204

Markusen JR, Venables AJ (1998) Multinational firms and the new trade theory. J Int Econ 46(2):183–203

Mkenda BK, Mkenda AF (2004) Determinants of FDI inflows to African countries: a panel data analysis, Economic and social research foundation, globalisation and East Africa, working paper series, no.11. Economic and Social Research Foundation, Globalisation and East Africa, Dar es Salaam

Mohamed SE, Sidiropoulos MG (2010) Another look at the determinants of foreign direct investment in MENA countries: an empirical investigation. J Econ Dev 35(2):75–95

Moosa IA, Cardak BA (2006) The determinants of foreign direct investment: an extreme bounds analysis. J Multinatl Financ Manag 16(2):199–211

Mottaleb KA, Kalirajan K (2010) Determinants of foreign direct investment in developing countries a comparative analysis. Margin J Appl Econ Res 4(4):369–404

Mundell RA (1957) International trade and factor mobility. Am Econ Rev 47(3):321–335

Nasser OMA, Gomez XG (2009) Do well-functioning financial systems affect the FDI flows to Latin America? Int Res J Finance Econ 29:60–75

Nonnemberg MB, Cardoso de Mendonça MJ (2004) The determinants of foreign investment in developing countries. http://www.anpec.org.br/encontro2004/artigos/A04A061.pdf

Noorbakhsh F, Paloni A, Youssef A (2001) Human capital and FDI inflows to developing countries: new empirical evidence. World Dev 29(9):593–1610

Noy I, Vu TB (2007) Capital account liberalization and foreign direct investment. Econ Finance 18:175–194
Pedroni P (1999) Critical values for cointegration tests in heterogeneous panels with multiple regressors. Oxford Bull Econ Stat 61:653–670
Pedroni P (2000) Fully modified OLS for heterogeneous cointegrated panels. Adv Econom 15:93–130
Pedroni P (2004) Panel cointegration: asymptotic and finite sample properties of pooled time series tests with an application to the purchasing power parity hypothesis. Econom Theory 20:597–625
Pesaran M (2007) A simple panel unit root test in the presence of cross-section dependence. J Appl Econom 22:265–312
Pesaran MH, Pesaran B (1997) Working with Microfit 4.0: an interactive econometric software package (DOS and Windows versions). Oxford University Press, Oxford
Pesaran MH, Shin Y (1998) Generalized impulse response analysis in linear multivariate models. Econ Lett 58:17–29
Pesaran MH, Shin Y, Smith RJ (2001) Bounds testing approaches to the analysis of level relationships. J Appl Econom 16:289–326
Pfefferman GP, Madarassy A (1992) Trends in private investment in developing countries, Discussion paper, no. 14. The World Bank, Washington, DC
Ramirez MD (2006) Economic and institutional determinants of foreign direct investment in Chile: a time series analysis 1960–2001. Contemp Econ Pol 24:459–471
Rodríguez X, Pallas J (2008) Determinants of foreign direct investment in Spain. Appl Econ 40:2443–2450
Rugman AM (1986) New theories of the multinational enterprise: an assessment of internalization theory. Bull Econ Res 38(2):101–118
Sachs J, McArthur JW, Schmidt-Traub G, Kruk M, Bahadur C, Faye M, McCord G (2004) Ending Africa's poverty trap. Brookings Pap Econ Act 69(1):117–240
Sahoo P (2006) FDI in South Asia: trends, policy, impact and determinants, Asian Development Bank Institute discussion paper series, no.56. Asian Development Bank Institute, Tokyo
Sahoo P (2012) Determinants of FDI in South Asia: role of infrastructure, trade openness and reforms. J World Invest Trade 13(2):256–278
Schneider F, Frey B (1985) Economic and political determinants of foreign direct investment. World Dev 13(2):161–175
Shah Z, Ahmed QM (2003) The determinants of foreign direct investment in Pakistan: an empirical investigation. Pak Dev Rev 42(4):697–714
Sin C, Leung W (2001) Impact of FDI liberalization on investment inflows. Appl Econ Lett 8:253–256
Smith V, Leybourne S, Kim TH (2004) More powerful panel unit root tests with an application to the mean reversion in real exchange rates. J Appl Econom 19:147–170
Taylor CT (2000) The impact of host country government policy on US multinational the role of governance infrastructure. World Dev 30(11):1898–1919
UNCTAD (1998) World investment report. United Nations, Geneva
UNCTAD (2000) World investment report. United Nations, Geneva
UNCTAD (2003) World investment report. United Nations, Geneva
UNCTAD (2009) Promoting investment and trade practices, investment advisory series, no. 4. United Nations, Geneva
Vadlamannati KC, Artur T, Irala LR (2009) Determinants of foreign direct investment and volatility in South East Asian economies. J Asia Pac Econ 14:246–261
Vernon R (1966) International investment and international trade in the product cycle. Q J Econ 80:190–207
Walsh JP, Yu J (2010) Determinants of foreign direct investment: a sectoral and institutional approach, IMF working paper, no.187. International Monetary Fund, Washington, DC
Wei S-J (2000) How taxing is corruption on international investors? Rev Econ Stat 82(1):1–11

Westerlund J (2007) Testing for error correction in panel data. Oxford Bull Econ Stat 69:709–748
Westerlund J, Edgerton D (2007) A panel bootstrap cointegration test. Econ Lett 97:185–190
Wheeler D, Mody A (1992) International investment location decisions: the case of U.S. firms. J Int Econ 33:57–76
World Bank (1993) World development report 1993. Oxford University Press for the World Bank, New York
Worth T (1998) Regional trade agreements and foreign direct investment. In: Burfisher ME, Jones EA (eds) Regional trade agreements and U.S. agriculture. US Department of Agriculture, Washington, DC, pp 77–86
Yanikkaya H (2003) Trade openness and economic growth: a cross-country empirical investigation. J Dev Econ 72:57–89
Zhang KH (2001) What attracts foreign multinational corporations to China? Contemp Econ Pol 19(3):336–346
Zhao H, Zhu G (2000) Location factors and country-of-origin differences: an empirical analysis of FDI in China. Multinatl Bus Rev 8(1):60–73

Chapter 7
Foreign Direct Investment (FDI) and Economic Growth in South Asia

7.1 Introduction

Economic growth in any country depends upon the sustained growth of productive capacity, supported by savings and investment. Low levels of savings and investment, particularly in developing countries and least developed countries (LDC), results in a low level of capital stock and economic growth. Therefore, FDI is considered a good substitute for debt in developing economies for higher investment and growth. The earlier growth models by Harrod (1939) and Domar (1946) explain that capital formation raises the standard of living, which in turn results in higher growth.

Criticising the growth models proposed by Harrod and Domar on the ground of the fixed proportion of factors of production and substitutability between labour and capital, Solow (1956) argued that capital formation increases labour productivity in a dynamic process of investment growth. Some recent growth theories, such as of Lucas (1988) and Rebelo (1991), broaden the definition of capital to include human capital and the accumulation of knowledge. Similarly, Romer (1986, 1991) and Grossman and Helpman (1991) incorporate knowledge capital gained through research and development to explain growth along with other variables. Overall, theoretical growth literature demonstrates the role of capital or changes in definition in capital (knowledge capital or human capital) in enhancing economic growth.

The recognition of the role of knowledge capital in economic growth creates a basis for analysing the role of FDI, which brings new technology and knowledge along with capital. In recent years, the need for FDI inflows has increased as multinational corporations (MNCs) have assumed significant importance as a source of economic growth and development (Bajpai and Sachs 2000). Since FDI may help developing or lower-income countries in South Asia by providing new knowledge and complementing domestic investment, it is important to empirically examine the growth impact of FDI. The FDI–growth connection has been examined by mainly examining the determinants of growth and FDI and the role of multinational firms in host countries. Many macro- and micro-studies examine the

P. Sahoo et al., *Foreign Direct Investment in South Asia*,
DOI 10.1007/978-81-322-1536-3_7, © Springer India 2014

relationship between FDI and economic growth, which is explained in the literature review of this chapter.

The issue of FDI interacting with economic growth in developing countries has become increasingly important because many developing countries have adopted a more liberal policy towards FDI since the mid-1980s to accelerate their economic growth. In particular, South Asian countries have been consistently improving their policy framework for attracting FDI. According to the 2012 World Investment Report of the United Nations Conference on Trade and Development (UNCTAD), FDI inflow to South Asia rose from US$68 million in the 1970s, crossed the US$1 billion mark in 1993, and after declining in 2009 and 2010, reached $39 billion in 2011. This happened mainly because these countries launched economic reform programmes. South Asia's share in FDI inflow to developing countries increased from 1.06 % in 1981 to 5.88 % in 2006, declined since, and stood at 5.2 % in 2011. Its share in global FDI inflows was 2.6 % in 2011.

An element key to supplement domestic investment in South Asian countries and improve their technological capability for sustainable, higher economic growth is FDI. However, debates and questions continue over its impact on growth, although growth depends on many factors—macroeconomic and political stability, investment, appropriate policy and regulatory frameworks, infrastructure development, and enhancement of regional cooperation. South Asian countries have experienced both increased FDI inflows and higher growth in the past two decades. South Asia has been one of the fastest-growing regions in the world in the past decade; it has grown almost 3.4 % per year since the 1980s, touched 4.5 % during 2000–2006, and grown at nearly 7 % per year on average during 2004–2012. This growth is one of the major factors of the increase in FDI. Although its ratio to GDP continues to be lower than in other regions, the evidence that higher FDI inflow has contributed to higher growth is overwhelming.

This book attempts to empirically examine the impact of FDI on economic growth for South Asia using both time series and panel data analysis and to test the absorption hypothesis that the growth impact of FDI is dependent on host country factors such as human capital development, trade openness, financial sector development, better infrastructure facilities, and better institutions. This book also presents a comparative analysis of FDI impact on China's economic growth at the national and provincial levels.

7.2 Theoretical Framework

A huge body of theoretical literature exists on the influence of FDI on economic growth. Theoretical views have evolved from the earlier capital accumulation arguments to recent support for the role of FDI in international technology transfer. However, the impact of FDI on economic growth can be decomposed into two channels: (1) the direct impact and (2) the indirect impact.

7.2.1 Direct Impact

In traditional Solow-type standard neoclassical growth models, FDI is considered an addition to the host economy's capital stock. It facilitates the incorporation of new inputs and new varieties of intermediate goods in production. As the size of the host country's physical capital stock per capita increases, its productive capacity and per capita output growth increase too. The impact of FDI on growth is similar to that of domestic capital, since there is no substantial difference between domestic and foreign capital. With diminishing returns to capital, FDI is expected to have a short-run impact on output growth, which depends on the transitional dynamics of capital to the steady-state growth path. Therefore, Solow-type models rule out capital as a source of long-run per capita growth. In such a framework, FDI directly affects growth through short-run capital inflow while the economy is in transition towards its steady state.

7.2.2 Indirect Impact

In contrast with the conventional neoclassical model, which postulates that long-run growth can happen only through both exogenous labour force growth and technological progress, the advent of endogenous growth models (Romer 1986, 1991; Barro and Martin 1995) made it possible to model FDI in promoting even long-run economic growth. Based on endogenous growth theories, and depending on the size of FDI and the spillover it creates for the host country, it can be argued that its impact on growth is substantial.

New or endogenous growth theories incorporate the role of knowledge or technology as an endogenous factor of production and provide for the reason of increasing returns to capital (Lucas 1988; Grossman and Helpman 1991; Romer 1994). Endogenous growth models predict that FDI can affect growth endogenously if it generates increasing returns to production via externalities and productivity spillovers. Lensink and Morrissey (2001a) discuss in detail various channels through which technology transfer influences growth—imitation, competition, linkages, and training. Therefore, the literature on technology transfer identifies four main channels of technological spillovers from FDI to host country—(1) learning by doing, (2) competition, (3) labour skills, and (4) linkage—although, in practice, it is rather difficult to distinguish between these four channels.

The operations of multinational enterprises (MNE) in the host country can result in technology spillovers from FDI if domestic firms improve their productivity by imitating the technology used by MNEs. This phenomenon is known as the imitation effect, or demonstration effect, or learning-by-watching effect (Gunther 2002). The higher the technology gap between foreign firms and domestic firms, the greater the spillover. As multinational firms (MNF) introduce new technologies, indigenous firms experience new actions, skills, and techniques and imitate or adopt these; productive efficiency improves as a result (Wang and Blomström 1992). Indeed, technical assistance, training of local staff, and the adoption of more effective organisational and management practices can improve the know-how, managerial skills, and productivity of local firms and the quality of domestic human capital (the learning-by-watching effect).

The *competition* channel emphasises that foreign firms' entry into domestic markets intensifies competition and encourages domestic firms to become more efficient by upgrading their technology base. This ensures that local firms operate more efficiently than in the absence of foreign firms (Kokko 1996; Wang and Blomström 1992). The positive externalities associated with FDI can occur through the competition channel where increased competition is likely to lead to increased productivity, efficiency, and investment in human and/or physical capital (Hermes and Lensink 2000). Increased competition may lead to changes in the industrial structure towards increased competitiveness and more export-oriented activities. Domestic firms are also forced invest more in in-house research and development (R&D) to survive and compete with foreign firms.

Through the linkages effect, FDI spillover may occur, and MNEs can have productivity spillover on domestic firms in the same industry through horizontal spillovers. Similarly, MNEs can have productivity spillovers on domestic firms in upstream and downstream industries through vertical spillovers (Rodriguez-Clare 1996; Hermes and Lensink 2000). Borensztein et al. (1998) argued that FDI increases the range and quality of intermediate goods, which in turn increases productivity. FDI also causes spillovers through the know-how and skills it brings into the host country. By transferring knowledge, FDI increases the stock of knowledge in the host country through labour training, transfer of skills, and the transfer of managerial and organisational best practices. The spillover effect can be argued to occur when workers and managers employed in foreign affiliates, with advanced technical and managerial skills, move to other domestic firms or their own enterprises (Lensink and Morrissey 2001a, b). Another important mechanism is that FDI raises the productivity of domestic research and development activities (Markusen 1995, 2002). Markusen (1995) argued that knowledge capital is important for MNEs as these tend to have large R&D budgets and many technical workers and produce technically advanced products.

Some other studies argue that FDI influences economic growth by promoting host country exports by:

1. Augmenting domestic capital for exports
2. Helping transfer of technology and new products for exports
3. Facilitating access to new and large foreign markets
4. Providing training for the local workforce and upgrading technical and management skills (UNCTAD 2003a,; Anwara and Nguyen 2010)

Studies also argue that the chosen mode of FDI affects its growth-enhancing ability. For example, technology spillovers and physical capital formation are expected to differ between greenfield FDI and brownfield FDI (Johnson 2006). In the case of greenfield FDI, MNEs construct new production facilities in the host country and conduct research and design. In the case of brownfield investment, the MNE acquires existing facilities in the host country. Therefore, greenfield FDI causes greater spillover and capital formation than brownfield FDI and should affect host country growth differently (Javorcik 2004).

7.3 FDI and Growth: Empirical Evidence

A huge volume of literature provides empirical evidence of the impact of FDI on economic growth, although the debate whether FDI is beneficial for growth continues.[1] Many researchers, using different data and methodologies, have concluded that FDI has a positive impact on growth, but the extent and degree of impact depends on the productivity spillovers of FDI to domestic firms and the characteristics of foreign investment, host countries, sectors, and firms. However, most studies assessed FDI influence on economic growth through econometric models that specify the rate of growth of real GDP or GDP per capita as a function of the stock or inflow of FDI. This section comprehensively reviews the empirical literature, which indicates that studies of FDI impact on economic growth can be divided into cross-country, country-level, industry-specific, and firm-specific studies.

7.3.1 Cross-Country Studies

The early works by De Gregorio (1992) for a panel of 12 Latin American countries and Blomström et al. (1996) for LDCs found a strong effect of FDI on economic growth. Their empirical result was supported by Borensztein et al. (1998), who tested the effect of FDI on economic growth in a framework of cross-country regressions for 69 developing countries over the past decade. Their results suggest that FDI was an important vehicle for technology transfer and that it contributed more to growth than domestic investment. The authors also found a strong complementary effect between FDI and human capital—FDI's contribution to economic growth was enhanced by the level of its interaction with human capital in the host country.

Blomström et al. (1994) found that ratios of FDI inflow to GDP among developing countries from 1960 to 1985 in a 5-year period were positively related to growth in the subsequent 5-year period. However, when the developing countries were

[1] Bhagwati (1978) suggested that the incentives offered by the trade policy of a host country determine the growth effects of inward FDI—an export promotion policy would increase the efficiency of FDI in promoting growth; an import substitution policy would decrease it. Balasubramanyam et al. (1996) tested this hypothesis; they found that higher inward FDI flows were associated with faster trade growth in 10–18 export-promoting countries but not in the others, presumably following import substitution trade policies.

divided between higher-income and lower-income countries, FDI was found to have promoted growth only in higher-income countries.

In their study of 69 developing countries between 1970 and 1989, Borensztein et al. (1995) found that while the impact of FDI inflow on economic growth by itself was only marginal, it was significant and positive when FDI inflow interacted with the education level of a country's labour force. In his study of 12 countries in Southeast Asia, Latin America, and sub-Saharan Africa over 1963–1992, Nyatepe-Coo (1998) found that FDI promoted economic growth in most countries.

De Mello (1999) attempted to find support for an FDI-led growth hypothesis with time series analysis and panel data estimation for a sample of 32 OECD and non-OECD countries over 1970–1990. The results suggest a positive impact on output growth and a dominant complementarity effect between FDI and domestic investment.

Xu (2000) investigated US MNEs as a channel of international technology diffusion in 40 countries over 1966–1994 by using panel data and found strong evidence of technology diffusion to developed countries but weak evidence of such diffusion to LDCs.

Wang (2002) reported a positive impact of FDI on economic growth using data from 12 Asian economies over 1987–1997. The study disaggregates the types of flows entering these economies and finds that FDI has a significant, positive impact on economic growth only in the manufacturing sector. The OECD (2002) documents that FDI increases economic growth by raising the efficiency of resources and factor productivity in the host country.

Similarly, Campos and Kinoshita (2002b) investigated the effects of FDI on 25 transitional economies of the former Soviet Bloc and found that FDI plays a significant factor in economic growth.

Lensink and Morrissey (2001a, b) utilise a standard model using cross section, panel data, and instrumental variables (IV) technique for 1975–1997 and found that while FDI has a positive effect on growth, the volatility of FDI has a negative impact. Also, importantly, the evidence of the positive effect of FDI on output growth in the recipient country is not conditional on any other explanatory variable.

Using a large cross-country sample for 1970–1999, Li and Liu (2005) also investigated the hypothesis in both developed and developing countries and found a strong complementary connection between FDI and economic growth. They accounted for the endogeneity issue and reported that FDI and economic growth had a significant complementary effect on each other, but that they formed an increasingly endogenous relationship only from the mid-1980s. Further, Li and Liu reported that FDI promoted economic growth both directly, by itself, and also indirectly, via human capital.

By using dynamic panel models, Baharumshah and Thanoon (2006) demonstrated how FDI contributed positively to East Asian economies' growth process—countries that attract FDI can finance more investment and grow faster than those that deter it.

Won et al. (2008) use panel vector autoregressive models to analyse newly industrialised Asian economies and show that inward FDI and exports were among the most important economic factors of these economies' rapid growth.

Kotrajaras (2010) examined the effect of FDI on the economic growth of 15 East Asian countries. The sample was divided into three groups:

1. High-income group (Hong Kong, Japan, South Korea, Singapore, and Taiwan)
2. Middle-income group (China, India, Indonesia, Malaysia, the Philippines, and Thailand)
3. Low-income group (Cambodia, Laos, Myanmar, and Vietnam).

The study used a fixed effect model and found a positive relationship between FDI and economic growth only in high-income and middle-income countries, which have the appropriate economic factors—well-educated workforce, investment in infrastructure, and trade openness.

Tiwari and Mutascu (2011) investigated the impact of FDI on economic growth in 23 Asian countries using panel data for the period 1986–2008. The study also examined the nonlinearities associated with FDI and exports. The result of this study indicates that FDI and exports enhance the growth process. In addition, labour and capital also play an important role in the growth of Asian countries.

7.3.2 Country-Specific Studies

On analysing the FDI-led growth hypothesis, Dees (1998) found that FDI affects growth in China through the diffusion of ideas; it affects long-term growth significantly and positively through its influence on technical change. Balamurali and Bogahawatte (2004) found the same results for Sri Lanka.

Shan (2002) examined the impact of FDI on economic growth in China over 1986–1998 using quarterly data and the vector autoregressive (VAR) method and documented a feedback relationship between FDI and output growth. However, the strength of causality is imbalanced: output growth affects FDI more than FDI affects output growth.

Hooi and Wah (2010) used time series analysis to examine the linkages between FDI, domestic investment (DI), and economic growth in Malaysia over 1970–2009. They found that FDI affects long-term economic growth positively, but DI affects it negatively and that an increase in FDI will positively affect DI.

7.3.3 Sectoral Studies

Few studies have examined the sectoral composition of FDI inflows and its impact on sectoral output growth recently, in contrast to the past. A few of these studies found that the positive impact of FDI inflow is greater on the manufacturing sector than on the services sector, which has a lower absorption capacity (Alfaro 2003; Aykut and Sayek 2007; Chakraborty and Nunnenkamp 2008; Dash and Parida 2012).

Nadia and Merih (2011) examined the growth effect of sectoral (manufacturing and service) FDI inflows in their own sector, their spillover to other sectors, and the overall economy for 60 countries. Manufacturing FDI stimulated activity in manufacturing in Latin America–Caribbean, Europe–Central Asia, middle- to low-income countries, and industrial economies. Service FDI stimulated the service industries but hurt manufacturing. Financial FDI enhanced growth in Southeast Asia and Pacific, high-income countries, and service-based economies by boosting activity in both sectors. However, nonfinancial service FDI drained resources and hurt manufacturing in the same group of countries due to its resource-draining effect.

7.3.4 Firm-Level Studies

Using firm-level data from Indonesia, SjoKholm (1999) found that while FDI does benefit locally owned firms, the benefits differ between groups of industries—larger technology gaps have bigger spillover effects for domestic producers. Using technology import data of US majority-owned affiliates in 33 developing countries, Kokko and Blomström (1995) showed that the affiliates' technology imports increase with the host country's DI and education levels. Therefore, productivity benefits may be highly dependent on the investment sector, the technology gap in a particular investment, and a host country's environment.

Some studies report a negative impact of FDI on economic growth (Singer 1950; Griffin 1970; Weisskopf 1972). These studies argued, mainly, that FDI flowed to the primary sector in LDCs, which promoted less market value for this sector. In a study of 16 developing countries over 1966–1988 based on a macro-econometric model with three-stage least squares methodology, Fry (1992) found no impact of FDI on DI and concluded that FDI exerts both a direct, positive effect on the current account and an indirect, negative effect.

Saltz (1992) examined the effect of FDI on economic growth for Third World countries over 1970–1980[2] and found a negative correlation. Carkovic and Levine (2002) empirically examined the FDI–economic growth relationship in 72 developed and developing economies over 1960–1995 using the generalised method of moments (GMM) panel estimator. They found no independent influence of FDI inflow on economic growth, even considering the recipient country's level of education, economic development, financial development, and openness to trade.

Townsend (2003) examined the effects of FDI on growth by using the Carkovic and Levine (2002) model that found no positive effect. The study, which uses a data set that contains LDCs only, found no robust FDI effect on growth. Durham (2004) also found no positive relationship and instead suggested that the host country's

[2] In his review of empirical studies of the macroeconomic effects of FDI on economic growth, Kumar (1996) concludes that most of such evidence is fraught with simultaneity problems and that causality runs more often from growth to FDI than the other way around.

ability to absorb FDI determines its effect. Mencinger (2003) suggested that the form of FDI could explain the negative FDI–growth relationship in transition economies, where investment has been mostly brownfield.

7.3.5 Studies on South Asia

A few studies have examined the FDI–growth relationship in South Asia. Pradhan (2002) estimated a Cobb–Douglas production function using aggregate data for 1969–1997 with FDI stocks as an additional input variable and found no significant impact of FDI on growth. However, a study using the Johansen co-integration technique over 1979–2001 found a long-run relationship between GDP, FDI, and exports (Sahoo and Mathiyazhagan 2003; Sahoo 2006, 2012). Using aggregate data for 1974–1996, Chakraborty and Basu (2002) reported that one-way causality runs from GDP to FDI and that FDI is positively related to GDP and openness to trade in the long run. Dua and Rasid (1998) report similar results. Kumar and Pradhan (2002) considered the FDI–growth relationship Granger-neutral for India as they did not find causality in either direction. Bhat et al. (2004) reported similar conclusions by applying Granger causality. By obtaining panel estimates for five South Asian countries including India over 1965–1996, Aggarwal (2005) found negligible growth impact of FDI. A study by Chakraborty and Nunnenkamp (2008) analysed the sector-specific hypothesis and found only transitory effects of FDI on output in the services sector in the case of India. The study, however, emphasised that FDI in the services sector may have promoted growth in the manufacturing sector through cross-sector spillovers. Bergman (2006) examined the intra-industry spillover effects of FDI in the pharmaceutical industry in India for 43 pharmaceutical firms. The results of this study are mixed. Spillover effects are visible in many of the spillover channels from FDI in foreign-owned firms. However, the correlation between FDI and productivity in domestic firms is insignificant, due to local firms' absorptive capability and factors such as market structure, competitiveness, trade, and technological policies.

Shahbaz et al. (2008) using the autoregressive distributed lag (ARDL)-bound testing approach examined the determinants of economic growth for Pakistan. The study finds that among other factors, FDI, financial development, remittances, and public investment have a positive effect on economic growth, while trade openness and inflation slow its pace. Shahbaz and Rehman (2010) identified the main determinants of economic growth, including FDI, for Pakistan. Using the ARDL method, they found that FDI, financial development, public investment, human capital, trade openness, and inflation have positive effects on economic growth. Jayachandran and Seilan (2010) examined the determinants of economic growth in the case of India. They found FDI and exports among the main factors of significant economic growth. However, reverse causality was not found. Ahamad et al. (2010) examine the FDI–GDP relationship using time series data over 1970–2006 for Bangladesh. The results reveal that growth stimulates FDI and not vice versa.

The argument rests on the fact that foreign investors invariably prefer to invest not only in large markets but also in economies experiencing ongoing high economic growth.

7.4 Conditions for Positive Impact of FDI on Growth

The literature review above reflects that FDI has a positive impact on growth, and that its extent and degree varies depending on productivity spillovers of FDI firms to domestic firms and the characteristics of foreign investment, host countries, sectors, and firms. The conditions for positive impact of FDI on growth can be categorised as follows.

7.4.1 Absorptive Capacities

One of the explanations proposed in the literature is that positive spillovers from FDI depend on a country's absorptive capacity, i.e. on the existence of various local conditions favourable to economic growth (Borensztein et al. 1998; Alfaro et al. 2003; Edison et al. 2002; Durham 2004). These initial conditions that capture the absorptive capacity of host countries include the initial level of development (Blomström et al. 1992) existing human capital development (Borensztein et al. 1998), trade policy (Balasubramanyam et al. 1996), financial development (Durham 2004; Alfaro et al. 2003), legal policy-based variables (Durham 2004; Edison et al. 2002), and general government policy (Edison et al. 2002). Recently, researchers recognised the fact that the quality of FDI is more important than the quantity alone (Enderwick 2005).

7.4.2 Human Capital

In a very influential paper, Borensztein et al. (1998) showed that it takes an educated labour force to spread the benefits of new technologies across all industries. Foreign investment was able to speed up growth in a host economy only if there is a minimum threshold of human capital. Their findings indicated that the gains from FDI come through technology diffusion rather than through capital accumulation. Campos and Kinoshita (2002a, b), who tested the effects of FDI on growth in transitional economies during the transitional period (1990–1998), supported these results. In 1999, UNCTAD analysed the impact of FDI on growth in developing countries and found it was only significantly positive when entered in interaction with the number of years of schooling. Li and Liu (2005) analysed panel data for 84 countries over the period 1970–1999 and observed that the interaction of

FDI with human capital exerted a strong positive effect on economic growth. Anwara and Nguyen (2010) examine the growth–FDI relationship for Vietnam. The results suggested that the impact of FDI on economic growth in Vietnam would have been larger if more resources were invested in education and training, developing the financial market, and in reducing the technology gap between foreign and local firms.

7.4.3 Trade Openness

Like better human capital, trade openness and an economy's export orientation can facilitate a greater transfer of know-how and managerial skills through FDI and 'crowd in' DI (Balasubramanyam et al. 1999). Therefore, the efficiency of FDI in promoting growth can be increased by export promotion policy and decreased by import substitution policy. Agrawal (2000) tested the economic impact of FDI in South Asia and found that the impact of FDI inflows on GDP growth rate was negative prior to the 1980s, slightly positive for the early 1980s, and strongly positive in the late 1980s and the early 1990s. From this, he concluded that a country must have an open economy to benefit from the positive effect that FDI can have on output growth. The importance of the trade regime's openness is further reinforced by Sadik and Bolbol's 2000 study, in which they investigated the effect of FDI on growth and productivity in six Arab economies (Egypt, Jordan, Morocco, Oman, Saudi Arabia, and Tunisia).

7.4.4 Financial Development

Well-functioning domestic financial markets are instrumental in efficiently allocating foreign financial flows, including FDI, to competing investment projects. Alfaro et al. (2004) argued that the effect of FDI on growth depends on the financial sector's degree of development. They concluded that countries with well-developed financial markets gain significantly from FDI. The results were robust to different measures of financial market development, the inclusion of other determinants of economic growth, and the consideration of endogeneity. Hermes and Lensink (2003) also conducted a broad country-panel study and found that a certain degree of development of the host country's financial system—measured as domestic credit provided by the banking sector to the private sector—is an important prerequisite for the positive effect of FDI on the host economy. Their results implied that domestic credit provided by the banking system should exceed 12 % of GDP for the host country to be able to absorb the potential technology diffusion of FDI. Kose et al. (2009) argued that there are certain 'threshold' levels of financial and institutional development that an economy needs to attain before it can derive the growth benefits of financial flows, including FDI.

7.4.5 *Infrastructure*

The effect of infrastructure investments on growth has received much attention since the seminal work by Aschauer (1989). According to Prüfer and Tondl (2008), infrastructure is likely a conditional factor for FDI to produce growth effects—apart from its independent contribution to growth. Good infrastructure can be considered complementary to FDI. If investors see poor telecommunication and transport infrastructure and unreliable electricity provision, FDI may not produce a high impact on productivity; in contrast, R&D collaboration and public infrastructure such as educational institutions, roads, ports, and airports can significantly support potential spillovers (Kinda 2007).

7.4.6 *Institutional Quality*

Institutional factors are also important in the FDI–growth connection. The quality of host country institutions, in particular the rule of law and the protection of property rights (North 1991; Rodrik 1999), is an oft-cited example of host country characteristics that determines the growth-enhancing effect of FDI. Using cross-sectional data, Olofsdotter (1998) found that an increase in FDI stock is positively related to growth. He also found a stronger effect for host countries with better institutional capability as measured by the degree of property rights protection and bureaucratic efficiency. Durham (2004) found that institutional factors have an important influence on the impact of FDI on growth. He used business regulation, property rights protection, and corruption as institutional indices. Finally, Bengoa and Sanchez-Robles (2003) investigated the relationship between FDI, economic freedom, and economic growth using panel data for Latin America. Comparing fixed and random effects estimations, they concluded that FDI has a significant positive effect on host country economic growth; however, the magnitude depends on host countries' conditions.

7.5 Data Source, Methodology, and Model Specification

Data have been collected from World Development Indicators (2012).

Annual data on real per capita income, real trade, real export, real gross capital stock, gross secondary enrolment ratio, labour force (ILO definition of the economically active population that includes both the employed and the unemployed), inflation rate (Consumer Price Index), banking sector credit to domestic sector as ratio of GDP, and government final expenditure as ratio of GDP over a period ranging from 1980 to 2010.

Infrastructure variables considered include air freight transport (million tons per km), electric power consumption (kwh per capita), rail density (per 1,000 population), energy use (kg of oil equivalent per capita), and total telephone lines (main line plus cellular phones) per 1,000 population are taken from World Development Indicators (various years).

Data on FDI inflows have been compiled from the UNCTAD online database and converted to real terms by using GDP deflator. Data on governance indicators (proxied by index of economic freedom) are collected from the Heritage Foundation. Both time series and panel data analysis have been used for getting a robust estimation. Given that only 31 observations were available per country, the ARDL technique is used. Two panel methods (system GMM and fully modified OLS (FMOLS) have been used to derive the long-run determinants of FDI for South Asia. First, unit root and co-integration tests are carried out; then, the long-run determinants of FDI are derived by using the appropriate methodology.

7.5.1 Model Specification

Since this study aims to examine the impact of FDI inflows on growth, we use a standard neoclassical production function framework with FDI as an additional variable along with domestic capital and labour (De Mello 1997):

$$Y_t = f\ (K,\ L,\ \text{FDIY})\ldots, \tag{7.1}$$

where Y_t denotes the output level (i.e. real GDP per capita),

K denotes the amount of domestic capital (which is measured by gross domestic capital formation (GCF) as a percentage of GDP), L denotes the amount of labour (measured by labour force of the country), and FDI is FDI as a ratio of GDP.

Following Grossman and Helpman (1990) and Barro and Martin (1995), this production function has been expanded according to the new growth theory. Trade theories (Krueger 1975; Bhagwati 1988) suggest that free trade enriches nations in various ways. In addition, the economic growth literature triggered by the endogenous growth theory (Grossman and Helpman 1990; Barro and Martin 1995) emphasises the importance of international trade in achieving a sustainable rate of economic growth by increasing labour productivity, generating greater capacity utilisation, bringing more technological progress, and opening up more employment opportunities. Following these studies, we include variables like trade openness and exports alternatively in the production function. Human capital is another source of growth in several endogenous growth models as well as one of the key extensions of the neoclassical growth model. A large number of studies have found that an educated population is the key determinant of economic growth (Barro 1991; Mankiw et al. 1992; Barro and Martin 1995). In addition, infrastructure development is one of the major determinants of economic growth, particularly in developing countries; this has been well recognised in the existing literature

(Aschauer 1989; World Bank 1994; Roller and Waveman 2001; Canning and Pedroni 2004; Sahoo and Dash 2012). Similarly, a well-developed financial system affects economic growth by helping the diversification of liquidity and investment risk, which attracts more savings into productive investment and prevents the premature withdrawal of capital from long-term projects. In this framework, financial intermediation has been shown to have both level effects and growth effects (Greenwood and Jovanvoic 1990; Bencivenga and Smith 1991; King and Levine 1993). Similarly, the inflation rate has been included to capture the effect of macroeconomic instability on economic growth. The effect of inflation on per capita income is expected to be negative as higher inflation negatively affects investment and its overall productivity and human capital accumulation (Barro and Sala-i-Martin 1990; Fischer 1993). On the other hand, empirical literature stresses that governance or the quality of institutions matters to economic development (Kaufmann et al. 2002). Introducing a number of conditional variables and taking logarithms, we can rewrite Eq. (7.1) as

$$\begin{aligned}\ln\ \text{PCI} = \alpha_i + \delta_i t + \beta_{1i}\ \ln\ \text{DBC} + \beta_{2i}\ \ln\ \text{TR} + \beta_{3i}\ \ln\ \text{INFRA} \\ + \beta_{4i}\ \ln\ \text{HUM} + \beta_{5i}\ \text{labourforce}\ (\text{LF}) + \beta_{6i} \ln \text{GCF} + \beta_{7i}\ \text{INF} \\ + \beta_{8i} \ln \text{FDI} + \beta_{9i} \ln \text{GOV} + u_{\text{it}}\end{aligned} \tag{7.2}$$

The expected sign of ($\beta_{1\text{i}}, \beta_{2\text{i}}, \beta_{3\text{i}}, \beta_{4\text{i}}, \beta_{5\text{i}}, \beta_{6\text{i}}, \beta_{8\text{i}}, \beta_{9\text{i}}$ is) > 0 and $B_{7\text{i}}$ is < 0 where PCI is real per capita income,
DBC is real domestic bank credit as a proxy for financial development,
TR is real trade,
INFRA is infra sector index,
FDI is real FDI,
HUM is human capital proxied by gross secondary enrolment,
GCF is real gross capital formation,
INF is inflation rate, and
GOV is governance indicator.

All variables are log transformed except inflation rate since some values are negative. The above growth model is compatible with endogenous growth theories, and we assume existence of scale economies and spillovers, and thus estimate the effect of FDI on growth, while factoring in scale economies and knowledge spillovers. The Eq. (7.2) is estimated in by using both time series as well as panel methodology.

7.6 Empirical Results

7.6.1 Time Series Analysis of Impact of FDI on Growth

The first test in the empirical analysis is the examination of properties of variables by using the ADF unit root test. First, we test the unit root by assuming that there is no trend but only intercept. Then, we test stationarity by assuming trend in the variable. It can be seen from Tables 7.A.1 and 7.A.2 that we have a mixture of $I(0)$ and $I(1)$ variables. Inflation rate and FDI are $I(0)$ variable; with the exception of the variable trade and LF, which is $I(0)$, for Bangladesh, others are $I(1)$ variables—per capita income, LF, infrastructure index, human capital, trade ratio, domestic capital formation, and governance indicator.

Given the mixture of $I(0)$ and $I(1)$ variables, ARDL procedure for co-integration is applied, and the result of co-integration test is presented in Table 7.A.2. It is clear from Table 7.A.2 that there exists a long-run relationship among the variables when real per capita income is the dependent variable, because the F-statistic exceeds the upper bound critical value (3.50) at the 5 % level for all the countries. Given that we have only 31 observations, we have considered two lags, which have been selected based on Akaike Information Criteria (AIC). Thus, the null hypothesis of non-existence of stable relationship is rejected in favour of a stable relationship.

Having found the long-run relationship between real per capita income and other variables, we estimate long-run coefficients of real per capita income by using ARDL model for five South Asian countries. The result of long-run coefficients is presented in Table 7.1.

7.6.1.1 India

The estimation results show the contribution to the growth of India made by GCF, LF, trade growth, infrastructure availability, FDI, and human capital development. Among other factors, trade development, capital formation, infrastructure development, financial development, and FDI inflows have significant positive impact on the economic growth of India. The impact of LF has been found to be positive but insignificant. In terms of relative importance, gross capital stock has the highest impact on growth, followed by trade and financial development. The impact of FDI inflows on economic growth is positive, but the magnitude is small. One unit increase in FDI increases economic growth by only 0.05 % in India. Other variables such as human capital and inflation rate have been found to be insignificant and hence dropped from final estimation.

7.6.1.2 Pakistan

For Pakistan, the relevant variables that significantly explain economic growth are LF, infrastructure development, human capital, trade development, FDI, and financial development. In terms of relative importance, LF has the highest impact on growth followed by financial development and trade. The impact of FDI is small although the coefficient is positive and statistically significant. The results indicate that 1 % increase in FDI inflows leads to a merely 0.03 % increase in economic growth in Pakistan. The result is not surprising since higher political instability has affected FDI inflows. This has reduced the impact of FDI on economic growth. The coefficient of inflation is negative, indicating that higher inflation retards economic growth. The coefficient of capital stock has been found to be negative and insignificant and, hence, was dropped from final estimation.

Table 7.1 Long-run coefficients of growth (1980–2010) (dependent variable LPCI)

	India	Pakistan	Sri Lanka	Bangladesh	Nepal
Variables	Coefficients	Coefficients	Coefficients	Coefficients	Coefficients
Constant	4.70* (1.99)	−1.49** (−4.44)	−8. 51** (−4.13)	−0.70* (−2.56)	−0.58 (−0.86)
LLF	0.020 (0.99)	0.27** (7.63)	0.90* (2.46)	−0.12 (−1.43)	0.38** (3.78)
LTR	0.18** (5.35)	0.07* (2.56)	0.25* (2.13)	0.06* (1.97)	0.08# (1.88)
LHUM	–	0.02# (1.83)	–		0.13** (3.12)
LGCF	0.31** (2.96)	–	0.26* (2.04)	0.28* (2.90)	0.12* (2.38)
LFDI	0.045* (2.78)	0.03* (2.25)	0.04# (1.84)	0.008# (1.94)	0.01 (0.50)
INFRA	0.09* (1.96)	0.06* (2.42)	0.04** (3.82)	0.03** (3.87)	0.02* (2.58)
INF	–	−0.03* (−2.25)	–		−002* (−2.56)
DBC	0.09* (2.22)	0.11** (4.26)	–	0.09** (3.02)	–
Model selection criteria (AIC)	(3,2,3,0,1,2.0)	(2,3,1,0,1,1,2)	(2,0,0,2,2,1,0)	(1,1,2,1,2,1,2)	(2,2,1,2,2,0,2)
Diagnostic test	ADJ. $R^2 = 0.91$, DW. Stat. =-1.07, LM = 0.9, ARCH = 1.54	ADJ. $R^2 = 0.86$, DW. Stat. = 1.7, LM = 2.1, ARCH = 1.8	ADJ. $R^2 = 0.92$, DW. Stat. = 2.02, LM = 2.3, ARCH = 1.21	ADJ. $R^2 = 0.89$, DW. Stat. = 2.1, LM = 1.59, ARCH = 1.6	ADJ. $R^2 = 0.75$, DW. stat. = 2.4, LM = 1.2, ARCH = 1.2
	Reset-0.54 (0.51)	Reset-0.79 (0.32)	Reset-1.7 (0.19)	Reset-1.4 (0.32)	Reset-1.1 (0.34)

Notes: ***, **, and # denote significant at 1, 5, and 10 % level, respectively. Figures in the parentheses are *t*-ratio

7.6.1.3 Sri Lanka

For Sri Lanka, major variables that explain economic growth are LF, infrastructure development, capital stock, trade development, and FDI. In terms of relative importance, LF has the highest impact on growth followed by capital stock and trade. The impact of FDI is small although the coefficient is positive and significant only at 10 % level of confidence. The results indicate that 1 % increase in FDI inflows leads to merely 0.04 % increase in economic growth in Sri Lanka. Other variables such as human capital, financial development, and inflation rate are found insignificant and hence dropped from final estimation.

7.6.1.4 Bangladesh

For Bangladesh, we have used two lags for deriving long-run coefficients as suggested by the AIC criterion. Important variables that explain economic growth in Bangladesh are capital stock, infrastructure development, trade development, FDI, and financial development. In terms of relative importance, capital stock has the highest impact on growth followed by financial development and trade. The impact of FDI is small, although the coefficient is positive and significant only at 10 % level of confidence. The results indicate that 1 % increase in FDI inflows leads to merely 0.008 % increase in economic growth in Bangladesh. The coefficient of LF is negative but insignificant. Other variables such as human capital and inflation rate are found insignificant and hence dropped from final estimation.

7.6.1.5 Nepal

For Nepal, we have used two lags for estimating long-run coefficients as suggested by the AIC criterion. The results indicate that LF, capital stock, infrastructure development, trade development, human capital, and inflation rate explain economic growth in Nepal. In terms of relative importance, LF, human capital, and capital stock have the highest impact on growth. The coefficient is positive but insignificant. The result supports the hypothesis that Nepal receives the least FDI—because of recent political instability.

The diagnostic test indicates that the model is free of the heteroscedasticity effect since the ARCH coefficient has been found to be insignificant for each country. Adjusted R^2 is high for all countries, indicating that the model has a very good explanatory power. Durbin–Watson (DW) statistics indicates that autocorrelation is not a problem for the model. In addition, Lagrange multiplier test statistics indicate that the model is free of the autocorrelation problem.

Overall, we find that the coefficient of FDI, which is the main focus of this study, is positive and significant for all countries except Nepal. More importantly, the coefficient of FDI is small—ranging from 0.021 to 0.05—indicating that a 1 %

increase in the FDI to GDP ratio leads to a 0.02–0.05 % increase in per capita income. Given that a small amount of FDI is coming into South Asian countries, it is expected that the impact of FDI on growth will be small. The results are in line with the findings of previous studies (Blomström et al. 1994; Borensztein et al. 1998; De Mello 1999; Lipsey 1999; Wang 2002). Other significant factors contributing to growth are trade, GCF, LF, inflation rate, human capital development, and infrastructure.

That trade and GCF contribute significantly to grow this consistent with the findings of several other studies (Harrison 1996; Krueger 1997; Edwards 1998; Frankel and Romer 1999; Apergis et al. 2007). Since infrastructure facilitates growth, the infrastructure index has been included in the growth function (Eq. 7.2), which is positive and significant. The impact of financial sector development is found positive for only two countries, Pakistan and Sri Lanka. Finally, the coefficient of inflation rate is negative and significant for India and Nepal, indicating that higher inflation rate increases macroeconomic instability. However, its coefficient is very small.

7.6.2 Panel Data Analysis

In the panel framework, we first conducted unit root test using the Pesaran (2007) CIPS test. The CIPS unit root test for both 'constant' and 'constant and trend' specifications and allowing for the lag order to be at maximum equal to 3 ($p = 1$, 2, 3) is presented in Table 7.A.3. It is clear that CIPS panel test does not reject the null of unit roots for the panel at level for all variables except inflation rate, LGFC and LFDI. On the contrary, the differenced series are stationary leading us to conclude that a panel unit root is present in the level series. Hence, the CIPS test indicates that we have mixture of $I(0)$ and $I(1)$ variables.

Having established the non-stationarity of the series, we then proceed to test for the existence of a long-run relationship between real per capita income and other relevant variables using error correction panel co-integration test developed by Westerlund (2007). The results of Westerlund (2007) co-integration test with the asymptotic p-values based on 500 replications are presented in Table 7.A.4. When using the asymptotic p-values, the no co-integration null is rejected by Gt in favour of existence of co-integration at 5 % level, indicating we have co-integration for at least one cross section. Similarly, with the asymptotic p-values, the no co-integration null is rejected by Pt at the 5 % level (i.e. when ρ_i is restricted to be homogenous), suggesting that the whole panel is co-integrated. Therefore, the long-run relationship between real per capita income and its determinants is stable.

Long-Run Coefficients of Growth: To derive long-run growth coefficients, we use both FMOLS and system GMM methodology to overcome possible endogeneity problems. According to Borensztein et al. (1998), the FDI–growth rate correlation could arise from an endogenous determination of FDI; in other words, FDI may be influenced by innovations in the stochastic process governing

Table 7.2 Long-run coefficients of growth (1980–2010)

	GMM system	FMOLS
Variables	Coefficients	Coefficients
Constant	0.90** (16.88)	–
LLF	–	0.43** (9.32)
LTRADE	0.32** (11.08)	0.09** (5.38)
LHUM	0.23** (13.08)	0.05 (0.78)
LFDI	0.02** (3.74)	0.01* (2.13)
LGCF	0.25** (11.24)	0.11** (3.77)
INFRA	0.08** (22.11)	0.02** (3.38)
LDBC	–	0.10** (6.21)
INF	−0.004** (−6.27)	−0.005* (−2.13)
Arellano–Bond test for AR(1) in first differences		$z = -3.19$, $\Pr > z = 0.00$
Arellano–Bond test for AR(2) in first differences		$z = -1.14$, $\Pr > z = 0.25$
Sargan test of overid. restrictions:		$\text{chi}^2(80) = 69.84$, $\Pr > \text{chi}^2 = 0.05$
GMM instruments for levels: Difference-in-Sargan tests of exogeneity of instrument subsets:		$\text{chi}^2(52) = 199.39$, $\Pr > \text{chi}^2 = 0.00$

Notes: *** and ** denotes Significant at 1 and 5 % level, respectively. Figures in the parentheses are *t*-ratio

growth rates. The results of panel estimation for 1980–2010 using two different methods are presented in Table 7.2.

It is clear from Table 7.2 that the impact of FDI on real per capita income is positive and significant. The GMM system passes all diagnosis tests related to Sargan test of overidentifying restrictions and the Arellano–Bond test of first-order and second-order autocorrelation. The results from the dynamic panel analysis validate the hypothesis that FDI is growth conducive in our sample of five countries. The coefficient of FDI is 0.02 %, indicating 1 % increase in FDI increase growth by 0.02 %. This hypothesis is further validated by the FMOLS result, although the coefficient is marginally lower and still at the lower end. In addition to FDI, other variables such as LF, human capital development, trade, infrastructure stock, and inflation rate affect economic growth significantly.

The coefficient of gross capital formation as ratio of GDP has been found to have positive impact for South Asia. The neoclassical theory highlights that an increase in investment raises the steady-state level of output per worker and, therefore, raises the growth rate of output. The coefficient of trade ratio is positive and significant. Therefore, the present study supports the finding in the previous literature that FDI is beneficial for countries following a trade-led growth strategy. In addition, a positive and significant impact of human capital on real per capita GDP is reported in estimations. This result confirms the findings in Mankiw et al. (1992) that a better-educated population augments a country's ability to absorb and adopt new technologies and to innovate; therefore, it is an important factor of growth, and human capital development affects economic growth positively. The inflation rate affects economic growth negatively as the coefficient of inflation rate is negative and significant. Thus, the analysis of the sample of five

South Asian developing economies shows that the FDI variable is robust in several different specifications, and that it has a significant positive effect on the host country's economic growth.

7.6.3 FDI and Absorptive Capacity

A large empirical literature suggests that the influence of FDI on economic growth depends on several factors (Durham 2004)—human capital development, financial development, trade, infrastructure development, and institutions. This section assesses how each factor influences the effect of FDI on economic growth (Table 7.3). The GMM system passes all diagnostic tests related to Sargan test of overidentifying restrictions and the Arellano–Bond test of first-order and second-order autocorrelation. Following Balusubramanyam et al. (1999), we use the FDI*Trade as an additional independent exogenous variable because countries with an open trade regime can benefit from the technological spillovers of FDI. The coefficient of FDI*Trade interaction term indicates that trade openness does not help FDI to influence growth for South Asia.

Similarly, we test the hypothesis (Borensztein et al. 1998) that, to reap the positive effects of FDI on growth, a country must have a minimum threshold of human capital stock. Thus, we include the FDI*HUM interaction term as an additional exogenous variable. Table 7.3 indicates that the coefficient of FDI*HUM interaction term is positive but insignificant, indicating that FDI is not conditional on human capital development in South Asia. This finding is in contrast to earlier findings by UNCTAD (1999) and Li and Liu (2005).

In addition to this, we also tested the hypothesis that better infrastructure facilities influence FDI impact on growth. The interaction term FDI*NFRA is included in the regression; the result is presented in column 3 of Table 7.3. As expected, the impact of FDI on economic growth is conditional to better infrastructure facilities since the interaction term is positive and statistically significant. However, the coefficient is very small. The study also tests the validity of the argument presented by Alfaro et al. (2003) that countries with well-developed financial markets gain significantly from FDI. To test this hypothesis, we rerun the regression using the interaction term FDI*Credit. The results, presented in column 4 of Table 7.3, reveal that the interaction term of FDI*Credit has a positive significant effect on economic growth. Thus, we find evidence supporting the argument of Alfaro et al. (2003) that the effect of FDI on growth depends on how well the host country's financial sector functions.

Finally, we test the hypothesis that better and quality institutions are necessary for favourable FDI impact on growth. The quality of host country institutions, in particular the rule of law and the protection of property rights, is an oft-cited example of host country characteristics that determine the growth-enhancing effect of FDI (North 1991; Rodrik 1999). We use the economic freedom index of the Heritage Foundation as a proxy for institution. The result is presented in the last

Table 7.3 FDI and absorptive capacity (GMM system)

Variables	Coefficients	Coefficients	Coefficients	Coefficients	Coefficients
Constant	0.14 (0.76)	1.86**(13.8)	1.80** (14.8)	1.43** (10.3)	1.97** (6.43)
LLF	–	–	–	–	–
LTRADE	0.33** (7.05)	0.63** (7.37)	0.64** (9.31)	0.44**(13.7)	0.08 (0.80)
LHUM	0.10** (3.34)	0.05* (2.06)	0.21** (5.13)	0.24**(9.92)	0.59**(12.81)
LFDI	0.06** (3.15)	0.05* (2.46)	0.02**(2.28)	−0.003 (−1.13)	0.08*(2.68)
LDGCF	0.36* (2.87)	0.16*(2.53)	0.37** (11.56)	0.39**(12.43)	−0.01 (−0.20)
INFRA	0.10** (22.34)	0.08** (33.6)	0.06* (2.41)	0.08** (9.90)	0.09** (14.16)
INF	−003** (−4.9)	−0.005**(−3.05)	−0.005**(−3.94)	−0.005**(−9.37)	−0.007**(−6.56)
FDI*TR	−0.01(−1.22)				
FDI*HUM		0.02 (0.86)			
FDI*INFRA			0.02* (2.24)		
FDI*DBC				0.004**(9.05)	
FDI*GOV					0.49*(2.63)
Arellano–Bond test for AR(1) in F.D.	$z = -3.85$ $Pr > z = 0.000$	$z = -3.85$ $Pr > z = 0.000$	$z = -3.68$ $Pr > z = 0.001$	$z = -3.34$ $Pr > z = 0.00$	$z = -1.51$ $Pr > z = 0.09$
Arellano–Bond test for AR(2) in F.D.	$z = -0.40$ $Pr > z = 0.68$	$z = -0.05$ $Pr > z = 0.96$	$z = -0.58$ $Pr > z = 0.67$	$z = -0.08$ $Pr > z = 0.89$	$z = -0.59$ $Pr > z = 0.55$
Sargan test of overid. restrictions:	$chi^2(80) = 427.84$	$chi^2(80) = 14.7$	$chi^2(83) = 88.84$	$chi^2(80) = 76.57$	$chi^2(26) = 93.4$
GMM instruments for levels:	$Pr > chi^2 = 0.00$	$Pr > chi^2 = 0.77$	$Pr > chi^2 = 0.05$	$Pr > chi^2 = 0.00$	$Pr > chi^2 = 0.00$
Difference-in-Sargan tests of exogeneity of instrument subsets:	$chi^2(52) = 12.79$ $Pr > chi^2 = 0.94$	$chi^2(52) = 21.9$ $Pr > chi^2 = 0.79$	$chi^2(52) = 14.34$ $Pr > chi^2 = 0.78$	$chi^2(52) = 20.74$ $Pr > chi^2 = 0.88$	$chi^2(52) = 90.34$ $Pr > chi^2 = 0.00$
Difference-in-Sargan tests of exogeneity of instrument subsets:	$chi^2(52) = 41.58$ $Pr > chi^2 = 0.00$	$chi^2(52) = 15.80$ $Pr > chi^2 = 0.12$	$chi^2(52) = 1.76$ $Pr > chi^2 = 0.43$	$chi^2(52) = 9.56$ $Pr > chi^2 = 0.03$	$chi^2(52) = 77.34$ $Pr > chi^2 = 0.00$

Notes: *** and ** denotes Significant at 1 and 5 % level, respectively. Figures in the parentheses are *t*-ratio column of Table 7.3. The coefficient of FDI*GOV interaction term is positive and significant, indicating that better institutions positively influence the FDI–growth impact. Therefore, from the above results, it is found that FDI in South Asia is conditional on financial development, better infrastructure facilities, and institutional quality.

7.7 Impact of FDI on China's Growth: A Comparative Analysis

7.7.1 Brief Review of Literature for China

Much of the literature supports the position that inward FDI has played an important role in both China's economy and its fast growth (Tseng and Zebregs 2002; Lemoine 2001; Berthelemy and Demurger 2000; Graham and Wada 2001; Liu 2002; Sun and Parikh 2001; Wei et al. 1999). Zhang (1999) argues that FDI is an important source of saving and an agent of technology transfer in the Chinese economy, in particular the growth of foreign trade, and has spillover effects on domestic industries. Whalley and Xian (2006) examined the contribution of inward FDI to China's recent rapid economic growth over the period 1996–2004. Results of the study suggest that the contribution of FDI to growth may have been large, and that without inward FDI China's growth rate may have been around 3.4 % points lower in the past few years. Yao and Wei (2007) examined the impact of FDI on economic growth for China using the augmented Cobb–Douglas production function framework. Results indicate that output is positively influenced by labour, capital, export, FDI, human capital, and the real foreign exchange rate. The positive impact of FDI operates mainly through technology transfer and capital formation.

Apart from the national level, some studies also paid attention to regional level and found that the effects of FDI vary across regions in China. A study that used panel data across 16 provinces in the eastern and western regions in China over 1986–1992 found a strong effect of FDI on economic growth in the eastern region but a weak effect in the western region, which reinforced interregional inequality (Sun and Chai 1998). Berthelemy and Demurger (2000) use an endogenous growth model to investigate the impact of FDI on economic growth across China's 24 provinces over 1985–1996. They argued that FDI has played a fundamental role in economic growth in China through technology spillover. Zhang (2006) examined FDI-led growth hypothesis for China using province-level data over 1992–2004. Using panel methodology, the study documents that FDI has a favourable effect on economic growth by raising productivity and promoting export. The study also found that FDI has higher marginal productivity than domestic capital. Ljungwall and Li (2007) examined the impact of FDI on economic growth for 28 Chinese provinces over 1986–2003. They found that FDI promotes economic growth conditional on financial development. Liu (2002) investigated empirically whether FDI generates

Table 7.4 Long-run coefficients using ARDL method

	China
Variables	Coefficients
Constant	6.70* (0.49)
LLF	0.14 (1.14)
LTR	0.13** (2.35)
LHUM	0.41* (2.09)
LGCF	0.38** (2.42)
LFDI	0.14* (2.69)
INFRA	0.22* (2.95)
Model selection criteria (AIC)	(1,2,1,1,2,1,1)
Diagnostic test	ADJ. $R^2 = 0.92$, DW. Stat. $= 1.57$, LM $= 1.9$, ARCH $= 1.78$, Reset-0.94 (0.31)

Notes: *** and ** denotes Significant at 1 and 5 % level, respectively. Figures in the parentheses are *t*-ratio

externalities in the form of technology transfer. Using data on 29 manufacturing industries over the period from 1993 to 1998 in the Shenzhen Special Economic Zone of China, the study found that FDI has large and significant spillover effects in that it raises both the level and growth rate of productivity of manufacturing industries, and domestic sectors are the main beneficiaries.

7.7.2 Empirical Results

The augmented Dickey–Fuller (1981) test is used to test for the existence of unit roots and determine the order of integration of the variables. The tests are done both with and without a time trend. Akaike method is used to choose the optimal lag length. The null hypothesis of the series, being non-stationary, is not rejected at the 5 % significance level, but the same null hypothesis is rejected in favour of the alternative at least at the 1 % significance level when first differences of the variables are taken (Table 7.A.5). Therefore, all variables are non-stationary in levels, but stationary at first difference except LF and inflation rate. This implies we have mixture of $I(0)$ and $I(1)$. Hence, the ARDL co-integration method is appropriate for examining a long-run relationship.

Having found the stationary properties of the variables, we examine for the existence of co-integrating relationship. We find a long-run relationship among the variables when real per capital income is the dependent variable because its F-statistic (6.64) exceeds the upper bound critical value (3.5) at the 5 % levels. Thus, the null of non-existence of stable long-run relationship is rejected in favour of co-integration. These results also warrant proceeding to the next stage of estimation—of model (7.2) for China by using the ARDL method. The long-run coefficient of real per capital income is presented in Table 7.4. Maximum lag length is used to derive long-run coefficients is 2 based on AIC criteria. Diagnostic tests are checked to ensure that it is the best model and there is no misspecification bias in the model. The diagnostic tests include the test of serial autocorrelation (LM), heteroscedasticity (ARCH test), and omitted variables/functional form (Ramsey Reset).

Results indicate that among other factors, trade development, gross stock of capital, infrastructure development, and FDI inflows have a significant positive impact on economic growth in China. The impact of LF is found to be positive but insignificant. In terms of relative importance, human capital and gross capital stock have the highest impact on growth followed by infrastructure and FDI. The coefficient of LF—positive but insignificant—indicates that China is a labour-surplus country. The impact of FDI inflows on economic growth is positive but statistically significant at 5 % level. One unit increase in FDI increases economic growth by only 0.14 % in China. This indicates that FDI impact on growth is three times higher in China compared to South Asian countries. Other variables such as inflation rate and financial development are found insignificant and hence dropped from final estimation. Our results are in line with other studies (Whalley and Xian 2006; Yao and Wei 2007) on China.

7.8 Causality Between FDI and Real Per Capita Income

Although there is a plethora of literature on documenting the positive relationship between FDI and economic growth, few studies have acknowledged causality evidence between the two. Even if one accepts the positive association, there is still the question of causality which is vital for designing policy. In literature, the causal relation between FDI and GDP growth can run in either direction. On the one hand, according to the 'FDI-led growth hypothesis', FDI inflows stimulate growth in the host countries by increasing their capital stock, creating new job opportunities, and easing the transfer of technology (UNCTAD 2003a, b; Tang et al. 2008; Anwara and Nguyen 2010). On the other hand, the 'market size hypothesis' predicts that higher GDP growth attracts increased FDI inflows as higher growth creates new investment opportunities in the host country. Thus, a large market size provides more opportunities for sales and also profits to foreign firms and therefore attracts FDI (Chakrabarti 2001; Ramirez 2006). Last but not least, it is also possible that a causal relationship between FDI and economic growth does not exist, supporting the so-called neutrality hypothesis (Carkovic and Levine 2002). Carkovic and Levine (2002) argue that if country-specific factors such as endogeneity of FDI inflows are taken into account, there is no robust impact of FDI on growth. Given the ambiguity in the direction of causality, we conduct a causality test between FDI and per capital income for South Asian countries.

7.8.1 Granger Causality

Following Granger (1969), an economic time series Y_t said to be 'Granger-caused' by another series X_t if the information in the past and present of X_t helps to improve the forecasts of the Y_t variable, i.e. if, MSE $(Y_t/\phi_t) < (Y_t/\phi_t')$ where MSE is the conditional mean square error of the forecast of Y_t, ϕ_t denotes the set of all : (relevant information up to time t), while ϕ_t' excludes the information in the past and present X_t. The conventional Granger causality test involves specifying a bivariate pth order VAR as follows:

$$Y_t = \alpha_0 + \sum_{i=1}^{p} \alpha_i Y_{t-i} + \sum_{j=1}^{p} \beta_j X_{t-j} + u_i \tag{7.3}$$

$$X_t = \mu_0 + \sum_{i=1}^{p-1} \mu_i Y_{t-i} + \sum_{j=1}^{p-1} \gamma_j X_{t-j} + v_t \tag{7.4}$$

where α_0 and μ_0 are constant drifts, u_t and v_t are error terms, and more generally. The equation may include any number of additional relevant variables. Then the null hypothesis the X_t does not Granger-cause Y_t amounts to testing of

$$\beta_1 = \beta_2 \cdots = \beta_k = 0 \tag{7.5}$$

This can be tested by standard methods, such as an F-test. Similarly, the null hypothesis that Y_t does not Granger X_t could be tested by

$$\mu_1 = \mu_2 \cdots = \mu_k = 0 \tag{7.6}$$

The direction of causality is judged as follows:

The result of F-test	Direction of causality
(a) Condition (7.5) holds but (7.6) does not hold:	X_t Causes Y_t $(X_t \rightarrow Y_t)$
(b) Condition (7.5) does not hold but (7.6) holds:	Y_t causes X_t $(Y_t \rightarrow X_t)$
(c) Both (7.5) and (7.6) hold:	Feedback between Y_t and X_t $(Y_t \leftrightarrow X_t)$
(d) Neither (7.5) nor (7.5) hold:	Y_t and X_t are independent

7.8.1.1 Granger Causality: The Vector Error Correction (VECM) Procedure

To ascertain the direction of causality between infrastructure development and output. If all the variables are found to be integrated of same order, Granger causality (Engle and Granger 1987) line can be used to see the direction of causality between output and infrastructure development in India. Since we found both GDP and infrastructure index are integrated of order one {$I(1)$, see Table 7.A.1}, we use vector error correction mechanism for testing the direction of causality. *The general model for Granger causality for (1)* (see Engle and Granger 1987): *variable is given as*

$$\Delta Y_t = \eta + \sum_{i=1}^{p-1} \alpha_i \Delta Y_{t-i} + \sum_{j=1}^{p-1} \beta_j \Delta X_{t-j} + \Theta(Y - \kappa X)_{t-1} + U_t \tag{7.7}$$

$$\Delta X_t = \eta' + \sum_{i=1}^{p-1} \gamma_i \Delta Y_{t-i} + \sum_{j=1}^{p-1} \delta_j \Delta X_{t-j} + \Phi(Y - \kappa X)_{t-1} + U'_t \tag{7.8}$$

where the lagged error correction terms (ECM) $(Y-\kappa X)_{t-1}$ are the lagged residuals from the co-integrating relation between Y and X (this term is not included in case the variables are not co-integrated). As Engle and Granger (1987) have argued, failure to include the ECM term will lead to misspecified models which can lead to erroneous conclusions about the direction of causality. Thus if Y_t and X_t are $I(1)$ and co-integrated, Granger causality tests can be carried out using (7.7) and (7.8). However, there are now two sources of causation of Y_t by X_t, either through the lagged dynamic terms ΔX_t if all the β_{i} are not equal to zero or through the lagged ECM term if θ is non-zero (the latter is also the test of weak exogeneity of Y; see Engle et al. 1983). Similarly, X_t is Granger caused by Y_t either through the lagged dynamic terms ΔX_t if all the γ_{i} are not equal to zero, or through the lagged ECM term if Φ is non-zero. Thus, this procedure has the additional advantage that the source of causation can be identified in the form of either short-run dynamics or disequilibrium adjustment.

7.8.2 Panel Causality Test

The choice of methodologies to test for causality with a panel is not very wide. Most works in this field use vector autoregression (VAR) panel models following the methods proposed by Holtz-Eakin et al. (1988). However, the methods proposed by Holtz-Eakin et al. (1988) ignore the potential heterogeneity of the individual cross sections.

Our methodology is an adaptation of the Granger causality panel data approach with fixed coefficient, proposed by Hurlin and Venet (2003) and Hurlin and Venet (2008) which addresses the problem of heterogeneity. To test for causality between per capita income and FDI. We first consider the following equations:

$$\ln \text{ LPCI}_{it} = \alpha_i + \sum_{k=1}^{K} \gamma_i^{(k)} \ln \text{ LPCI}_{it-k} + \sum_{k=1}^{K} \beta\text{i}^{(k)} \ln \text{ LFDI}_{it} - k + \varepsilon_{it}, \tag{7.9}$$

$$i = 1, \ldots, N, \ t = 1, \ldots, T,$$

$$\ln\ \mathrm{LFDI}_{it} = \delta_i + \sum_{k=1}^{K} \lambda_i{}^{(k)} \ln\ \mathrm{LPCI}_{it-k} + \sum_{k=1}^{K} \psi_i{}^{(k)} \ln\ \mathrm{LFDI}_{it-k} + \nu_{it}, \tag{7.10}$$

$$i = 1,\ldots,N,\ t = 1,\ldots,T,$$

Individual effects α_i and δ_i are assumed to be fixed; K is the lag order and assumed identical for all cross-sectional units of the panel. The autoregressive parameters $\gamma_i{}^{(k)}$ and regression coefficients slopes $\beta_i{}^{(k)}$ in Eq. (7.9) and autoregressive parameters $\lambda_i^{(k)}$ and regression coefficients slopes $\psi_i{}^{(k)}$ in Eq. (7.10) differ across series. Since the coefficients (autoregressive parameters and regression coefficients slopes) differ across countries, the test allows for heterogeneity among individual countries. We examine for Granger non-causality from FDI to PCI by testing the null hypothesis,

$$H_0 :\ \beta_i = 0 \quad \text{for all} \quad i = 1,\ldots,N,$$

tested against the alternative

$$H_a :\ \beta_i \neq 0 \text{ for some } i \in \{1,\ldots,N,\},$$

where $\beta_i \equiv [\beta_i^{(1)},\ldots,\beta_i^{(k)}]'$. Here the null hypothesis is a homogeneous non-causality hypothesis, while the alternative which 'allows for the causality from FDI to PCI for some but not all individuals' is a heterogeneous non-causality. Similarly, to examine for Granger non-causality from PCI to FDI, we test the null hypothesis (7.10),

$$H_0 : \lambda_i = 0 \quad \text{for all} \quad i = 1,\ldots,N,$$

against the alternative

$$H_a :\ \lambda_i \neq 0 \quad \text{for some} \quad i \in \{1,\ldots,N,\}$$

The Hurlin and Venet (2008) test proceeds in two steps. In the first step, we estimate the regression Eqs. (7.9) for each country i and compute the Wald statistic for the null hypothesis that $\beta_i{}^{(1)} = \ldots = \beta_i{}^{(k)} = 0$, denoted $W_{i,T}$. Then, in the second step, we compute the average of the Wald statistics from the previous step:

$$W_{N,T}^{\mathrm{HNC}} = \frac{1}{N} \sum_{i=1}^{N} W_{i,T} \tag{7.11}$$

As shown by Hurlin and Venet (2008), the average Wald statistic $W_{N,T}^{\mathrm{HNC}}$ sequentially converges (i.e. $T \to \infty$ first and then $N \to \infty$) in distribution. More specifically,

$$Z_{N,T}^{\mathrm{HNC}} = \sqrt{\frac{N}{2K}}\left(W_{N,T}^{\mathrm{HNC}} - K\right) \xrightarrow{d} N(0,1) \qquad (7.12)$$

If T is small, the last asymptotic result does not hold. Nevertheless, Hurlin and Venet (2008) shows that for small samples, $T > 5 + 2K$, we can write

$$\tilde{Z}_{N,T}^{\mathrm{HNC}} = \sqrt{\frac{N}{2K} \times \frac{T-2K-5}{T-K-3}}\left[\frac{T-2K-3}{T-2K-1} W_{N,T}^{\mathrm{HNC}} - K\right] \xrightarrow{d} N(0,1) \qquad (7.13)$$

The statistic $\tilde{Z}_{N,T}^{\mathrm{HNC}}$ follows the same distribution as the standardised average Wald statistic $Z_{N,T}^{\mathrm{HNC}}$ as $N \to \infty$. The Hurlin tests require that $T > 5 + 2K$. In other words, a country must have at least $6 + 2K$ consecutive observations to be selected for inclusion in the sample. As such, the sample size depends on the selection of K. A greater K will shorten the distance between T and $6 + 2K$ and thus lead to an inaccurate approximation of finite sample moments of the test statistic $\tilde{Z}_{N,T}^{\mathrm{HNC}}$. Hurlin and Venet (2008) shows that if N and T are fixed, the average statistic $W_{N,T}^{\mathrm{HNC}}$ and the standardised statistic $\tilde{Z}_{N,T}^{\mathrm{HNC}}$ do not converge to standard distributions under the HNC hypothesis and accordingly Hurlin and Venet (2008) computed exact sample critical values for finite N and T. For each test, two statistics are calculated and reported: the standardised statistic $Z_{N,T}^{\mathrm{HNC}}$ based on the asymptotic moments and the standardised $\tilde{Z}_{N,T}^{\mathrm{HNC}}$ based on the approximation of the finite sample moments.

Since real FDI and real per capita income are found $I(1)$ except for Sri Lanka, we carry out the causality analysis in the error correction framework. For Sri Lanka, since both are $I(0)$ series, we conduct a simple Granger causality. The presence of co-integration relationship between the variables suggests that there exists a causal relationship between exports and GDP at least in one direction and possibly in both directions (Engle and Granger 1987). The result of VECM causality test is presented in Table 7.5. It is clear that the null hypothesis of no causality from FDI growth to per capita income growth is rejected by the lagged ECM term (the long-term causality), in favour of FDI-led growth in India. On the other hand, we find weak causality in the opposite direction (growth to FDIY) only through dynamic terms ΔPCI. Therefore, we find the evidence of one-way causality from FDI to income growth for India. On the other hand, we find two-way causality between FDI growth per capita income growth for Pakistan, Bangladesh, and Nepal. In the case of Pakistan and Nepal, causality from FDI to income is significant only at 10 % level. The causality result for Sri Lanka is presented in Table 7.6. It is clear that in the case of Sri Lanka, there is one-way causality from FDI to income and not the vice versa.

In addition to time series causality, panel causality is also conducted by using Hurlin and Venet (2008). Results are presented in Table 7.7. Results indicate that when lag one is selected, null of no causality from FDI to per capita income is rejected at 5 % level. Similar causality results are also found at lag 2. However,

Table 7.5 Causality between FDIY and LPCI using VECM approach

Dependent variable	$\sum_{j=1}^{p} \Delta \ln \mathrm{PCI}_{t-j}$ $\sum \beta_i = 0$: F-stat (p-value)	$\sum_{j=1}^{p} \Delta \ln \mathrm{FDI}$ $\sum \beta_i = 0$: F-stat (p-value)	Lagged ECM term $\Theta = 0$: t-stat (p-value)
India			
$\Delta\ell$nLPCI		0.41 (0.62)	−2.06* (0.04)
$\Delta\ell$nLFDI	3.24# (0.06)		−1.15 (0.15)
Pakistan			
$\Delta\ell$nLPCI		0.78 (0.50)	−1.64# (0.08)
$\Delta\ell$nLFDI	1.12 (0.25)		−3.17** (0.00)
Bangladesh			
$\Delta\ell$nLPCI		2.78 (0.14)	−1.97** (0.04)
$\Delta\ell$nLFDI	0.87 (0.43)		−3.18** (0.00)
Nepal			
$\Delta\ell$nLPCI		3.73# (0.07)	−1.65# (0.08)
$\Delta\ell$nLFDI	0.67 (0.51)		−1.84# (0.06)

**Denotes significance a 1 % level
*Denotes significance a 5 % and # at 10 % level. Optimal lag length is selected on the basis of Akaike Information Criteria (AIC)

Table 7.6 Granger causality between FDIY and LPCI for Sri Lanka

Null hypothesis	Optimal lag	$\sum \beta_i = 0$: F-statistic	(p-value)
LFDI → growth	3(AIC)	5.62*	0.02
growth → LFDI	2(AIC)	0.19	0.66

*Denotes rejection of null hypothesis at 10 % level

Table 7.7 Panel causality test between LPCI and FDIY

Direction of causality		$k = 1$	$k = 2$	$k = 3$
LFDI → LPCI	Z_{HNC}	2.86*	2.74*	1.67#
	$\tilde{Z}_{\mathrm{HNC}}$	2.57*	2.39*	1.16
LPCI → LFDI	Z_{HNC}	3.43*	2.65*	1.42
	$\tilde{Z}_{\mathrm{HNC}}$	2.26*	2.44*	1.27

Notes: * and # denote rejection of null hypothesis of no causality at 5 and 10 % level

when lag 3 is selected, null of no causality from FDIY to GFC is rejected at 10 % level. On the other hand, causality from per capita income to FDI is found only at lag 1 and 2. At lag 3; the causality evidence is absent. Therefore, panel causality test supports bidirectional hypothesis between FDI and real per capita income. This indicates that higher FDI inflows will stimulate economic growth in South Asia and higher economic growth also in turn leads to higher FDI inflows.

7.9 Summary and Conclusion

In this chapter, we have tried to assess the impact of FDI on the economic growth of South Asia using both time series and panel data analysis and annual data over 1980–2010. Five major South Asian countries—India, Pakistan, Sri Lanka, Bangladesh, and Nepal—were chosen as their economic structure, growth patterns, and policy approaches towards FDI are similar. The empirical literature suggests that economic growth is significantly affected by LF, trade openness and exports (TRADE), human capital (HUM), infrastructure development (INFRA), financial sector development (DBC), quality of institutions (GOV), macroeconomic instability (INF), and productivity of investment (GCF). In other words, these factors help us test the absorption hypothesis that the growth impact of FDI in any country is conditioned on the overall health of that country's economy as indicated by these variables.

First, unit root was tested by assuming no trend, only intercept and then by assuming trend in the variable. The test indicates the presence of a mixture of $I(0)$ and $I(1)$ variables. Thus, the ARDL procedure for co-integration resulted in the presence of a long-term stable relation between the variables when real per capita income is the dependent variable.

The long-run coefficients of real per capita income were estimated using the ARDL model for all five countries. The results indicate that the coefficient of FDI is small but positive and significant for all countries except Nepal (where the coefficient was negative). The FDI coefficient is highest in the case of India—0.05—indicating one unit increase in FDI, leading to a 0.05 % increase in economic growth, followed by Sri Lanka (0.04), Pakistan (0.03), and Bangladesh (0.008). This could be because India receives the most FDI in South Asia. Trade development, capital formation, infrastructure development, financial development, and FDI inflow have a significant positive impact on economic growth in India, which indicates that its capacity to absorb FDI is good, and that it has a favourable environment for FDI to have a positive impact on the economy's growth. The impact of macroeconomic stability has been found negative, as expected, and statistically insignificant. Thus, its impact on India's economic growth is negligible, and, therefore, it provides FDI an environment to flourish. The results for Sri Lanka and Bangladesh are similar to that of India. The impact of macroeconomic instability is significant in Pakistan, where political instability is high. These factors lower the impact of FDI on its economic growth. Similarly, in Nepal, which receives the least FDI in South Asia and suffers from high political instability, FDI has a very small, negative impact on economic growth.

Thus, a country must have a sound economy for FDI to positively, substantially impact growth. This result confirms the results of the existing literature—positive spillovers from FDI depend on the absorptive capacity of a country, i.e. on the existence of various local conditions favourable to economic growth (Borensztein et al. 1998; Alfaro et al. 2003; Edison et al. 2002; Durham 2004).

Our panel data analysis found a long-term stable relationship between real per capita income and its determinants as indicated by the Westerlund error correction panel co-integration test. The null hypothesis, that there exists no co-integration, was rejected by P_t in favour of the existence of co-integration at 5 % level of confidence. The long-run coefficients of growth have been derived using both FMOLS and GMM system methodology to overcome possible endogeneity problems, which could arise because the stochastic process governing growth rates may be influencing FDI. The results of these tests confirm that FDI has a positive impact on the economic growth in our sample of five countries. In addition, it also supports our absorption hypothesis that other associated factors such as LF, human capital development, trade, infrastructure stock, and inflation rate also affect economic growth significantly. The coefficient of inflation rate indicating macroeconomic stability is statistically significant and has a negative sign as assumed, thus reflecting a negative impact on economic growth. The coefficient of human capital, trade openness, and gross capital formation as a ratio of GDP are significant and positive. Thus, the findings of the previous studies have been substantiated by the fact that FDI favours countries that follow a trade-led growth strategy and have better investment environment and an educated population.

We also presented a comparative analysis by estimating the impact of FDI on China's economy. Again, the ARDL co-integration test confirms the presence of a long-term stable relation between variables when real per capita income is the dependent variable. We then estimated the long-term coefficients of the variables using the ARDL method, as was done earlier. The coefficient of FDI has been found to be positive and statistically significant at 5 % level. Apparently, FDI's impact on China's economic growth is three times that of South Asia. This could be because 8.1 % of the global FDI inflow in 2010 went to China but only 2.4 % to South Asia. In addition, macroeconomic instability as reflected by the inflation rate, which was statistically significant in South Asia, was statistically insignificant in China; this was a factor of its economic growth and reflects a better environment for FDI. Also, human capital, gross capital formation, and infrastructure development positively significantly affect China's growth and provide FDI a supportive environment.

Thus, overall, the above results confirm that the impact of FDI on a country's economic growth is determined by trade openness, human capital, gross capital formation, financial development, infrastructure development, and LF. This is true of all countries, as confirmed above by South Asian countries and China. However, the importance of these factors may vary from country to country depending upon the overall economic performance. The 1980–2010 period is of importance as large sums of FDI flowed into South Asian countries after these opened up trade and changed trade and investment policy.

To augment economic growth, South Asian governments should identify the factors of a positive relationship with FDI and emphasise these. They should also identify the factors that negatively impact FDI and correct these. A politically stable region with strong macroeconomic fundamentals would attract huge sums of FDI and positively impact growth; political instability would set it back. Also, countries should cooperate with each other to project the region as an attractive FDI destination instead of competing with each other and projecting each individual country. Increasing intra-regional trade in South Asia and promoting peace and security will make it the most attractive FDI destination in the world.

Appendix

Table 7.A.1 Unit root test for using ADF test

Variables	At level with constant	Optimal lag	At level with constant and trend	Optimal lag	At first difference with constant	Optimal lag	Order of integration
India							
LPCI	2.68	2	−0.25	2	−3.36[a]	0	*I*(1)
LLF	1.34	1	0.56	1	−3.67[a]	1	*I*(1)
LHUM	−1.33	3	−3.36	2	−4.79[a]	1	*I*(1)
LFDI	−3.93[a]	1					*I*(0)
LGCF	0.51	3	−1.63	3	−4.12[a]		*I*(1)
LDBC	1.47	1	−0.24	1	−3.19	1	*I*(1)
LTRADE	0.99	3	−2.72	2			
Pakistan							
LPCI	2.68	2	−0.25	2	−3.36[a]	0	*I*(1)
LF	1.91	3	−0.81	2	−3.86[a]	0	*I*(1)
LHUM	−1.27	1	−1.54	1	−5.97[a]	0	*I*(1)
LFDI	−1.96	3	−2.14	1	−4.59[a]	1	*I*(1)
LGCF	−1.42	0	−1.54	0	−412[a]	0	*I*(1)
LDBC	−1.04	3	−2.31	2	−3.89[a]	1	*I*(1)
LTRADE	−1.49	3	−2.20	2	−3.98[a]	0	*I*(1)
Sri Lanka							
LPCI	1.75	3	−1.11	3	−3.78[a]	0	*I*(1)
LF	−1.25	1	−0.95	3	−3.29[a]	3	*I*(1)
LHUM	−1.56	1	−2.54	2	−5.65[a]	0	*I*(1)
LFDI	−0.32	1	−4.10[a]	1			*I*(0)
LGCF	0.61	2	−2.51	2	−3.14[a]	0	*I*(1)
LDBC	0.22	3	−2.54	3	−4.87[a]	1	*I*(1)
LTRADE	−1.52	3	−0.88	3	−4.65[a]	1	*I*(1)
Bangladesh							
LPCI	4.12	1	2.35	1	−3.25[a]	1	*I*(1)
LF	−5.45[a]	0					*I*(0)
LHUM	−2.02	1	−1.73	2	−4.08[a]	0	*I*(1)
LFDI	−1.34	1	−2.86	1	3.54[a]	1	*I*(1)
LGCF	0.91	3	−2.81	3	−4.52[a]	0	*I*(1)
LDBC	0.77	2	−1.32	3	−3.63[a]	0	*I*(1)
LTRADE	0.63	2	−4.10[a]				*I*(0)
Nepal							
LPCI	0.54	2	−2.40	1	−4.02[a]	1	*I*(1)
LF	0.92	2	−2.01	2	−3.21[a]	0	*I*(1)
LHUM	−1.60	1	−3.46	2	−3.92[a]	0	*I*(1)
LFDI	−1.71	1	−2.09	2	4.10[a]	1	*I*(1)
LGCF	−1.89	2	−1.36	3	−5.12[a]	0	*I*(1)
LDBC	0.48	3	−2.52	2	5.45[a]	0	*I*(1)
LTRADE	−1.46	3	−1.18	2	−4.74[a]	1	I(1)

[a]Denotes rejection of null of unit root

Table 7.A.2 ARDL co-integration test (1980–2010)

Country	Dependent variable	*F*-stat	5 % critical value[a]	Result
India	LPCI	638[b]	3.50	Rejection of null of no co-integration
Pakistan	LPCI	7.68[b]	3.50	Rejection of null of no co-integration
Sri Lanka	LPCI	5.22[b]	3.50	Rejection of null of no co-integration
Bangladesh	LPCI	5.73[b]	3.50	Rejection of null of no co-integration
Nepal	LPCI	6.21[b]	3.50	Rejection of null of no co-integration

Notes: The order of ARDL is selected on the basis of AIC
[a]Denotes upper bound critical values with seven independent variables
[b]Denotes rejection of null hypothesis of no co-integration in favour of co-integration

Table 7.A.3 Panel unit root test using Pesaran (2007)

	At level		First difference	
Variables	Constant	Constant and trend	Constant	Conclusion
LPCI	−1.67	−1.95	−3.51*	*I*(1)
LF	−1.03	−2.00	−2.99*	*I*(1)
LTRADE	−1.16	−1.29	−3.14*	*I*(1)
LFDI	−2.12	−3.18*		*I*(0)
LGFC	−1.86	−1.83	−4.23*	*I*(1)
LDBC	−2.48*			*I*(0)
LHUM	−1.15	−2.21	−3.06*	*I*(1)
INF	−3.42*			*I*(0)
LGOV	−1.00	−1.34	−2.53*	*I*(1)

Notes: The null hypothesis is that the panel has a unit root. Critical values are tabulated by Pesaran (2007). In Table II (a–c), we report the ones for $T = 30$ and $N = 10$
'**' and '*' indicate significance of the test at 1 and 5 % level, respectively

Table 7.A.4 Westerlund (2007) error correction model panel co-integration tests

	Dependent variable LPCI	
Dependent variable LPCI	Value	*P*-value
Gt	−4.18*	0.02
Ga	−6.17	0.77
Pt	−7.17*	0.04
Pa	−6.75*	0.05

Notes: The Westerlund (2007) tests assume no co-integration as the null. The test regression is fitted with constant and one lag and lead
*Denotes rejection of null of unit root at 5 % level

Table 7.A.5 Unit root test using ADF

	At level		First difference	
Variables	Constant	Constant and trend	Constant	Conclusion
LPCI	0.85	−1.32	−5.12*	*I*(1)
LLF	−9.12*			*I*(0)
LFDI	−2.19	−1.19	−4.32*	*I*(1)
LGFC	−0.09	−1.98	−4.23*	*I*(1)
LTRADE	−1.01	−2.78	−5.84*	*I*(1)
LHUM	−0.68	−2.33	−3.87*	*I*(1)
INF	−3.54*			*I*(0)
Infra	1.34	−1.38	−3.57*	*I*(1)

* denotes rejection of null of Unit Root at 5 % level

References

Aggarwal A (2005) The influence of labour markets on FDI: some empirical explorations in export oriented and domestic market seeking FDI across Indian States, University of Delhi, Delhi. http://knowledgeforum.tifac.org.in/IndexServer/tifac.article/22.doc

Agrawal P (2000) Economic impact of foreign direct investment in South Asia. Indira Gandhi Institute of Development Research, Mumbai

Ahamad, MG, Tanin F, Uddin Z (2010) Does FDI intensify Economic Growth? Empirics from Bangladesh? MPRA paper no. 21022. Munich

Alfaro L (2003) FDI and growth: does the sector matter? Working paper, Harvard Business School, Boston

Alfaro L, Areendam C, Kalemli-Ozcan S, Selin S (2003) FDI and economic growth: the role of local financial markets. J Int Econ 61(1):512–533

Alfaro L, Chanda A, Kalemli-Ozcan S, Sayek S (2004) FDI and economic growth: the role of local financial markets. J Int Econ 64:113–134

Anwara S, Nguyen L (2010) FDI and economic growth in Vietnam. Asia Pac Bus Rev 16(1–2):183–202

Apergis N, Lyroudia K, Vamvakidis A (2007) The relationship between foreign direct investment and economic growth: evidence from transitional countries, Working paper SSRN no. 990251. New York

Aschauer DA (1989) Is public expenditure productive? J Monet Econ 23:177–200

Aykut D, Sayek S (2007) The role of the sectoral composition of FDI on growth. In: Piscitello L, Santangelo GD (eds) Do multinationals feed local development and growth? Elsevier, Amsterdam

Baharumshah AZ, Thanoon MAM (2006) Foreign capital flows and economic growth in East Asian countries. China Econ Rev 17:70–83

Bajpai N, Sachs JD (2000) FDI in India: issues and problems. Harvard Institute of International 1029 Development

Balamurali N, Bogahawatte C (2004) FDI and economic growth in Sri Lanka. Sri Lankan J Agric Econ 6:37–50

Balasubramanyam VN, Salisu MA, Sapsford D (1996) Foreign direct investment and growth in EP and IS countries. Econ J 106(434):92–105

Balasubramanyam VN, Salisu M, Sapsford D (1999) FDI as an engine of growth. J Int Trade Econ Dev 8(1):27–40

Barro RJ (1991) Economic growth in a cross-section of countries. Q J Econ 106(2):407–443

Barro R, Martin SI (1995) Economic growth. MIT Press, Cambridge

Barro RJ, Sala-i-Martin X (1990) Economic growth and convergence across the United States, Working paper 3419, Cambridge, MA

Bencivenga V, Smith BD (1991) Financial intermediation and endogenous growth. Rev Econ Stud 58:195–209
Bengoa M, Sanchez-Robles B (2003) FDI, economic freedom and growth: new evidence from Latin America. Eur J Polit Econ 19(3):529–545
Bergman A (2006) FDI and spillover effects in the Indian pharmaceutical industry. School of Economics and Management, Department of Economics, Master's thesis. Lunds Universitet
Berthelemy JC, Demurger S (2000) FDI and economic growth: theory and applications to China. Rev Dev Econ 4(2):140–155
Bhagwati J (1978) Anatomy and consequences of exchange control regimes. Balinger Publishing, New York
Bhagwati JN (1988) Export-promoting trade strategy: issues and evidence. World Bank Res Obs 125:27–57
Bhat KS, Sundari TCU, Raj KD (2004) Causal nexus between FDI and economic growth in India. Indian J Econ 85(337):171–185
Blomström M, Kokko A, Zejan M (1992) Host country competition and technology transfer by multinationals, Working paper no. 4131. NBER, Cambridge, MA
Blomström M, Lipsey RE, Zejan M (1994) What explains growth in developing countries? NBER discussion paper No. 1924, Cambridge, MA
Blomström M, Lipsey R, Zejan M (1996) Is fixed investment the key to economic growth? Q J Econ 111(1):269–276
Borensztein E, Gregorio J, Lee J (1995) How does FDI affect economic growth? J Int Econ 45(1):115–135
Borensztein E, Gregorio JD, Lee JW (1998) How does foreign direct investment affect economic growth? J Int Econ 45:115–135
Campos N, Kinoshita Y (2002a) Foreign direct investment as technology transferred: internalization theory. Bull Econ Res 38(2):101–118
Campos N, Kinoshita Y (2002b) FDI as technology transferred: some panel evidence from the transition countries. Manch Sch 70(3):398–419
Canning D, Pedroni P (2004) The effect of infrastructure on long run economic growth. Harvard University, Mimeo, Williamstown
Carkovic M, Levine R (2002) Does FDI accelerate economic growth? Working paper, University of Minnesota Department of Finance. Available at: www.ssrn.com/abstract=314924
Chakrabarti A (2001) The determinants of foreign direct investment: sensitivity analysis of cross-country regressions. Kyklos 54:89–114
Chakraborty C, Basu P (2002) FDI and growth in India: a cointegration approach. Appl Econ 34(9):1061–1073
Chakraborty C, Nunnenkamp P (2008) Economic reforms, FDI, and economic growth in India: a sector level analysis. World Dev 36(7):1192–1212
Dash RK, Parida PC (2012) Services trade and economic growth in India: an analysis in the post-reform period. Int J Econ Bus Res 4(3):326–345
De Gregorio J (1992) Economic growth in Latin America. J Dev Econ 39:58–84
De Mello LR (1997) Foreign direct investment in developing countries and growth: a selective survey. J Dev Stud 34(1):1–34
De Mello LR (1999) Foreign domestic investment-Led growth: evidence from time series and panel data. Oxford Econ Pap 51:133–151
Dees S (1998) FDI in China: determinants and effects. Econ Plan 31:175–194
Dickey DA, Fuller WA (1981) Likelihood ratio statistics for autoregressive time series with a unit root. Econom: J Econom Soc, 1057–1072
Domar E (1946) Capital expansion, rate of growth and employment. Econometrica 14:137–147
Dua P, Rasid AI (1998) FDI and economic activity in India. Indian Econ Rev 33(2):153–168
Durham JB (2004) Absorptive capacity and the effects of FDI and equity foreign portfolio investment on economic growth. Eur Econ Rev 48(2):285–306

Edison H, Klein M, Ricci L, Sløk T (2002) Capital account liberalization and economic performance: survey and synthesis. IMF Mimeo, International Monetary Fund, Washington, DC

Edwards S (1998) Capital flows, real exchange rates and capital controls: some Latin American experiences, NBER working paper 6000, National Bureau of Economic Research, Cambridge, MA. Also in author's web page: http://www.anderson.ucla.edu/faculty/sebastian.edwards/

Enderwick P (2005) Attracting "desirable" FDI: theory and evidence. Transnatl Corp 14(2):93–119

Engle RF, Granger CW (1987) Cointegration and error correction: representation, estimation and testing. Econometrica 55:251–276

Engle RF, Hendry DF, Richard JF (1983) Exogeneity. Econometrica 51:277–304

Fischer S (1993) The role of macroeconomic factors in growth. J Monet Econ 32:485–512

Frankel J, Romer D (1999) Does trade cause growth? Am Econ Rev 89(3):379–399

Fry MJ (1992) Foreign direct investment in a macroeconomic framework: finance, efficiency, incentives and distortions, PRE working paper. The World Bank, Washington, DC

Graham EM, Wada E (2001) FDI in China: effects on growth and economic performance. In: Drysdale P (ed) Achieving high growth: experience of transition economies in East Asia. Oxford University Press, Oxford

Granger CWJ (1969) Investigating causal relation by econometric and cross-sectional method. Econometrica 37:424–438

Greenwood J, Jovanvoic B (1990) Financial development, growth, and the distribution of income. J Polit Econ 98(5):1076–1107

Griffin KB (1970) Foreign capital, domestic savings and development. Oxford Bull Econ Stat 32(2):99–112

Grossman G, Helpman E (1990) Innovation and growth in the global economy. MIT Press, Cambridge, MA

Grossman G, Helpman E (1991) Trade, knowledge spillovers, and growth. Eur Econ Rev 36:237–267

Gunther J (2002) FDI as a multiplier of modern technology in Hungarian industry. Intereconomics: Rev Eur Econ Pol 37(5):263–269

Harrison A (1996) Determinants and consequences of foreign investment in three developing countries. In: Roberts M, Tybout J (eds) Industrial evolution in developing countries: micro patterns of turnover, productivity, and market structure. Oxford University Press, Oxford

Harrod RF (1939) An essay in dynamic theory. Econ J 49:14–33

Hermes N, Lensink R (2000) Foreign direct investment, financial development and economic growth, SOM research report 00E27, University of Groningen, Groningen

Hermes N, Lensink R (2003) FDI, financial development and economic growth. J Dev Stud 40:142–163

Holtz-Eakin D, Newey W, Rosen H (1988) Estimating vector autoregressions with panel data. Econometrica 56(6):1371–1395

Hooi LH, Wah TB (2010) Linkages between FDI, DI and economic growth in Malaysia. Prosiding Perkem 2:48–57

Hurlin C, Venet B (2003) Granger causality tests in panel data models with fixed coefficients. Mimeograph, Universitie Paris I, Paris

Hurlin C, Venet B (2008) Financial development and growth: a re-examination using a panel Granger causality test, Working paper. Laboratoired' EconomieD'Orleans, University of Orleans, Orleans

Javorcik BS (2004) Does foreign direct investment increase the productivity of domestic firms? In search of spillovers through backward linkages'. Am Econ Rev 94(3):605–627

Jayachandran G, Seilan A (2010) A causal relationship between trade, FDI and economic growth for India. J Finance Econ 42:74–88

Johnson A (2006) FDI inflows to the transition economies in Eastern Europe: magnitude and determinants, CESIS working paper no. 59, Stockholm

Kaufmann D, Kraay A, Zoido P (2002) Governance matters II: updated indicators for 2000–01. World Bank policy research working paper, No. 2772, Washington, DC
Kinda T (2007) Increasing private capital flows to developing countries: the role of physical and financial infrastructure, MPRA paper no. 19163, Munich
King RG, Levine R (1993) Finance and growth: Schumpeter might be right. Q J Econ 108 (3):717–737
Kokko A (1996) Productivity spillovers from competition between local firms and foreign affiliates. J Int Dev 8(4):517–530
Kokko A, Blomström M (1995) Policies to encourage inflows of technology through foreign multinationals. World Dev 23:459–468
Kose MA, Prasad ES, Taylor AD (2009) Thresholds in the process of financial integration, NBER working paper no. 14916. National Bureau of Economic Research, Cambridge, MA
Kotrajaras P (2010) Foreign direct investment and economic growth: a comparative study among East Asian countries. Appl Econ J 17(2):12–26
Krueger AO (1975) Foreign trade regimes and economic development: Turkey. National Bureau of Economic Research, New York, pp 271–339
Krueger AO (1997) Trade policy and economic development: how we learn. Am Econ Rev 87(1):1–22
Kumar N (1996) Foreign direct investment and technology transfer in development: a perspective on recent literature. UNI/INTECH discussion papers, no. 9606, UNI/INTECH, Maastricht
Kumar N, Pradhan JP (2002) Foreign direct investment, externalities and economic growth in developing countries: Some empirical explorations and implications for WTO negotiations on investment, RIS discussion paper, no.27. Research and Information System for the Non-Aligned and Other Developing Countries, New Delhi
Lemoine F (2001) FDI and the opening up of China's economy, CEPII working paper, number 2000–11. Centre d'études prospectives et d'informations internationales, Paris
Lensink R, Morrissey O (2001a) FDI: flows, volatility and growth in developing countries, SOM research report 01E16. SOM Research School, University of Groningen, Groningen
Lensink R, Morrissey O (2001b) FDI: flows, volatility and growth in developing countries, Research report no. 01.16. Graduate School Research Institute Systems, Organisations, and Management, Groningen
Li X, Liu X (2005) FDI and economic growth: an increasingly endogenous relationship. World Dev 33(3):393–407
Lipsey RE (1999) The location and characteristics of U.S. Affiliates in Asia, NBER working papers, no.6876. National Bureau of Economic Research, Cambridge, MA
Liu Z (2002) FDI and technology spillover: evidence from China. J Comp Econ 30:579–602
Ljungwall C, Li J (2007) Financial sector development, FDI and economic growth in China, Centre for Economic Research (CCER), Perking University. Working paper series, No. E2007005, Beijing
Lucas REJ (1988) On the mechanics of economic development. J Monet Econ 22:3–42
Mankiw NG, Romer D, Weil DN (1992) A contribution to the empirics of economic growth. Q J Econ 107:407–437
Markusen JR (1995) The boundaries of multinational enterprises and the theory of international trade. J Econ Perspect 9(2):169–189
Markusen JR (2002) Multinational firms and the theory of international trade. The MIT Press, Cambridge, MA/London
Mencinger J (2003) Does FDI always enhance economic growth? Kyklos 56(4):493–510
Nadia D, Merih U (2011) Does the worldwide shift of FDI from manufacturing to services accelerate economic growth? A GMM estimation study. J Int Money Finance 30(3):410–427
North D (1991) Institutions, institutional change and economic development. Cambridge University Press, Cambridge

Nyatepe-Coo A (1998) FDI and economic growth in selected LDCs, 1963–1992, Handbook on the globalization of the world economy Chapter 4 edited by Amnon Levy-Livermore, Edward Elgar Publishing Inc., Northampton, pp 87–100
OECD (2002) Foreign direct investment for development: maximising benefits, Minimising costs. OECD, Paris
Olofsdotter K (1998) Foreign direct investment, country capabilities and economic growth. Rev World Econ 134(3):534–547
Pesaran M (2007) A simple panel unit root test in the presence of cross-section dependence. J Appl Econom 22:265–312
Pradhan JP (2002) Foreign direct investment and economic growth in India: a production function analysis. Indian J Econ 82(327):582–586
Prüfer P, Tondl G (2008) The FDI-Growth Nexus in Latin America: the role of source countries and local conditions. Discussion Paper 2008–61, Tilburg
Ramirez MD (2006) Economic and institutional determinants of foreign direct investment in Chile: a time series analysis1960-2001. Contemp Econ Pol 24:459–471
Rebelo S (1991) Long run policy analysis and long run growth. J Polit Econ 99:500–521
Rodriguez-Clare A (1996) Multinationals, linkages, and economic development. Am Econ Rev 86:852–873
Rodrik D (1999) The new global economy and developing countries: making openness work policy essay 24. Overseas Development Council Johns Hopkins University Press, Washington, DC
Roller L-H, Waverman L (2001) Telecommunications infrastructure and economic development: a simultaneous approach. Am Econ Rev 91(4):878–909
Romer P (1986) Increasing returns and long term growth. J Polit Econ 94:1002–1037
Romer PM (1991) Increasing returns and new developments in the theory of growth. In: Barnett WA, Cornet B, d'Aspremont (eds) Equilibrium theory and applications. Cambridge University Press, Cambridge
Romer P (1994) New goods, old theory, and the welfare costs of trade restrictions. J Dev Econ 43:5–38
Sahoo P (2006) FDI in south Asia: trends, policy, impact and determinants, Asian development bank institute discussion paper series, no.56. Asian Development Bank Institute, Tokyo
Sahoo P (2012) Determinants of FDI in south Asia: role of infrastructure, trade openness and reforms. J World Invest Trade 13(2):256–278, Geneva, Switzerland
Sahoo P, Dash RK (2012) Economic growth in south Asia: role of infrastructure. J IntTrade Econ Dev Int Comp Rev 21(2):217–252
Sahoo D, Mathiyazhagan MK (2003) Economic growth in India: does FDI inflow matter? Singap Econ Rev 48:151–171
Saltz I (1992) The negative correlation between FDI and economic growth in the third world: theory and evidence. Rivista Internazionale di Scienze Economiche e Commerciali 39:617–633
Shahbaz M, Rehman MM (2010) Foreign capital inflows-growth nexus and role of domestic financial sector: an ARDL cointegration approach for Pakistan. J Econ Res 35:207–231
Shahbaz M, Ahmad K, Chaudhary AR (2008) Economic growth and its determinants in Pakistan. Pak Dev Rev 47:471–486
Shan J (2002) A VAR approach to the economics of FDI in China. Appl Econ 34:885–893
Singer H (1950) The distributions of gains between investing and borrowing countries. Am Econ Rev 40:473–485
SjoKholm F (1999) Productivity growth in Indonesia: the role of regional characteristics and direct foreign investment. Econ Dev Cult Chang 47(3):559–584
Solow R (1956) A contribution to the theory of economic growth. Q J Econ 70:65–94
Sun H, Chai J (1998) Direct foreign investment and inter-regional economic disparity in China. Int J Soc Econ 25:424–447

Sun HS, Parikh A (2001) Exports, inward FDI, and regional economic growth in China. Reg Stud 35(3):187–196
Tang S, Selvanathan EA, Selvanathan S (2008) FDI, domestic investment and economic growth in China: a time series analysis. World Econ. doi:10.1111/j.1467-9701.2008.01129.x
Tiwari AK, Mutascu M (2011) Economic growth and FDI in Asia: a panel data approach. Econ Anal Pol 41(2):173–187
Townsend I (2003) Does FDI accelerate economic growth in less developed countries? Ph.D. thesis, Department of Economics, St. Olaf College, Northfield, MN
Tseng W, Zebregs H (2002) FDI in China: some lessons for other countries. IMF policy discussion paper, PDP/02/3, Washington, DC
UNCTAD (1999) Trends in international investment agreements: an overview. United Nations Publication, New York, Sales No. E.99.11.D.23
UNCTAD (2003a) World investment report. United Nations, Geneva
UNCTAD (2003b) World investment report. United Nations Conference on Trade and Development, Geneva
Wang M (2002) Manufacturing FDI and economic growth: evidence from Asian economies. Department of Economics, University of Oregon Mimeo, Eugene
Wang JY, Blomström M (1992) Foreign investment and technology transfer: a simple model. Eur Econ Rev 36(1):137–155
Wei Y, Liu X, Parker D, Vaidya K (1999) The regional distribution of foreign direct investment in China. Reg Stud 33:857–867
Weisskopf TE (1972) The impact of foreign capital inflow on domestic savings in underdeveloped countries. J Int Econ 2:25–38
Westerlund J (2007) Testing for error correction in panel data. Oxford Bull Econ Stat 69:709–748
Whalley J, Xian X (2006) China's FDI and non-FDI economies and the sustainability of future high Chinese growth, NBER working paper, no. 12249. National Bureau of Economic Research, Cambridge, MA
Won Y, Hsiao F, Yang D (2008) FDI inflows, exports and economic growth in first and second generation analysis: panel data causality analyses. KIEP Work Pap 08(02):11–86
World Bank (2007, 2011, 2012) World development indicators CD, World Bank, Washington, DC
World Bank (1994) World development report 1994: infrastructure for development. Oxford University Press, New York
Xu B (2000) Multinational enterprises, technology diffusion, and host country productivity growth. J Dev Econ 62:477–493
Yao S, Wei K (2007) Economic growth in the presence of FDI: the perspectives of newly industrializing economies. J Comp Econ 35:211–234
Zhang KH (1999) How does FDI interact with economic growth in a large developing country? The case of China. Econ Syst 23(4):291–303
Zhang KH (2006) How does foreign direct investment affect economic growth in China? Econ Transit 9(3):679–693

Chapter 8
Impact of Foreign Direct Investment and Domestic Investment in South Asia: Time Series and Panel Evidence

8.1 Introduction

Investment is a crucial intermediate variable for economic growth; therefore, the relationship between FDI and domestic investment (DI) is widely debated in economic literature. In the neoclassical growth model, FDI promotes economic growth by increasing the volume of investment and/or its efficiency. Therefore, the impact of FDI on economic growth depends on the relationship between FDI and DI (de Mello 1999). Like growth, the effect of FDI on DI depends on several factors: domestic country economic policy, specific kinds of FDI received by the host country, and the strength and financial situation of domestic enterprise. The impact of FDI on economic growth will be positive/negative if FDI has complementary/ substitution effects on DI, respectively. There are two hypotheses in this regard: (1) FDI crowds in DI; (2) FDI crowds out DI.

According to the 'crowding in' hypothesis, FDI is expected to 'crowd in' FDI as FDI inflows would lead to positive spillovers to the domestic economy. Such spillovers occur because foreign investment lowers the costs of adopting new technologies, which in turn enhances the rate of growth (Borensztein et al. 1998).[1] For example, greenfield FDI contributes directly to DI. FDI may produce investment spillovers beyond the direct increase in capital stock through linkages among firms. The operation of an MNC may have an impact on the profitability of DI. For example, foreign investors may be directly involved in providing necessary infrastructure such as transportation, logistics, and telecommunications, thus increasing the profitability of DI. Increase in the profitability of domestic firms leads to higher DI. Further, MNCs may provide new investment opportunities for local firms through the provision of machinery, technology, training and managerial skills, and finance (Sun 1998). FDI may also generate demand for specialised inputs, thus increasing the marginal productivity of

[1] Based on Romer's (1993) endogenous growth model, it is assumed that FDI may contribute to the capital formation of the host country through introducing new goods and technologies.

P. Sahoo et al., *Foreign Direct Investment in South Asia*,
DOI 10.1007/978-81-322-1536-3_8,

investments in those inputs. Higher productivity increases profit and induces higher investment in the host country. Further, the relationship between FDI and DI is likely to be complementary when the investment is in an undeveloped sector of the economy (Agosin and Mayer 2000). Operation of an MNC increases government tax revenue, which may boost higher public investment and thereby DI.

Gallagher and Zarsky (2007) classify four channels of FDI crowding in DI. These channels operate through backward and forward linkages. FDI crowds in DI through backward linkages created through the provision of inputs to foreign investors by local firms. Forward linkages can be formed when foreign firms provide goods and services to domestic industries to use as efficiency-enhancing inputs. Crowding in may occur due to knowledge spillovers from multinational firms to domestic firms that gain access to new technologies and tacit knowledge. In addition, demand for local inputs such as labour and suppliers create local demand of domestically produced goods and services. This increases DI through multiplier effects (investment multiplier). Finally, FDI, foreign loans, and portfolio investment may reduce interest rates or increase credit available to finance new DI (Harrison et al. 2004).

On the other hand, crowding out of DI might occur in several ways. Domestic firms may not be as competitive as foreign investors since foreign companies may be more efficient or may form oligopolies and sell at cheaper prices than domestic firms (Agosin and Mayer 2000). This is because multinational firms have access to global inputs and capital markets whereas domestic firms have to rely on domestic markets and inputs. This results in displacement of DI by FDI. In addition, when foreign investors borrow from domestic financial markets to finance their investment, the interest rate may rise in domestic markets and crowd out domestic firms. The operation of MNCs raises both the domestic wage rate and local input cost. This increases the cost of investment and reduces profit in the host country, thereby reducing DI. Furthermore, foreign investors can bring about adverse knowledge spillovers if they start 'hiring domestic entrepreneurs and skilled workers away from domestic firms' (Gallagher and Zarsky 2007). This effect crowds out investment though negative investment multipliers.

Securing the supply of raw materials and other natural resources has been acknowledged as an important objective of MNCs since the earliest work on international investment. In the case of such resource-seeking or rent-seeking FDI, no correlation is to be expected with DI. The literature on the Dutch disease and on the resource 'curse' shows that natural resource abundance rarely stimulates DI (Lautier and Moreaub 2012).

Therefore, understanding the dynamic relationship between FDI and DI is vital for developing countries. Previous empirical studies do not provide any clear evidence. In fact, the empirical evidence varies from country to country and region to region because of differences in national/regional policies, response of domestic enterprises, the type of FDI inflow in the recipient country, and the econometric methodology used for the study[2] (De Mello 1999; Agosin and Mayer 2000; Apergis et al. 2006). Hence, this section intends to contribute to the FDI–DI connection by examining the issue empirically for five South Asian countries by using both time series and panel data analysis.

8.2 Empirical Literature

The literature on the effects of inward FDI on growth, exports, productivity, employment, and wages is vast (De Mello 1999; Lipsey 2002; Görg and Greenaway 2004), but the evidence on the effects of inward FDI on DI is much more limited. Noorzoy (1979) examines the impact of FDI (outward and inward) on DI in Canada between 1957 and 1971. The results indicate that outward FDI in Canada had a positive effect on DI. The evidence is thus consistent with that of Caves and Reuber (1971), who show a complementary relationship between US FDI in Canada and capital formation in Canada.

Nwanna (1986) empirically estimates the impact of FDI on DI for Nigeria using a structural model over 1960–1980. The study finds that FDI had a displacing impact in the short run and a complementary impact in the long run. In the short run N1 of inflow resulted to a decline in DI by N2.90, but an addition of N3.7 in the long run. Part of the negative impact was explained as resulting largely from a positive effect of FDI on imports, a fact well demonstrated by the unprecedented increase in consumption of imported goods since the mid-1970s. On the other hand, the long-run positive impact was explained as resulting from a possible positive multiplier effect on invested funds.

Fry (1993a, b) empirically examines the effects of FDI in a four-equation macroeconomic model containing investment, savings, growth, and current account equations for 16 developing countries over the period 1975–1991. This study finds that in 11 countries, FDI is associated with reduced DI—indicating that it is a close substitute for other capital inflows. For the five Pacific Basin market economies, however, FDI raises DI by the full extent of the FDI inflow.

De Mello (1999) analyses the impact of FDI on capital accumulation, output, and total factor productivity growth in the recipient countries using panel data for both OECD and non-OECD country samples over 1970–1990. He finds 'no time series evidence of linear endogenous growth derived from FDI' for the OECD sample. He highlights that FDI has a twofold effect on growth. It is supposed to foster growth through capital formation. Bosworth and Collins (1999) provide evidence on the effect of capital inflows on DI for 58 developing countries during

[2] More importantly, the effects of FDI on domestic capital accumulation may vary from country to country depending on the domestic policies, degree of financial development (Alfaro et al. 2004), educational level (Borensztein et al. 1998), the size of the technological gap between multinational and domestic firms (De Mello 1999), the types of FDI a country receives, and the sectoral distribution of FDI (Agosin and Mayer 2000).

the period 1978–1995. The study provides evidence that an increase of a dollar in capital flows is associated with an increase in DI of about 50 %. The study further shows that FDI appears to bring a one-for-one increase in DI but there is no discernible relationship between portfolio investment and DI, and the impact of loans falls below those of the other flows. On the other hand, Bosworth and Collins (1999) examined the implications of capital inflows for recipient countries in a panel set of 23 industrialised countries and 62 developing countries for the period 1978–1995. The study revealed that FDI crowds in DI. However, when the model controlled for other variables such as the accelerator term in the developing countries, it found FDI crowded out DI.

Agosin and Mayer (2000) investigate the extent to which FDI in developing countries crowds in or crowds out DI based on panel data for the years 1970–1996. They find that FDI crowds in DI in Asian countries but crowds it out in Latin American countries, while in Africa the relationship is neutral (or one to one between FDI and total investment). Therefore, they conclude that effects of FDI are not always favourable and simplistic policies are unlikely to be optimal. These regional patterns tend to corroborate the findings of Fry (1993a, b).

Kumar and Pradhan (2002) analysed the relationship between FDI, growth, and DI for a sample of 107 developing countries for the period 1980–1999. The results suggest that crowding out effect seems to dominate the relationship between FDI and DI in the Latin America and Caribbean group and only seven countries reported a crowding in. In Asia and Africa the patterns of crowding in and crowding out are more evenly distributed. Braunstein and Epstein (2002) examined the effect of FDI on DI for 1986–1999 using province-level panel data for China. They find that FDI crowds out DI in China. The study points out that the social benefits of FDI are dissipated at least at the provincial level due to intense competition for FDI among the regions in China. The study finds that FDI crowds in DI in Bangladesh, Sri Lanka, and Nepal but crowds out in India.

Misun and Tomsik (2002) test the hypotheses of crowding in and crowding out of FDI on DI in the Czech Republic, Hungary, and Poland in the 1990s. They find that there was evidence of a crowding out effect in Poland (1990–2000) and a crowding in effect in Hungary (1990–2000) and the Czech Republic (1993–2000). Razin (2003) examined the interactions between FDI inflows, DI, international loans, and international portfolio investment for a sample of 64 developing countries for the period 1976–1997. The study analysed the interaction in a four-equation system. The study found a significant role of FDI on DI process compared to other types of capital inflows such as portfolio flows and loans. Agosin and Machado (2005) tested for crowding out or crowding in effects of FDI inflows using 36 developing countries (12 countries in each of three developing regions (Africa, Asia, and Latin America) over 1971–2000. The results indicate that, at best, FDI has left DI unchanged in all three developing regions, and FDI displaces DI in several subperiods for specific regions. In particular, FDI seems to crowd out DI in Latin America, and FDI has led to a one-to-one increase in total investment in Africa and Asia in the chosen period. They conclude that the effects of FDI on DI are by no means always favourable; simplistic policies towards FDI are unlikely to be optimal; and more attention needs to be paid to economic policies that foster the domestic component of total investment.

Mody and Murshid (2005) empirically examine the impact of capital inflows on DI for 60 developing countries over 1977–1998. They obtain coefficients of 0.72 for FDI, 0.61 for foreign loans, and 0.46 for portfolio investment and a long-run coefficient of above 3 for FDI from the dynamic specification. Mody and Murshid also divide their data set into two periods and find that the impact of both FDI and loan inflows declined in the 1990s relative to the 1980s even as developing countries relaxed their capital account restrictions in the 1990s. The relatively high coefficient of FDI, compared with those of portfolio investment and foreign loans, suggests that FDI contributes more appreciably to the productivity of domestic capital than other types of foreign capital.

Apergis et al. (2006) analyse the dynamic linkages between FDI and DI using panel co-integration techniques for 30 countries from America, Asia, Europe, and Africa over 1992–2002. The bivariate model proves a positive long-run relationship, which is evident for Asian and African countries in the multivariate model but not evident for American and European countries. Causality results indicate a two-way feedback relationship between FDI and DI. Further, the study provides evidence that FDI inflow crowds in DI in a univariate model but crowds it out in a multivariate model—accounting for other variables. These findings are parallel to those of de Mello (1999) for a group of developed countries and of Lipsey (2000) and Agosin and Mayer (2000) in terms of their results for Latin America.

Udomkerdmongkol and Morrissey (2008) studied the effect of FDI on private investment in different developing regions over 1995–2001. The study controlled for the political regime and included 13 Latin American countries, 8 Caribbean countries, 8 Asian countries, 10 European transition countries, and 5 African countries. The study revealed that FDI tends to crowd out domestic private investment. This crowding out effect is greater in countries with high governance scores and lower in Latin America compared to Asia, Europe, and Africa. Ndikumana and Verick (2008) investigate whether DI promotes FDI and is in turn affected by FDI in 38 African countries over 1970–2005 and find that the FDI–DI relationship runs both ways. But the positive impact of DI on FDI is stronger and more robust than the reverse relation especially in the case of private investment.

Another study on the sub-Saharan African (SSA) nations by Mutenyo et al. (2010) indicates that FDI crowds out domestic private investment in the selected SSA sample. This finding seems to suggest that although increased FDI leads to economic growth in SSA, the effect of FDI on economic growth is derived from the overall higher induced level of investment rather than efficiency gains. This study is based on the standard panel models (i.e. fixed effects, between effects, and random effects regressions) and 2SLS econometric technique.

Wu et al. (2012) examine the impact of FDI inflows on China's Yangtze River Delta area over 2000–2008. The study, based on panel regression analysis, documents that FDI crowds in DI. Kamaly (2012) examines the dynamic relationship between FDI and DI for 16 emerging countries over 30 years using the 3SLS technique and finds no clear relationship.

There are few country-level studies of the FDI–DI linkage. Using a panel of more than 4,000 Venezuelan firms, Aitken and Harrison (1997) found that the impact of FDI on DI depends on the ownership structure. In particular, FDI that participates with domestic firms in a joint venture arrangement enhances DI profitability. By contrast, FDI negatively affects the productivity of firms with full domestic ownership. On balance, the study shows FDI has a positive impact on DI.

Driffield and Hughes (2003) examined the impact of FDI on DI over 1984–1997 in the UK. The results indicated that FDI's impact on DI is mixed. While FDI had a positive impact on manufacturing investment in the domestic sector, it had a negative effect on other industries. Some other studies find that FDI crowds in DI (Misun and Tomsik (2002) for Hungary and the Czech Republic and Kim and Seo (2003) for South Korea). Kim and Seo (2003) analyse the dynamic relationship between inward FDI, economic growth, and DI in Korea over 1985–1999. Using the vector autoregression model (VAR) and innovations accounting techniques, the study finds that FDI does not crowd out DI in Korea. However, an increase in DI appears to crowd out the inflow of FDI.

Titarenko (2006) examined the influence of FDI inflow on DI in Latvia using quarterly data over 1995–2004 and found that FDI crowded out DI. Using industry-level data, Arndt et al. (2007) examined the effect of FDI inflow on domestic capital stock in Germany over 1991–2004. Using panel co-integration method for different industries, the study documents a positive impact of FDI inflows on the domestic capital stock. This holds for the capital stock owned by domestic investors and the stock of inward FDI. The study concludes that the effects of FDI on the domestic capital stock are driven mainly by intra-sector effects.

Tang et al. (2008) also studied the casual link between FDI, DI, and economic growth in China over 1988–2003 and found only one-way causality from FDI to DI and FDI to GDP in China, while the causal link between DI and economic growth is bilateral. Therefore, FDI had a complementary effect on DI in China. Ang (2009) examined the long-run relationship between private DI, public investment, and FDI in Malaysia over 1960–2003. Using multivariate co-integration techniques, the study finds a robust co-integrated relationship between these variables over 1960–2003. Both public investment and FDI are found to be complementary rather than competing with private DI.

Some studies examine the impact of outward FDI on DI. In a seminal paper, Feldstein (1994) found a negative effect of outward FDI on DI in OECD countries in the 1970s and 1980s. Similarly, replicating Feldstein's estimations methodology, Desai et al. (2005a) confirm that higher outward FDI causes lower DI for 26 OECD countries. However, based on estimations using aggregated plant-level time series data for US MNCs, Desai et al. (2005a) find positive effects. Interestingly, Herzer and Schrooten (2007), using aggregate data, find negative effects of outward FDI in Germany, but positive effects in the US.

Agrawal (2000) examined the impact of FDI on DI in India, Pakistan, Bangladesh, Sri Lanka, and Nepal using annual data over 1965–1996. Using the fixed effect model, the study found that FDI inflows in South Asia were associated with a manifold increase in investment by national investors. This suggests complementarity between FDI and DI, possibly through various backward and forward linkages. Sahoo (2010) finds similar results for five South Asian countries.

Shah et al. (2010) examine the impact of foreign capital inflows on DI in Pakistan over 1990–2010. Using the structural equation model, the study finds more than a one-on-one relation between FDI and DI. On the other hand, the role of portfolio and loan in stimulating DI is found negligible. The empirical result further indicates that the impact of FDI on DI is stronger than the role of DI in attracting FDI in the case of Pakistan.

8.3 Model Specification and Data Sources

The investment function specified here as the ratio of investment to GDP is based on the flexible accelerator model as developed in Fry (1993a, b). According to the accelerator model, the desired capital stock K^* is *proportional* to real output Y:

$$K^* = \alpha Y. \tag{8.1}$$

This can be expressed in terms of a desired ratio of investment to output $(I/Y)^*$:

$$\left(\frac{I}{Y}\right)^* = \alpha\, g, \tag{8.2}$$

where I/Y denotes gross domestic fixed investment in current prices, Y denotes GDP in current prices, and g is the rate of growth of real GDP, Y. The adjustment mechanism allows the actual investment rate to adjust partially in any one period to the difference between the desired investment rate and the investment rate in the previous period:

$$\Delta\left(\frac{I}{Y}\right) = \lambda\left[\left(\frac{I}{Y}\right)^* - \left(\frac{I}{Y}\right)_{t-1}\right] \tag{8.3}$$

$$\text{Or}\quad \frac{I}{Y} = \lambda\left(\frac{I}{Y}\right)^* + (1-\lambda)\left(\frac{I}{Y}\right)_{t-1} \tag{8.4}$$

where λ is the coefficient of adjustment. The flexible accelerator model allows economic conditions to influence the adjustment coefficient λ (Fry 1998). Specially,

$$\lambda = \beta_0 + \left[\frac{(\beta_1 X_1 + \beta_2 X_2 + \beta_3 X_3 + \cdots)}{((I/Y)^* - (I/Y)t - 1)}\right] \tag{8.5}$$

where X_i are the variables (including an intercept term for a constant depreciation rate) that affect 1 and β_i are their respective coefficients. The explanatory variables used for this study are GDP growth rate (Gr) over the previous year, bank credit to domestic sector as share of GDP (DBC), FDI inflows as share of GDP (FDIY), real exchange rate (RER), and the real lending rate of banking sector (RL). Based on these explanatory variables, the investment function is

$$\mathrm{GFC} = \alpha_0 + \alpha_1\,\mathrm{GFC}_{t-1} + \alpha_2\,\mathrm{Gr} + \alpha_3\,\mathrm{FDIY} + \alpha_4\,\mathrm{DBC} + \alpha_5\,\mathrm{RER} + \alpha_6\,\mathrm{RL} + \varepsilon \quad (8.6)$$

where GFC is gross fixed capital as ratio of GDP,

Gr is the growth rate over previous year,
FDIY is the ratio of inflows of FDI to GDP,
DBC is domestic credit by banking sector as ratio of GDP,
RER is the real exchange rate[3] and RL real interest on bank landing, and ε is a serially uncorrelated error.

The model is estimated for five South Asian countries using both time series and panel methodology. Gross fixed capital formation is used as proxy to DI, which is widely used in the literature (see, e.g. Agosin and Mayer 2000; Apergis et al. 2006). The expected sign of (α_1, α_2, α_3, $\alpha_{4,}$) > 0, whereas the coefficient of α_5 and α_6 is ambiguous. The GFC has been increasing for all South Asian countries considered for this study except Pakistan (Fig. 8.1), where political instability and uncertainty has wrecked the business environment.

8.3.1 GDP Growth Rate (Gr)

Neoclassical investment theory suggests that the growth rate of real GDP influences private investment in a positive manner (Greene and Villanueva 1991). This is also known as the 'accelerator effect'. Therefore, the real GDP growth rate (Gr) over the previous year is an important determinant of investment since higher growth would imply higher capital requirement and hence higher investment rate. Further, the growth rate lagged by one period could also be construed as a proxy for expectations about future demand for, and returns from, the output of investments (Jayaraman 1996). The expected sign of Gr is positive.

8.3.2 Availability of Credit (DBC)

The availability of formal sector credit as a ratio of GDP (proxied by domestic credit by banks) is another important determinant of the investment rate in developing countries (Fry 1995; Bontempi et al. 2010). The quantity of credit is likely to be important in a credit market where the interest rates are controlled at below

[3] RER is defined as RER = $e.P^f/P$, where e is the exchange rate (number of domestic currency units per dollar), P is the domestic price level (the GDP deflator), and P^f is the foreign price level (proxied here by the US GDP deflator, given that the USA is the most important trading partner of South Asian countries).

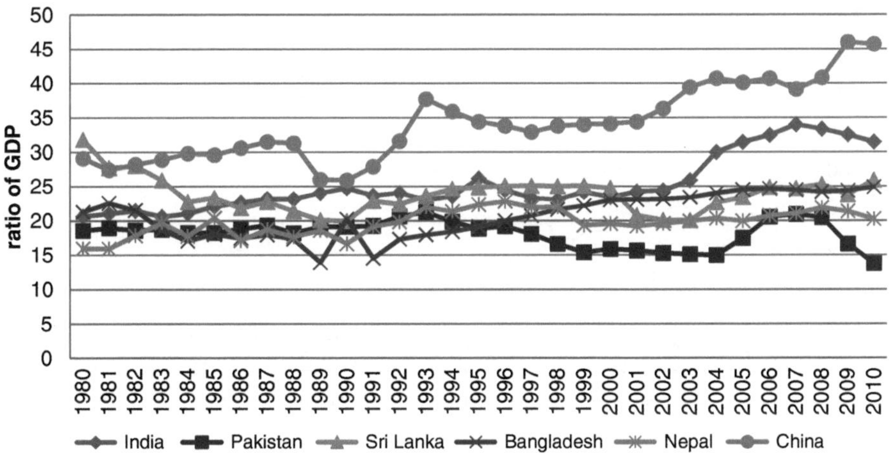

Fig. 8.1 Gross fixed capital formation: South Asia and China

market clearing levels and/or directed at credit programmes that exist for selected industrial sectors. Hence, financial sector development increases credit supply, and the sign of bank credit as a ratio of GDP is expected to be positive (Agrawal 2000). Figure 8.2 explains the trends in bank credit to domestic sector in South Asia along with China. Though DBC is relatively low compared to China, the credit flows have been increasing in five South Asian countries since the early 1990s.

8.3.3 Real Lending Rate (RL)

True domestic costs of borrowings are very difficult to measure in developing countries because of selective credit policies and disequilibrium institutional interest rates (Fry 1992). Therefore, here we use the RL rate of banks as a proxy for capital cost. The RL rate is obtained by subtracting the inflation rate from the nominal prime lending rate of the banks. The user cost of capital is an important factor in any decision by the private sector to invest. Investment declines when the cost of bank credit or retained earnings—which is the main source of finance for investment—is raised, as it increases the user cost of capital.

The findings of various empirical studies are not, however, consistent. While certain studies (Greene and Villanueva 1991) have found a negative relationship between interest rates and investment, studies by others have shown that the credit policy affects investment in a distorted manner in repressed financial markets (Servén and Solimano 1993). However, based on the financial liberalisation hypothesis of McKinnon (1973) and Shaw (1973a, b) and in contrast to neoclassical theory, investment is expected to be positively related to the real rate of interest because a rise in interest rates increases the volume of financial savings through financial intermediaries and thereby raises investible funds. Therefore, the expected sign of RL is ambiguous.

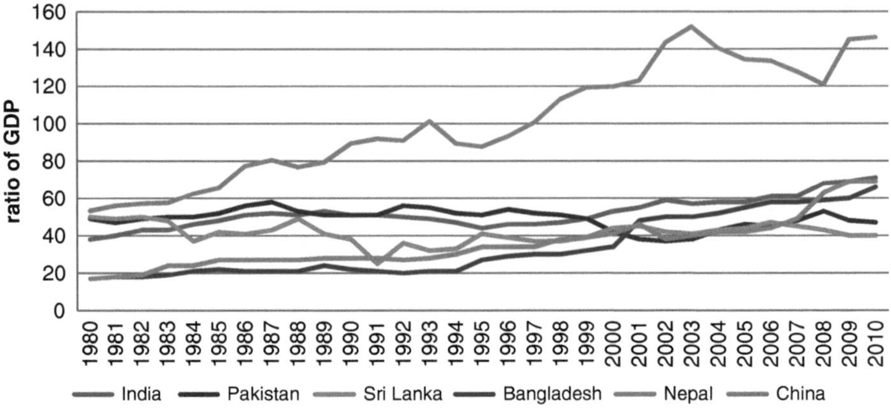

Fig. 8.2 Bank credit to domestic sector, South Asia and China

8.3.4 RER

The effect of real exchange rate on investment is ambiguous, since an increase in RER (depreciation) would increase the price of imported capital and intermediate goods and reduce investment (Servén and Solimano 1992; Fry 1992; Agrawal 2000). On the other hand, an appreciating RER may stimulate investment through higher inflows of capital. Similarly, Van Wijnbergen (1985) shows that the net effect of a real depreciation on investment is ambiguous—investment increases in tradable goods but decreases in domestic goods. The real exchange in South Asian countries witnessed appreciation over the period (Fig. 8.3).

8.3.5 Foreign Direct Investment Ratio (FDIY)

Finally, the coefficient of FDIY is expected to be positive since FDI promotes DI through the backward and forward linkages with the domestic industries (de Mello 1999; Gallagher and Zarsky 2007). FDI may also generate demand for specialised inputs, thus increasing the marginal productivity of investments in those inputs. Higher productivity increases profit and induces higher investment in the host country.

In our model, we are testing for the long-term crowding in or crowding out effect. For this purpose, the relevant coefficient is:

$$\alpha_{\mathrm{LT}} = \frac{\alpha_3}{1 - \alpha_1} \tag{8.7}$$

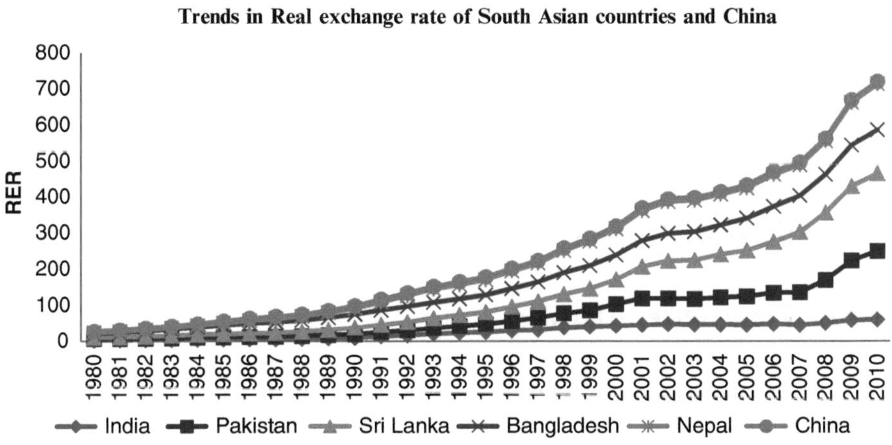

Fig. 8.3 Trends in real exchange rate of South Asian countries and China

where α_{LT} is the long-run impact of FDI on DI. The criteria used to determine crowding in and crowding out are the value and significance of $\alpha_{LT.}$ There are three possibilities:

1. If $\alpha_{LT} = 1$, this means that, in the long run, an increase in FDI of 1 percentage point of GDP results in an increase in total DI amounting to 1 percentage point of GDP. This implies that FDI neither crowds in DI nor crowds it out.
2. If $\alpha_{LT} > 1$, there is the evidence of a crowding in effect. In the long term, an additional \$1 of FDI generates more than an additional \$1 in total investment.
3. If $\alpha_{LT} < 1$, this implies the evidence of crowding out effect. In the long term, an additional \$1 of FDI results in less than a \$1 increase in total DI. In other words, FDI displaces DI.

In the long term, if FDI crowds in DI, long-term macroeconomic externalities are positive for South Asian countries. On the other hand, evidence of crowding out implies that FDI inflow has negative long-term macroeconomic externalities.

8.3.6 Data Sources

Annual data on GDP growth rate, inflation rate (consumer price index), interest rate on bank lending, banking sector credit to domestic sector as ratio of GDP, exchange rate, and GDP deflator are collected from World Development Indicators 2012. Gross fixed capital formation and FDI as ratio of GDP are collected from the UNCTAD online database. The analysis is limited to the period 1980–2010.

The study uses both time series and panel data analysis for getting robust estimation. Given that we have only 31 observations per country, the autoregressive distributed lag (ARDL) technique is used for co-integration analysis. The study uses dynamic OLS (DOLS) developed by Saikonnen (1991) and Stock and Watson (1993) for deriving long-run coefficients. The advantage of the methods is that the endogeneity of any of the regressors has no effect, asymptotically, on the robustness of the estimates. Two panel methods (system GMM and fully modified OLS (FMOLS)) are used to derive long-run determinants of FDI for South Asia. We conduct unit root and co-integration test before using the above methodologies to derive the long-run determinants of FDI.

8.4 Analysis of Empirical Results

8.4.1 Time Series Analysis

The first step in the empirical analysis is the examination of time series properties of variables by using ADF unit root test. First, we test unit root by assuming there is no trend but only intercept. Then we test stationarity by assuming trend in the variable. The result of ADF unit root test is given in Table 8.A.1. It is seen from Table 8.A.1 that we have a mixture of $I(0)$ and $I(1)$ variables. Gross fixed capital is $I(0)$ for Bangladesh and Sri Lanka but $I(1)$ for other countries. Similarly, RL is $I(1)$ for all countries except Nepal. Similarly, GDP growth rate (Gr) is $I(0)$ variable. On the other hand, RER and FDIR are $I(1)$ for all countries except for Sri Lanka and Bangladesh. Therefore, ADF unit root test results suggest that we have a mixture of $I(0)$ and $I(1)$ variables.

8.4.1.1 Co-integration Results

Since we have a mixture of $I(1)$ and $I(0)$ variables, co-integration procedures are applicable and can be used to examine the existence of a long-run relation between the variables, which is the second step in exploring the long-run determinants of FDI. We use autoregressive distributed lag (ARDL) method developed by Pesaran et al. (2001) to find out the long-run relationship among the relevant variables. The result of ARDL co-integration test is presented in Table 8.A.2. When GFC is the dependent variable, a long-run relationship among the variables is clear (Table 8.A.2), because its F-statistic exceeds the upper bound critical value (3.50) at the 5 % level for all countries. Given that we have only 31 observations, we have considered maximum three lags and selected these based on the Akaike Information Criteria (AIC). Thus, the null of non-existence of stable long-run relationship is rejected in favour of a long-run stable relation. These results also warrant proceeding to the next stage of estimation.

Having found the long-run relationship between gross fixed capital and other variables, we estimate determinants of DI by using the DOLS model. A dynamic version of the linear model was estimated, by including the lagged dependent variable of dependent variable. The result is presented in Table 8.1. The diagnostic test indicates that the serial correlation and heteroscedasticity are not a problem. Adjusted R^2 is also very high, indicating that the model fits the data very well.

Table 8.1 Estimated result of DI (DOLS)

	India	Pakistan	Sri Lanka	Bangladesh	Nepal
Variables	Coefficients	Coefficients	Coefficients	Coefficients	Coefficients
Constant	11.37* (2.85)	5.79** (2.67)	3.91 (1.65)	13.75** (6.26)	9.01* (2.78)
GFC_{t-1}	0.05 (0.23)	0.64** (6.03)	0.53**(4.93)	0.15 (1.15)	0.54** (3.18)
FDIY	1.15* (2.36)	0.88** (4.43)	1.07* (2.89)	2.74** (3.74)	5.44* (1.96)
RER	−0.04 (−0.25)	−0.02** (−3.79)	−0.01* (−2.46)	−0.02 (−0.37)	0.012 (0.86)
RL	−0.41* (−2.82)	−0.01 (−0.34)	0.08* (2.21)	−0.06 (−0.77)	−0.06 (−0.88)
DBC	0.24** (3.37)	0.17* (2.75)	0.07# (1.65)	0.12* (2.03)	−0.04 (−0.74)
GR	0.38* (2.38)	0.19* (2.37)	0.72** (4.51)	−0.08 (−0.32)	0.14* (1.97)
	Adj. $R^2 = 0.93$,	Adj. $R^2 = 0.90$,	Adj. $R^2 = 0.86$,	Adj. $R^2 = 0.91$,	Adj. $R^2 = 0.66$,
	SE = 0.75,	SE = 0.63,	SE = 0.90,	SE = 0.95,	SE = 0.97,
	DW stat = 2.74	DW stat = 1.98	DW stat = 1.89	DW stat = 1.83	DW stat = 1.48
	LM = 1.52	LM = 0.12	LM = 0.66	LM = 0.09	LM = 3.51
	ARCH = 0.45	ARCH = 0.13	ARCH = 2.12	ARCH = 0.38	ARCH = 0.46

Notes: *** and ** denote significance at 1, 5, and 10 % level, respectively. Figures in the parentheses are *t*-ratio. # denotes significance at 10 % level.

8.4.1.2 The Dynamic OLS (Or DOLS) Procedure

This procedure, developed by Saikonnen (1991) and Stock and Watson (1993), has the advantage that the endogeneity of any of the regressors has no effect, asymptotically, on the robustness of the estimates. Further, statistical inference on the parameters of the co-integrating vector is facilitated by the fact that the t-statistics of the estimated coefficient have asymptotic normal distribution, even with endogenous regressors (Stock and Watson 1993). This procedure also allows for direct estimation of a mixture of $I(1)$ and $I(0)$ variables. The DOLS procedure incorporates the lags and leads of the first differences of the $I(1)$ variables. Thus, estimation of the long-run relation between Y and X is carried out with a regression of the type

$$Y = \lambda^{d'} X + S_{-n}{}^{n}\ a_i \Delta X_{t-i} \tag{8.8}$$

where λ^d denotes the vector of long-run coefficients of X using the DOLS procedure. The inclusion of ΔX_{t+j} terms takes care of the possibility of endogeneity of X, i.e. feedback from Y to future values of X—see Stock and Watson (1993).

8.4.1.3 Determinants of DI in India

The estimated results of India are presented in column 1 in Table 8.1. It is evident that all the variables have expected signs although RER is not statistically significant. Further, the coefficient of RER is very small, and it cannot be a policy variable to boost investment in India. The coefficient of growth rate is positive and statistically significant, supporting the accelerator model. Therefore, higher economic growth in 1990s and 2000s has stimulated DI in India. Similarly, the availability of credit also boosts DI, as the coefficient of DBC is positive and significant. In India, with progressive financial liberalisation, the bank credit to domestic sector has increased significantly. This has played a significant role in promoting DI. This result confirms that financial liberalisation leads to higher investment as proposed by McKinnon (1973) and Shaw (1973a, b). The coefficient of RL is negative and statistically significant. Higher interest rate on lending, therefore, increases cost of borrowing and discourages investment.

Early studies (e.g. Greene and Villanueva 1991) have also found a negative relationship between interest rates and investment. The coefficient for the key variable (FDI) turned out to be positive and significant. The short-run coefficient of FDIY is found at 1.15 for India. This indicates that one unit rise in FDI will lead to more than one unit rise in DI, supporting the crowding in hypothesis. The long-run coefficient is obtained by dividing the coefficient of FDIY by 1—the coefficient of the lagged dependent variable. Using this result, the long-run coefficient of FDIY is found to be more than 1 (1.21). This suggests complementarity between FDI and DI, possibly through various backward and forward linkages.

8.4.1.4 Pakistan

All the exploratory variables have the expected sign but RL rate does not have significant impact on DI. The coefficient of growth rate one period lag has positive impact on investment, indicating the operation of the accelerator model for Pakistan. However, the coefficient is lower than for India. This is mainly due to lower economic growth in Pakistan during the 2000s. The availability of credit also boosts DI, as the coefficient of DBC is positive and significant. This supports the hypothesis that availability of credit is an important factor for investment in developing countries. The coefficient of RER is negative and statistically significant. This implies that the appreciation of RER has increased the price of imported capital and intermediate goods and resulted in a contraction of investment in Pakistan. The coefficient of FDIY is found positive and significant. The short-run coefficient of FDI is less than 1 (0.88). However, the long-run coefficient of FDI is more than one, supporting the crowds in hypothesis. This implies that as FDI increases by one unit, DI increases by more than a unit in the case of Pakistan. This positive relationship seems to suggest that any appreciation in terms of FDI will improve the DI in Pakistan.

8.4.1.5 Sri Lanka

All the variables except RL rate have the expected sign. The coefficient of RL rate is positive and significant. Historically, the interest rate in Sri Lanka has been very high due to the higher inflation rate. In addition, Sri Lanka was the first country in South Asia to liberalise its economy—in the late 1970s. Liberalisation led to increased domestic savings, investment, and interest rate, as proposed by the McKinnon (1973) and Shaw (1973a, b) hypothesis. The impact of lag growth rate on DI was found to be positive and significant. Higher economic growth in the 1990s and 2000s stimulated DI in Sri Lanka, as proposed by the accelerator model. Credit availability also boosted DI, as the coefficient of DBC is positive and significant at 10 % level. The coefficient of RER is negative and statistically significant. This indicates that the appreciation of RER has increased the prices in Sri Lanka. The lagged dependent variable is highly significant in all specifications, indicating an inertia effect. The coefficient of FDIY is found positive and significant at 5 % level. The short-run coefficient of FDI is more than one (1.07). The long-run coefficient of FDI is more than 1, supporting the crowding in hypothesis through backward and forward linkage effect. The long-run coefficients indicate that if FDI increases by one unit, DI increases by more than two units.

8.4.1.6 Bangladesh

All the variables except the lagged growth rate have the expected sign. However, the growth rate coefficient is found insignificant. Similarly, the coefficients of RL rate and RER are insignificant. The coefficient of bank credit to domestic sector is positive, indicating that credit availability is an important factor in boosting DI in Bangladesh. The coefficient of the key variable (FDI) is positive and significant. The short-run coefficient of FDIY is 2.74 and the long-run coefficient is 3.22, supporting the crowding in hypothesis possible through backward and forward linkage effect. The long-run coefficients indicate that if FDI increases by one unit, DI increases by more than three units.

8.4.1.7 Nepal

DI in Nepal is determined by FDI, and lagged growth rate as other variables is found to have insignificant impact. The coefficient of RL is negative and statistically not significant as anticipated. Similarly, the coefficient of bank credit to domestic sector is negative but insignificant. This indicates that the financial sector remained underdeveloped in Nepal. The crucial variable, the ratio of FDI inflows to GDP (FDIY) has a strong positive effect with the short-run coefficient in the range of 5.41 for Nepal. Short-run coefficients of FDI indicate that FDI crowds in DI in Nepal. The long-run coefficients indicate that if FDI increases by one unit, DI increases by more than 11 units. Therefore, FDI has the highest impact on DI in Nepal in South Asia.

The long-run coefficient is obtained by dividing the coefficient of FDIY by 1—the coefficient of the lagged dependent variable. Using this result, the long-run coefficient of FDIY is between 12.6 and 1.9. This implies that a 1 % increase in FDI is associated with a 1.12 % increase DI in India, 1.44 % in Pakistan, 1.9 % increase in Bangladesh, and 12.6 % increase in Nepal. This suggests complementarity between FDI and the DI, possibly through various backward and forward linkages. In other words, one dollar inflow of FDI creates more than one dollar capital formation in South Asia except Sri Lanka. Therefore, time series evidence suggests that FDI crowds in DI in South Asia.

8.4.2 *Panel Analysis*

Time series analysis is further corroborated by panel analysis. The result of panel unit root test is presented in Table 8.A.3. The results indicate that most of the variables are $I(1)$ or stationary at first difference. However, FDI ratio, RL rate, and growth rate are $I(0)$ series.[4] Having established the nonstationarity of the series, we then proceed to test for the existence of a long-run relationship between real per capita income and other relevant variables using error correction panel co-integration test developed by Westerlund (2007). The results of Westerlund (2007) co-integration test with the asymptotic p-values based on 500 replications are presented in Table 8.A.4. When using the asymptotic p-values, except for G_a and Gt, the no co-integration null is rejected in favour of the existence of co-integration at 5 % level. Therefore, we find that the DI and its determinants are having long-run stable relationship in South Asia.

8.4.2.1 Estimated Coefficients of DI

The third step in our panel analysis is the estimation of Eq. (8.6) using various panel methods (pooled, fixed effect, GMM system, and FMOLS). The estimated short-run coefficients are presented in Table 8.2. The GMM system passes all diagnostic tests related to the Sargan test of overidentifying restrictions and the Arellano–Bond test of 1st-order and 2nd-order autocorrelations. The Arellano–Bond test of 1st-order autocorrelation is significant, and 2nd-order autocorrelation is insignificant. Results indicate that growth rate, FDI inflows, RER, and domestic credit provided by banking are major determinants of DI in South Asia. In the pooled regression, both FDIY and growth rate have positive significant impact on DI. On the other hand, the coefficient of RL rate is positive and significant as found in the literature. This result confirms that financial liberalisation leads to higher investment through higher savings mobilisation, as proposed by McKinnon (1973) and Shaw (1973a, b). The lagged dependent variable is highly significant in all specifications, indicating an inertia effect. Similar results are found in other specifications. The effect of RER is negative but significant in fixed effect and FMOLS estimation. The short-run coefficient of

[4] However, we considered these variables in our analysis given their importance in the functions. Since most of the variables are nonstationary, we could use co-integration analysis.

Table 8.2 Estimated coefficients of DI (1980–2010)

	POOL	Fixed effect	GMM system	FMOLS
Variables	Coefficients	Coefficients	Coefficients	Coefficients
Constant	0.66 (0.34)	5.12** (5.05)	2.58 (1.46)	–
GFC_{t-1}	0.86**(22.3)	0.60** (10.42)	0.81**(12.74)	0.58**(11.78)
FDIY	0.26* (2.26)	0.77** (4.00)	0.37* (2.80)	0.63** (3.43)
RER	−0.001 (−0.48)	−0.006* (−1.96)	−0.005 (−1.31)	−0.02** (−3.09)
DBC	0.04 (1.10)	0.05** (2.98)	0.04*(2.49)	0.03* (2.79)
Gr	0.21** (3.45)	0.20** (3.65)	0.17* (2.67)	0.14** (4.66)
RL	0.06* (2.34)	0.05# (1.84)	0.05 (1.08)	0.07** (3.30)
R^2	0.89	0.83		
Hausman test		$Pr > Chi^2 = 0.00$		
Arellano–Bond test for AR(1) in first differences				$z = -4.94$, $Pr > z = 0.00$
Arellano–Bond test for AR(2) in first differences				$z = -1.67$, $Pr > z = 0.08$
Sargan test of overid. restrictions				$chi^2(80) = 86.24$
GMM instruments for levels				$Pr > chi^2 = 0.06$
Difference-in-Sargan tests of exogeneity of instrument subsets				$chi^2(52) = 43.85$, $Pr > chi^2 = 0.06$
Difference-in-Sargan tests of exogeneity of instrument subsets:				$chi^2(52) = 81.96$, $Pr > chi^2 = 0.12$

Notes: ***, **, and # denote significance at 1, 5, and 10 % level, respectively. Figures in the parentheses are *t*-ratio

Table 8.3 Long-run coefficients of FDI for South Asian countries

Variable	Pool	Fixed	GMM	FMOLS
FDIR	1.85	1.92	1.95	1.5

Long-run coefficients are estimated using Eq. (8.7)

FDI ratio is positive and statistically significant but less than one in all procedures. This implies FDI crowds out DI in the short run. In other words, one dollar FDI inflows result in less than one dollar capital formation in South Asia in the short run (Agosin and Machado 2005). The panel result corroborates time series findings.

The long-run coefficient of FDI is estimated using Eq. (8.7) and presented in Table 8.3. It is clear that the long-run coefficient is positive and more than one, indicating FDI inflows stimulate DI in the long run for South Asia. For example, \$1 of FDI inflow increases domestic capital formation by \$1.85 in pooled estimation, \$1.92 in fixed effect, \$1.95 in GMM, and \$1.5 in FMOLS, respectively. The results are in line with findings by Agrawal (2000) and Kumar and Pradhan (2002) for South Asian countries. Therefore, FDI seems to crowd in DI in South Asia. This positive relationship seems to suggest that any appreciation in the terms of FDI will improve DI in South Asia.

8.5 Impact of FDI on DI in China: A Comparative Analysis

Of developing countries, China has received the most FDI. This section attempts to find the FDI–DI relationship in China for comparative purposes.

Several studies—at macro and province level—have documented the positive impact of FDI inflows on DI (Braunstein and Epstein 2002; Tang et al. 2008; Wu et al. 2012). Xu and Wang (2007) use the structural model to test the effects of inward FDI on China's domestic capital formation, exports, imports, and GDP growth over 1980–1999. A key finding was that inward FDI began to exert a significant effect in the Chinese economy in the 1990s. In addition, the growing presence of FDI appears to have enhanced investment efficiency in the Chinese economy. Using the Feldstein and Horioka (1980) model, Choy et al. (2009) estimate the relationship between FDI and gross capital formation for 25 regions of China over 2004–2007. The results of this study indicate that FDI inflows crowd in DI in China through higher productivity caused by transfer of managerial and technical know-how. On the other hand, outward FDI has no impact on capital formation.

8.5.1 Empirical Results

For assessing FDI impact on DI for China, we estimate Eq. (8.6). Annual data on gross fixed capital, RL rate, RER, inflation rate, and growth rate of GDP is collected from World Development Indicators of the World Bank. Data on FDI inflows are collected from UNCTAD online database. Like for South Asian countries, we first started time series properties of variables by using the ADF unit root test. For China, the test indicates that gross fixed capital ratio, RER, bank credit to domestic sector as ratio of GDP, and FDI as ratio of GDP are nonstationary in level but stationary at first difference or $I(1)$. On the other hand, growth rate of GDP and RL rate are stationary at level. Therefore, we have a mixture of $I(1)$ and $I(0)$ variables (Table 8.A.5). Hence, the ARDL co-integration procedure is appropriate. The results of the ARDL co-integration test are presented in Table 8.A.6.

The result of ARDL co-integration test suggests that there exists a long-run equilibrium relationship between DI and its determinants as F-stat (4.89) exceeds the upper bound critical value (3.5) at the 5 % levels. Thus, the null of non-existence of stable long-run relationship is rejected in favour of co-integration. The co-integration results warrant proceeding to the next stage of estimation, i.e. estimation of long-run coefficients.

Having seen a long-run equilibrium relationship, we proceed to the estimation of model (8.8) for China by using the DOLS method. The long-run coefficient of gross fixed capita rate is presented in Table 8.4. Maximum lag length used to derive long-run coefficients is 2 based on AIC criteria. Diagnostic tests are checked to ensure that

Table 8.4 Estimated result of DI of China (DOLS)

	China
Variables	Coefficients
Constant	10.28* (2.34)
GFC_{t-1}	0.49** (3.31)
FDIY	0.74* (2.66)
RER	−2.01** (−3.79)
RL	−0.24* (−2.33)
DBC	0.14**(5.07)
GR	0.63** (4.35)
	Adj. R^2 = 0.95, SE = 1.25, DW stat = 1.79, LM =0.22, and ARCH = 0.05

Notes: *** and ** denote significance at 1, and 5 % level, respectively. Figures in the parentheses are *t*-ratio

it is the best model and there is no misspecification bias in the model. The diagnostic tests include the test of serial autocorrelation (LM), heteroscedasticity (ARCH test), omitted variables/functional form (Ramsey RESET). The estimated long-run coefficients indicate that lagged growth rate boosted DI in China. China's economic growth rate is one of the highest in the 1990s and 2000s. Higher economic growth created higher expectations about future demand, boosting higher DI.

The impact of bank credit on the domestic sector also boosted DI in China. Bank credit to domestic sector as a ratio of GDP increased from a mere 50 % in the early 1980s to above 125 % in 2000s. This was further boosted in the early 1990s as China liberalised its financial system. The coefficient of RER is significantly negative, indicating that domestic currency appreciation increases the cost of capital goods and reduces investment. The coefficient of RL rate is also negative and statistically significant, contrary to the expectation of the McKinnon (1973) and Shaw (1973a, b) liberalisation hypothesis. This is expected, as the Chinese authorities kept the interest rate low to finance DI. The short-run coefficient of FDI ratio is positive and statistically significant but less than 1. This implies FDI crowds out DI in the short run. The long-run coefficient of FDI is estimated using Eq. (8.7); it is more than 1 (1.47). This indicates FDI inflows stimulate DI in the long run for China.

8.6 Causality Between DI and FDI Using VECM Approach

The co-integration result provides the degree of association but not the direction of causality. Therefore, we also test causality between DI and FDI to find its direction. Since FDI and between domestic are found $I(1)$ except Sri Lanka, we carry our causality in the error correction framework. For Sri Lanka, since both are $I(0)$ series, we conduct a simple Granger causality test. The presence of a co-integration relationship between the variables suggests a causal relationship between export and GDP at least in one direction and possibly in both directions (Engle and

Table 8.5 Causality between DI and FDI using VECM approach

	$\sum_{j=1}^{p} \Delta GFC_{t-j}$	$\sum_{j=1}^{p} \Delta FDIY_{t-j}$	Lagged ECM term
Dependent variable	$\sum \beta_i = 0$: F-stat (p-value)	$\sum \beta_i = 0$: F-stat (p-value)	$\Theta = 0$: t-stat (p-value)
India			
ΔGFC		6.41* (0.02)	−2.65* (0.012)
ΔFDIY	2.24 (0.34)		0.18 (0.89)
Pakistan			
ΔGFC		2.78 (0.13)	−2.32* (0.03)
ΔFDIY	3.12 (0.11)		−3.02** (0.00)
Bangladesh			
ΔGFC		0.78 (0.67)	−2.46** (0.03)
ΔFDIY	0.32 (0.73)		0.08 (0.91)
Nepal			
ΔGFC		4.73* (0.04)	−2.82* (0.04)
ΔFDIY	1.27 (0.18)		−0.84 (0.26)

** Denotes significance at 1 % level, and * denotes significance at 5 %. Optimal lag length is selected on the basis of AIC

Table 8.6 Causality between DI and FDI using VECM approach

Null hypothesis	Optimal lag	$\sum \beta_i = 0$: F-statistic	(p-value)
FDIY → GFC	2(AIC)	2. 09#	0.08
GFC → FDIY	2(AIC)	0.76	0.24

# Denotes rejection of null hypothesis at 10 % level

Granger 1987). The result of VECM causality test is presented in Table 8.5. It is clear that the null hypothesis of no causality from FDI growth to growth of GFC is rejected by both the lags of ΔFDIY terms (the short-term causality) as well the lagged ECM term (the long-term causality), in favour of FDI-led DI in India. On the other hand, we do not find causality in opposite direction (GFC to FDIY) either through dynamic terms ΔGFC or through error correction term. Therefore, we find the evidence of one-way causality from FDIY to GFC for India. Similar results are found for Bangladesh and Nepal. For Pakistan, there is evidence of two-way mutual feedback between DI and FDI. In Sri Lanka, there is one-way causality from FDI to DI as the null of no causality is rejected at the 10 % level.

Panel causality was also conducted by using Hurlin and Venet (2008). Results are presented in Table 8.6 to 8.7. Results indicate that when lag one is selected, null of no causality from FDIY to GFC is only rejected at the 10 % level. When higher lags are selected, null of no causality from FDIY to GFC is only rejected at the 5 % level. On the other hand, causality from GFC to FDI is found at any lag. The null of no causality from GFC to FDIY is rejected at the 5 % level. Therefore, panel causality test supports bidirectional hypothesis between FDI and DI. This indicates that higher FDI inflows will increase DI and lead to higher FDI inflows to South Asia (Table 8.7).

Table 8.7 Panel causality test between GFC and FDIY

Direction of causality		$k = 1$	$k = 2$	$k = 3$
FDIY → GFC	Z_{HNC}	1.86[#]	3.74*	3.05*
	$\tilde{Z}_{HNC}$	1.77[#]	2.89*	2.56*
GFC → FDIY	Z_{HNC}	2.13*	3.39	2.71*
	$\tilde{Z}_{HNC}$	2.13*	3.08	2.27*

Notes: * and [#] denote rejection of null hypothesis of no causality at 5 and 10 % level

8.7 Conclusion

The chapter deals with the impact of FDI on DI in the context of five South Asian countries, which is a sparsely researched area in empirical literature, and examines the FDI–DI nexus in China for comparative purpose. There is no consistent answer to the question of crowding in or crowding out of DI as a result of FDI, as it results in crowding in through:

- Spillovers in terms of lower cost of new technologies
- Spillover of knowledge
- Backward linkages—inputs that foreign producers provide local firms
- Forward linkages—efficiency-enhancing inputs provided to domestic firms
- Infrastructure enhancement
- Generating demand for specialised inputs
- Increasing government revenues and, thereby, public investment

However, there are also fears that domestic firms may be crowded out by:

- More competitive foreign firms' cost/price and technology terms.
- Foreign firms' entry into the domestic financial sector to borrow, which may increase the interest rate.
- Foreign entities' operation, which may increase the wage cost.
- Poaching—foreign firms may hire skilled HR away from domestic industry.

A survey of various empirical literatures reveals several factors of the impact of FDI on DI—apart from various controlling variables such as growth of GDP, interest rate, exchange rate, and domestic bank credit as a share of GDP. Important differences in outcome crop up when the issue is studied in the context of different areas (Asia, Latin America) or different developmental levels (OECD, LDCs, developing countries). The impact in the short run differs from that in the long run. Crucially, few studies have examined the use of different methodologies on the same set of data to test the consistency of results. This study tries to fill that gap. Based on the previous literature, we tried to examine the issue of impact of FDI on DI in five South Asian nations—India, Pakistan, Sri Lanka, Bangladesh, and Nepal.

We used an empirical version of flexible accelerator model which allows control variables to empirically test the crowding out and crowding in hypotheses. Here, the desired capital stock is proportional to the real output. Explanatory variables used are:

- DI with 1 year lag
- GDP growth rate over the previous year

- Bank credit to domestic sector as a share of GDP
- FDI inflows as a share of GDP
- RER and RL rate of banking sector

The expected signs of the first four variables are positive, while the last two are ambiguous. In our model, we also tested for long-term crowding in or crowding out effect. The estimation technique used both time series and panel method to derive inference. The result suggests both stationary and nonstationary series, and the co-integration test tells us that variables have long-run stable relations.

The empirical test shows that all the explanatory variables except RER have expected signs for India. Our variable of interest is FDI as a share of GDP; it shows that FDI crowds in DI in both the short and long run. This suggests complementarities between FDI and DI. The long-run coefficient is 1.21.

For Pakistan, all variables have the expected signs, but the RL rate has no significant impact. While the short-run impact is less than 1, the long-run impact is greater than 1, indicating crowding in. If FDI increases by one unit, DI increases by more than two units.

For Sri Lanka, all the variables except the RL rate have the expected sign. Both the short-run and long-run coefficients of FDI are more than 1, indicating the crowding in of DI through backward and forward linkage effects. The long-run coefficient indicates that if FDI increases by one unit, DI increases by more than two units.

For Bangladesh, all the variables except the lagged growth rate have the expected signs. Both the short-run and long-run coefficients are more than 1, indicating crowding in. The long-run coefficient indicates that if FDI increases by one unit, DI increases by more than three units.

In Nepal, only FDI and the lagged growth rate are significant determinants of DI. Both short-run and long-run coefficients are more than 1, indicating crowding in. The long-run coefficient indicates that if FDI increases by one unit, DI increases by more than 11 units. The FDI has the highest impact on DI in Nepal in South Asia. The results of the time series test indicate that FDI generally improves DI in South Asian nations and that the impact is inversely related to the level of development. China is a special case, where FDI crowds out DI in the short run and stimulates it in the long run.

From the panel estimation, which used four types of estimation technique, it is observed that for South Asian countries, one unit increase in FDI results in more than one unit increase in DI in the long run. The causality test indicates one-way causality from FDI to DI in all South Asian nations except Pakistan, where there is a two-way mutual feedback between FDI and DI.

Based on the current study, the policy to enhance FDI should be implemented to stimulate DI. More FDI should encourage DI in less-developed regions, as the positive impact of FDI on DI is more pronounced there. But sectors should be selected so that backward and forward linkages through spillovers increase rather than displacing domestic firms. Overall, FDI has played a significant complementary role to DI in developing South Asian countries. Therefore, these countries must make every effort to get FDI and, thereby, improve DI—which is crucial for sustaining high economic growth.

Appendix

Table 8.A.1 Unit root test for using ADF test

Variables	At level with constant	Optimal lag	At level with constant and trend	Optimal lag	At first difference with constant	Optimal lag	Order of integration
India							
GFC	−0.83	3	−1.91	2	−3.23*	1	*I*(1)
FDIY	−1.33	1	−2.6	1	−3.78*	1	*I*(1)
RL	0.09	3	−1.23	3	−4.10*	1	*I*(1)
DBC	−0.21	1	−1.78	3	−3.75*	2	*I*(1)
Gr	−3.50*	1					I(0)
RER	0.02	3	−3.07	3	−2.87*		*I*(1)
Pakistan							
GFC	−2.29	2	−3.03	3	−2.97*	1	*I*(1)
RL	−1.63	2	−2.48	1	−4.38*	1	*I*(1)
DBC	−1.80	3	−2.19	2	−3.87*	1	*I*(1)
Gr	−2.86*						*I*(0)
RER	1.76	2	0.28	2	−2.69*	1	*I*(1)
FDIY	−2.26	1	−3.2	1	−4.37*	2	*I*(1)
Sri Lanka							
GFC	−3.12*	2					*I*(0)
RL	−3.45*	1					*I*(0)
DBC	−2.79*	2					*I*(0)
Gr	−3.19*						*I*(0)
RER	2.26	2	1.21	3	−3.61*	1	*I*(1)
FDIY	−3.93*	1					*I*(0)
Bangladesh							
GFC	−0.54	3	−4.19*	2			*I*(0)
RL	−1.91	3	−1.60	2	−3.43*	2	*I*(1)
DBC	0.94	2	−1.26	2	−3.41	1	*I*(1)
Gr	−1.36	2	−4.12*				*I*(0)
RER	2.45	2	0.85	3	−3.93*	1	*I*(1)
FDIY	−1.23	1	−3.13	3	−4.34*	1	*I*(1)
Nepal							
GFC	−2.44	2	−2.61	2	−3.02*	0	*I*(1)
RL	−2.83*	1					*I*(0)
DBC	0.64	1	−1.25	1	−3.41*	1	*I*(1)
Gr	−7.72*						*I*(0)
RER	0.91	1	−2.42	1	−3.28*	1	*I*(1)
FDIY	−2.64	2	−3.05	2	−3.67*	2	*I*(1)

*Denotes that the null hypothesis that the variable concerned is nonstationary can be rejected at 5 % significance level. Asymptotic cut-off values for 5 % significance level are −3.41 when the trend term is included and −2.86 when the trend term is not included (see Davidson and Mackinnon 1993). L stands for log transformation

Table 8.A.2 ARDL co-integration test (1980–2010)

Country	Dependent variable	F-stat	5 % Critical value[a]	Result
India	GFC	5.87[b]	3.50	Rejection of null of no co-integration
Pakistan	GFC	4.95[b]	3.50	Rejection of null of no co-integration
Sri Lanka	GFC	4.65[b]	3.50	Rejection of null of no co-integration
Bangladesh	GFC	5.06[b]	3.50	Rejection of null of no co-integration
Nepal	GFC	7.24[b]	3.50	Rejection of null of no co-integration

Notes: The order of ARDL is selected on the basis of AIC.
[a]Denotes upper bound critical values with seven independent variables.
[b]Denotes rejection of null hypothesis of no co-integration in favour of co-integration

Table 8.A.3 Panel unit root test using Pesaran (2007)

	At level		First. difference	
Variables	Constant	Constant and trend	Constant	Conclusion
GFC	−1.80	−2.22	−3.38**	$I(1)$
FDIY	−2.78*	–	–	$I(0)$
RL	−2.57*	–	–	$I(0)$
DBC	−2.04	−2.29	−3.67**	$I(1)$
RER	0.12	−0.82	−2.45*	$I(1)$
GR	−3.50*	–	–	$I(0)$

Notes: The null hypothesis is that the panel has a unit root. Critical values are tabulated by Pesaran (2007)
In both Tables 8.1 and 8.2, we report the ones for $T = 30$ and $N = 10$. '**' and '*' indicate significance of the test at 1 and 5 % level, respectively

Table 8.A.4 Westerlund (2007) error correction model for panel co-integration test

	Dependent variable GFC	
Test statistics	Value	p-Value
Gt	−2.18	0.18
Ga	−9.61[a]	0.02
Pt	−5.82[a]	0.03
Pa	−9.14[a]	0.02

Notes: The Westerlund (2007) tests take no co-integration as the null. The test regression is fitted with constant, and one lag and lead
[a]Denotes rejection of null of no co-integration at 5 % level

Table 8.A.5 Unit root test using ADF

	At level		First. difference	
Variables	Constant	Constant and trend	Constant	Conclusion
GFC	−0.46	−3.32	−5.12*	$I(1)$
RER	−2.62	−1.96	−4.11	$I(1)$
DBC	−1.19	−2.82	−4.38*	$I(1)$
RL	−3.34*	–	–	$I(0)$
GR	−4.17*	–	–	$I(0)$
FDIY	−2.06	−1.81	−3.32*	$I(1)$

*Denotes that the null hypothesis that the variable concerned is nonstationary can be rejected at 5 % significance level

Table 8.A.6 ARDL co-integration test (1980–2010)

Country	Dependent variable	F-stat	5 % critical value[b]	Result
China	GFC	6.64*	3.50	Rejection of null of no co-integration

[b]Denotes rejection of null hypothesis of no co-integration in favour of co-integration

References

Agosin M, Machado R (2005) Foreign investment in developing countries: does It crowd in domestic investment? Oxford Dev Stud 33(2):149–162

Agosin MR, Mayer R (2000) Foreign investment in developing countries: does it crowd-in domestic investment? UNCTAD discussion paper, no. 146. UNCTAD, Geneva

Agrawal P (2000) Economic impact of foreign direct investment in South Asia. Indira Gandhi Institute of Development Research, Mumbai

Aitken BJ, Harrison AE (1997) Do domestic firms benefit from foreign direct investment? Evidence from Panel Data. Columbia University, Mimeo

Alfaro L, Chanda A, Kalemli-Ozcan S, Sayek S (2004) FDI and economic growth: the role of local financial markets. J Int Econ 64:113–134

Ang JB (2009) Foreign direct investment and its impact on the Thai economy: the role of financial development. J Econ Finance 33:316–323

Apergis N, Katrakilidis CP, Tabakis NM (2006) Dynamic linkages between FDI inflows and domestic investment: a panel cointegration approach. Atl Econ J 34:385–394

Arndt C, Buch C, Schnitzer M (2007) FDI and domestic investment: an industry-level view, CEPR discussion papers, no. 6464. Centre for Economic Policy Research, London

Bontempi ME, Golinelli R, Parigi G (2010) Why demand uncertainty curbs investment: evidence from a panel of Italian manufacturing firms. J Macroecon 32(1):218–238

Borensztein E, Gregorio JD, Lee JW (1998) How does foreign direct investment affect economic growth? J Int Econ 45:115–135

Bosworth BP, Collins SM (1999) Capital flows to developing economies: implications for saving and investment. Brookings Pap Econ Act 1:143–169

Braunstein E, Epstein G (2002) Bargaining power and foreign direct investment in China: can 1.3 billions consumers tame the multinationals? CEPA working paper, no. 13. Center for Economic Policy Analysis, New York

Caves RE, Reuber G (1971) Capital transfers and economic policy. Canada, 1951–62. Harvard University Press, Cambridge, MA

Choy HT, Winkey KO, Stephen WK (2009) On *FDI* and domestic capital stock: a panel data study of Chinese region, Hong Kong Polytechnic University. Downloaded from http://www.bre.polyu.edu.hk/BRE_workshop/pdf/FDI_China.pdf

Davidson R, MacKinnon JG (1993) Estimation and inference in econometrics. Oxford University Press, New York

De Mello LR (1999) Foreign domestic investment-led growth: evidence from time series and panel data. Oxford Econ Pap 51:133–151

Desai MA, Foley CF, Hines JR (2005) Foreign direct investment and domestic capital stock, NBER working paper, no.11717. National Bureau of Economic Research, Cambridge, MA

Driffield N, Hughes D (2003) Foreign and domestic investment: regional development or crowd out? Reg Stud 37(3):227–228

Engle RF, Granger CW (1987) Cointegration and error correction: representation, estimation and testing. Econometrica 55:251–276

Feldstein M (1994) The effects of outbound foreign direct investment on the domestic capital stock, NBER working paper no. 4668. Cambridge, MA

Feldstein M, Horioka C (1980) Domestic saving and international capital flows. Econ J 90:314–329

Fry MJ (1992) Foreign direct investment in a macroeconomic framework: finance, efficiency, incentives and distortions, PRE working paper. The World Bank, Washington, DC

Fry MJ (1993a) Foreign direct investment in a macroeconomic framework: finance, efficiency, incentives and distortions, Working paper series, no.1141. World Bank, Washington, DC

Fry MJ (1993b) Foreign direct investment in southeast Asia: differential impacts. Institute of Southeast Asian Studies, Singapore

Fry MJ (1995) Money, interest and banking in economic development. Johns Hopkins University Press, Baltimore

Fry MJ (1998) Saving, investment, growth and financial distortions in Pacific Asia and other developing areas. Int Econ J 12(1):1–25

Gallagher KP, Zarsky L (2007) The enclave economy: foreign investment and sustainable development in Mexico's silicon valley. The MIT Press, Cambridge, MA

Görg H, Greenaway D (2004) Much ado about nothing? Do domestic firms really benefit from foreign investment? World Bank Res Obs 19(2):171–197

Greene J, Villanueva D (1991) Private investment in developing countries: an empirical analysis, IMF staff papers 38, no. 1. International Monetary Fund, Washington, DC, pp 33–58

Harrison A, Love I, McMillan M (2004) Global capital flows and financing constraints. J Dev Econ 75:269–301

Herzer D, Schrooten M (2007) Outward FDI and domestic investment, Discussion papers of DIW Berlin 679, DIW Berlin

Hurlin C, Venet B (2008) Financial development and growth: a re-examination using a panel Granger causality test

Jayaraman TK (1996) Private investment and macroeconomic environment in the South Pacific Island countries: a cross-country analysis, Occasional paper no.14. Asian Development Bank, Manila

Kamaly A (2012) Does FDI crowds in or out domestic investment? New Evidence from Emerging Economies. Available at SSRN: http;//ssrn/abstract=2154525

Kim DD, Seo J (2003) Does FDI inflow crowd out domestic investment in Korea? J Econ Stud 30(6):605–622

Kumar N, Pradhan JP (2002) Foreign direct investment, externalities and economic growth in developing countries: Some empirical explorations and implications for WTO negotiations on investment, RIS discussion paper, no.27. Research and Information System for the Non-Aligned and Other Developing Countries, New Delhi

Lautier M, Moreaub F (2012) Domestic investment and FDI in developing countries: the missing link. J Econ Dev 37(3):1–23

Lipsey RE (2000) Interpreting developed countries' foreign direct investment, NBER working paper no. 7810. Cambridge, MA

Lipsey RE (2002) Home and host country effects of FDI, NBER working paper, no. 9293. National Bureau of Economic Research, Cambridge, MA
McKinnon RI (1973) Money & capital in economic development. Brookings Institution Press, Washington, DC
Misun J, Tomšík V (2002) Does foreign direct investment crowd out or crowd in domestic investment? East Eur Econ 40(2):38–56
Mody A, Murshid AP (2005) Growing up with capital flows. J Int Econ 65:249–266
Mutenyo J, Asmah E, Kalio A (2010) Does foreign direct investment crowd-out domestic private investment in Sub-Saharan Africa. Afr Finance J 12(1):27–53
Ndikumana L, Verick S (2008) The linkages between FDI and domestic investment: unravelling the developmental impact of foreign investment in Sub-Saharan Africa. Dev Pol Rev 26(6):713–726
Noorzoy MS (1979) Flows of direct investment and their effects on investment in Canada. Econ Lett 2:257–261
Nwanna I (1986) The impact of foreign direct investment on domestic capital formation in a developing country: Nigeria. Sav Dev 10(3):265–278
Pesaran M (2007) A simple panel unit root test in the presence of cross-section dependence. J Appl Econometr 22:265–312
Pesaran MH, Shin Y, Smith RJ (2001) Bounds testing approaches to the analysis of level relationships. J Appl Econometr 16:289–326
Razin A (2003) FDI flows and domestic investment: overview. CESifo Econ Stud 49:415–428
Romer PM (1993) Idea gaps and object gaps in economic development. J Monet Econ 32:543–573
Sahoo P (2010) FDI in south Asia: impact on growth, investment and exports. In: Bhattacharya S et al (eds) Globalization, foreign capital and development. Regal Publications, New Delhi. ISBN 9788184840841
Saikonnen P (1991) Asymptotically efficient estimation of cointegration regressions. Econometr Theor 7:1–21
Servén L, Solimono A (1992) Private investment and macroeconomic adjustment: a survey. World Bank Res Obs 7(1):95–114
Servén L, Solimano A (1993) Debt crisis, adjustment policies and capital formation in developing countries: where do We stand? World Dev 21(1):127–140
Shah H, Hasnat, H, Li J (2010) Does foreign capital inflows really stimulate domestic investment: a case study of Pakistan? MPRA paper no. 35737, Munich
Shaw ES (1973a) Financial deepening in economic development, vol 39. Oxford University Press, New York
Shaw ES (1973b) Financial deepening in economic development. Brookings, Washington, DC
Stock JH, Watson MW (1993) A simple estimator of cointegrating vectors in higher order integrated systems. Econometrica 61:783–820
Sun H (1998) Macroeconomic impact of direct foreign investment in China: 1979–1996. World Econ 21(5):675–694
Tang S, Selvanathan EA, Selvanathan S (2008) FDI, domestic investment and economic growth in China: a time series analysis. World Econ. doi:10.1111/j.1467-9701.2008.01129.x
Titarenko D (2006) The influence of foreign direct investment on domestic investment processes in Latvia. Transp Telecommun 7(1):76–83
Udomkerdmongkol M, Morrissey O (2008) Political regime, private investment and foreign direct investment in developing countries, UNU-WIDER research paper, no. 109. UNU-WIDER, Helsinki
Van Wijnbergen S (1985) Trade reform, aggregate investment and capital flight. Econ Lett 19:369–372
Westerlund J (2007) Testing for error correction in panel data. Oxford Bull Econ Stat 69:709–748
Wu G, Sun Y, Li Z (2012) The crowding-in and crowding-Out effects of FDI on domestic investment in the Yangtze delta region. China Int J 10(2):119–133
Xu G, Wang R (2007) The effect of foreign direct investment on domestic capital formation, trade, and economic growth in a transition economy: evidence from China. Glob Econ J 7(2):1–23

Chapter 9
Impact of Foreign Direct Investment on Domestic Exports: Time Series and Panel Evidence from South Asia

9.1 Introduction

The favourable impact of exports on economic growth has been well established in literature as exports facilitate better resource allocation, efficient management style, economies of scale, and efficiency of production (Krueger 1975; Balassa 1978; Bhagwati 1982; Awokuse 2003). Another important factor for growth in recent years has been FDI, which enhances export competitiveness (Helpman et al. 2003; Aitken et al. 1997). Thus increase in investment in the export sector, even at the cost of other sectors, is expected to have positive impact on the economy. Further, exports enable imports of essential raw materials and capital goods, thus increasing investment in the economy and thereby resulting in higher output (Rana and Dowling 1990).

Following the export-oriented growth argument, many developing countries, particularly East Asian countries, changed their development strategy from import substitution to export promotion during the 1970s. Consequently, the East Asian countries have experienced sustained increase in exports as well as economic growth[1] over the last three decades. Several studies have established the effectiveness of trade liberalisation strategies in promoting higher economic growth in East Asian countries (Krugman 1986; Bhagwati 1988; Dornbusch 1992 and Krueger 1998). The remarkable success of East Asian countries led by higher exports in general and manufacturing exports in particular was possible due to market reforms, particularly investment reforms allowing for foreign investment. The FDI inflows to East Asia helped modernisation of the exports sector, more so the manufacturing sector, leading to growth in exports as well as overall economic growth (Riedel 1993; Krueger 1997). FDI can help integrate developing countries into the global economy by easing access to foreign markets and including local enterprises in global production chains.

[1] Except the few years following the East Asian currency crisis.

P. Sahoo et al., *Foreign Direct Investment in South Asia*,
DOI 10.1007/978-81-322-1536-3_9, © Springer India 2014

In East Asia, efficiency-seeking and export-oriented FDI mainly from Japan and the USA have played a major role in export-led growth strategy followed in the 1970s and 1980s (Fukao et al. 2003).

FDI contributes in a big way in improving export competitiveness and volume of exports particularly technology-intensive manufacturing exports in developing countries. In fact, lately one can also see a link between FDI and technology exports enhancing the export competitiveness of a country. A considerable body of research by UNCTAD, ESCAP, and World Bank shows that the late industrialising countries (e.g. Japan and subsequently South Korea) acquired technology from abroad instead of 'reinventing the wheel' in each case, thereby saving time and resources. FDI is the cheapest and most effective way of obtaining latest technology from abroad instead of direct purchasing of capital goods or licensing. It is essential that proper bargaining take place between the host country and foreign investor with regard to conditions of investment including local content, the transfer of R&D activities as part of FDI, and the technology to be transferred.

To upgrade the primary and labour-intensive exports into higher value added items, developing countries required to move into new, more advanced inputs and technology. The developing countries can attain these objectives by improving and deepening the capabilities of domestic enterprises, by tapping into transnational corporation (TNC) networks and conduits of trade, or by attracting FDI into export activities. Considering the beneficial effects such as creation of new employment, transfer of technology, and strengthening of domestic capabilities and enhancement of marketing expertise, FDI is encouraged in these countries as TNCs bring technology, which helps the host country to improve its export competitiveness and economic growth (see Parida and Sahoo 2007; Sahoo 2004a; Sharma 2003; Lall 1999; Bhalla 1995; Fry 1993). South Asian countries have also made earnest efforts in recent years to sell itself as an attractive destination for FDI not only to acquire advanced technology but also to enhance its export potential and export competitiveness with emphasis on value-added manufacturing-intensive exports. The experience of China, Singapore, and other East Asian countries support FDI-led export growth theory and show that international competitiveness and export capabilities are closely linked to R&D, innovation capabilities of FDI, and technology exports in a country.

Both Singapore and China have successfully directed foreign investment in high value-added exports, particularly manufacturing exports, through different industrial policies like directing FDI into high value-added activities, emphasising MNCs and TNCs to increase R&D expenditure, allowing public sector for FDI, and pushing FDI into specialised high export market. As a result, there has been a dramatic increase in the share of foreign companies in the total industrial investment, output and in total exports of the country. Overall, China, Singapore, and also East Asian countries followed three broad policies to give a boost to high value-added export industry such as (1) open-door policies on FDI without any substantial government intervention, particularly in export-oriented industries; (2) allowed participation of TNCs in manufacturing but intervened selectively to guide investors in directions towards industrial upgrading; and (3) allowed collaborative arrangements with set of policies to deepen the manufacturing sector, promote local linkages, and increase local innovative capabilities.

It has been widely recognised that FDI can positively impact domestic firms, either through forward and backward linkage, labour mobility, or imitation and competition effects (UNCTAD 2003a, b; Zhang 2006; Sun et al. 2012). In general, FDI effect on host country exports can be direct and indirect. Direct effects refer to exports by foreign affiliates themselves. For example, vertical FDI directly boosts host country exports, since output resulting from FDI is typically intended for export. On the other hand, horizontal FDI is oriented primarily to the host country market, so it does not directly contribute to host country exports. Similarly, the impact of FDI on export activities of local firms makes up the indirect effects (Zhang 2006; Xuan and Xing 2008).

It has been shown that the exports by FFEs in China increased dramatically to 32 % in 1995 from a mere 3 % in 1987 (Zhang and Song 2000). Export by FFEs has become an increasingly important part of China's total export. It suggests that China's exports are closely associated with inward FDI, though the structure of FDI promoting exports could be changing through decades due to China's rapid economic development.

The direct effects of FDI on host country exports, particularly labour-surplus developing countries, can be divided into three categories according to production characteristics: (a) local raw materials processing, (b) new labour-intensive final product exports, and (c) labour-intensive processes and component specialisation within vertically integrated international industries (Zhang and Song 2000). As for the indirect effects of FDI on host country exports, it involves the influence of FDI on the competitiveness of host country firms and the diffusion of new technologies. With the MNCs firm-specific assets, MNCs may increase competition in host country markets and force existing firms to adopt more efficient methods. FDI thus may improve the efficiency of host country firms through the diffusion of new technologies and management practices in host countries. The third indirect effect is related to the linkage structure between foreign and local firms. Multinational corporations (MNCs) that engage in FDI have a key role in channelling products from host countries to the international markets through their global distribution networks. Multinational corporations, therefore, are considered among the important ingredients in an economy's exporting success. Further, local firms may increase their exports by observing the export activities of MNCs and by making use of the infrastructure of transport, communications, and financial services that develop to support those activities (Haddad and Harrison 1993). FDI flows into the service sectors (e.g. telecommunications, banking) can support countries in their efforts to diversify production and exports. By slashing transaction costs, they also raise export competitiveness and increase exports in goods. However, the actual effects of FDI on the host economy and possibly on its exports depend on the type of the investment as well as on the specific host country initial economic conditions.

Similar to East Asia, South Asian countries followed export-led growth strategy in 1990s, and FDI was considered vital for the success of this policy. Empirical evidence also suggests that export-led growth strategy is highly successful in the

South Asian context (Parida and Sahoo 2007). However, role of FDI in export-led strategy has not been examined in detail for South Asia. An empirical assessment of the role of FDI on host country's export performance is important, since exports for a long time have been viewed as an engine of economic growth (Edwards 1998; Krueger 1998). In this chapter, we empirically examine the role of FDI inflows in augmenting exports for South Asian countries.

9.2 Export Performances of South Asian countries

Various trade liberalisation measures taken in the 1980s and 1990s by South Asian countries have had positive impact on their exports. During the 1970s, the average annual growth of exports of goods and services for Nepal was highest (18.4 %), and Sri Lanka (1.9 %) was lowest among South Asian countries. India and Bangladesh's export growth was impressive and higher than the growth rate of world exports. However, the export growth decelerated for all the counties except Pakistan and Sri Lanka during the 1980s. In the 1980s, Pakistan recorded an export growth of 10.7% followed by Sri Lanka at 6.5 %, Bangladesh at 7.2 %, and India at 5.2 %. In the 1990s, all the countries accelerated their export growth except Pakistan. India, Bangladesh, and Nepal recorded a robust export growth at 13.0, 12.0, and 13.9 %, respectively (see Table 9.1). The garment quota provided by the USA also encouraged exports from Nepal, as well as a gradual increase in exports of other products. Germany was a major importer of carpets from Nepal, which made Germany another major export destination for Nepal. The decline in Nepal's exports in the 2000s was mainly due to decline in exports to America and Germany in garments following phasing out of quotas for garments. Similarly, Sri Lanka's export growth and world share have been declining post 2000s mainly due to its heavy reliance on textile and tea exports. The share of textiles in total manufacturing exports declined from 70 % in 2000 to 45 % in 2010.

During 2000–2010, both India and Bangladesh managed to keep their export growth momentum intact, while other countries such as Nepal, Pakistan, and Sri Lanka lost pace. Interesting fact to note is that average growth rate of export for South Asian countries as a whole was above the world export growth rate for the entire period of the analysis. Overall, we find that export growth for India and Bangladesh accelerated during post-liberalisation (1991 onwards) period, and other countries like Sri Lanka and Nepal have performed decently on the export front.

Higher export growth, particularly during the 1990s and 2000s, resulted in increase in export intensity (export as ratio of GDP) for all South Asian countries. India and Bangladesh had lowest trade ratio (5.5), and Sri Lanka had highest export ratio (27.9) during pre-liberalisation period (1970–1990) among South Asian countries. However, India's export ratio increased from 8 % in 1991 to 13 % in 2000 and further to 23 % in 2010. On the other hand, export ratio for Sri Lanka after rising from 29 % in 1991 increased to 39 % in 2000 and again declined to 21 % in

Table 9.1 Annual average decadal growth rate of export

Countries	1970–1980	1981–1990	1991–2000	2000–2010
Bangladesh	8.7	7.2	12.3	10.1
India	10.5	5.2	12.7	13.6
Nepal	18.4	5.8	13.9	5.4
Pakistan	2.3	9.1	5	6.3
Sri Lanka	1.9	6.5	8.2	4.5
South Asia	8	6.2	10.8	12.3
World	6.2	5	7	4.1

Source: World Development Indicators 2011, World Bank

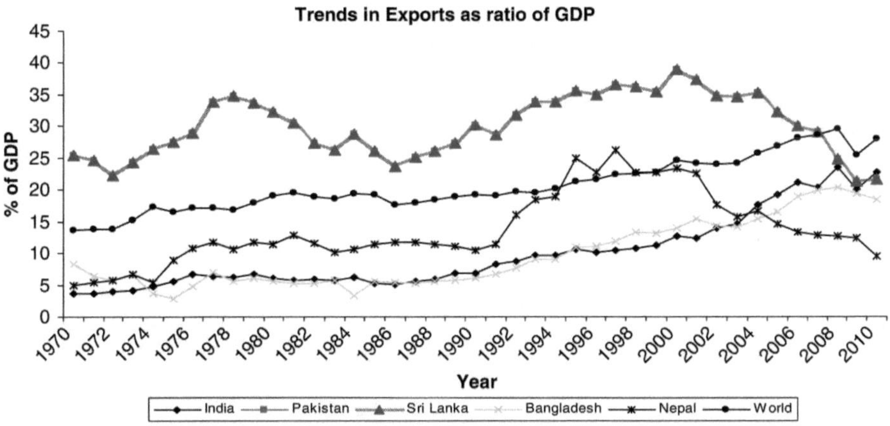

Fig. 9.1 Export intensity of South Asian countries (*Source*: World Development Indicators 2011, World Bank)

2010 (see Fig. 9.1). On the other hand, export ratio for Pakistan increased during 1990s and declined during the 2000s.

Although, export ratio has increased for all South Asian countries over time except Nepal and Sri Lanka in the 2000s, South Asia's share in world exports remains very insignificant compared to other regions. The share of South Asia in world export increased from 0.8 % during the 1980s to 0.9 % in the 1990s and further to above 1.5 % during the 2000s. Europe and Central Asia had the highest export share followed by East Asia and Pacific. More importantly, share of all other regions fluctuated during 1980–2010, and only the share of South Asia and East Asia and Pacific showed an upward trend (Fig. 9.2).

The export share of South Asian countries also shows different trends for different countries. For example, both India and Bangladesh have doubled their exports share during the 1980s–2000s, whereas share of other countries such as Pakistan, Sri Lanka, and Nepal have remained or declined over the period 1980–2010. India's export share increased from 0.5 % in the 1980s to 0.6 % in the 1990s and further to 1.25 % in the 2000s. Similarly, Bangladesh has increased its share from 0.04 % in the 1980s to 0.06 % in the 1990s and further to 0.085 % in

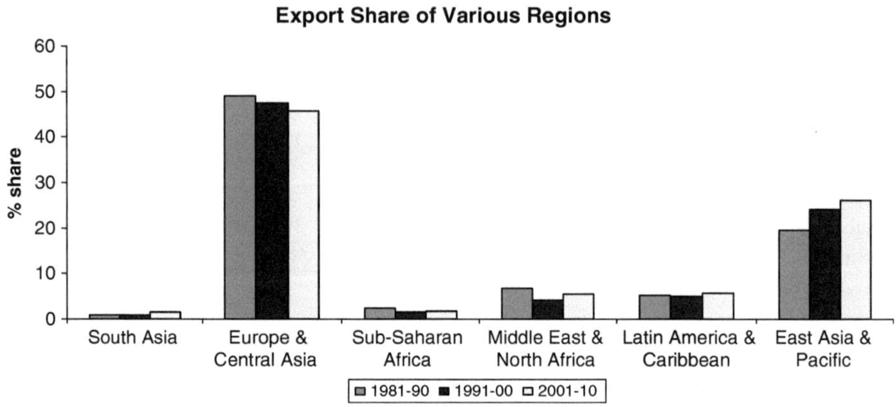

Fig. 9.2 Export share of various regions in the world (*Source*: World Development Indicators 2011, World Bank)

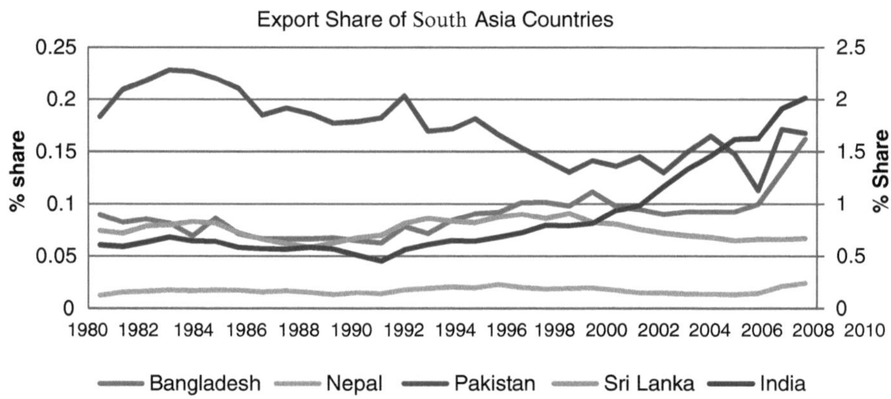

Fig. 9.3 Trends in export share of South Asian countries

the 2000s. On the other hand, export share of Pakistan marginally increased from 0.145 % in the 1980s to 0.151 % in the 1990s and again declined to 0.13 % in the 2000s. Similarly, share of Sri Lanka marginally increased from 0.06 % in the 1980s to 0.07 % in the 1990s and declined to 0.063 % in the 2000s (Fig. 9.3).

Not only has the share of South Asia increased over time, but its export composition has also changed over time. In the 1970s and 1980s, primary commodity export was dominant for all the countries except Pakistan, but after 1991, the share of manufacturing goods increased significantly.

Now, the share of manufacturing goods accounts for around 70 % of total exports. Sri Lanka, which was mainly primary commodity exporter in the 1970s and 1980s, turned exporter of manufactured goods since the early 1990s. Interestingly, Bangladesh

Fig. 9.4 Manufacturing export as ratio of total merchandise exports (*Source*: World Development Indicators 2011)

exports higher amount of manufacturing goods in South Asia compared to other countries. However, the share of manufacturing sector has declined since the global economic crisis in 2007–2008 (Fig. 9.4).

9.3 Theoretical Background

There has been, traditionally, a divergence in terms of the development of the theories on FDI and international trade. Trade theories attempt to explain why countries trade with each other and FDI theory tries to understand why firms produce abroad and invest in particular countries. In the neoclassical approach of trade theory, the paper of Mundell (1957) was the first to focus on the relationship between capital movements and trade of commodities. In the Heckscher–Ohlin–Samuelson (HOS) framework, in taking account of the assumptions of perfect competition and constant economies of scale, Mundell (1957) argued that a tariff protection would generate a perfect substitution between capital movements and trade of commodities. Vernon's product cycle model also suggested a substitution relationship between FDI and trade (Vernon 1966). Dunning (1977) used firm organisation theory to discuss whether FDI should serve a foreign market through exports or local production. Exports and FDI are fundamentally substitutes in his framework.

Some earlier theoretical work has predicted either a substitute or complementary relationship between FDI and trade. These models are based on imperfect competition, the economies of scale, the difference in production technologies, etc. Some have focused mainly on either vertical or horizontal FDI.[2] In the first case, firms separate geographically their different stages of the value-added chain. In the second case, firms duplicate the entire production process in several countries with an exception for headquarter activities. The models of Helpman (1984) and Helpman and Krugman (1985) integrate vertical FDI into international trade theory. They show that FDI generates complementary trade flows of finished goods from foreign affiliates to parent companies or to the home country and intra-firm transfers of intangible headquarter services from parent companies to foreign affiliates. On the other hand, in the models based on horizontal FDI, such as Markusen (1983), Brainard (1993), Horstmann and Markusen (1992), Markusen (1995), and Markusen and Venables (1998), foreign investment is alternative modality. The choice of multinational firms depends on the interaction between these key elements: the firm-specific advantages (activities of research and development, managerial knowhow, etc.), the plant-level scale economies, and transport costs and geographical and cultural distance costs. In these models, the substitutability between FDI and trade prevails over complementarity. According to the models of Brainard (1993) and Horstmann and Markusen (1992), when countries are identical in technologies, preferences, and factor endowments, the higher the value of firm-level scale economies and tariffs and transport costs relative to that of plant-level scale economies, the more likely is the presence of horizontal FDI. These models based on the trade-off between proximity and concentration postulate a substitution relationship between horizontal FDI and trade.

Markusen and Venables (1998) further elaborated the theory to introduce asymmetries between countries in terms of market size, factor endowments, and technologies. Countries' asymmetries make it possible for national and multinational firms and, therefore, trade and FDI to coexist. However, as countries become more similar in market size, relative factor endowments, and technical efficiency, FDI will increase and international economic activity will become increasingly dominated by MNEs, which displace trade, provided that transport costs are not very small.

In a recent survey article, Helpman (2006) argued that the traditional classification of FDI into vertical and horizontal forms has become less meaningful as MNEs' outsourcing and FDI practices become more complicated. In particular, utilising developing countries as an export platform is another motivation for MNEs' FDI. China is the classic example of an export platform for MNEs. Foreign-invested firms accounted for more than 60 % of China's exports, and they are the essential driving force behind China's rapid export expansion (Liu et al. 2002; Xing 2006).

[2] Horizontal FDI is defined as investment in the same industry abroad as a firm operates in at home. In contrast, vertical FDI takes two forms: (1) backward vertical FDI, where an industry abroad provides inputs for a firm's domestic production process, and (2) forward vertical FDI, in which an industry abroad sells the outputs of a firm's domestic production processes.

The theoretical literature shows the ambiguity of the relationship between FDI and international trade. The conclusions of the models revolve around substitutability and complementarity. However, conclusions ought to be determined by empirical findings.

9.4 Review of Empirical Literature

The role of FDI in the export performance of host country industries has received considerable attention in recent years, especially in the context of liberalisation and globalisation. Empirical research has come up with different conclusions on the relationship between FDI and foreign trade. For example, Balasubramanyam et al. (1996) asserts that endogenous growth theory provides a new conceptual framework to analyse the effect of FDI on growth through its effect on host countries exports. Indeed, Bhagwati (1978) explains that volume and efficiency of FDI are more pronounced in export-oriented host countries. Aitken et al. (1997) conducting a study on Mexican manufacturing firms for the period 1986–1990 found that export decision of Mexican firms is positively related to foreign firms' presence that is measured using two separate variables: MNCs' output (production) and their exports. They found that the presence of MNCs with their production and export activities reduces export costs for domestic firms. Haddad and Harrison (1993) find some evidence of FDI spillover on Moroccan firms.

There are studies on other countries and blocks of countries in this regard. For instance, Zhang and Song (2000) find support for the widely held belief that increased levels of FDI have positively affected export performance of China. Using an augmented export demand model and a panel data set for 11 OECD countries, Pain and Wakelin (1998) find that inward FDI has a positive effect on export. Other studies too indicate that FDI has a positive effect on export performance of host countries as found in Ireland (O'Sullivan 1993), Portugal (Cabral 1995), UK (Blake and Pain 1994), etc.

A cross-country analysis of 52 countries by UNCTAD (1999) found that there is a positive relationship between FDI and manufactured exports, and the relationship is stronger for developing countries than developed countries and in high- and low-tech industries than in medium-tech ones. Metwally (2004) tests the relationship between FDI, exports, and economic growth in three countries, namely, Egypt, Jordan, and Oman, during the period 1981–2000 by using a simultaneous equation model. The result suggests that the export of goods and services is strongly influenced by inward FDI in these three countries. Zhang and Song (2000) found that FDI is an important factor affecting export performance in the case of China. FDI can help channel capital into industries that have the potential to compete internationally, and the global linkages of MNCs can facilitate their access to foreign markets. FDI can also promote exports through the teaching of proper marketing strategies, methods, procedures, and channels of distribution. In contrast, Wen (2005) finds that in east China, geographical advantage in export attracts FDI inflow, which in turn promotes export. However, FDI impact on export is negative in central China. Zhang (2006) examines the impact of FDI on exports using cross-sectional analysis at industry-level data for China. Results based on 186 industries indicate that the effect of FDI on exports is larger in labour-intensive industries than capital-intensive industries.

In addition, other studies have emphasised the motives of FDI in explaining FDI and export linkages. For example, Pradhan and Abraham (2005) argue that export-oriented FDI can be expected to generate strong links with local economy compared to local market-oriented FDI in the host country specifically because it is motivated to exploit the location advantages offered by the host country like low-cost labour, raw materials, components, and parts, among others. The experience of countries like China and Mexico shows that these countries were able to increase their international market shares mostly by attracting export-oriented FDI (UNCTAD 2002). Therefore, it is expected that spillover effects will be larger from the presence of more export-oriented MNEs compared to domestic market-seeking ones. The impact of FDI on exports, however, may differ according to the source of FDI. The importance of the source of FDI in export promotion was first discussed by Kojima. The theoretical framework developed by Kojima (1982) shows that 'American-type FDI' is a substitute for trade, but 'Japanese-type FDI' enhances trade in the host country.

A number of studies have attempted to analyse the impact of FDI on the export performance in the case of South Asia, particularly in the case of India. In India, earlier studies for the period of restrictive policy regimes could not find any significant difference in the export performance of foreign and domestic firms (e.g. Kumar and Siddharthan 1994). However, a number or recent studies for the post-1991 liberalisation period suggest that foreign firms show higher export performance as compared to domestic firms (e.g. Aggarwal 2002; Kumar and Pradhan 2003). Aggarwal (2002) compared the export performance of MNC affiliates and domestic firms in Indian manufacturing after the 1991 liberalisation by analysing the determinants of their export intensities. The study examined the relationship between FDI and export performance using Tobit model for 916 Indian manufacturing firms for the period 1996–2000. The study found that the liberalisation measures of the 1990s enhanced the export role of MNC affiliates, especially in the late 1990s. However, the author could not find any evidence of positive relationship between foreign equity share and export performance of firms. Sharma (2003) examines the determinants of export performances of India using annual data for 1970–1998 in a simultaneous equation framework. Results suggest that the real appreciation of the rupee adversely affects India's export performance. Export supply is positively related to the domestic relative price of exports, while higher domestic demand reduces export supply. Foreign investment appears to have had no statistically significant impact on export performance although its coefficient has a positive sign.

Kumar and Pradhan (2003) have examined the important factors that influence the export competitiveness of Indian manufacturing firms with emphasis on knowledge-based industries. They found that younger firms drive export competitiveness in the high-technology and low-technology industries, whereas in the medium-technology industries, older firms are more competitive. The study also found that foreign affiliates are better achievers on export front compared to their domestic counterparts in Indian manufacturing. The study concluded that the liberalisation policies of 1990s have definitely improved the export competitiveness of Indian manufacturing, especially technology-intensive segments. Banga (2003) examines the export-diversifying impact of FDI using panel data for 52 industries over the period 1994–1995 to 1999–2000 in the case of India. The results of this study suggest that FDI from the USA has led to diversification of India's exports both directly as well as indirectly. On the other hand, Japanese FDI has had no significant impact on India's exports. In a descriptive analysis of firm-level data for Indian manufacturing firms for the period from 1989–1990 to 2000–2001, Pradhan and Abraham (2005) found that foreign firms having 65–75 and 40–55% of ownership tend to export more as a percentage of sales than any other group. Using a simple Tobit analysis, the study finds that firms with modest levels of foreign equity participation have shown higher export performance following the implementation of economic reforms. However, firms with majority foreign ownership have not yet shown any significant improvement in their export behaviour, supporting the earlier findings that firms with larger foreign equity participation in Indian manufacturing are relatively local market oriented.

In addition to macro studies, there are number of micro- or firm-level studies. For instance, Kokko et al. (2001) examined the association between FDI spillovers and the export behaviour of domestic firms in Uruguay using a cross-sectional firm-level data. They found that domestic firms are more likely to export if they operate in sectors where the presence of foreign firms is relatively high. Their study also pointed out that the type of trade regime (controlled or liberalised) may influence the ability of MNEs in generating positive export spillovers. On the other hand, Barrios et al. (2003) found no evidence of export spillovers to local firms from the existence of MNCs in the case of Spain. Ruane and Sutherland (2004) find no evidence of export spillovers from MNCs to local firms in Ireland. While FDI has the potential to help host countries' exports, the benefits do not accrue automatically or uniformly across countries. National policies and host government bargaining powers relative to MNCs matter for attracting export-oriented FDI and for reaping its full benefits for exports. Greenaway et al. (2004), using a two-step Heckman selection model to determine the influence of FDI spillovers on the export decision of domestic firms, found positive FDI spillovers on the probability of a UK firm being an exporter. They found that the most important channel of export spillovers is the increased competition resulting from foreign firms. Sun (2012) investigates the impact of FDI on domestic exporting firms in the case of China using panel data for 3,260 firms over the period 2000–2010. They find that domestic firms respond to an increase in the presence of FDI by increasing their exports even though the increase in foreign presence can drive up production costs and make the domestic market more profitable.

There have been a large number of studies in the recent years that technical and technology export capabilities and performance are increasingly important factors in enhancing the international competitiveness of a nation and of an enterprise in the emerging knowledge-driven economy (Helpman et al. 2003; Aitken et al. 1997). This explains the importance, which the MNCs and TNCs have in increasing the export share of several developing countries, particularly shifting the export composition from primary and labour-intensive products to high-technology manufacturing products (Helpman et al. 2003; Aitken et al. 1997). One of the primary objectives of attracting FDI in South Asia is to enhance the international competitiveness of industries and thereby exports, besides bringing long-term additional capital for economic growth.

Several cross-country studies also find support for the hypothesis of a negative relationship between FDI and export. Using trade equations for the US and Swedish firm-level data, Blomström et al. (1988) find that the relationship between FDI and export sales is complementary; hence, a negative relationship exists. Several cross-country studies find support for the hypothesis of a negative relationship between FDI and export (Jeon 1992). However, there are still few middle grounders who find no significant relationship between FDI and trade. Studies on import–FDI relationship are not as common as that of export–FDI. Even some authors take trade as a synonym for export. Studies like Culem (1988) identify existence of a long-run positive relationship between host country import and FDI inflow.

9.4.1 Studies on Casualty Between FDI and Exports

Khan and Leng (1997) examine the interactions among inward FDI, exports, and economic growth for Singapore, Taiwan, and South Korea, at the aggregate level during the period from 1965 to 1995 by using Granger causality test. They claim that there is no evidence to support the causal relationship between FDI and exports in Taiwan and South Korea. Moreover, a one-way causal relationship that flows from exports to inward FDI is found in Singapore. Zhang and Felmingham (2001) examine the causal relationship between inward FDI and export performance using both national- and provincial-level data for China over the period 1986–1999. The result reveals that there is a two-way causality between inward FDI and exports at the country and province levels. Baliamoune-Lutz (2004) examines the causal relationship between FDI, exports, and economic growth in Morocco from 1973 to 1999 by using the Granger causality test. The result shows that there is a two-way causal relationship between FDI and exports at a national level. Alici and Ucal (2003) investigate the causal links among inward FDI, exports, and economic growth in the Turkish economy during the period of 1987–2002 on a quarterly basis. The linkage of FDI-led export growth is not found in Turkey. Liu et al. (2002) investigate the causal links between GDP, FDI, exports, and imports in China with the methods developed by Johansen (1988) and Hall and Milne (1994). They show each of these variables with the tests proposed by Hall and Milne (1994). They also provide evidence to support the presence of bidirectional short-run causal links between GDP, FDI, and exports. However, unidirectional causal link can be found from GDP, FDI, and exports to imports. Sahoo (2004a, b) uses the co-integration and causality analysis with an error correction model (ECM) and finds a bidirectional causality between FDI and manufacturing exports both in long run as well as in short run in India. Dash and Sharma (2011) examine the direction of causality between FDI and exports for four South Asian countries using quarterly data for the period 1990 Q1–2007 Q4. The results of this study indicate that there exist bidirectional causality between FDI and export for three countries, namely, India, Bangladesh, and Pakistan. However, the study does not find any causality between FDI and exports in Sri Lanka.

Overall, we find that FDI inflows have positive impact on host countries' exports. Although, FDI has the potential to help host countries' exports, the benefits do not accrue automatically or uniformly across countries. National policies, host government bargaining powers relative to MNCs matter, and availability of infrastructure facilities are important for attracting export-oriented FDI and for reaping its full benefits for exports.

9.5 Model Specification

9.5.1 Possible Determinants of Export Function

In the traditional export function, demand-side factors were given more importance assuming supply is not a constraint on exports. Such models have generally been unsuccessful in explaining long-run trends in export performance. However, Goldstein and Khan (1978) pointed out that unless export production is subject to constant or increasing returns to scale, an increase in the demand for a country's exports cannot be met without generating a rise in the price of exports. Arize (1990) and Funke and Holly (1992) show that for developing countries, demand and supply factors are equally important in determining their export growth pattern. Therefore, one should consider both demand-side and supply-side factors. In this section, we briefly review possible determinants of both export demand and supply.

In order to assess the impact of FDI on exports for South Asian countries, we estimate both demand for and supply of export function. Export demand function can be written as

$$\mathrm{Xd} = \beta_0 - \beta_1\left(\frac{\mathrm{PX}}{\mathrm{PWX}}\right) + \beta_2\mathrm{WY} \tag{9.1}$$

$$\beta_1 < 0 \text{ and } \beta_2 > 0$$

where Xd is real exports demanded, PX is price of export, PWX is world export price, and WY is net world real income. In the export demand function, real exports can be regarded as a decreasing function of relative prices (the price of a country's exports relative to the foreign price of related goods). All other things being equal, an increase in the price of exports lowers the demand for exports, while a rise in the price of the competing goods would increase demand for exports. Empirical results suggest that the average long-run price elasticity is found to be approximately -1, but there is a wide diversity of experiences (Goldstein and Khan 1982; Arize 1987; Senhadji and Montenegro 1999). Apart from relative price effect, the export demand is also influenced by conditions prevailing in the world market (Goldstein and Khan 1978). The demand for exports increases with the rise in the income of the rest of the world. That is, the higher the level of foreign real income, the larger would be the foreign demand for a nation's export, *ceteris paribus*. Empirical results suggest that the average long-run income elasticities are found to be approximately 1.5, but there is a wide diversity of experiences (Arize 1990; Senhadji and Montenegro 1999). The measurement of world demand variable has often varied across studies. Generally, three income measures are used in the literature: GNP or GDP, industrial production, and world real import of major export destinations of particular products.

Export supply function can be written as

$$\mathrm{Xs} = \alpha_0 + \alpha_1\left(\frac{\mathrm{PX}}{\mathrm{Pd}}\right) + \alpha_2\mathrm{DD} + \alpha_3\mathrm{INFRA} + \alpha_4\mathrm{HUM} + \alpha_5\mathrm{FDI} \tag{9.2}$$

$$\alpha_1, \alpha_3, \alpha_4, \alpha_5 > 0 \quad \text{and} \quad \alpha_2 < 0$$

where Xs is real exports supplied, PX is price of exports, Pd is price of export in the domestic market expressed in local currency, DD domestic demand is taken as ratio of GDP, INFRA is infrastructure stock, HUM is human capital stock proxied by gross enrolment ratio, and FDI is foreign direct investment as ratio of GDP. On the supply side, export decision mainly depends upon relative price changes, i.e. export price relative to domestic prices. This reflects relative profitability of selling in foreign markets. We expect that an increase in the relative price will have a favourable impact on the incentive for exports, i.e. the ratio should be above unity. On the other hand, a better domestic price reduces this incentive and domestic manufactures will be interested in catering to domestic demand, *ceteris paribus*. Empirically, it is found that the estimated supply price elasticity is significant for most of the countries, but the magnitude varies (Goldstein and Khan 1982; Arize 1990; Muscatelli et al. 1992). Increase in domestic demand diverts export supply towards domestic consumption, leading to a fall in exports. In addition, domestic demand signifies the cyclical effect, as the industry is very sensitive to them. Here the hypothesis is that during high domestic demand pressure, firms will operate at full capacity and will export little, while during domestic recession, capacity utilisation will be low, and firms will attempt to export as much machines as possible (Joshi and Little 1994).

FDI influences supply-side determinants of exports and imports, reflecting to some extent the quality of physical capital as well as worker skills and market penetration potential (De Gregorio 1992). There is consensus among development economists that FDI inflows are likely to play an important role in explaining growth of recipient countries (De Mello 1999). However, the World Bank (1993) notes that the role of FDI in export promotion depends crucially on the motive for such investment: if the motive behind FDI is to capture the domestic market (tariff-jumping type of investment), it may not contribute to export growth. On the other hand, if the motive is to tap export markets by taking advantage of a country's comparative advantage, then FDI may contribute to export growth. Thus, whether FDI contributes to export growth or not depends on the nature of the policy regime (Sharma 2003). Like the theoretical views, the existing empirical studies of the role of FDI in export performance also report mixed findings. Some studies found a negative relationship between FDI and export (Ancharaz 2003; Gu et al. 2008). In contrast, others indicate that FDI has a positive effect on the export performance of host countries (Fugazza 2004; UNCTAD 2005; Gu et al. 2008). Another major factor affecting export supply capacity is the domestic infrastructure. To sustain the rapid growth of exports, it is necessary to have a well-functioning infrastructure, including electric power, road and rail connectivity, telecommunications, air transport, and efficient ports (UNCTAD 2005). Infrastructure can refer to the financial system that facilitates and supports trade or the education and training system that produces skilled labour. Most of the South Asian countries are characterised by poor infrastructure facilities, which is a major impediment to trade, competitiveness, and sustainable development (Jones 2006; Sahoo and Dash 2012). Empirical studies also support the positive relationship between infrastructure development and export performance (Bougheas et al. (1999) and Fugazza (2004)). Therefore, improvements in infrastructure can lead to better export performance (Fugazza 2004; UNCTAD 2005). Finally, low human capital is hindrance for technology transfer and learning in low-income countries that have been shown to hamper export growth and diversification (Hausmann et al. 2006; Biggs et al. 1996). A country's level of human development indicators is an important and useful barometer of how much it is likely to benefit from international trade. The current export success of the East Asian countries and PR China can be explained, at least partially, by its achievement of relatively good human capital. A healthier and more skilled and educated workforce is also likely to contribute to productivity increases and higher exports. Therefore, higher human capital stock will increase higher export capacity of domestic economy.

In equilibrium Xd = Xs = X, therefore, Eqs. (9.1) and (9.2) can be solved for equilibrium export[3]:

$$X = \sigma_0 + \sigma_1\,\mathrm{RER} + \sigma_2\,\mathrm{WY} - \sigma_3\mathrm{DD} + \sigma_4\,\mathrm{INFRA} + \sigma_5\mathrm{HUM} + \sigma_6\mathrm{FDI} + u \quad (9.3)$$

[3] A number of empirical studies (e.g. Goldstein and Khan 1985; Bushe et al. 1986; Arndt and Hueme 2004, Athukorala 2004; Chinn 2005) have examine export behaviour using a single-equation approach where both demand and supply equations are solved together to yield an expression for the equilibrium volume of exports.

where $\sigma_0 = (\alpha_0\beta_1+\alpha_1\beta_0)/(\beta_1+\alpha_1)$, $\sigma_1 = (\alpha_1\beta_1)/(\beta_1+\alpha_1)$, $\sigma_2 = (\alpha_1\beta_2)/(\beta_1+\alpha_1)$, $\sigma_3 = (\beta_1\alpha_2)/(\beta_1+\alpha_1)$, $\sigma_4 = (\beta_1\alpha_3)/(\beta_1+\alpha_1)$, $\sigma_5 = (\beta_1\alpha_4)/(\beta_1+\alpha_1)$, $\sigma_6 = (\beta_1\alpha_5)/(\beta_1+\alpha_1)$,

$$\sigma_1, \sigma_2, \sigma_4, \sigma_5, \sigma_6 > 0 \text{ and } \sigma_3 < 0$$

Therefore, a number of empirical studies in this research area (e.g. Goldstein and Khan 1985; Bushe et al. 1986; Arndt and Hueme 2004, Athukorala 2004; Chinn 2005) examine export behaviour using a single-equation approach where both demand and supply equations are solved together to yield an expression for the equilibrium value of real exports.

9.6 Data Sources and Methodology

Annual data on exports, unit value of exports, and exchanger rate are collected from IFS database of International Monetary Fund (IMF). Data on manufacturing exports, world income, gross enrolment ratio, inflation rate (Consumer Price Index), domestic credit by banking sector, and domestic final consumption as ratio of GDP are collected from World Development Indicators of World Bank. The study uses both time series and panel data analysis for getting robust estimation. Given that we have only 31 observations per country, autoregressive distributed lag (ARDL) technique is used for co-integration analysis. In addition to time series analysis, we also present panel data analysis. Unit of export price for China is estimated by dividing export value index with export volume index.

9.6.1 Analysis of Empirical Results: Times Series Analysis

The first step in the empirical analysis is the examination of time series properties of variables by using augmented Dickey–Fuller (ADF) unit root test (see Chap. 6 for details). The result of ADF unit root test is given in Table 9.A.1. It is seen from Table 9.A.1 (Appendix) that we have mixture of $I(0)$ and $I(1)$ variables. All the variables are $I(1)$ for India, Bangladesh, and Pakistan. However, manufacturing export, FDI ratio, and domestic demand as ratio of GDP are $I(0)$ for Sri Lanka. Similarly, exports and domestic demand ratio are $I(0)$ for Nepal. After establishing the order of integration of variables, the test for co-integration has been conducted to examine the long-run properties of an estimated econometric model and its adjustment process towards the long-run equilibrium. ARDL procedure (see Chap. 6 for details) for co-integration is applied, and the result of co-integration test is presented in Table 9.A.2. It is clear from Table 9.A.2 is that there exists a long-run relationship among the variables when real export is the dependent variable because the F-statistic exceeds the upper bound critical value (3.50) at the 5 % levels for all the countries. Similarly, the results also indicate that real manufacturing export and other variables are having long-run equilibrium relationship since F-stat rejects the null non-co-integration. Given that we have only 31 observations, 2 lags were considered and selected based on the AIC. Thus, the null of non-existence of stable long-run relationship is rejected in favour of a stable relationship.

9.6.1.1 Determinants of Export

Having found the long-run relationship between real export and other relevant variables, we estimate long-run coefficients of real per capita income by using ARDL model. The result of long-run coefficients is presented in Table 9.2. Diagnostic test indicates that the serial correlation, ARCH effect, and heteroscedasticity are not a problem. Further, Ramsey test also suggest there is no misspecification problem for the model. Adjusted R^2 is also very high, indicating the model fits the data very well.

9.6.1.2 India

The estimated long-run coefficients of export equation estimated by ARDL and DOLS for India are presented in column 2 of Table 9.2. The results show that as expected real world income has positive significant effect on real exports in India. The coefficient of real world income is greater than one, indicating income elasticity is more than 1. This is in line with previous empirical studies (Arize 1990; Senhadji and Montenegro 1999). Therefore, exports from India are more likely to be affected by external shocks like any kind of changes in major export destination markets. The coefficient of real exchange rate (RER) is found to have negative impact on real exports as appreciation of domestic currency adversely affects exports. It is well known that the appreciation of the real effective exchange rate (REER) reduces export (Joshi and Little 1994; Srinivasan 1998; Sharma 2003); hence, a negative link between the appreciation of REER and export demand is expected. Supply-side factors such as infrastructure stock, human capital, domestic final consumption, and FDI have expected signs. The impact of domestic consumption real export is negative and statistically significant. The negative elasticity of domestic demand pressure indicates that the export supply declines as domestic demand increases (Joshi and Little 1994; Sharma 2003). The availability of higher human capital and infrastructure stock increases export supply, as their coefficient is positive (UNCTAD 2005; Hausmann et al. 2006). However, human capital stock as proxied by gross secondary enrolment is significant at 10 % level only in DOLS estimation. Finally, the impact of FDI on exports is found to be positive, but the coefficient is higher in ARDL estimation which is the focus variable in our analysis. One unit increase in FDI inflows increases around 0.2 % of export in India. Our results are similar to the existing empirical studies about the role of FDI in export performance (UNCTAD 2005; Gu et al. 2008; Sun et al. 2012).

Table 9.2 Determinants of total export performances dependent variable: log of real exports

	India		Pakistan		Sri Lanka		Bangladesh		Nepal	
Variables	ARDL	DOLS	ARDL	DOLS	ARDL	DOLS	ARDL	DOLS	ARDL	DOLS
Constant	−12.15	−16.34**	−3.26	5.55**	2.02	−15.43**	12.4	−24.22*	−12.34**	3.04
	(−1.56)	(−3.14)	(−0.96)	(3.99)	(1.15)	(−5.86)	(0.91)	(−2.33)	(−3.37)	(1.02)
LRWY	2.37*	2.93**	2.28**	2.49**	0.61**	2.78**	1.58**	2.12**	0.59*	0.82*
	(2.26)	(5.75)	(11.63)	(16.34)	(3.20)	(7.59)	(3.01)	(9.14)	(2.53)	(2.92)
LRER	−0.58*	−1.62**	0.07	−0.57**	1.46**	−0.59*	−0.65	−0.53*	1.48**	0.28
	(−2.10)	(−5.15)	(0.46)	(3.36)	(3.92)	(−2.04)	(−1.31)	(−2.17)	(4.62)	(1.02)
LHUM	0.44	0.76#	−0.66	−0.10	0.71*	0.65*	−0.71	0.07	0.39	0.64*
	(1.36)	(1.78)	(−1.36)	(−0.60)	(2.53)	(2.51)	(−1.41)	(0.78)	(1.34)	(2.28)
INFRA	0.33*	0.17*	0.10*	0.09**	–	0.04*	0.18**	0.03	–	0.05
	(2.47)	(2.83)	(2.55)	(4.65)		(2.52)	(3.70)	(0.89)		(0.76)
LDom	−6.37*	−0.60	−4.68**	−4.09**	−3.80**	0.21	−9.01*	−5.03**	5.15	3.13**
	(−2.74)	(−0.83)	(−3.30)	(5.23)	(−5.55)	(0.28)	(2.18)	(−3.68)	(1.63)	(3.53)
FDIy	0.30**	0.15*	0.05**	0.045**	0.14**	0.07*	0.047	0.039*	0.11	−0.04
	(3.10)	(2.13)	(3.23)	(5.29)	(4.91)	(2.33)	(0.96)	(2.32)	(0.87)	(−0.95)
MSC (AIC)	(1,1,0,2,2,1,2)		(0,3,1,2,2,0)		(2,3,2,3,3,3)		(1,1,2,0,2,0,1)		(0,2,1,2,2,2	
Diagnostic test	ADJ $R^2 = 0.91$ DW = 1.7 LM = 1.35 ARCH = 1.4 Reset-0.76	ADJ $R^2 = 0.96$ DW = 1.7 LM = 0.7 ARCH = 0.04 Reset-0.37	ADJ $R^2 = 0.98$ DW = 1.76 LM = 2.8 ARCH = 0.09 Reset-1.87	ADJ $R^2 = 0.97$ DW = 2.56 LM = 1.54 ARCH = 1.09 Reset-0.17	ADJ $R^2 = 0.62$ DW = 2.3 LM = 1.9 ARCH = 1.57 Reset-2.3	ADJ $R^2 = 0.98$ DW = 2.09 LM = 0.3 ARCH = 0.12 Reset-0.45	ADJ $R^2 = 0.94$ DW = 2.4 LM = 2.5 ARCH = .15 Reset-0.05	ADJ $R^2 = 0.96$ DW = 2.3 LM = 2.1 ARCH = 0.88 Reset-0.75	ADJ $R^2 = 0.75$ DW = 1.95 LM = 0.05 ARCH = 2.2 Reset-2.4	ADJ $R^2 = 0.73$ DW = 2.03 LM = 0.91 ARCH = 0.64 Reset-2.23

Notes: ***, **, and # denote significance at 1, 5, and 10 % level, respectively. Figures in the parentheses are *t*-ratio. *MSC* model selection criteria

9.6.1.3 Pakistan

Like India, coefficients of real exports indicate that all the variables have expected sign except human capital for Pakistan. The coefficient of real world income is greater than one, indicating income elasticity is more than 1. Therefore, one unit change in real world income will result in more than two unit change in Pakistan exports. The coefficient of RER is found to be negative and significant only in DOLS estimation, indicating depreciation of Pakistan currency will boost exports. Supply-side factors such as infrastructure stock, domestic final consumption, and FDI have expected signs. Increase in domestic consumption will reduce real export as goods are diverted to meet domestic demand. Availability of infrastructure stock increases exports by improving export supply, as the coefficient of infrastructure stock is positive and statistically significant. However, human capital stock has no significant on exports for Pakistan. Finally, the impact of FDI inflows on exports is found to be positive but statistically significant. The magnitude of coefficient indicates that one unit increase in FDI inflows increases around 0.05 % of export in Pakistan. Therefore, recent slowdown in FDI inflows to Pakistan is found to be an important factor in export performances.

9.6.1.4 Sri Lanka

The estimated long-run coefficients of export for Sri Lanka indicate that export is determined by real world income, RER, domestic final consumption, human capital stock, and FDI inflows. The coefficient of world income is positive but greater than one for DOLS estimation. Similarly, the coefficient of real exchange has positive sign in ARDL estimation but negative sign in DOLS estimation.

Supply-side factors such as human capital, domestic final consumption, and FDI have expected signs. Results indicate that increase in domestic consumption will reduce real export as exportable goods are diverted to meet domestic demand. On the other hand, availability of infrastructure stock and human capital increases exports by improving export capacity and reducing transaction cost. Finally, the impact of FDI inflows on exports is found to be positive. The magnitude of coefficient indicates that one unit increase in FDI inflows increases around 0.14 and 0.07 % of export in ARDL and DOLS estimations, respectively.

9.6.1.5 Bangladesh

For Bangladesh, both demand-side and supply-side factors are major determinates of exports. Among demand-side factors, while real world income increases real exports of Bangladesh, depreciation of RER will boost exports by increasing competitiveness of exports in the world market. The income elasticity is greater than one and that of RER is less than one.

Among supply-side factors, infrastructure stock, domestic consumption, and FDI inflows have necessary impact on exports. Higher domestic consumption in Bangladesh will reduce exportable amount available for exports. On the other hand, availability of better facilities such as power, road, and telecom facilities will stimulate exports by reducing transaction cost and increasing competitiveness. FDI inflows increase exports by augmenting supply of exports. The magnitude of coefficient indicates that one unit increase in FDI inflows increases around 0.04 % of exports. This is comparable to its other counterparts in South Asia. Recent FDI inflows to textile sectors have increased competitiveness of Bangladesh textile sector. As a result, exports of textile and textile products increased significantly.

9.6.1.6 Nepal

For Nepal, major determinants of real exports are world income, domestic consumption, and human capital stock. The impact of FDI on real exports is negative. This is because in recent times, FDI inflows to Nepal have declined mainly due to political instability. Further, Nepal's main exports are textile and textile products, and since 2000, textile exports have been declining due to phase out of quota system. The coefficient of domestic consumption is positive which is in contrast to economic theory. Other variables such as infrastructure facilities and RER do not have significant impact on exports.

The results of ARDL and DOLS estimation of manufacturing exports are presented in Table 9.3. It is clear that real income of rest of the world, RER, human and infrastructure capital stock, and domestic consumption are major determinants of real manufacturing exports in South Asia. Like real exports, FDI impact on manufacturing exports are found to be positive for India, Pakistan, Sri Lanka, and Bangladesh and negative and insignificant for Nepal. The magnitude of the coefficient of FDI is similar to the findings for real exports. Therefore, from time series analysis, we find that the FDI inflows have contributed export growth significant in India, Sri Lanka, and Pakistan. On the other hand, FDI has not contributed significantly to export growth in Nepal.

9.6.2 Panel Data Analysis

In addition to time series analysis, we also present panel data analysis. In the panel framework, we first conducted unit root test using Pesaran (2007) CIPS test which not only takes into account country heterogeneity but also serial dependency among countries (see Chap. 6 for details). The CIPS unit root test for both 'constant' and 'constant and trend' specifications and allowing for the lag order to be at maximum equal to 3 ($p = 1, 2, 3$) is presented in Table 9.A.3. It is clear that CIPS panel test does not reject the null of unit roots for the panel at level for all the variables except FDIR. On the contrary, the differenced series are stationary leading us to conclude

Table 9.3 Determinants of manufacturing export Dependent variable: log of real manufacturing exports

	India		Pakistan		Sri Lanka		Bangladesh		Nepal	
Variables	ARDL	DOLS	ARDL	DOLS	ARDL	DOLS	ARDL	DOLS	ARDL	DOLS
Constant	−20.58	−4.50	8.02*	−5.67*	16.99**	−15.9**	−6.86	−27.56*	2.34	11.3**
	(−1.07)	(−1.05)	(2.15)	(−1.98)	(3.11)	(−4.32)	(−0.68)	(2.44)	(1.23)	(3.62)
LRWY	1.77*	1.69**	1.67**	1.56**	2.93**	1.03*	3.05**	2.76**	−1.67*	−1.20*
	(2.12)	(3.83)	(11.26)	(9.61)	(4.86)	(2.26)	(8.04)	(9.24)	(−2.69)	(−2.34)
LRER	−0.62*	−0.81**	−0.39	−0.41#	2.80**	−0.93*	−1.06*	−0.24	0.38	0.48
	(−2.12)	(−3.93)	(−.18)	(−1.94)	(3.45)	(−2.59)	(−2.44)	(−0.86)	(0.60)	(1.24)
LHUM	2.22*	0.64	–	0.35*	7.16**	4.53**	−0.63	0.38*	1.70*	1.12**
	(2.07)	(1.26)		(1.96)	(11.16)	(6.59)	(−1.53)	(2.44)	(2.42)	(3.20)
LINFRA	0.19*	0.16*	0.09**	0.06*	–	0.13**	–	–	–	–
	(2.27)	(2.06)	(3.01)	(2.16)		(4.16)				
LDom	−0.76	−0.58	−8.31**	−2.18#	−5.66**	−2.34*	−5.14	−4.97*		−1.22
	(−1.44)	(−0.81)	(−5.85)	(−1.88)	(−3.66)	(2.53)	(−1.45)	(−2.64)		(−1.19)
FDIY	0.30**	0.15* (2.40)	0.03#	0.03*	0.25**	0.04*	0.09*	0.07*	−0.21	−0.03
	(2.90)	(2.45)	(1.95)	(2.71)	(3.51)	(1.97)	(2.27)	(2.88)	(−1.30)	(−0.39)
MSC (AIC)	(2,2,1,2,2,2,0)		(0,0,1,0,3,2)		(3,3,3,1,3,3)		(1,1,0,2,1,2)		(2,2,0,0,2)	
Diagnostic test	ADJ $R^2 = 0.97$	ADJ $R^2 = 0.90$	ADJ $R^2 = 0.92$	ADJ $R^2 = 0.92$	ADJ $R^2 = 0.62$	ADJ $R^2 = 0.92$	ADJ $R^2 = 0.87$	ADJ $R^2 = 0.98$	ADJ $R^2 = 0.72$	ADJ $R^2 = 0.77$
	DW = 1.68	DW = 1.8	DW = 2.2	DW = 2.2	DW = 2.7	DW = 2.7	DW = 2.3	DW = 2.5	DW = 2.4	DW = 1.8
	LM = 2.2	LM = 0.5	LM = 2.3	LM = 2.3	LM = 2.9	LM = 2.3	LM = 1.09	LM = 2.23	LM = 1.9	LM = 0.4
	ARCH = 0.4	ARCH = 2.3	ARCH = 1.3	ARCH = 1.3	ARCH = 0.66	ARCH = 0.09	ARCH = 1.8	ARCH = 0.8	ARCH = 1.7	ARCH = 0.14
	Reset-0.61	Reset-0.68 (0.32)	Reset-0.47 (0.52)	Reset-0.47 (0.52)	Reset-2.6 (0.10)	Reset-0.48	Reset-2.4 (0.12)	Reset-0.06	Reset-2.1 (0.14)	Reset-2.6

Notes: ***, **, and # denote significance at 1, 5, and 10 % level, respectively. Figures in the parentheses are *t*-ratio. *MSC* model selection criteria

Table 9.4 Estimated coefficients of real exports (demand)

	Pool	Fixed effect	GMM system
Variables	Coefficients	Coefficients	Coefficients
Constant	−31.2** (−7.85)	−8.64** (−3.46)	−15.98** (−17.34)
LRPd	−0.91** (−8.03)	−0.08 (−1.28)	−0.25** (−7.78)
LWY	5.51** (9.49)	1.78** (8.13)	3.46** (26.47)
RER	−2.91** (−9.13)	−0.51** (−3.46)	−3.58** (−40.27)
R^2	0.44	0.83	
Hausman test		Pr > chi^2 = 0.00	
Arellano–Bond test for AR(1) in first differences			$z = 2.39$, Pr > z = 0.00
Arellano–Bond test for AR(2) in first differences			$z = 0.96$, Pr > z = 0.34
Sargan test of overid. restrictions:			Chi^2(80) = 282.9
GMM instruments for levels:			Pr > Chi^2 = 0.00
Difference-in-Sargan tests of exogeneity of instrument subsets:			Chi^2(52) = 32.4, Pr > Chi^2 = 0.21
Difference-in-Hansen tests of exogeneity of standard "IV" instrument subsets			Chi^2(52) = 281, Pr > chi^2 = 0.00

Notes: *** and ** denote significance at 1 and 5 % level, respectively

that a panel unit root is present in the level series for all variables except FDIY and domestic credit by banking sector (DBC). Hence, the CIPS test indicates that we have mixture of $I(0)$ and $I(1)$ variables. Given that panel data increases number of observation, we have added additional variables such relative demand (RPd) and supply price (RPs), financial infrastructure variable represented by domestic credit by banking sector (DBC).

Having established the non-stationary of the series, we then proceed to test for the existence of a long-run relationship between demand for and supply of real and manufacturing exports using error correction panel co-integration test developed by Westerlund (2007). The results of Westerlund (2007) co-integration test with the asymptotic p-values based on 500 replications are presented in Table 9.A.4. When using the asymptotic p-values, except for G_a, no co-integration null is rejected in favour of existence of co-integration at 5 % level for real exports. On the other hand, for manufacturing exports, the null of no co-integration is rejected by both Gt and Pt in favour of existence of co-integration at 5 % level (Table 9.A.5). Therefore, we find that real export, manufacturing export, and their determinants have a stable long-run relationship.

Third step in our panel analysis is the estimation of Eqs. (9.1) and (9.2) using various panel methods (pooled, fixed effect, and GMM system). The estimated coefficients of demand for and supply of real exports are presented in Tables 9.4 and 9.13. The GMM system passes all diagnosis test related to Sargan test of overidentifying restrictions and the Arellano–Bond test of first-order and second-order autocorrelation. The results of export demand equation indicate that relative price of demand and world income have expected sign and significant at 1 % level (Table 9.4). The coefficient of relative price (PX/PWX) is negative and less than one in all specifications. Empirical results suggest that the average long-run price elasticity is found to be approximately −1, but there is a wide diversity of experiences (Goldstein and Khan 1982; Arize 1987; Senhadji and Montenegro 1999). Apart from relative price effect, the export demand is also influenced by conditions prevailing in the world market (Goldstein and Khan 1978). The coefficient of real world income is positive and more than one. This is expected, as the demand for exports increases with the income of the rest of the world. That is, the higher the level of foreign real income, the larger would be the foreign demand for a nation's export, *ceteris paribus*. Empirical results suggest that the average long-run income elasticities are found to be approximately 1.5, but there is a wide diversity of experiences (Arize 1990; Senhadji and Montenegro 1999). The coefficient of RER is negative and significant as per our expectation. This indicates that real depreciation of domestic currency increases real exports.

The result of export supply equation indicates that coefficients of all the variables are on the expected line. The coefficient of relative price of supply (Px/Pd) is positive but less than one. This reflects relative profitability of selling in foreign markets. On the other hand, a better domestic price reduces this incentive, and domestic manufactures will be interested in catering domestic demand, *ceteris paribus*. Empirically, it is found that the estimated supply price elasticity is significant for most of the countries, but the magnitude varies (Goldstein and Khan 1982; Arize 1990; Muscatelli et al. 1992). Similarly, the coefficient of infrastructure is positive and significant at 1 % level. Therefore, to sustain the rapid growth of exports, it is necessary for South Asian countries to have a well-functioning infrastructure, including electric power, road and rail connectivity, telecommunications, air transport, and efficient ports (UNCTAD 2005). Similarly, the coefficient of financial development (bank credit to domestic sector) is positive and significant. Therefore, access to finance at reasonable cost can be important for export development in South Asia (Biggs 2007; Aghion and Griffith 2005). The impact of domestic consumption on export supply is negative and statistically significant. The negative elasticity of domestic demand pressure indicates that the export supply declines as domestic demand increases (Joshi and Little 1994; Sharma 2003). The coefficient of domestic consumption is more than unity for South Asia (Table 9.5).

Finally, the impact of FDI on export supply in South Asia is positive and statistically significant. The magnitude of the coefficient suggests that a $1 of FDI inflows may increase real exports by $0.03 in South Asia, which is very small. However, contrary to mixed result found in the empirical literature, our results suggest that FDI has positive impact on real exports in South Asia.

The estimated results of demand for and supply of manufacturing export are presented in Tables 9.6 and 9.7. Like real exports, the coefficient of relative price (PX/PWX) is negative and statistically significant. Further, the rise in real world income on manufacturing export is positive. The income elasticity of manufacturing export is more than unity, indicating that 1 % increase in world demand leads to more than 1 % rise in manufacturing export in South Asia.

An examination of supply equation reveals that relative price is positively related manufacturing export supply (Table 9.7). The positive price elasticity of

Table 9.5 Estimated coefficients of real exports (supply)

	Pool	Fixed effect	GMM system
Variables	Coefficients	Coefficients	Coefficients
Constant	33.28** (15.88)	12.75** (10.3)	21.3** (20.93)
LRPs	0.09* (2.22)	−0.09** (−3.58)	0.045* (2.43)
FDIY	−0.07* (−1.97)	0.10** (6.48)	0.03* (2.40)
INFRA	0.27** (9.38)	0.07** (3.43)	0.22** (20.33)
DBC	0.07 (0.38)	−0.23* (−2.24)	0.23** (2.61)
DD	−15.5** (−15.5)	−4.49** (−7.17)	−9.45** (19.30)
R^2	0.78	0.63	
Hausman test		Pr > chi^2 = 0.00	
Arellano–Bond test for AR(1) in first differences			z = 2.02, Pr > z = 0.04
Arellano–Bond test for AR(2) in first differences			z = 0.21, Pr > z = 0.83
Sargan test of overid. restrictions:			Chi^2(80) = 752.9
GMM instruments for levels:			Pr > chi^2 = 0.00
Difference-in-Sargan tests of exogeneity of instrument subsets:			Chi^2(52) = 116.4, Pr > Chi^2 = 0.00
Difference-in-Hansen tests of exogeneity of standard "IV" instrument subsets:			Chi^2(52) = 643, Pr > chi^2 = 0.00

Notes: *** and ** denote significance at 1 and 5 % level, respectively

Table 9.6 Estimated coefficients of real manufacturing exports (demand)

	Pool	Fixed effect	GMM system
Variables	Coefficients	Coefficients	Coefficients
Constant	−29.21** (−6.97)	−4.71* (−2.71)	−15.98** (−17.34)
LRPd	−0.86** (−7.33)	0.02 (0.35)	−0.15** (−4.52)
LWY	5.09** (8.44)	1.07** (4.39)	1.78** (14.287)
RER	−2.55** (−7.22)	0.19 (1.20)	−0.08** (−0.81)
R^2	0.37	0.83	
Hausman test		Pr > chi^2 = 0.00	
Arellano–Bond test for AR(1) in first differences			z = 3.21, Pr > z = 0.00
Arellano–Bond test for AR(2) in first differences			z = 1.05, Pr > z = 0.29
Sargan test of overid. restrictions:			Chi^2(80) = 256.9
GMM instruments for levels:			Pr > chi^2 = 0.00
Difference-in-Sargan tests of exogeneity of instrument subsets:			Chi^2(52) = 26.4, Pr > Chi^2 = 0.22
Difference-in-Hansen tests of exogeneity of standard "IV" instrument subsets			Chi^2(52) = 268, Pr > chi^2 = 0.00

Notes: *** and ** denote significance at 1 and 5 % level, respectively

export supply implies that a rise in export prices in relation to domestic prices increases export supply. Therefore, it can be argued that improved domestic profitability might act as a significant deterrent for domestic manufactures to go for export business. On the other hand, an improvement in infrastructure facilities

Table 9.7 Estimated coefficients of real manufacturing exports (supply)

Variables	Pool Coefficients	Fixed effect Coefficients	GMM system Coefficients
Constant	25.75** (12.31)	8.80** (7.55)	22.23** (28.54)
LRPs	0.11* (2.66)	−0.14** (−5.13)	0.03* (2.36)
FDIY	−0.09* (−2.55)	0.05** (4.24)	0.034* (2.68)
INFRA	0.28** (9.71)	−0.007 (−0.38)	0.21** (16.45)
DBC	0.87** (3.51)	0.52** (6.25)	−0.12 (−1.23)
DD	−12.27** (−12.29)	−3.03** (−5.43)	−9.58** (−24.64)
R^2	0.77	0.51	
Hausman test		$Pr > chi^2 = 0.00$	
Arellano–Bond test for AR(1) in first differences			$z = 3.06$, $Pr > z = 0.00$
Arellano–Bond test for AR(2) in first differences			$z = 0.11$, $Pr > z = 0.96$
Sargan test of overid. restrictions:			$Chi^2(80) = 152.9$
GMM instruments for levels:			$Pr > chi^2 = 0.12$
Difference-in-Sargan tests of exogeneity of instrument subsets:			$Chi^2(52) = 56.4$, $Pr > chi^2 = 0.23$
Difference-in-Hansen tests of exogeneity of standard "IV" instrument subsets:			$Chi^2(52) = 43$, $Pr > chi^2 = 0.34$

Notes: *** and ** denote significance at 1 and 5 % level, respectively

positively affects the supply of manufacturing exports as the coefficient of INFRA is positive and statistically significant. Further, financial development in South Asia also affects supply function positively. The impact of domestic consumption on manufacturing export supply is negative and statistically significant. Therefore, rise in domestic consumption reduces export supply. Finally, the impact of FDI on manufacturing export supply in South Asia is positive and statistically significant. The magnitude of the coefficient suggests that a $1 of FDI inflows may increase real exports by $0.034 in South Asia, which is very small. Therefore, it can be said that FDI has contributed to export performance in South Asia partially.

9.6.3 Causality Between Exports and FDI

Although the positive spillover of FDI to host country exports is documented in the literature, the causality result is yet to be settled. The direction of causality between FDI and export could run in either direction. Initially, firms trade in the foreign market, and after learning more about the economic, social, political, and ruling conditions of their trading partners, they may establish a subsidiary in the host country (Liu et al. 2001; Pacheco-López 2005) or they may embark on joint ventures with local enterprises. This implies FDI inflows, and after some period, multinational corporations (MNCs) may start to export (UNCTAD 1996). The role of MNCs in expanding exports in host countries derives from the additional capital, new technology, and better management and marketing strategies that they can bring with them (UNCTAD 2002). Thus, there may be a bidirectional causal

Table 9.8 Causality between LREX and FDIY using VECM approach

	$\sum_{j=1}^{p} \Delta \ln \text{REX}_{t-j}$	$\sum_{j=1}^{p} \Delta \text{FDIY}_{t-j}$	Lagged ECM term
Dependent variable	$\Sigma\beta_i = 0$: F-stat (p-value)	$\Sigma\beta_i = 0$: F-stat (p-value)	$\Theta = 0$: t-stat (p-value)
India			
ΔℓnREX		1.34 (0.32)	−2.13* (0.03)
ΔFDIY	0.64 (0.58)		−0.76 (0.41)
Pakistan			
ΔℓnREX		2.37 (0.14	−3.51** (0.08)
ΔFDIY	1.48 (0.21)		−1.27 (0.24)
Bangladesh			
ΔℓnREX		1.78 (0.29)	−4.07** (0.00)
ΔFDIY	0.77 (0.56)		−1.50 (0.13)
Causality between LMREX and FDIY using VECM approach			
	$\sum_{j=1}^{p} \Delta \ln \text{MREX}_{t-j}$	$\sum_{j=1}^{p} \Delta \text{FDIY}_{t-j}$	Lagged ECM term
India			
ΔℓnMREX		1.37 (0.34)	−2.29* (0.03)
ΔFDIY	1.54 (0.31)		−2.28* (0.03)
Pakistan			
ΔℓnMREX		3.37# (0.08)	−4.14** (0.00)
ΔFDIY	1.02 (0.52)		−0.62 (0.53)
Bangladesh			
ΔℓnMREX		0.75 (0.65)	−3.55** (0.00)
ΔFDIY	1.06 (0.51)		−0.06 (0.97)
Nepal			
ΔℓnMREX		0.42 (0.75)	−0.69 (0.52)
ΔFDIY	1.21 (0.40)		−2.73* (0.02)

**Denotes significance at 1 % level, *Denotes significance at 5 % and # at 10 % level. Optimal lag length is selected based on AIC

link: exports stimulate FDI and FDI promotes exports. However, empirical studies indicate that causality between exports and FDI is complicated and depends largely on the types of exports and FDI being considered. It is country, industry, and even firm specific (Zhang and Felmingham 2001; Liu et al. 2002; Girma et al. 2008; Dash and Sharma 2011). This suggests the importance of empirical investigations in assessing true FDI–export relationship.

Since real FDI and total exports are found $I(1)$ for all countries except Sri Lanka and Nepal, we carry our causality in the error correction framework (see Chap. 6 for details). For Sri Lanka, since both FDIY is $I(0)$ series, we conduct simple Granger causality. Similarly, for Nepal, total exports is $I(0)$, but manufacturing export is $I(1)$. Hence, simple Granger causality tests are conducted for total exports. The result of VECM causality test is presented in Table 9.8. It is clear that the null hypothesis of no causality from FDI growth to total exports growth is rejected by lagged ECM term (the

Table 9.9 Granger causality between LREX and FDIY for Sri Lanka

Null hypothesis	Optimal lag	$\Sigma\beta_i = 0$: F-statistic	p-value
FDIY → LnΔREX	4(AIC)	3.56[a]	0.02
LnΔREX → FDIY	4(AIC)	0.25	0.90
FDIY → LMREX	4(AIC)	4.71[a]	0.00
LMREX → FDIY	1(AIC)	2.24	0.12
	Nepal		
ΔFDIY → LREX	2	0.19	0.92
LREX → ΔFDIY	2	1.91	0.17

[a]Denotes rejection of null hypothesis at 5 % level

Table 9.10 Panel causality test between LPCI and FDIY

Direction of causality		$k = 1$	$k = 2$	$k = 3$
FDIY → LREX	Z_{HNC}	3.16*	2.14*	1.17
	$\tilde{Z}_{HNC}$	3.07*	1.49	1.01
LREX → FDIY	Z_{HNC}	3.43*	2.95*	2.32*
	$\tilde{Z}_{HNC}$	3.26*	2.74*	2.12*
FDIY → LMREX	Z_{HNC}	2.28*	2.69*	1.47
	$\tilde{Z}_{HNC}$	2.07*	2.56*	1.43
LMREX → FDIY	Z_{HNC}	3.43*	1.72	1.22
	$\tilde{Z}_{HNC}$	3.26*	1.61	1.12

Notes: * denote rejection of null hypothesis of no causality at 5 % level

long-term causality) in favour of FDI-led export for India, Pakistan, and Bangladesh. On the other hand, we do not find causality in the opposite direction (exports to FDIY) either through short-run dynamics or through lagged ECM term. The causality result for Sri Lanka and Nepal is presented in Table 9.9. It is clear that, in the case of Sri Lanka, there is one-way causality from FDI total exports and not the vice versa. In the case of Nepal, we find the evidence of no causality in either direction.

Similarly, the causality between manufacturing exports and FDI is presented in Table 9.7 (lower section). It is clear that there exists two-way causality between FDI and manufacturing exports for India and one-way causality from FDI to manufacturing exports for Pakistan and Bangladesh. On the other hand, there exists one-way causality from manufacturing exports to FDI for Nepal.

In addition to time series causality, panel causality results (Table 9.10) indicate that when lag one is selected, we have two-way causality between total and manufacturing exports and FDI. On the other hand, when lag 2 is selected, we have the evidence of one-way causality from exports to FDI. However, when lag 3 is selected, null of no causality from FDIY to GFC is rejected at 10 % level. On the other hand, causality from per capita income to FDI is found only at lag 1 and 2. At lag 3, the causality evidence is mostly absent in either direction. Therefore, panel causality test supports bidirectional hypothesis between FDI and exports for South Asia. This indicates that higher FDI inflows will stimulate exports in South Asia and higher exports will also lead higher FDI inflows.

9.7 FDI and Exports in China

China has been hugely successful in attracting FDI than any other developing country in history. Motivation as well as impact of FDI can be multiple. Two main motivations behind FDI in a host country are exploiting the domestic market of the host country by avoiding high tariff wall as well as high transport cost and exploiting the comparative advantage the host country in terms of resource endowment, low labour cost, skilled manpower, and other benefits and incentives. China's domestic market is huge, and its export share is rapidly increasing in world market both in labour-intensive as well as high-end manufacturing products. Does FDI have any role in this achievement of China in export? China's export as share of GDP grew from an average of 12.2 % during 1980–1990 to 29.5 % during 2010. Likewise, China's total trade as share of world trade rose from an average of 1.43 to 9.7 % during 2010 (WDI 2012). China's total FDI rose from mere $4.5 billion in 2001 to $123 billion in 2011. Foreign-invested enterprises' exports percentage increased from 32 % in 1995 to over 58 % in 2005. Exports by foreign institutional enterprises (FIEs) have become an important part of China's total export. It suggests that China's exports are closely associated with inward FDI (Gu et al. 2008).

Research on China's inward FDI and exports relationship has been a more recent addition to the literature. Although some authors have examined the impact of FDI on China's exports, most of them depend on the use of aggregated national or provincial data (Zhang and Song 2000; Sun 2001; Gu et al. 2008; Sun et al. 2012). Compared to aggregate studies, Gu et al. (2008) examine the impact of FDI on China's exports in subsectors in manufacturing over the period from 1995 to 2005. The empirical results suggest that FDI has a statistically significant and positive impact on China's exports for 13 out of 14 sectors. Overall studies on China indicate that FDI inflows in China not only increased productivity but also helped in technology upgradation through technology spillover, employment generation, and export competitiveness (Zhang 2006; Gu et al. 2008; Sun et al. 2012). In recent years, China is increasingly exporting more and more high value-added technical products in the field of electronics, information, aerospace, optics, digital or computer programmed machinery, and space and ocean engineering technologies. Some of these commodities are principal exports in the Chinese export basket contributing substantially to its total exports. More than half of China's major electronics, telecommunication equipment, and engendering firms are foreign-invested firms. The export competitiveness of China has improved substantially over the years and its domestic industry established in the international market due to appropriate policies of the Chinese government in attracting FDI. In this section, we examine role of FDI in augmenting export by estimating export function of China using Eq. (9.3).

Table 9.11 Determinants of total and manufacturing exports

	Total exports		Manufacturing exports	
Variables	ARDL	DOLS	ARDL	DOLS
Constant	−10.22** (−30.07)	−10.58** (−10.07)	−13.19** (3.87)	−13.45** (−4.43)
LRWY	2.16** (4.18)	2.12** (7.47)	2.36** (4.15)	3.19** (7.49)
LRER	0.06# (1.89)	0.01 (0.89)	0.06 (1.43)	0.01 (0.69)
LHUM	0.82** (3.03)	1.12* (2.54)	0.87** (3.07)	1.07* (2.38)
LINFRA	0.04* (2.32)	0.09* (3.17)	0.04* (2.19)	0.09* (3.10)
LDom	−1.46* (−2.47)	−2.88** (−4.87)	−1.49* (−2.49)	−2.88** (−4.16)
FDIY	0.09* (2.44)	0.07* (2.81)	0.11* (2.76)	0.09* (2.89)
MSC (AIC)	(1,1,0,1,1,1,1)			
Diagnostic test	ADJ	ADJ	ADJ	ADJ
	$R^2 = 0.98$	$R^2 = 0.98$	$R^2 = 0.98$	$R^2 = 0.98$
	DW = 2.39	DW =2.16	DW =2.34	DW = 2.11
	LM = 2.3	LM = 1.1	LM = 2.1	LM = 1.2
	ARCH = 2.5	ARCH = 0.5	ARCH = 1.6	ARCH = 0.76
	Reset-1.6	Reset-1.23	Reset-1.7	Reset-1.34

Notes: ***, **, and # denote significance at 1, 5, and 10 % level, respectively. Figures in the parentheses are *t*-ratio. *MSC* model selection criteria

9.7.1 Empirical Results

The ADF test is used to test for the existence of unit roots and determine the order of integration of the variables. The tests are done both with and without a time trend. Akaike method is used to choose the optimal lag length. It can be seen in Table 9.A.6 that most of the variables are non-stationary or $I(1)$. Only RER is stationary at level. This implies we have mixture of $I(0)$ and $I(1)$. Hence, ARDL co-integration method is appropriate for examining long-run relationship between the variables. The results of ARDL co-integration test is presented in Table 9.A.7.

As can be seen from Table 9.A.7 is that there is a long-run relationship among the variables when total and manufacturing exports are the dependent variable because its F-statistic (6.18 and 5.67) exceeds the upper bound critical value (3.5) at the 5 % levels. Thus, the null of non-existence of stable long-run relationship is rejected in favour of co-integration.

9.7.1.1 Long-Run Coefficients of Exports

After establishing long-run equilibrium relationship between total and manufacturing exports and its determinants, we then proceed to the estimation of model (3) for China by using ARDL and DOLS method. The long-run coefficient of real per capita income is presented in Table 9.11. Maximum lag length used to derive long-run coefficients is 2, based on AIC criteria. Diagnostic test is checked to ensure that it is the best model, and there is no misspecification bias in the model.

The diagnostic tests include the test of serial autocorrelation (LM), heteroscedasticity (ARCH test), and omitted variables/functional form (Ramsey Reset).

The results indicate that among other factors, world income, infrastructure development, human capital stock, domestic consumption, and FDI inflows have significant impact on export performances of China. The impact of FDI inflows on total and manufacturing exports is positive and statistically significant at 5 % level. The coefficients of FDIY indicate that one unit increase in FDI increases total exports by only 0.09 % in China. This indicates that FDI impact on exports is higher in China as compared to South Asian countries. In addition, infrastructure facilities have positive impact on Chinese exports. Our results are in line with findings of previous studies like Zhang and Song (2000) and Sun (2001).

9.8 Conclusion

FDI impact on host country exports can be direct and indirect. Direct refers to exports by foreign affiliates themselves. For example, vertical FDI directly boosts host country exports, since output resulting from FDI is typically intended for export. On the other hand, horizontal FDI is oriented primarily to the host country market, so it does not directly contribute to host country export. Again, the direct effect can be divided into three categories according to production characteristics: (1) local raw material processing, (2) new labour-intensive final product exports, and (3) labour-intensive processes and component specialisation within vertically integrated international industries. Indirect effect can be in the form of influence of FDI on the competitiveness of the host country firms and diffusion of new technologies. The indirect effect can also be through the linkage structure between foreign and local firms. South Asia's growth in export is impressive as it grew at a rate of 12.3 % per annum during 2000–2010, which is higher than previous decade.

Theoretical literature shows the ambiguity of the relationship between FDI and export. The models that focused on vertical FDI show that FDI generates complementary trade flows of finished goods from foreign affiliates to parent companies or to the home country. However, models such as which focused on horizontal FDI and substitutability between FDI and trade prevail over complementarity. Traditional classification of FDI into vertical and horizontal forms has become less meaningful as MNEs' outsourcing and FDI practices become more complicated. In particular, utilising developing countries as an export platform has emerged as another motivation behind FDI. Empirical studies show that impact of FDI on exports can differ based on region, category, or industry, i.e. labour intensive or capital intensive. There are studies that find support for positive effect of FDI on export and support for negative effect of FDI on export. Spillover effects will be larger from the presence of more export-oriented MNEs compared to domestic market-seeking FDI. The impact of FDI may also differ according to the source of FDI.

This study examines impact of FDI on export performance of five South Asian countries in a form of equation derived after solving export demand function and export supply function for equilibrium state. Both time series and panel estimation were employed to check for the robustness of the result. The data set was tested for stationary and non-stationary property, and co-integration test is performed which found that there exists stable relationship among variables. In India, Pakistan, Sri Lanka, and Bangladesh, coefficient for FDI was positive and significant showing that increase in FDI results in positive increase in export. Only Nepal showed negative and insignificant coefficient. The explanation for this is that because of phasing out of quota in textile, which is main export of Sri Lanka and decline of FDI inflow into Nepal due to political instability, the negative coefficient is plausible. Panel data analysis also shows that the impact of FDI on export supply in South Asia is positive and statistically significant. The magnitude of the cocfficient suggests that one unit increase in FDI results in 0.03 percentage increase in real export in South Asia. The same estimation was run taking manufacturing export as dependent variable, and FDI impact on manufacturing export was found to positive and significant for India, Bangladesh, Pakistan, and Sri Lanka and negative and insignificant for Nepal. Causality test performed indicates that for India, Pakistan, Sri Lanka, and Bangladesh, FDI causes export, which is one way and causality is not found in other direction. For Nepal, there is no causality in either direction. For manufacturing export, India exhibits two-way causality, whereas Pakistan and Bangladesh show one-way causality from FDI to export. For Nepal, it is from export to FDI. A special case of China was taken to compare with South Asia, and it was found that 1 unit increase in FDI in China results in 0.09 % increase in export, which is higher compared to South Asian countries. The analysis highlights the fact that by emulating the policies followed by China and Singapore and with the right mix of domestic policies for FDI by South Asian countries, India can substantially enhance its export competitiveness in the international market and total exports.

Appendix

Table 9.A.1 ADF unit root test

Variables	At level with constant	Optimal lag (AIC)	At level (constant and trend)	Optimal lags (AIC)	(First difference) (constant)	Optimal lags (AIC)	Order of integration
India							
LREXP	0.95	2	−1.25	1	−6.43*	0	*I*(1)
LRMEXP	0.63	1	−1.82	3	−4.80*	1	*I*(1)
LRER	−2.03	1	−1.48	1	−4.97*	0	*I*(1)
LRWY	0.34	1	−2.46	2	−4.04*	1	*I*(1)
LINFRA	1.16	3	−1.56	3	−3.29*	2	*I*(1)
LHUM	−1.67	3	−3.16	2	−4.39*	1	*I*(1)
FDIY	−0.39	2	−2.41	3	−5.43*	1	*I*(1)
LDOM	−0.72	3	−1.83	2	−3.16*	1	*I*(1)
Bangladesh							
LREXP	0.23	1	−2.54	2	−5.71*	0	*I*(1)
LRMEXP	−0.22	1	−2.97	3	−6.69*	0	*I*(1)
LRER							*I*(1)
LRWY	−1.29	3	−3.46	1	−4.13*	1	*I*(1)
LINFRA	−0.07	1	1.88	2	−3.15*	1	*I*(1)
LHUM	−2.02	1	−1.73	2	−4.08*	0	*I*(1)
FDIY	−1.23	1	−3.13	3	−4.34*	1	*I*(1)
LDOM	−1.01	3	−1.82	0	−4.92*	1	*I*(1)
Pakistan							
LREXP	−0.93	2	−2.28	2	−6.12*	0	*I*(1)
LRMEXP	−1.43	0	−1.07	1	−4.39*	0	*I*(1)
LRER	−1.65	2	−1.45	3	−3.34*	1	*I*(1)
LRWY	−1.32	2	−2.60	2	−4.13*	1	*I*(1)
LINFRA	−0.07	1	1.88	2	−3.15*	1	*I*(1)
LHUM	−1.27	1	−1.54	1	−5.97*	0	*I*(1)
FDIY	−2.26	1	−3.2	1	−4.37*	2	*I*(1)
LDOM	−1.71	1	−0.76	1	−4.12*	1	*I*(1)
Sri Lanka							
LREXP	−2.24	2	−0.35	1	−4.21*	0	*I*(1)
LRMEXP	−4.25*	2					*I*(0)
LRER	−1.22	2	−2.08	1	−4.42*	4	*I*(1)
LRWY	−1.26	2	−2.45	2	−4.87*	1	*I*(1)
LINFRA	0.93	1	2.84	3	−3.21*	1	*I*(1)
LHUM	0.86	1	−1.47	1	−3.58*	1	*I*(1)
FDIY	−2.05	2	−3.92*	1			*I*(0)
LDOM	−3.07*	0					*I*(0)
Nepal							
LREXP	−3.10*	1					*I*(0)

(continued)

Table 9.A.1 (continued)

Variables	At level with constant	Optimal lag (AIC)	At level (constant and trend)	Optimal lags (AIC)	(First difference) (constant)	Optimal lags (AIC)	Order of integration
LRMEXP	−1.06	2	−1.69	3	−4.69*	0	$I(1)$
LRER	−0.99	1	−1.16	3	−4.27*	0	$I(1)$
LRWY	−1.21	2	−2.66	2	−4.44*	1	$I(1)$
LINFRA	2.48	3	1.18	3	−3.29*	2	$I(1)$
LHUM	−1.60	1	−3.46	2	−3.92*	0	$I(1)$
FDIY	−2.64	2	−3.05	2	−3.67*	2	$I(1)$
LDOM	−3.10*	0					$I(0)$

*Denotes that the null hypothesis of the variable concerned is non-stationary and can be rejected at 1 % significance level. *L* stands for logarithms

Table 9.A.2 ARDL co-integration test

Country	Dependent variable	*F*-stat	5 % critical value[a]	Result
India	LREXP	7.33	3.50	Rejection of null of no co-integration
Pakistan	LREXP	18.1[b]	3.50	Rejection of null of no co-integration
Sri Lanka	LREXP	5.80[b]	3.50	Rejection of null of no co-integration
Bangladesh	LREXP	5.67[b]	3.50	Rejection of null of no co-integration
Nepal	LREXP	6.81[b]	3.50	Rejection of null of no co-integration
India	LRMEXP	6.08[b]	3.50	Rejection of null of no co-integration
Pakistan	LRMEXP	5.30[b]	3.50	Rejection of null of no co-integration
Sri Lanka	LRMEXP	5.33[b]	3.50	Rejection of null of no co-integration
Bangladesh	LRMEXP	4.80[b]	3.50	Rejection of null of no co-integration
Nepal	LRMEXP	5.78[b]	3.50	Rejection of null of no co-integration

Notes: The order of ARDL is selected based on Akaike Information Criteria (AIC)

[a]Denotes upper bound critical values with seven independent variables. The relevant critical value bounds are obtained from Table C1.iii (with an unrestricted intercept and no trend; with three regressors) in Pesaran et al. (2001)

[b]Denotes rejection of null hypothesis of no co-integration in favour of co-integration

Table 9.A.3 Panel unit root test using Pesaran (2007)

	At level		First difference	
Variables	Constant	Constant and trend	Constant	Conclusion
LREX	−1.76	−1.97	−3.84*	$I(1)$
LRMEX	−2.07	−2.37	−3.50*	$I(1)$
RPd	−1.97	−2.49	−3.44*	$I(1)$
RPs	−1.69	−1.96	−3.76*	$I(1)$
DD	−1.79	−1.90	−3.82*	$I(1)$
LWY	−0.32	−1.14	−4.21*	$I(1)$
INFRA	−1.54	−1.88	−4.24**	$I(1)$
FDIY	−2.77*	–	–	$I(0)$
LHUM	−1.15	−2.21	−3.06**	$I(1)$
LRER	−1.20	−1. 98	−3.69**	$I(1)$
DBC	−2.48*	–	–	$I(0)$

Notes: The null hypothesis is that the panel has a unit root. Critical values are tabulated by Pesaran (2007)
In Table II(a–c), we report the ones for $T = 30$ and $N = 10$. '**' and '*' indicate significance of the test at 1 and 5 % level, respectively

Table 9.A.4 Westerlund (2007) error correction model panel co-integration tests

	Dependent variable LREX (demand)	
Dependent variable LPI	Value	*p*-value
Gt	−2.99*	0.03
Ga	−10.1	0.50
Pt	−6.41*	0.02
Pa	−12.12*	0.05
Dependent variable LREX (supply)		
Gt	−3.08*	0.02
Ga	−6.29	0.60
Pt	−6.41*	0.02
Pa	−12.12*	0.05

Notes: The Westerlund (2007) tests take no co-integration as the null. The test regression is fitted with constant and one lag and lead
*Denotes rejection of null of no co-integration at 5 % level

Table 9.A.5 Westerlund (2007) error correction model panel co-integration tests

	Dependent variable LRMEX (demand)	
Dependent variable LPI	Value	*p*-value
Gt	−1.97*	0.04
Ga	−7.32	0.87
Pt	−7.30*	0.03
Pa	−6.42	0.63
Dependent variable LRMEX (supply)		
Gt	−2.49*	0.05
Ga	−6.88	0.60
Pt	−4.73*	0.05
Pa	−6.01	0.05

Notes: The Westerlund (2007) tests take no co-integration as the null. The test regression is fitted with constant and one lag and lead
*Denotes rejection of null of no co-integration at 5 % level

Table 9.A.6 Unit root test using ADF

	At level		First difference	
Variables	Constant	Constant and trend	Constant	Conclusion
LREX	−0.04	−2.36	−3.38*	*I*(1)
LMREX	−0.21	−2.43	−3.45	*I*(1)
LRER	−2.69*			*I*(0)
FDIY	−2.06	−1.81	−4.52*	*I*(1)
LRWY	−1.26	−2.45	−4.13*	*I*(1)
LHUM	−0.68	−2.33	−3.87*	*I*(1)
LDOM	−0.52	−1.93	−2.97	*I*(1)
Infra	1.34	−1.38	−3.57*	*I*(1)

*Denotes that the null hypothesis that the variable concerned is non-stationary and can be rejected at 1 % significance level. *L* stands for logarithms

Table 9.A.7 ARDL co-integration test (1980–2010)

Country	Dependent variable	*F*-stat	5 % critical value[#]	Result
China	LREX	6.18*	3.50	Rejection of null of no co-integration
China	LMREX	5.67*	3.50	Rejection of null of no co-integration

[#]denotes upper bound critical value.

References

Aggarwal A (2002) Liberalization, multinational enterprises and export performance: evidence from Indian manufacturing. J Dev Stud 38(3):119–137

Aghion P, Griffith R (2005) Competition and growth: reconciling theory and evidence. MIT Press, Cambridge, MA

Aitken B, Hansen GH, Harrison AE (1997) Spillovers, foreign investment and export behaviour. J Int Econ 43:103–132
Alıcı AA, Ucal MS (2003) Foreign direct investment, exports and output growth of Turkey: causality analysis. Paper presented at the European Trade Study Group (ETSG) fifth annual conference, Madrid.
Ancharaz VD (2003) Determinants of trade policy reform in Sub-Saharan Africa. J Afr Econ 12(3):417–443
Arize A (1987) The supply and demand for imports and exports in a simultaneous model. Appl Econ 19:1233–1247
Arize A (1990) An econometric investigation of export behaviour in seven Asian developing countries. Appl Econ 22(7):891–904
Arndt SW, Hueme A (2004) Trade, production networks and the exchange rate. Lowe Institute of Political Economy, Claremont McKenna College, Claremont. Available: ssrn.com/abstract = 900416
Athukorala P (2004) Post-crisis export performance in Thailand. ASEAN Econ Bull 211:19–36
Awokuse TO (2003) Is the export-led growth hypothesis valid for Canada? Can J Econ/Revue canadienne d'économique 36(1):126–136
Balassa B (1978) Exports and economic growth: further evidence. J Dev Econ 5(2):181–189
Balasubramanyam VN, Salisu MA, Sapsford D (1996) Foreign direct investment and growth in EP and IS countries. Econ J 106(434):92–105
Baliamoune-Lutz MN (2004) Does FDI contribute to economic growth? Knowledge about the effects of FDI improves negotiating positions and reduces risk for firms investing in developing countries. Bus Econ 39(2):49–56
Banga R (2003) Impact of government policies and investment agreements on FDI inflows, Working paper, no. 116. Indian Council for Research on International Economic Relations, New Delhi
Barrios S, Görg H, Strobl E (2003) Explaining firms' export behaviour: R&D, spillovers and the destination market. Oxford Bull Econ Stat 65(4):475–496
Bhagwati J (1978) Anatomy and consequences of exchange control regimes. Balinger Publishing, New York
Bhagwati JN (1982) Introduction to "import competition and response". In: Bhagwati JN (ed) Import competition and response. University of Chicago Press, Chicago, pp 1–8
Bhagwati J (1988). Is free trade passe after all? Weltwirtschaftliches Archiv 125: 17–44; reprinted as Chapter I in J. Bhagwati, Political Economy and International Economics (ed. Douglas Irwin). MIT Press, Cambridge, MA
Bhalla AS (1995) Recent economic reforms in China and India. Asian Surv 35(6):555–572
Biggs T (2007) Export promotion and diversification: what DO we learn from the DTISs in low-income countries? Unpublished, World Bank, Washington, DC
Biggs T, Shah M, Srivastava P (1996) Technological capability and learning in African firms. Regional program for enterprise development, technical paper, World Bank, Washington, DC
Blake AP, Pain N (1994) Investigating structural change in UK export performance: the role of innovation and direct investment, NIESR discussion paper, no.71, London
Blomström M, Lipsey RE, Kulchycky K (1988) US and Swedish direct investment and exports. In: Baldwin RE (ed) Trade policy issues and empirical analysis. Chicago University Press, Chicago
Bougheas S, Demetriades PO, Morgenroth ELW (1999) Infrastructure, transport costs and trade. J Int Econ 47:169–189
Brainard SL (1993) A simple theory of multinational corporations and trade with a trade-off between proximity and concentration, NBER working paper, no. 4269. National Bureau of Economic Research, Cambridge, MA
Bushe DM, IKravis IB, Lipsey RE (1986) Prices, activity, and machinery exports: an analysis based on new price data. Rev Econ Stat 682:248–255
Cabral S (1995) Comparative export behaviour of foreign and domestic firms in Portugal. Banco de Portugal Econ Bull 96:69–78

Chinn MD (2005) Supply capacity. Vertical specialization and tariff rates: the implications for aggregate US trade flow equations. National Bureau of Economic Research, Working paper, no. 11719, Cambridge, MA
Culem CG (1988) The location determinants of direct investments: among industrialized countries. Eur Econ Rev 32(4):885–904
Dash RK, Sharma C (2011) FDI, trade, and growth dynamics: New evidence from the post-reform India. Int Trade J 25(2):233–266
De Gregorio J (1992) Economic growth in Latin America. J Dev Econ 39:58–84
De Mello LR (1999) Foreign domestic investment-Led growth: evidence from time series and panel data. Oxford Econ Pap 51:133–151
Dornbusch R (1992) The case for trade liberalization in developing countries. J Econ Perspect 6(1):69–85
Dunning JH (1977) Trade, location of economic activity and the MNE: a search for an eclectic approach. In: Ohlin B, Hesselborn PO, Wijkmon PM (eds) The international location of economic activity. Macmillan, London, pp 395–418
Edwards S (1998) Capital flows, real exchange rates and capital controls: some Latin American experiences, National Bureau of Economic Research, Working paper, no. 6000, Cambridge, MA
Fry MJ (1993) Foreign direct investment in a macroeconomic framework: finance, efficiency, incentives and distortions, Working paper series, no.1141. World Bank, Washington, DC
Fugazza M (2004) Export performance and its determinants: supply and demand constraints, Policy issues in international trade and commodities study series no. 26. UNCTAD, New York/ Geneva
Fukao K, Ishido H, Ito K (2003) Vertical intra-industry trade and foreign direct investment in East Asia. J Jpn Int Econ 17(4):468–506
Funke M, Holly S (1992) The determinants of West German exports of manufactures: an integrated demand and supply approach. Weltwirtschaftliches Archive 128:498–512
Girma S, Görg H, Hanley A (2008) R&D and exporting: a comparison of British and Irish firms. Rev World Econ 144(4):750–773
Goldstein M, Khan MS (1978) The supply and demand for exports: a simultaneous approach. Rev Econ Stat 60(2):275–286
Goldstein M, Khan M (1982) Effects of slowdown in industrial countries on growth in Non-oil developing countries, IMF occasional paper, no.12. International Monetary Fund, Washington, DC
Goldstein M, Khan M (1985) Income and price effects in foreign trade. In: Jones R, Kenen P (eds) Handbook of international economics, vol 2. Elsevier, Amsterdam
Greenaway D, Sousa N, Wakelin K (2004) Do domestic firms learn to export from multinationals? Eur J Polit Econ 20(4):1027–1043
Gu W, Awokuse TO, Yuan Y (2008) The contribution of foreign direct investment to China's export performance: evidence from disaggregated sectors. Paper prepared for presentation at the American Agricultural Economics Association annual meeting, Orlando
Haddad M, Harrison A (1993) Are there positive spillovers from direct foreign investment? J Dev Econ 42:51–74
Hall S, Milne A (1994) The relevance of p-star analysis to UK monetary policy. Econ J 104:597–604
Hausmann R, Hwang J, Rodrik D (2006) What you export matters, NBER working paper no. 11905, Cambridge, MA
Helpman E (1984) A simple theory of international trade with multinational corporations. J Polit Econ 92:451–471
Helpman E (2006) Trade, FDI, and the organization of firms, NBER working paper, no. 12091. National Bureau of Economic Research, Cambridge, MA
Helpman E, Krugman PR (1985) Market structure and foreign trade: increasing returns, imperfect competition, and the international economy. The MIT press, Cambridge

Helpman E, Melitz MJ, Yeaple SR (2003) Export versus FDI with heterogeneous firms. Am Econ Rev 94(1):300–316
Horstmann I, Markusen JR (1992) Endogenous market structures in international trade. J Int Econ 20:225–247
Jeon Y (1992) The determinants of Korean foreign direct investment in manufacturing industries. Weltwirrtschaftliches Archiv 128(3):527–542
Johansen S (1988) Statistical analysis of cointegration vectors. J Econ Control 12:231–254
Jones S (2006) Infrastructure challenges in East and South Asia. IDS bull 37(3):28–44
Joshi V, Little IMD (1994) India: macroeconomics and political economy 1964–1991. The World Bank, Washinton, DC
Khan K, Leng K (1997) Foreign direct investment, exports and economic growth. Singap Econ Rev 42(2):40–60
Kojima K (1982) A macroeconomic approach to foreign direct investment. Hitosubashi J Econ 14(1):1–21
Kokko A, Zejan M, Tansini R (2001) Trade regimes and spillover effects of FDI: evidence from Uruguay. Weltwirtschaftliches Archiv 137:124–149
Krueger AO (1975) Foreign trade regimes and economic development: Turkey. National Bureau of Economic Research, New York, pp 271–339
Krueger AO (1997) Trade policy and economic development: how we learn. Am Econ Rev 87(1):1–22
Krueger A (1998) Why trade liberalisation is good for growth. Econ J 108(450):1513–1522
Krugman PR (ed) (1986) Strategic trade policy and the new international economics. MIT Press, Cambridge, MA
Kumar N, Pradhan JP (2003) Export competitiveness in the knowledge-based industries: a firm-level analysis of Indian manufacturing. Research and Information System for Developing Countries (RIS), New Delhi
Kumar N, Siddharthan NS (1994) Technology, firm size, and export behavior in developing countries: the case of Indian enterprises. J Dev Stud 31(2):289–309
Lall S (1999) India's manufactured exports: comparative structure and prospects. World Dev 27(10):1769–1786
Liu X, Wang C, Wei Y (2001) Causal links between foreign direct investment and trade in China. China Econ Rev 12(2):190–202
Liu XH, Burridge P, Sinclair PJN (2002) Relations between economic growth. FDI and trade: evidence from China. Appl Econ 34:1433–1440
Markusen JR (1983) Factor movements and commodity trade as complements. J Int Econ 13(3):341–356
Markusen JR (1995) The boundaries of multinational enterprises and the theory of international trade. J Econ Perspect 9(2):169–189
Markusen JR, Venables AJ (1998) Multinational firms and the new trade theory. J Int Econ 46(2):183–203
Metwally MM (2004) Impact of EU FDI on economic growth in middle eastern countries. Eur Bus Rev 16:381–389
Mundell RA (1957) International trade and factor mobility. Am Econ Rev 47(3):321–335
Muscatelli VA, Srinivasan TG, Vines D (1992) Demand and supply factors in the determination of NIE exports: a simultaneous error correction model for Hong Kong. Econ J 102(415):1467–1477
O'Sullivan PJ (1993) An assessment of Ireland's export-led growth strategy via foreign direct investment: 1960–80. Weltwirtschaftliches Archiv 129:139–158
Pain N, Wakelin K (1998) Export performance and the role of foreign direct investment. Manch Sch Econ Soc Stud 66(3):62–89
Pacheco-López P (2005) Foreign direct investment, exports and imports in Mexico. World Economy 28(8):1157–1172
Parida P, Sahoo P (2007) Export-led growth hypothesis in South Asia: a panel cointegration analysis. Int Econ J, Rutledge 21(2):155–175

Pesaran M (2007) A simple panel unit root test in the presence of cross-section dependence. J Appl Econom 22:265–312
Pesaran MH, Shin Y, Smith RJ (2001) Bounds testing approaches to the analysis of level relationships. J Appl Econom 16:289–326
Pradhan JP, Abraham V (2005) Attracting export-oriented FDI: can India win the race? Working paper, no.156. Gujarat Institute of Development Research, Ahmedabad
Rana PB, Dowling JM (1990) Foreign capital and Asian economic growth. Asian Dev Rev 8(2):77–102
Riedel J (1993) Vietnam: on the trail of the tigers. World Econ 16(4):401–422
Ruane F, Sutherland M (2004) Ownership and export characteristics of Irish manufacturing performance, IIIS discussion paper, 32, Dublin
Sahoo P (2004a) FDI and technology exports in India. ICFAI J Appl Econ 3(3):25–36
Sahoo P (2004b) Fiscal federalism in India: a review. Asian Econ Rev 48(4):25–36
Sahoo P, Dash RK (2012) Economic growth in South Asia: role of infrastructure. J Int Trade Econ Dev 21(2):217–252
Senhadji A, Montenegro C (1999) Time-series analysis of export demand equations: a cross-country analysis. IMF Staff Pap 46(3):259–273, International Monetary Fund :Washington D. C
Sharma K (2003) Factors determining India's export performance. J Asian Econ 14(3):435–446
Srinivasan TN (1998) India's Export performance: a comparative analysis. In: Ahluwalia IJ, Little IMD (eds) India's economic reforms and development essay for Manmohan Singh. Oxford University Press, Delhi
Sun H (2001) Foreign direct investment and regional export performance in China. J Reg Sci 41(2):317–336
Sun S (2012) The role of FDI in domestic exporting: evidence from China. J Asian Econ 23(4):434–441
Sun SL, Peng MW, Ren B, Yan D (2012) A comparative ownership advantage framework for cross-border M&As: the rise of Chinese and Indian MNEs. J World Bus 47(1):4–16
UNCTAD (1996) World investment report 1996. United Nations, Geneva
UNCTAD (1999) Trends in international investment agreements: an overview. United Nations Publication, New York, Sales No. E.99.11.D.23
UNCTAD (2002) World Investment Report, annual. UN Publications, Geneva
UNCTAD (2003a) World investment report. United Nations, Geneva
UNCTAD (2003b) World investment report. United Nations Conference on Trade and Development, Geneva
UNCTAD (2005) World investment report. United Nations Conference on Trade and Development, Geneva
Vernon R (1966) International investment and international trade in the product cycle. Q J Econ 80:190–207
Wen M (2005) Foreign direct investment, regional geographical and market conditions, and regional development: a panel study on China, ANU working paper on trade and development, no.12. Australian National University, Canberra
Westerlund J (2007) Testing for error correction in panel data. Oxford Bull Econ Stat 69:709–748
World Bank (1993) World development report 1993. Oxford University Press for the World Bank, New York
World bank (2011) World development indicator, 2011. World Bank, Washington, DC
World Development Indicator (2012) World Bank, Washington, DC
Xing Y (2006) Exchange rate policy and the relative distribution of FDI between host countries, Working papers EMS, no.10. Research Institute, International University of Japan, Helsinki
Xuan NT, Xing Y (2008) Foreign direct investment and exports: the experience of Vietnam. Econ Trans 16(2):183–197

Zhang KH (2006) How does foreign direct investment affect economic growth in China? Econ Transit 9(3):679–693

Zhang Q, Felmingham B (2001) The relationship between inward direct foreign investment and China's provincial export trade. China Econ Rev 12:82–99

Zhang KH, Song S (2000) Promoting exports: the role of inward FDI in China. China Econ Rev 11:385–396

Chapter 10
FDI Reforms in South Asia: Unfinished Agenda, Future Reforms, and Challenges

10.1 Introduction

In the past two decades, South Asian countries have largely liberalised their FDI environment and made it conducive to attract foreign investment. However, prior to the 1980s, South Asia's policy towards FDI was selective with varying degrees of restrictions, and only India used to attract FDI. However, things have improved: South Asia is now considered a safe haven for FDI and one of the most attractive destinations for FDI in the world.[1]

The inflow of FDI depends both on policy and on other factors[2]: rate of return on investment and the certainty or uncertainty surrounding that return and a host of economic, institutional, regulatory, and infrastructure-related factors at both the macroeconomic and microeconomic level.[3] Though South Asian countries have been receiving increasing amounts of FDI in recent years, those are still lower than other country regions like East Asia, Southeast Asia, and Latin America.

There are many difficulties for foreign investors in South Asia as reflected by the *Doing Business* indicators of the World Economic Forum. China and East Asian countries perform better than South Asian nations in the annual business and macroeconomy indicators in the Global Competitiveness Report, World Economic Forum. In the overall index, Singapore ranks highest at seventh while Bangladesh is at the bottom at 107. China performed better than India (Table 10.A.1). India fares

---

[1] Kearney (XXX) ranks India as the second most important FDI destination since 2005.

[2] For theories of FDI, see Hymer (1976), Dunning (1977), and Rugman (1986).

[3] These can be called pull factors (for an elaboration, see Markusen and Venables 1999; Globerman and Shapiro 1999; Bajpai and Sachs 2000; Hanson 2001; Kinoshita and Campos 2003; Sahoo 2006; Sahoo and Nataraj 2008). However, there are also push factors such as recession, low international interest rates, and stringent environmental norms in developed economies.

P. Sahoo et al., *Foreign Direct Investment in South Asia*,
DOI 10.1007/978-81-322-1536-3_10, © Springer India 2014

better than China on business sophistication and institutions but worse on infrastructure and much worse on macroeconomy. In South Asia, Bangladesh and Nepal have not performed very satisfactorily; Sri Lanka's indicators are relatively better. In East Asia, Singapore and Malaysia are better performers. In case of basic requirement provision, China betters India.

In East Asia, China lags behind Singapore, Korea, Malaysia, and Thailand. India fares better than China on efficiency enhancement, innovation, and sophistication. In South Asia, Bangladesh and Nepal are laggards as usual. In East Asia, Singapore, Korea, and Malaysia are better performers, sometimes better than China (Table 10.A.2). India fares better than China on goods market efficiency, financial market efficiency, and technological readiness (Table 10.A.3); on labour market efficiency, China is ahead of India. As usual, Singapore is far ahead overall in East Asia and South Asia. Korea and Malaysia also fare better. Notably, despite high labour market rigidity, Sri Lanka is one of the better performers on South Asia (Table 10.A.3).

In case of export and import cost, China has a clear advantage over South Asian countries. Even within South Asia, Pakistan and Sri Lanka are less costly than India. This shows that trade and transaction costs are higher in South Asian countries than in China. In case of enforcing commercial contracts, India's situation is not as good as in most nations in South Asia and China. While in India, it is easier to hire personnel, it is not the case while firing. In terms of financial costs, it is of course less burdensome on employers in India compared to other countries, e.g. China and other nations in South Asia (Table 10.A.4).

Hence, the objective of the present chapter is to understand both FDI policies and the constraints to implementing these policies that affect FDI inflows to the region. The chapter has also attempted to put forth the future reforms that need to be carried out in each of the economies of the region for increasing FDI inflows. Key questions being asked include the following: (1) What are the constraints to FDI inflows into India at present? (2) What are the policy priorities/reforms relevant in the present context?

10.2 FDI in India: Unfinished Agenda

In this section, we analyse major policies and issues that directly and indirectly affect FDI inflows into India.[4] These include labour rules and regulations, infrastructure development, special economic zones (SEZ), and further trade reforms.

[4] This section on India heavily draws from Sahoo (2012).

10.2.1 Labour Rules and Regulations

Among the 47 central and 200 state labour laws that apply to the organised sector, three main acts affect the labour market in India. The Industrial Disputes Act (1947) has rigid provisions such as compulsory and prior government approval in the case of layoffs, retrenchment, and closure of industrial establishments employing more than 100 workers. Rigid labour laws also discourage firms trying to introduce a new technology that would require some workers to be retrenched. This deters greenfield FDI because of the fear that it would not be possible to dismiss unproductive workers or to downsize during a downturn in business.[5] The objective of getting FDI into export-oriented labour-intensive sectors in India has not been fully achieved because of rigid labour laws. By contrast, China has been hugely successful in attracting FDI into export-oriented labour-intensive manufacturing, in part because of its flexible labour laws such as the contract labour system implemented in 1995.

10.2.2 Infrastructure Development: A Major Obstacle to FDI

The availability of quality infrastructure, particularly electricity, transportation, telecommunications, and water, is an important determinant of FDI. However, poor infrastructure facilities have deterred foreign investors from coming to India. In India, infrastructure projects have traditionally been initiated, owned, and managed by the state. The role of the private sector has been relatively limited, usually restricted to subcontracting in the construction phase. However, the ability of governments to exclusively fund infrastructure projects is increasingly limited by their resource constraints and the sheer scale of demand for both maintenance of existing infrastructure and provision of additional services (Noel and Brzeski 2004; Grimsey and Lewis 2005; Nataraj 2007; NCAER-HOLCIM 2010). As a result, governments are increasingly looking to the private sector to both finance and build and operate infrastructure assets.

One of the major infrastructure issues in India has been the inadequacy of public–private partnerships (PPPs) in meeting the supply–demand gap in infrastructure facilities. This is because of a lack of the following: a clear and stable legal framework, information dissemination and guidance materials, competent institutional mechanisms to prioritise investment projects, efficient mechanisms for dispute resolution, and well-developed financial markets.

Financing infrastructure is a complex and difficult matter as infrastructure projects need high initial capital cost and involve a complex and varied mixture

[5] A number of studies suggest that rigid labour regulations end up doing more harm than good in terms of employment generation, exports, and investment (Besley and Burgess 2004; Planning Commission 2001).

of financial and contractual arrangements. Some of the major constraints for financing infrastructure in India are (1) limited exit options for investors and weaknesses in corporate governance, (2) interest caps and lack of deep forward foreign exchange markets, (3) lack of depth in the government bond market, (4) regulatory uncertainty which increases the risk profile of infrastructure projects, and (5) weak fiscal positions of the governments making them less bankable business partners for infrastructure projects.

Government can facilitate infrastructure investment and reduce cost by giving fiscal incentives such as reducing the customs duty on capital goods and giving tax concessions on long-term investment in infrastructures. There are other serious constraints on infrastructure financing such as time-consuming multiple government approvals, red tape, and administrative hurdles.

10.2.3 SEZ: Objectives and Issues

SEZ are important channels of attracting FDI into a country. Emulating the experience of China and other emerging economies, India also set up several SEZs in the country in the last decade. In 2000, the government of India announced the SEZ policy with the objective of making SEZs an engine of growth by providing quality infrastructure with minimum regulation. Foreign investors and developers get a number of fiscal incentives such as exemptions from direct and indirect taxes.[6] There is single window clearance for SEZs and all approvals for establishment and management are granted by a unit approval committee, which has a Development Commissioner and centre and state nominees as members.

To attract FDI into SEZs, a number of other policy measures have been taken. Foreign ownership of up to 100 % is allowed under the automatic route for all manufacturing activities, except those under the reserved and negative list. Foreign ownership of up to 100 % is allowed for development of townships (including housing, commercial, and recreational facilities) on a case-by-case basis. There is a facility for foreign companies to set up manufacturing units in SEZs as branch operations on a stand-alone basis without approval from the Reserve Bank of India. Foreign ownership of up to 100 % is permitted under the automatic route for setting up 100 % export-oriented units and industrial parks, subject to sectoral policies. Proposals for FDI for non-resident Indian investment in EHTP units are eligible for approval under the automatic route. Finally, proposals for FDI or non-resident Indian investment in software technology park units are also eligible for approval under the automatic route.[7]

[6] Tax exemptions cover income tax, central sales tax, excise duty, export profit, capital gains, dividend and customs duties on imported goods, and local excise.

[7] Proposals not covered under the automatic route would be considered and approved by the Foreign Investment Promotion Board.

The major concern in setting up SEZs has been the acquisition of the required land. There is no specific provision for the acquisition of land for SEZ. The centre has advised the states about priorities for land acquisition.[8] But since land acquisition is under state law, state government cooperation is important to ensure the required land proposed for SEZs.

The experience of SEZs in China provides lessons for India. China set up SEZs to attract investors into labour-intensive manufacturing exports and to experiment with market-oriented economic reforms. The Chinese SEZs were very large and housed activities such as commerce, tourism, housing, agriculture, and industrial production as well as export processing. The SEZs were given special status with minimum bureaucracy, good infrastructure, and generous tax holidays for manufacturing units and unlimited duty-free imports of raw, intermediate, and final goods as well as capital goods. Unlike in India where the powers for foreign investment approval in SEZs are vested with the Development Commissioners who are the representatives of the central government, in China the provincial and local authorities were made partners and stakeholders by delegating power to them to approve foreign investment. The delegation of authority to the provincial governments allowed them to introduce their own legislation to attract foreign investment in SEZs by providing incentives and giving faster clearances and approvals. Thus, a conducive policy environment, along with infrastructure, cheap labour and flexible labour laws, and low cost of capital, made Chinese SEZs a viable proposition for foreign investors.

10.2.4 Land Acquisition

The land acquisition in India has become the major problem for industrialisation. This section reviews the land acquisition laws and problems.

10.2.4.1 Land Acquisition Act, 1894

To facilitate the acquisition of privately held land for public purposes, the 'Land Acquisition Act' was enacted in 1894, which extends to the whole of India except the state of Jammu and Kashmir. The law defines the term 'land acquisition' as acquiring land for some public purpose by government/government agency, as authorised by law, from the individual landowner(s) after paying a fixed compensation in lieu of losses incurred by landowner(s) due to surrendering of his/her land

[8] The first priority should be for the acquisition of waste and barren land. If necessary, single-crop agricultural land could be acquired for SEZs. If a portion of double-cropped agricultural land has to be acquired to meet the minimum area requirements, especially for multiproduct special economic zones, it should not exceed 10 % of the total land required for the SEZ.

to the concerned government agency. The Act defines the expression 'public purpose' as the acquisition of land for:

1. The provision of village sites or the extension, planned development, or improvement of existing village sites
2. The provision of land for town or rural planning
3. The provision of land for planned development of land from public funds in pursuance of any scheme or policy of the government and subsequent disposal thereof in whole or in part by lease, assignment, or outright sale with the object of securing further development as planned
4. The provision of land for a corporation owned or controlled by the state
5. The provision of land for residential purposes to poor or landless or to persons residing in areas affected by natural calamities or to persons displaced or affected by the reason of the implementation of any scheme undertaken by the government, any local authority, or a corporation owned by the state
6. The provision of land for any other scheme of development sponsored by the government or with prior approval of the appropriate government or local authority
7. The provision of any premises or building for locating a public office, but does not include the acquisition of land for companies
8. The provision of land for carrying out any educational, housing, health, or slum clearance scheme sponsored by the government

However, the Land Acquisition Act of 1894 has been criticised on ground of low compensation, lack of proper relief and rehabilitation (R&R), and excessive use of state eminence for land. All these problems acted as impediment in land acquisition and industrialisation. Therefore, after many efforts the new land acquisition has finally proposed in 2011.

10.2.4.2 Land Acquisition and Resettlement and Rehabilitation (LARR) Bill, 2011

The first draft of the new Land Acquisition Bill was put out in July 2011, the primary focus of which is social inclusiveness. The LARR Bill 2011 is expected to affect rural families in India whose primary livelihood is derived from farms. LARR Bill 2011 proposed to compensate rural households—both landowners and livelihood losers. The Bill goes beyond compensation; it mandates guaranteed series of entitlements to rural households that are affected. LARR Bill 2011 mandates higher payments for land as well as guaranteed entitlements from India's non-agriculture-derived GDP to the people supported by agriculture-derived GDP. It is expected that the Bill will directly affect 132 million hectares (326 million acres) of rural land in India, over 100 million landowners, with an average land holding of about 3 acres per landowner. For a typical rural household that owns the average of 3 acres of land, the LARR Bill 2011 is expected to replace the loss of annual average per capita income of Rs 11,136 of the rural household, with:

- Four times the market value of land.
- An upfront payment of Rs 1,36,000 (US$3,000) for subsistence, transportation, and resettlement allowance.
- An additional entitlement of a job to the family member, or a payment of Rs 50,000 (US$11,000) up front, or a monthly annuity totalling Rs 24,000 (US $550) per year for 20 years with inflation adjustment for inflation – the option from these three choices shall be the legal right of the affected landowner family, not the land acquirer.
- A house with no less than 50 m^2 in plinth area.
- Additional benefits may apply if the land is resold without development, used for urbanisation, or if the landowner belongs to SC/ST or other protected groups as per rules of the Government of India.

10.2.4.3 Implications for the Private Sector and Issues

The Bill provides that R&R provisions are mandatory for all private purchases through private negotiations if the land purchased is over 100 acres in rural areas or 50 acres in urban areas. The Bill requires a social impact assessment (SIA) study to be conducted for every acquisition of land. The Bill provides for an independent multidisciplinary expert group, which shall evaluate the SIA. This group would be required to assess whether (1) the project serves the stated public purpose, (2) it is in larger public interest, and (3) the potential benefits outweigh the costs and adverse impact. There are no guidelines to determine the methodology for such assessment and the Bill does not provide for such guidelines to be delegated to the rules. This could lead to lack of consistency in the assessment of projects by different expert groups.

The proposed Land Acquisition Bill is likely to sharply inflate business cost for companies from mining, metal, and infrastructure sectors. At the same time, the Bill might speed up land acquisition for companies by reducing the number of hurdles and disputes in the process. The Bill places no limit on the total compensation or number of claimants; nor does it place any statute of limitations on claims or claimants. The beneficiaries of the Bill, with guaranteed jobs for 26 years, will have no incentive to be productive. The proposed Bill severely curtails free market transactions between willing sellers and willing buyers. Direct land transactions with owners on a willing voluntary basis, at market-determined rate, should be kept out of the purview of the Bill. This is self-defeating; industries are based near cities, rivers, coastlines, expressways, and other places of logistical necessities, quality of life for workers, cost of operations, and various reasons. History of urbanisation and global distribution of industry hubs show that the locations of great industry were all on fertile land. The proposed Bill prohibits the acquisition of fertile agriculture land beyond 5 % per district. The Bill inflates the cost of land to help a small minority of Indians at the cost of vast majority of Indian citizens, as less than 10 % of Indian population owns rural or urban land. The Bill favours a privileged minority of landowners as the Bill mandates above market prices for their land plus an expensive rehabilitation package.

However, the version that was passed by the Cabinet is slightly different from the draft issued in July, according to Indian media reports. One change is that companies acquiring land in rural areas will have to pay four times the market rate, rather than six times the rate, as earlier suggested. In urban areas, companies will have to pay twice the market price—as the draft suggests. There are few other points from the draft that seem to have stayed untouched—on every transfer of land within 10 years of the date of acquiring it, 20 % of the appreciated value shall be shared with the original owner. One member per affected family must be offered a job or Rs 200,000 if employment is not offered.

The Bill seeks to update India's 118-year-old land acquisition laws and overhaul its rehabilitation and resettlement policy, a hot-button issue that has stalled several projects in India. So far, Indian law has kept rehabilitation a separate exercise from land acquisition. However, this could change.

10.2.5 Environmental Clearances

The continuously growing industrial sector, without giving much attention to the harmful effects of its activities on the environment and natural resources, became a cause of primary concern for both the people and the government. Along with the land acquisition, getting environmental clearances for industrial and infrastructure projects has become very debatable. In 1986, the Environment (Protection) Act was enacted for the protection and improvement of the environment and empowering the Central Government to take necessary actions to prevent, control, and abate environmental pollution. The Act stipulates that no person performing any industrial activity or carrying out operation or process should discharge or emit environmental pollution in excess of the prescribed limit. Under the provision of the Act, the process of environmental impact assessment (EIA) was made mandatory in 1994. The MoEF grants environmental clearances required to set up the developmental projects. Projects up for consideration at the MoEF are divided into two categories, A and B, based on the spatial extent of potential impacts on human health and natural and manmade disasters. For matters listed under 'Category A', prior environmental clearance is given by the Central Government (MoEF) on recommendations of an Expert Appraisal Committee (EAC), which is constituted by the Central Government. The matters listed in 'Category B' are considered at the state level by the State Environment Impact Assessment Authority (SEIAA) to grant environmental clearances.

Despite the larger agenda of safeguarding the environment, there are significant drawbacks in the Indian system that needs further scrutiny. For instance, certain industries are excluded from the list of industries that require EC, even though their technological processes could have negative effects on the environment. Small-scale industries are not included in the list but they contribute to environmental pollution. Investment value should not be a criterion of exemption of industries from EIA requirements.

A significant cause of concern is that the EIA is commissioned by the project proponents. The assessment is funded by the agency or individual seeking the clearance. It is more likely that the report is biased, as the prime objective of the proponent is to obtain the clearance. Moreover, significant information is generally missing in the report. In many cases, the EC has been granted despite objections from people. Public opinions are invited only in the later stages of the process with leads to conflict. Several industrial projects are based in the resource-rich tribal and rural areas. The land is easily acquired by convincing the tribals who are illiterate and lack knowledge on the legal procedures. The local environmental and social groups take the challenge to educate people about the actual impact of the activities and push them to raise objections. In addition, the information on the MoEF website is updated much after the decision is taken. Those without access to Internet are not informed. The redressal mechanism is weak and has limited scope. In the past few years, only a handful of cases have been heard by the National Appellate Authority. People with low bargaining power cannot stand against the giant and powerful project proponents. It has been suggested to create an independent EIA authority consisting of representatives from communities, citizens' group, scientists, sociologists, and environmentalists, independent of the MoEF.

The latest National Environment Policy (NEP) was passed in 2006, despite protests and opposition. In order to facilitate speedy clearances, the EIA notification was re-engineered, reducing public involvement in the decision-making, thereby making the process less transparent. From 1986 to 2006, the MoEF cleared 4,016 projects; between September 2006 and August 2008, the MoEF granted 2,019 project clearances. For the period between January 2008 and February 2009, the number of clearances was highest at 2,586. The decision-making has been limited to the identification of mitigation measures and the public consultation process is turned into merely a forum to improve an EIA report.

The EIA process requires a huge amount of information on diverse environmental and social parameters, which stands as a challenge for both clearance givers and seekers. The collection and analysis of all these aspects of environment and people and their interaction over time demands a great amount of time and effort. To expedite the clearance process, the experts in the Finance Ministry's committee recommended the standardisation of Terms of Reference (ToRs) for 'repetitive projects'. ToRs perform the function of listing all the aspects that an EIA for a project should cover, based on characteristics, location, and other specifications. In addition, expert committee suggested that in case the MoEF is unable to complete the procedure of clearance within the stipulated time, the process will automatically turn to a clearing house for the grant of clearance.

To bring about a change in the process of granting EC in the wake of controversies related to the clearance given to the developmental projects, Prime Minister Manmohan Singh announced the government's plan to set up an independent environmental regulator, the National Environment Assessment and Monitoring Authority (NEAMA). It would be manned by dedicated professionals and would work towards forming better methods of environmental assessment.

10.2.6 Trade Reforms and FDI Inflows

Bhagwati (1978) theorised that FDI would be more growth enhancing in countries that pursued an export promotion strategy than an import-substituting development strategy. At a microeconomic level, studies find that the net welfare gain associated with FDI projects is positively correlated with the degree of openness of the recipient country (Balasubramanyam et al. 1996; Lal and Streeten 1977; Encarnacion and Wells 1986). Realising the fact, India has been persistently following open trade policies by bringing down tariffs, allowing current account convertibility and taking gradual steps towards capital account convertibility. Although India has been a strong supporter of the multilateral trading system, it has started taking a keen interest in regional agreements for promoting trade and investment.[9] However, as Kalirajan and Singh (2008) suggest, India needs to address behind-the-border constraints such as reforms in domestic policies and infrastructure to improve its exports and to catch up with China.

10.2.7 The Unfinished Agenda and Way Forward

The analysis of FDI policy and trends shows that many difficulties still prevent India being a prime destination for foreign investors. With all the advantages India has, there are still factors and issues that hinder FDI flow into India, including:

- Infrastructure bottlenecks
- Rigid and complicated labour laws
- Lack of coordination between the centre and states
- FDI caps/ceilings in many sectors where 100 % FDI equity is not allowed for feasible investment projects
- Difficult bureaucratic controls and procedures to get the necessary clearances and approvals and first-time investors in India are always sceptical about whether projects will progress from screening to operation

In this backdrop, a few reforms that are essential to sustain and increase FDI into India include the following:

[9] This is mainly because of slow progress in the WTO. Currently, India is among the top countries having regional trade agreements either in place or under negotiation. See Jaumotte (2004) for the impact of regional trade agreements on FDI inflows. However, Dee (2006) concludes that the trade provisions of preferential trade agreements, not the investment provisions, have had a positive impact on FDI activity in Asia.

10.2.7.1 Infrastructure Development

The environment for both public and private infrastructure development needs improvement by having a more stable and secure policy framework (including pricing and subsidy policies) and protection of property rights. A major obstacle for infrastructure development is cost and time overruns in major projects arising from contractual and intuitional failures (Ram Singh 2010). For example, there is often a failure to make precise calculations of the cost and time required to complete projects. There is often also a lack of (or delay in) cooperation by state-level departments for land acquisition and environmental clearance.

On-time completion of infrastructure projects for better utilisation funds requires a two-pronged approach: (1) better designed projects with proper estimation before contracts are awarded and (2) clearance from the proper institutional bodies, including politicians from the major political parties and administrative heads of relevant ministries at both the centre and the states. The land acquisition requirements and availability of utilities (power, water, etc.) should be studied properly so that project implementation takes place effectively. Land acquisition in India is a major problem because of the process for valuing and acquiring land and paying for compensation, rehabilitation, and resettlement. Though there have been amendments, there is a need to revisit land acquisition issues and environmental issues and there should be efforts to adopt more decentralised process for negations.

Infrastructure projects are capital intensive and the ability of foreign investors to finance and mobilise resources and global expertise can expedite infrastructure investment. To attract foreign investors, foreign equity limits should be increased to 100 % in most infrastructure sectors, subject to appropriate regulatory mechanisms being put in place. The success of investment in telecommunications shows the benefits of having autonomous bodies for regulation and governance. Allowing cost-recovery pricing is also important for attracting private investment into infrastructure sector. Increased private investment in the power sector, for example, will require policy and regulatory reforms of user charges, along with a reduction of theft and allowing private entry into distribution.

Since the actual investment takes places at the state level, any special investment law in infrastructure should integrate the many state laws, rules, and regulations applicable to investment in and production of infrastructure services. The Andhra Pradesh Infrastructure Act and the success of the Gujarat government in attracting private investment and FDI in ports and other infrastructure could be taken as reference cases.

Another major problem in infrastructure development is infrastructure financing. Certain steps that could boost infrastructure financing are:

- Removing interest rate caps on external commercial borrowing (ECB)
- Relaxing bank's investments in corporate bonds (investment and regulatory guidelines for financial intermediaries which will encourage them to participate in infrastructure projects)

- Allowing financial intermediaries to invest in reasonably rated infrastructure projects
- Giving to use pension funds, insurance, and FIIs; to invest in infrastructure projects
- Creating special infrastructure financial institutions which would get involved in the design and planning of the projects
- Creating a debt recovery tribunal to create confidence in making large investments

Some of these steps could be gradual. All would improve infrastructure financing.

10.2.7.2 Flexible Labour Laws

It has often been highlighted that laws should be made simple and flexible if India is to achieve the same level of FDI inflows as China. Apart from constitutional provisions, there are separate state regulations for different kinds of workers and types of labour. There should be efforts to unify all the definitions into a Uniform Labour Code where, for instance, all provisions related to social security or wages can come under a single statute. There should also be efforts to remove the rigid provisions affecting labour markets that were discussed in the previous section.

The reason for lack of labour reforms in India is the lack of political consensus. Trade unions only protect organised labour, which constitutes less than 10 % of the total labour force, but unions are vocal and politically affiliated. Thus, labour reform is a very sensitive issue and has to be dealt with gradually after bringing all stakeholders on board. The first step should be to set up a commission to revisit the innumerable provisions in central and state laws and their present relevance for labour welfare at large in a market economy. The commission should have experts including representatives of labour unions. Once there is consensus about changes for the unification and harmonisation of labour laws across states, government can consult with different political parties to consolidate and implement labour reforms.

10.2.7.3 Better Coordination Between the Centre and the States

Investment projects require clearances from both the central and state government, which involve many bureaucratic procedures and delay.[10] Though the centre is very proactive in reforming FDI policy from time to time, actual implementation takes place at state level (Palit 2009). Bureaucratic hassles, mainly at the state level, are one of the major reasons for the slow realisation of FDI relative to approvals.

[10] India is a federal country and there are many issues between centre and states and also among the states which make the reform process and also implementation slow. For fiscal federalism issues in India, see Sahoo (2001, 2004).

Although the Foreign Investment Implementation Authority tries to solve problems through regional meetings of foreign investors, there should be an autonomous body in charge of getting clearances from both centre and state governments within a stipulated time frame. Other useful steps would be (1) to encourage every state to have a single window nodal agency for approval and clearances and (2) to have coordination between central government institutions (such as the Foreign Investment Promotion Board, the Foreign Investment Implementation Authority, and the Secretariat for Industrial Assistance) and these state-level nodal agencies to reduce duplication and the number of clearances.

If there is a complex matter between the centre and the states, the relevant ministries and other related institutions must be available at the problem-solving stage to find solutions and make quick decisions. For this to happen, it is necessary to have an autonomous body with members from the states who would be accountable in the case of delays in project implementation. Some of the major causes of delay are state-level issues such as land acquisition, land use change, power connection, and building plan approval. Therefore, coordination on these issues between the centre and the states before the approval of investment projects is required to avoid unnecessary delays at state level. Reforms at the state level to simplify and modernise policy and rules and to keep in step with policy changes at the centre are also necessary for better realisation of FDI and speedier implementation.[11]

10.2.7.4 Making SEZs More Effective

Chinese competitiveness in manufacturing was helped by developing zones as industrial clusters of specific products. Therefore, policy measures to enhance the performance of the SEZs in India should include the proper design and operation of SEZs as clusters of specific products. To do this, the government needs to rethink the size of SEZs, which are currently relatively small. Proper planning and design should also include providing sufficient infrastructure connectivity to domestic and external markets.

In recent years, establishing SEZs has faced increasing difficulties because of the regulatory framework for land acquisition.[12] In most cases, land acquisition becomes a political battle when landowners ally with opposition parties. Since land, water, power, and other utilities are basic requirements for SEZs, the first priority before granting approval should be the proper planning and analysis by an independent agency of the viability of the project and then consultation with

[11] The Govindarajan Committee report recommending simplification of regulatory procedures and investment norms, including the removal of archaic laws at the state level, was submitted to the Government of India in November 2002.

[12] SEZs in Nandigram (WB), Kalinganagar (Orissa), Kakinada (Andhra Pradesh), and Nandagudi (Karnataka) have faced stiff resistance from landowners (Mukherji 2008).

stakeholders including political parties. The examples of Andhra Pradesh and Tamil Nadu show that it is possible to develop SEZs and attract FDI without stiff resistance. It is possible to get the consent of the majority of landowners provided there is proper and generous relief package worked out, along with social entrepreneurship.[13]

Though the Development Commissioner is the centre's single window nodal agency for approving SEZs, the actual regulatory clearances lie with states. Therefore, the Development Commissioner needs to have proper consultation with state agencies before giving approval. Further, states trying to attract investment into SEZs need to make proactive policies in different sectors where they want to attract FDI. The best example is the policy of the Andhra Pradesh government for textile and apparel promotion in 2005, which resulted in significant FDI in its SEZs in this sector. If governments find it difficult to provide the required infrastructure connectivity, the private sector should be allowed (with automatic 100 % ownership of FDI) and encouraged to develop infrastructure to service the SEZs. Since connecting infrastructure such as roads and railways are problematic in India, SEZs should be established in the coastal regions, as was done in China.

10.2.7.5 Increasing FDI Equity Ceilings

Relaxation of ceilings for foreign equity in many sectors would certainly increase FDI inflows. Some of the sectors which have huge potential to attract FDI by increasing FDI caps are (1) telecommunications and the civil aviation sector, subject to independent and autonomous regulatory systems to control market distortions and allow fair competition; (2) civilian goods used by defence forces or dual use equipment used in the production of civilian goods[14]; (3) power generation, subject to regulatory mechanisms to avoid monopoly in power generation; and (4) food retailing (Virmani 2004).[15]

The important reforms required in manufacturing are increasing the FDI equity cap and allowing entry into more sectors under the automatic route. The FDI ceiling can also be raised in public sector refineries and oil marketing, from 26 %

[13] The Sri City SEZ in Andhra Pradesh is an example. It did not witness a single litigation case while acquiring 2,700 acres of land.

[14] Since most of the defence equipment used for making weapons domestically is imported from foreign private companies, therefore allowing FDI with higher equity to produce defence equipment should be allowed.

[15] More FDI in food retailing would increase the productivity and efficiency of the supply chain, thereby reducing the gap between prices received by farmers and paid by consumers. Over time, increases in income of farmers would generate employment opportunities for intermediaries. In the short run, governments can compensate the losers through direct budgetary subsidies.

at present. The current foreign equity limit of up to 24 % in small-scale industry (though a higher equity proportion is permitted if 50 % of output is exported) is not justified when small-scale industry needs funds to expand and modernise. All the sectors where 100 % FDI equity has been allowed should be put on the automatic route.[16]

In services also, FDI limits can be raised in sectors such as insurance, banking, investment companies, and the real estate sector. The experience of opening up insurance to a 26 % FDI equity limit has been beneficial in terms of efficiency, given an effective Insurance Regulatory Authority. Given effective regulation of the banking sector by the Reserve Bank of India, FDI limits for private banks should also be raised to 100 %, as public sector banks have been successfully competing and improving their efficiency. Similarly, the equity limit for FDI should be raised to 100 % from 49 % for investment companies (for infrastructure and social sectors). India could attract a huge amount of FDI in real estate, provided the plethora of controls was removed and rules and regulations were properly designed and clear. In the non-retailing sector also, 100 % FDI can be allowed through the automatic route with clearly spelt out conditions.

Overall, FDI reform in India is largely accepted across political parties, levels of bureaucracy, and different sections of Indian society. There are enough successful examples of large benefits from reforms to continue the reform impetus. It is therefore expected that policymakers in India would carry on with FDI reforms, with due consultation with different stakeholders.

The post-liberalisation period has been remarkable for FDI in India. It has created a conducive environment for foreign investment by abolishing industrial licensing, establishing institutions, lifting FDI equity ceilings, shifting more sectors to the automatic route, providing incentives, and liberalising foreign exchange regulations. Consequently, FDI inflows, which used to be negligible before 1991, have increased substantially.

The establishment of FDI institutions to facilitate FDI moving beyond approval to implementation has certainly helped to enhance inflows and give a higher realisation of approvals. Further, the post-reform period has also witnessed FDI inflows from a growing number of countries and more greenfield investment, confirming improved investment norms and the preference of foreign investors for new business start-ups.

However, FDI is still concentrated in a few sectors and a few states because of unresolved issues and India is yet to receive FDI inflows to its full potential. The factors that hinder FDI flows into India include infrastructure bottlenecks, rigid and complicated labour laws, lack of coordination between the states and the centre,

[16] For example, production of drugs using recombinant DNA, courier services, and in airports is on the Foreign Investment Promotion Board approval route even though 100 % FDI equity is allowed. Since these sectors are well regulated and monitored with appropriate terms and conditions, there is no justification for keeping these on the Foreign Investment Promotion Board route.

lack of reforms at the state level except in a few states, FDI equity caps/ceilings in many potential sectors, and delay in getting multiple clearances and approvals.

The next level of reforms and policies need to address these issues and set up appropriate institutions. Some of the necessary reforms are:

- A better environment for infrastructure development with an appropriate institutional framework such as a dispute resolution mechanism, independent regulatory authority, and special investment law
- A Uniform Labour Code after an independent review and proper consultation with stakeholders
- Proper design and planning of SEZs, including local-level solutions for land acquisition and sector-specific policies with incentives to attract FDI into SEZs
- Proper infrastructure connectivity to SEZs and allowing the private sector to provide infrastructure services to SEZs
- Increasing FDI caps in sectors with FDI potential and allowing more sectors under the automatic route
- Revisiting outdated laws, controls, regulatory systems, and government monopolies affecting the investment environment
- Encouraging non-governmental facilitation services for foreign investors
- Further trade reforms and reforms in public services to attract foreign investment

Overall, India needs to address its lack of adequate infrastructure, rigid labour laws, bureaucratic delays, and state-level reforms to realise its FDI potential.

10.3 FDI in Pakistan: Unfinished Agenda and Challenges

Apart from India, Pakistan happens to be another country that has been attracting a fair amount of FDI in South Asia. In fact, Pakistan has the potential to be Asia's premier trade, energy, and transport corridor. Its geographical location suits transit trade given its proximity to West Asia, Central Asia, China, and South Asia. However, Pakistan is a troubled economy and there are several challenges that come in the way of enhancing its FDI inflows. These include both international factors and domestic factors. Among the international factors which are more recent include the global financial crisis (recession in Eurozone and the USA), global commodity prices (upsurge in food and oil prices), and regional security situation. There are several domestic factors also which hinder FDI into the country. These are macroeconomic stability, energy shortages, infrastructure (railroad transportation and ICT), contract enforcement, regulatory quality, financial and capital markets, taxation and tariff structure, innovation and competition, quality and flexibility of labour markets, government footprints in markets, and political stability and policy continuity. Some of these factors are explained in detail below.

10.3.1 Difficulties and Challenges for FDI

As mentioned above, there are several factors both domestic and international, which pose immediate challenges for FDI into Pakistan. Further, terrorist violence and natural disasters are keeping investors at bay. Therefore, it is vital that the government of Pakistan retains the faith and confidence of its investors and makes determined efforts to realise its considerable market potential. Based on its efforts to globalise, Pakistan has a decent foreign investment policy in place that encourages foreign investors in almost all economic sectors, based on a single window clearance. However, given its image as an extremely corrupt country, with overprotective labour laws and political and military strife and with no likelihood of democracy in the near future, Pakistan needs to ensure that all its FDI policies are implemented smoothly to facilitate the foreign investment that is much needed.

Pakistan is an important and strategic country in South Asia and its growth and development has far-reaching implications for the Asian region in general and the South Asian region in particular. Foreign business and industrial houses have confirmed their plans to continue to invest in Pakistan despite certain difficulties. These difficulties relate to an uncertain law and order situation on the back of terrorist activities in the country's western region. However, 74 % of the foreign investors already operating in Pakistan are interested in going ahead with new investments over the next 2 years and beyond given the country's considerable market potential. Some of the challenges to Pakistan's FDI inflows are given below.

10.3.2 Land Acquisition in Pakistan

The Land Acquisition Act 1894 is the principal act administering the acquisition of land for public purpose in Pakistan. Various amendments have been made in the act from time to time. As per the act, 'public purpose' constitutes provision of village sites in the districts upon a notification by the provincial government for the intended acquisition.

One of the shortcomings of the Land Acquisition Act (LAA) is that the land compensation is only for titled landowners or holders of customary rights. However, the Punjab Jinnah Abadis for non-proprietors in Rural Areas Act 1986 promises to address the rights of the title less, by providing a replacement plot in compensation. Projects such as Chotiari Dam, Ghazi Barotha Hydropower, and National Highways Improvement have awarded compensation and assistance to unregistered tenants and other forms of AP (sharecroppers/squatters) (NTDC 2006).

Pakistan laws are not clear on the rehabilitation of the displaced persons. The LAA itself does not necessitate the rehabilitation and assistance for the poor displaced families, vulnerable groups, or severely affected APs. The steps for ad hoc arrangements for the provision of rehabilitation are taken by the local governments and specific project proponents at their own discretion (NTDC 2006).

The LAA and its implementation rules require that following an impact assessment/valuation effort, land and crops are compensated in cash at market rate to titled landowners and registered land tenants/users, respectively. The LAA mandates that land valuation is to be based on the latest 5–3 years average registered land sale rates, though in several recent cases, the median rate over the past 1 year, or even the current rates, has been applied. Due to widespread land undervaluation by the Revenue Department, current market rates are now frequently applied with an added 15 % compulsory acquisition surcharge as provided in the LAA (NTDC 2006).

The problems with the Act do not end here. Another one is regarding the only pre-litigation final authority that is the land acquisition collector (LAC) to decide disputes and address complaints regarding quantification/compensation for the affected lands and other assets (NTDC 2006).

As noted above, exceptions to the rule are intrinsic to the fact that the law is elastic and is broadly interpreted at the provincial level depending on operational requirements, local needs, and socio-economic circumstances. Recourse is often taken to ad hoc arrangements, agreements, and understandings for resettlement in difficult situations. The above is also influenced by the fact that an amendment of the LAA has been considered necessary by the Ministry of Environment. Accordingly, a National Resettlement Policy (NRP) and a Resettlement Ordinance have been drafted to broaden LAA provisions and current practices to widen the scope of eligibility and tightening up loopholes (i.e. regarding definitions of malpractices, cut-off dates, political influence on routing). But both these documents are still awaiting governmental approval for implementation (NTDC 2006).

10.3.3 Pending Reforms and Way Forward

In 2011, Pakistan has emerged as the third largest country in South Asia with FDI inflows of $1.3 billion says the World Investment Report 2012. Even though Pakistan's economy is in shambles, the government of Pakistan has been proactive and continues to liberalise the FDI policy in the country. Some of the key reforms carried out so far include all major economic sectors open to foreign investors, foreign equity up to 100 % allowed, no government permissions required by investors, and import of raw material for export manufacturing zero rates. Further, Pakistan has aggressively pursued bilateral agreements. It has signed investment protection treaties with 48 countries and has avoidance of double taxation treaties with 52 countries.

Moreover, Pakistan recently announced a new investment policy strategy. The strategy covers the period 2010–2015. Some key features are public–private sector dialogue (PPDs), investment promotion, investment facilitation, SEZ, tax holidays, duty-free imports of plant and machinery, and one window facility offered by BOI.

Undoubtedly, Pakistan is in a transition phase and has tough challenges ahead. Efforts to sustain and increase FDI inflows largely hinge on efforts made by the

Government of Pakistan to retain the confidence of investors. These include potential as well as exiting investors, some of whom have been operating in Pakistan for many years. They also include domestic investors, whose actions shape perceptions of new investors. Determined efforts need to be made through dialogue and partnership with private sector and tap into the country's substantial resource capacity and its considerable market potential.

In sum, if the Pakistan government implements new FDI strategy in a determined and systematic manner by speeding up its implementation, Pakistan will soon be on the track to recovery and may go on to become the second largest recipient of FDI into the region.

10.4 FDI in Bangladesh: Unfinished Agenda and Challenges

Bangladesh has been promoting FDI for decades with the most liberal investment policy and incentive regime in South Asia. The Foreign Private Investment (Promotion and Protection) Act, 1980, ensures equal treatment for local and foreign investors. This act also provides legal protection to foreign investment in Bangladesh against nationalisation and expropriation. It also gives the guarantee of repatriation of capital and dividend.

Although Bangladesh is trying to be as friendly as possible to FDI, the country is facing problems attracting foreign investment. The problems that have restricted FDI potentials in the country are as follows:

- Bureaucratic interference
- Irregularities in processing papers
- Overlapping administrative procedures
- Absence of a transparent system of formalities
- Continuity and prevention of timely implementation of strategic, procedural, and even routine duties
- Frequent power failures

Some of the problems and challenges to FDI in Bangladesh are explained in the section below.

10.4.1 Difficulties and Limitations

Bangladesh has one of the worst infrastructures in South Asia. The constraints to infrastructure in Bangladesh and other factors are explained in the following section.

10.4.1.1 Infrastructure Constraints

Similar to India and Pakistan, lack of infrastructure remains a major obstacle to FDI in Bangladesh. Nasrin et al. (2010) identify infrastructure constraints, bureaucratic procedure, and political stability as major barriers to FDI inflows in Bangladesh. According to Global Competiveness Report (2011–2012), Bangladesh ranked 134 out of 142 countries in terms of infrastructure facilities with the score of 2.2. Power and telecom sector remained major areas of concern with scores of 1.6 and 0.6, respectively. In addition, road sector also ranked 129 with score of 2.8. In addition, structural and institutional weaknesses remain serious impediments to attracting higher FDI inflows.

Corruption: Corruption remains one of the most important impediments for FDI inflows to Bangladesh. This is not surprising given that Bangladesh holds the dubious distinction of one of the most corrupt countries in the world. In fact, Transparency International ranked Bangladesh as the most corrupt country in the world for five consecutive years from 2001 to 2005. The most recent Corruption Perception Index published by Transparency International (2010) ranked Bangladesh 134 out of 178 countries with the score of 2.4 in a scale of 0–10.

Political Stability: Political instability of a host country changes the rules of the game under which businesses operate and has an impact on profit and future FDI inflows. Lack of democracy and governance remained major concern areas. According to economic freedom index (2010), economic freedom score of Bangladesh is 51.1, making its economy the 137th freest economy out of 178 countries. This indicates Bangladesh has very low score on governance.

10.4.1.2 Land Acquisition in Bangladesh

The principal legal instrument governing land acquisition in Bangladesh is the Acquisition and Requisition of Immovable Property Ordinance 1982 (Ordinance II of 1982 including amendments up to 1994) and other land laws and administrative manuals relevant to alluvion/diluvion land, char, and khas land administration in Bangladesh.[17] The 1982 Ordinance requires that compensation be paid for (1) land and assets permanently acquired (including standing crops, trees, houses) and (2) any other damages caused by such acquisition. The Deputy Commissioner (DC) determines (a) market value of acquired assets on the date of notice of acquisition (based on the registered value of similar property bought and/or sold in the area over the preceding 12 months) and (b) 50 % premium on the assessed value (other than crops) due to compulsory acquisition. However, it is well known

[17] Alluvial, deluvion, and char land survey and settlement (No. 2-2/87/90(1060)/1987); Settlement of char land (No. 2L-3/73/86(19)-R.L/1973); Settlement of Diluviated Lands Reformed in Situ (Memo No. 196(36)-V-177/77-L.S /1978), State Acquisition and Tenancy (Amendment) Act, 1994); Transfer of Khas Land between GOB departments (M:/Sha-10/HUD/general-1/94/345 (64)/1994) (Source: Land Administration Manual, Vol. 1, Ministry of Land, GOB)

in Bangladesh that people devalue land during transactions to pay lower registration fees. As a result, compensation for land paid by DC including premium remains less than the real market price or replacement value. The 1994 amendment made provisions for payment of crop compensation to tenant cultivators.

The Ordinance, however, does not cover project-affected persons without title or ownership record, such as informal settler/squatters, occupiers, and informal tenants and leaseholders (without registration document), and does not ensure replacement market value of the property acquired. The act has no provisions for resettlement of the affected households/businesses or any assistance for restoration of livelihoods of the affected persons. As a result, land acquisition potentially diminishes productive base of farm families and those affected and displaced by development projects.[18]

Since the 1982 Ordinance falls short of the requirements of the World Bank safeguard policies on some grounds, the project land acquisition and resettlement policy has been harmonised with the World Bank's social safeguard requirements. The harmonisation has also benefited from the RTIP-I experience in resettlement.

10.4.2 Unfinished Agenda and the Way Forward

In Bangladesh FDI plays a very important role in increasing GDP. In order to sustain the economic growth and continue the present status of FDI inflows, Bangladesh needs to take some effective steps to promote FDI. The administrative system of the country requires reforms through appropriate and effective measures. The bureaucracy needs to be reorganised in such a way that the control of the bureaucracy is minimised.

Government should look into the law and order situation to ensure business friendly environment. A social consciousness is much more needed to ensure the rule of law and reduce the various effects of corruption. Both the government and private sector need to take a lead in infrastructure development. Appropriate policy measures would ensure that the private sector runs smoothly. If both public and the private sector work together with the objective of implementing economic reforms, Bangladesh will surely upgrade its position. In order to stimulate domestic and foreign investments, the privatisation programme ought to be initiated on a large scale.

With respect to pending reforms, it is important for a developing country like Bangladesh to modernise the laws relating to business and investment. It should be done focusing on international practices. The development of new industrial parks can play an important role in attracting foreign investment in Bangladesh. The government can also think of improving the image of the country abroad. Setting up

[18] Afsana Rahman (2012), 'Foreign Direct Investment in Bangladesh, Prospects and Challenges and its Impact on Economy', Project Submitted to Asian Institute of Technology School of Management, Thailand.

of an investment promotion agency to facilitate investment generation and policy advocacy will help Bangladesh catch up with the rest of the region fast. Bangladesh can also look to improving bilateral relations with potential investors in the region and outside.

The prospects of Bangladesh becoming a preferred destination of FDI in South Asia are quite possible if it overcomes its challenges of corruption and weak bureaucracy. Recently Bangladesh has taken steps to simplify various processes to encourage increased FDI. The government, total financial sector, and foreign investors would need to work together to achieve the goal of making Bangladesh a progressive economy by the end of this decade.

10.5 FDI in Sri Lanka: Unfinished Agenda and Challenges

The end of Sri Lanka's long-running civil war in May 2009 has opened a new era of economic opportunities and prospects of rebounding economic growth. The Government of Sri Lanka (GSL) has set very ambitious goals for economic development, aspiring to achieve GDP growth rates of over 8 % and developing economic hubs in ports, aviation, commercial, knowledge, and energy. Sri Lanka also provides very strong prospects in tourism and infrastructure. The country can still be a difficult place to do business, however, with a dynamic policy environment and cumbersome bureaucracy. Nonetheless, compared to other South Asian countries, Sri Lanka is relatively open to foreign investment. It offers a relatively open financial system, moderately good infrastructure, and generally capable workers.

However, the challenges to enhancing FDI in the country remain. A few of them are workers' declining English language skills, inflexible labour laws, overburdened infrastructure (although the GSL is moving to improve roads and ports), and an unreliable court system. Sri Lanka boasts a 90 % literacy rate in the local Sinhala and Tamil languages, but English, which was once widely spoken, is now far less prevalent. Sri Lanka's labour laws include many model protections but can make it nearly impossible for companies to lay off workers even when market conditions fully warrant doing so. The cost of dismissing an employee in Sri Lanka is, percentage-wise, one of the highest in the world. Until recently, Sri Lanka has not invested in infrastructure to keep pace with its growth. Its roads are narrow and congested. With the conclusion of the war, Sri Lanka is renovating and constructing roads in the North and East. Multiyear projects to expand the ports in Colombo and Hambantota are underway.

Sri Lanka's electricity supply is generally reliable but can fail to meet peak demand in years of low rainfall. Electricity costs are priced higher than in other Asian countries, and the GSL has recently raised electricity tariffs. Businesses in Sri Lanka also face high interest rates, although rates have come down in the past few months. Sri Lanka's courts cannot be relied upon to uphold the sanctity of contracts. The courts are not practical for resolving disputes or obtaining remediation, because their procedures make it possible for one side in a dispute to prolong cases indefinitely. Aggrieved investors (especially those dealing with the government on projects) have frequently pursued out-of-court settlements, in hopes of speedier resolution. A few of the key problems affecting foreign investment are explained in detail below.

10.5.1 Difficulties and Limitations

Though Sri Lanka approves 100 % foreign ownership in most of the manufacturing and some service sector activities like banking, insurance, telecommunication, and construction, it omits certain sectors for strategic purpose. These are railway freight transportation, electricity transmission, and distribution, costal fishing, and education. Some primary sector activities like mining oil and gas have a cap of 40 %. In media sector, television and print media have also 40 % caps. Foreign equity in retail sector is approved only if it satisfies eligibility criteria of more than $1,000,000. In 1990, the ownership restrictions were removed on units located outside the EPZs.

While in 2000, Sri Lanka notified WTO that its investment regime is TRIM compliant, investment in certain sectors requires approval from multiple agencies contrary to the information that BOI is a one-stop clearance for foreign investors. Some of the benefits provided by the BOI incentive schemes like tax holidays are contingent upon achieving certain export commitment, which is a limiting factor on the incentives (Athukorala 2013). A general condition is that the manufacturing enterprise has to export 80 % of output while service sector has to export 70 % of its output, with required minimum investment and employment levels to qualify for preferential incentives, which vary across sectors.

While Sri Lanka does not have a national investor protection and treatment law, Sri Lanka has investor protection agreement with about 28 countries and double taxation agreement with 38 countries. The arbitration process is hampered by its overburdened courts and results in delay in enforcing arbitration awards. On average it takes about 103 weeks to enforce arbitration awards from filing an application to a writ of execution attaching assets (World Bank Group 2010).

Sri Lanka is one of the most hospitable countries' to FDI in South Asia. However, political instability has hampered this after mid-1980s. Some authors have argued that overall investment climate which includes macroeconomic, political, and social stability is far more important than incentives, which has cost in terms of revenues foregone and BOP constraint.

Sri Lanka passed a law that provides for the appointment of a competent authority to control, administer, and manage 37 domestic and foreign enterprises. The legislation aims to revive underperforming companies and underutilised assets in places where the land belongs to the government (UNCTAD 2012).

10.5.2 Land Acquisition

The LAA No. 9 of 1950 applies to the whole of Sri Lanka for government acquisition of land for public purpose. However, the Government of Sri Lanka adopted the National Involuntary Resettlement Policy (NIRP) in May 2001 to:

- Minimise and mitigate the impacts of involuntary resettlement
- Ensure that people adversely affected by development projects are fully compensated and successfully resettled, the livelihoods of displaced people are re-established, and the standard of living improved
- Ensure that people are not impoverished when the state compulsorily acquires land for development and to assist affected persons in dealing with the psychological, cultural, social, and other stresses
- Make all affected persons aware of grievance redressal processes available and make those processes easily accessible and immediately responsive
- Institute a consultative, transparent, and accountable involuntary resettlement process with a time frame agreed to by the project proponent and the affected persons

The NIRP applies to all development-induced involuntary resettlement, where the option to stay behind does not exist. It also applies to cases where people do not have to be physically relocated (NIRP 2003). The process of acquisition is clearly laid down in the Act; however, it is not followed in the same way in some cases. This is evident in the cases of the construction of an outer circular road and power plant in Trincomalee. In the case of the construction of road, public notifications were not issued; so there was no clarity on the legal basis for the acquisition.

Another example is related to the acquisition of land to set up a coal-based thermal power plant in Trincomalee by Ceylon Electrical Board. The Government of Sri Lanka issued a notification under the LAA to begin the process of acquisition of land to set up the power plant. However, not much information was provided to the IDPs other than the offer of new lands in relocation sites. In fact, the people even failed to fully understand the implications of the notice. The notice confused the people greatly by providing rather incorrect and contradictory information (COHRE 2009). Not to mention, one of the common issues is the settlement of claims. More than 42,000 people await settlement of claims for land acquisition. In total, approximately 8.5 billion rupees are owed.

According to the Doing Business Report 2011 elaborated by the World Bank, Sri Lanka was placed 102nd out of 183 economies in the ranking on the ease of doing business, which is higher than 111th of Bangladesh or 134th of India but lower than East Asian countries like Vietnam and China.

10.5.3 Labour Regulations and Higher Wages

One of the biggest problems that companies face in Sri Lanka is the tight labour regulations. With reference to the Termination of Workmen Act (TEWA), the cost

Table 10.1 Payment of compensation

Number of years of services completed at the date of termination	Number of months salary to be paid as compensation for each year of service	Maximum compensation (cumulative) month salary
1–5	2.5	12.5
6–14	2.0	30.5
15–19	1.5	38.0
20–24	1.0	43.0
25–34	0.5	48.0

of severance payments for a worker is very high especially for those who have worked in a company for a longer term (see Table 10.1). Protection of workers is the main concern for the government; however, the rigid labour regulations are disadvantageous for a company considering setting up a factor in Sri Lanka.

The Labour Commissioner has absolute discretion to approve involuntary terminations and to determine the compensation payable. The Labour Commissioner's decisions can take a long time even though TEWA stipulates a maximum period of 3 months. Affected employees remain on the payroll until the decision is made. The decision is final and cannot be repealed. TEWA creates two severe difficulties for investors:

- Uncertainty as to their ability to restructure their labour force in response to changed future market conditions or technological change
- Uncertainty, when planning their investments, as to the true cost of labour (a significant operating cost in most sectors), because restructuring and exits costs is unknown and may be very high.

Such practices harm the investment climate. They unnecessarily increase business risks and thus, by raising the rate of return required by investors, reduce the amount of investment committed to the economy and number of jobs created. The key provisions of TEWA must be changed if private investment is to play a full part in Sri Lanka's development.

Increase in wages also cause problem in hiring labour. The average monthly wages of workers in Sri Lanka is USD 120, which is higher than Vietnam, Cambodia, Bangladesh, and Myanmar where labour-intensive manufacturing sector has the competitiveness with its cheaper labour force. Compared with China, Indonesia, and India enjoying large scale of economy as well as having huge domestic market and countries like Vietnam and Bangladesh enjoying lower cost of labour and a large younger population, the competitiveness of Sri Lankan labour market is rather weak.

10.5.4 Taxation

The principal taxes that affect businesses in Sri Lanka are taxes on corporate profits and dividends, value-added tax (VAT), and import and excise duties. Sri Lanka has a transparent, low-tax regime and has signed double taxation relief agreements with 26 countries. These arrangements provide for reduced tax rates on dividends, interests, and royalties. All Sri Lankan businesses, except for BOI companies and enterprises that qualify for special concessions under the Inland Revenue Law, are liable to taxation. Recently completed agreements include special provisions to ensure that foreign investors receive the benefits arising from various tax incentives.

Despite the incentives given out, it has a number of pitfalls in the taxation policy:

- It discriminates against small- and medium-sized enterprises (SMEs) in most cases of incentives. Yet investors not eligible for incentives face a tax burden that is 50–100 % higher than that of incentive companies.
- It requires substantial bureaucracy to approve and monitor size-based incentives. Any lowering thresholds to curb discrimination against SMEs would increase bureaucracy.
- It has masked the true investment attraction performance of the BOI. Many investors would approach the BOI as a gateway to incentives and not because of leads generated by the BOI.
- It has almost certainly led to structuring business to reduce tax in unanticipated ways. For example, there is an obvious incentive for banks to lend to zone companies (deemed to be non-resident) through their tax-advantaged foreign currency banking units.
- The BOI does not provide facilitation services to SMEs because they are too small to become BOI companies via entitlement to tax incentives.

The application of broad tax concessions to most large investors over many years contributes to weak budget revenues and a high fiscal deficit. This results in clearly inadequate public expenditures on infrastructure, which is the most serious constraint on private investment. The current approach to tax design is characterised by an uncompetitive standard fiscal regime that is relieved by a patchwork of discriminatory and bureaucratic incentives.

In respect of paying taxes and the tax burden for local enterprises, Sri Lanka is ranked as 166th, one of the worst countries due to complexity of tax or mandatory contribution in setting up business. Sixty-two separate tax payments and 256 h of compliance a year are required to enterprises, as said in the report. East Asian countries have simplified tax payments by unifying the accounting methods and introducing electronic tax filing system, which has taken decades to reach the current level.

10.5.5 Unfinished Agenda and Way Forward

Sri Lanka can take the advantage of favourable trends in global FDI flows by making investment climate better. It requires improving government policies, approaches to regulation and taxation, the provision of infrastructure, the functioning of finance and labour markets, and achieving political and economic stability and broader governance. Labour regulations are restrictive that hinder smooth business operation. Inflexible and arbitrary labour regulations create uncertainty about hiring and firing of workers and thereby discourage investment. The termination of Employment of Workers Act (1971) is a most restrictive labour regulation.

The bottom line is that if Sri Lanka is to attract substantial FDI, then there are many preconditions to be established to attract the expected increase in foreign investment flows with renewed growth of the international economy. The prospects of Sri Lanka after the end of the civil war have improved substantially and a determined effort by the country will go a long way in making Sri Lanka one of the preferred destinations of FDI in South Asia.

10.6 FDI in Nepal: Unfinished Agenda and Challenges

Nepal remains one of the worst performers in the region in terms of FDI despite a robust growth of 125 % attained in 2011 according to the UNCTAD data. In terms of the FDI potential index, Nepal ranks the lowest in the region, i.e. 175 out of 182 countries ranked globally.

While there are some typical challenges that each post-conflict LDC like Nepal faces in terms of attracting as well as retaining investment, Nepal faces constraints that are neither common nor explained by any theory. Given the fact that there is need to utilise FDI to achieve the development objectives such as poverty alleviation and inclusive economic growth pursued by the government, these challenges become even starker. Like all other developing and least developed economies, the constraints to FDI in Nepal are too many. These include weak infrastructure, weak governance, procedural hurdles, weak economic diplomacy, lack of identification of viable sectors of FDI, weak negotiation capacity, weak coordination among line ministries, and high cost of doing business, too many entities for investment approval, concession, facilitation, and promotion. A few of the other problems and challenges related to FDI in Nepal are explained below.

10.6.1 Land Acquisition in Nepal

The LAA of 1977, enacted by the King Birendra Bir Bikram Shah Dev with the advice and approval of Rastriya Panchayat, governs the acquisition of land in Nepal. As per the Act, 'land' means any land belonging to any person and walls, buildings, trees, etc. permanently installed thereon.

The Act precisely defines the 'public purposes' as undertaken in the interest of or for the benefit or use of the general public or functions to be undertaken by Government of Nepal and the term also included the following:

1. Project approved by Government of Nepal
2. Project undertaken by local bodies in different levels

Since the purpose is not stated clearly, the government can modify it at its own discretion.

The Act empowers the Government of Nepal to acquire any land at any place for public purpose if it finds it necessary for the development of the country, subject to compensation under this Act.

The Act also provides for the acquisition of land for institutions by the Government of Nepal for any of the following purposes, subject to payment of compensation and all other expenses under this Act, and Government of Nepal may decide to have the land acquired for such institution:

(a) To construct residential quarters for the staff, workers, or labourers of the institution, or otherwise provide for their welfare, or undertake any function in the interest of the general public
(b) To operate a project connected with an institution fully owned by the Government of Nepal or to construct a godown for the storage of any commodes or material connected with or manufactured by any such institution

10.6.1.1 Criteria for the Estimation of Compensation

To acquire lands for Government of Nepal, local bodies, and institutions fully owned by Government of Nepal, the compensation fixation committee shall follow the criteria laid down below for the estimation of compensation:

(a) The guidelines issued by Government of Nepal from time to time in respect to the fixation of compensation
(b) The losses suffered by the concerned person as a result of his having been required to shift the residence or the place of his/her business by reason of acquisition of the land

However, in case of acquisition of land for institutions other than local bodies, and institutions fully owned by Government of Nepal, the compensation fixation committee shall take the following criteria into consideration for the determination of compensation:

(a) The price of the land at the time of the publication of a notice of land acquisition under Section 9
(b) The value of the crops, houses, walls, sheds, etc., if any, acquired along with the land
(c) The losses which the concerned person will suffer as a result of shifting his/her residence or the place of his/her business, because of the acquisition of his/her land

Presently, according to Nepal Law Commission, the new legislative framework for land acquisitions is going through the parliament, so it is unlikely that the Board of Investment in Nepal is going to change much.

10.6.2 Taxation

Business taxation is a serious impediment to attracting FDI in Nepal. Nepal's taxation is not competitive when account is taken of additional burdens imposed by statutory payments to or on behalf of employees. Poor tax administration imposes additional burdens and uncertainties. Uncertainty is heightened by increasing recourse to taxation through flat charges without direct regard to the profitability of investment. From a taxation standpoint, the foreign investor may not feel that there is a welcoming environment. Nepal has a penchant for the frequent introduction of new taxes in the form of fees and flat charges. This record increases uncertainties for investors, especially since new taxes can be introduced in forms which have no bearing on profitability and hence ability to pay.

10.6.3 Foreign Exchange Regulation

Nepal maintains a formal foreign exchange control regime that requires the surrender of foreign currency export proceeds. Current account transactions are delegated to the commercial banks while capital account transactions require the approval of the Central Bank. One useful concession is the ability of exporters to maintain foreign currency accounts at commercial banks—although at interest rates controlled by the Central Bank. Investors wishing to retain funds abroad in order to satisfy international project loan requirements must put a case to the Central Bank. It has been seen in the past that in larger investments (e.g. large hydropower generation investments), these arrangements have been given contractual force in agreements between the investor(s) and the government.

At present, the Nepalese currency is pegged to the Indian rupee and is convertible completely. It should be noted that the foreign exchange provisions of the foreign investment law do not suffice to remove convertibility risk. The foreign investment law provisions cover convertibility only for capital, dividend repatriation, and foreign debt service. They do not cover normal import and foreign services payments. Moreover, the foreign investment law provisions could be overturned by a subsequent law and are often deemed not to provide adequate protection for large, long-term foreign investment.

From an FDI attraction standpoint, the regime is thus of a traditional kind which falls below best practices of an increasing number of developing countries that have abolished exchange controls. The foreign investor faces more risk under an exchange control regime and certainly more bureaucracy.

10.6.4 Labour Law

The Labour Act was overhauled in 1992 but remains a highly restrictive code from an investor standpoint. By modern commercial standards, it impedes business flexibility in many instances:

- The labour office can direct a business as to job classification.
- The new owner of a business may not change the conditions of service of employees.
- Labour department permission is required in order to retrench workers if the business is in slowdown or ceases production. The department is entitled to take up to 2 months to decide. Severance pay is set by statute, not by employment contract.
- Permanent employees have a mandatory minimum annual pay rise.
- There are lengthy procedures for dismissal for misconduct.
- There is no provision for departmental review of a decision by the labour office on wage or bonus issues. The only recourse is to appeal to a court, which can be time-consuming.

It is suggested that Nepal should change labour policies towards a more market-driven approach under which wages and benefits are more consensual and flexible, with safeguards as appropriate for all parties concerned.

10.6.5 Unfinished Agenda and Way Forward

Nepal does not seem to offer a hospitable investment climate for foreign investors. Although there are several reasons that could deter investors from making long-term investment in Nepal, three problems stand out. First, the political instability and resultant policy and legal uncertainty means foreign investors would think twice before investing in Nepal. Second, poor infrastructure, in particular electricity and road network, which raises the cost of doing business in Nepal, works as a strong disincentive not only for foreign investors but also for local investors to invest in Nepal. Third, militancy of trade unions, which have become emboldened particularly in the aftermath of the declaration of Nepal as a republic, has created havoc for the overall business climate of the country (Adhikari 2013).

The Government of Nepal has been trying hard to address the challenges. It introduced a new Industry Policy in 2010. Some of its other reform measures include:

- Setting up of Nepal Business Forum by executive order for PPD and investment climate reforms
- SEZ Bill submitted to the parliament
- BOI chaired by the PM, a one-stop service centre

- Reform of existing foreign investment policy, act regulation, and procedures to create an investment-friendly environment
- Commitment to bring in a flexible labour and economic diplomacy policy to attract FDI
- Simplification of procedures and regulations

Despite various interlocked issues, controversies, and transitional political circumstances, Nepal is well positioned among low-income economies to move emphatically on development policy and spending priorities in the coming years. Above all, conclusion of political settlement, labour unrest, and power crisis are the critical factors. Political agenda and economic agenda need to be synchronised to achieve Nepal's objectives.

10.7 Conclusion: FDI in South Asia—The Way Forward

Undoubtedly, South Asia has grown in influence and is currently one of the fastest growing regions in the world. FDI has been a key determinant facilitating both FDI and growth of the region. However, FDI inflows into region have remained low as compared to its counterparts in the emerging economies of Central and Latin America and a few countries in Africa as well. According to the UNCTAD, 2012, the prospects of South Asia in attracting FDI are good. However, the success of FDI in the region largely depends on whether countries in the region can overcome old challenges and grasp new opportunities to attract investment and this will depend largely on government's efforts to further open their economies and deepen regional economic integration. The challenges facing the region are the poor business climate, poor infrastructure, restrictive labour policy and labour unrest, political uncertainties and civil conflicts, weak regulatory systems, and rampant corruption. The perception of investors of the business climate in host countries is a primary determinant of FDI. This is in turn dependent on economic and political conditions in host countries, such as the development of infrastructure, labour relations, the political situation, and enforcement of regulations and laws. At the individual country level, high political risks have also been a major deterrent to FDI inflows.

In the above context, the book has made a modest attempt to highlight the major challenges and prospects of FDI in South Asia. The book provides a comprehensive coverage of the FDI policies in each of the South Asian countries and the FDI policy in China with the objective of drawing some useful lessons for the region. The book also presents the current FDI trends for the South Asian region as a whole and FDI trends and prospects in each of the individual countries of the region. A sector attracting the most FDI along with the top sources of FDI in each of the countries of the region has also been detailed. The book with the help of empirical estimations has also tried to assess the impact of FDI on growth and exports in the region simultaneously analysing the determinants of FDI in South Asia. Based on the prevailing environment for FDI in the region, the book also highlights the pending reforms in each of the countries and the challenges that the region needs to overcome to be able to carve a path of making itself the most preferred FDI destination in the world.

It is evident that most of the South Asian countries are keen on attracting FDI and since the 1990s have been proactive not only liberalising their trade environment but also have been increasingly open to trade. The positive stance taken by the policymakers of the South Asian countries has encouraged foreign investors to enter the region and therefore the FDI inflows in to the region have improved in recent times as indicated by the UNCTAD 2012.

To conclude, further liberalisation of the FDI policies, improvement in infrastructure and reducing procedural hassles to FDI, flexible labour policy, and simplified tax laws are the key to sustaining South Asia's FDI flows and thereby growth and development of the region.

Appendix

Table 10.A.1 Indicators of business and macroeconomy

	Overall index		Institution		Infrastructure		Macroeconomy		Business sophistication	
Country	Rank	Score	Rank	Score	Rank	Score	Rank	Score	Rank	Score
India	51	4.3	58	4.0	86	3.5	73	4.5	44	4.3
China	27	4.8	49	4.4	50	4.4	4	6.1	41	4.3
Bangladesh	107	3.6	115	3.2	133	2.1	80	4.5	105	3.4
Sri Lanka	62	4.2	55	4.1	70	3.8	124	3.6	39	4.4
Pakistan	123	3.5	112	3.3	110	2.8	133	3.2	79	3.7
Nepal	130	3.3	130	3.0	139	1.8	86	4.4	132	3.0
Republic of Korea	22	4.9	62	4.0	18	5.6	6	5.8	24	4.8
Singapore	3	5.5	1	6.1	5	6.2	33	5.2	15	5.1
Indonesia	44	4.4	61	4.0	82	3.6	35	5.2	37	4.4
Malaysia	26	4.9	42	3.6	30	5.0	41	5.0	25	4.8
Thailand	38	4.5	64	4.0	35	4.8	46	4.9	48	4.2
Philippines	85	4.0	125	3.1	104	2.9	68	4.6	60	4.0

Source: The Global Competitiveness Report, 2010–2011, World Economic Forum

Table 10.A.2 Indicators of business and macroeconomy

	Basic requirements		Efficiency enhancers		Innovation and sophistication	
Country	Rank	Score	Rank	Score	Rank	Score
India	81	4.3	38	4.4	42	4.0
China	30	5.3	29	4.6	31	4.1
Bangladesh	114	3.7	97	3.6	109	3.0
Sri Lanka	73	4.4	69	4.0	40	4.0
Pakistan	132	3.4	95	3.7	76	3.6
Nepal	125	3.5	131	3.1	133	2.7
Republic of Korea	23	5.4	22	4.8	18	4.8
Singapore	3	6.1	1	5.5	10	5.1
Indonesia	60	4.6	51	4.2	37	4.1
Malaysia	33	5.2	24	4.7	25	4.4
Thailand	48	4.8	39	4.4	49	3.8
Philippines	99	4.0	7.8	3.9	75	3.4

Source: The Global Competitiveness Report, 2010–2011, World Economic Forum

Table 10.A.3 Indicators of business and macroeconomy

	Goods market efficiency		Labour market efficiency		Financial market development		Technological readiness	
Country	Rank	Score	Rank	Score	Rank	Score	Rank	Score
India	71	4.1	92	4.2	17	4.9	86	3.9
China	43	4.4	38	4.4	57	4.3	48	3.4
Bangladesh	102	3.8	108	4.0	66	4.2	126	2.7
Sri Lanka	47	4.4	104	4.0	52	4.4	84	3.4
Pakistan	91	3.9	131	3.5	73	4.1	109	2.9
Nepal	122	3.6	126	3.6	106	3.6	134	2.5
Republic of Korea	38	3.5	78	4.3	83	4.0	19	5.0
Singapore	1	5.7	1	5.9	2	5.8	11	5.3
Indonesia	49	4.3	84	4.2	63	4.2	91	3.2
Malaysia	27	4.8	35	4.7	7	5.3	40	4.2
Thailand	41	4.5	24	4.8	51	4.4	68	3.6
Philippines	97	3.9	111	3.9	75	4.0	95	3.2

Source: The Global Competitiveness Report, 2010–2011, World Economic Forum

Table 10.A.4 Indicators of business and macroeconomy

	India	Bangladesh	Nepal	Pakistan	Sri Lanka	China
Measures of tax burden						
Profit tax (%)	22.9	27.3	20.3	13.9	26.5	12
Labour tax and contributions (%)	18.2	0	11.3	12.6	16.9	58.9
Other taxes (%)	30.4	12.2	2.5	2.3	20.3	9
Total tax rate (% profit)	71.5	39.5	34.1	28.9	63.7	79.9
The costs imports and exports						
Cost to export (US$ per container)	945	970	1,764	611	865	460
Cost to import (US$ per container)	960	1,375	1,900	680	895	545
Difficulty of enforcing commercial contracts						
Procedures (number)	46	41	39	47	40	34
Duration (days)	1,420	1,442	735	976	1,318	406
Cost (% of claim)	39.6	63.3	26.8	23.8	22.8	11.1
Hiring and firing						
Difficulty of Hiring Index	0	44	56	78	0	11
Difficulty of Firing Index	70	40	70	30	60	50
Firing costs (weeks of salary)	56	104	90	90	169	91

References

Athukorala, P-c (2013) Intra-regional FDI and economic integration in South Asia: trends, patterns and prospects. Departmental working papers 2013–05, The Australian National University, Arndt-Corden Department of Economics

Bajpai N, Sachs JD (2000) FDI in India: issues and problems. Harvard Institute of International Development, DDP no. 759. Harvard University, Cambridge, USA

Balasubramanyam VN, Salisu MA, Sapsford D (1996) Foreign direct investment and growth in EP and IS countries. Econ J 106(434):92–105

Besley T, Burgess R (2004) Can education hinder economic performance? Evidence from India. Q J Econ 119(1):91–134

Bhagwati JN (1978) Anatomy and consequences of exchange control regimes, Studies in international economic relations. NBER, New York

Centre on Housing Rights & Evictions (COHRE) (2009) High security zones and the rights to return restitution in Sri Lanka – a case study of Trincomalee District, Sri Lanka

Dee P (2006) Multinational corporations and pacific regionalism. Crawford School of Economics and Government, Australian National University, Canberra

Dunning JH (1977) Trade, location of economic activity and the MNE: a search for an eclectic approach. In: Ohlin B, Hesselborn PO, Wijkmon PM (eds) The international location of economic activity. Macmillan, London, pp 395–418

Encarnacion DJ, Wells LT (1986) Evaluating foreign investment. In: Moran TH et al (eds) Investing in development: new roles for private capital. Transaction Books, New Brunswick, pp 61–86

Globerman S, Shapiro D (1999) The impact of government policies on foreign direct investment: the Canadian experience. J Int Bus Stud 30(3):513–532

Grimsey D, Lewis M (2005) The economics of public private partnerships, vol 183. Edward Elgar Pub, Northampton
Hanson HG (2001) Should countries promote foreign direct investment? G-24 discussion paper, no. 9. United Nations, New York
Hymer S (1976) The international operations of national firms: a study of direct foreign investment, vol 14. MIT Press, Cambridge, MA, pp 139–155
Industrial Disputes Act (1947) Ministry of labour and Employment, Government of India. http://pblabour.gov.in/pdf/acts_rules/industrial_disputes_act_1947.pdf
Jaumotte F (2004) Foreign direct investment and regional trade agreements: the market size effect revisited, vol 4. International Monetary Fund, Washington, DC
Kalirajan KP, Singh K (2008) A comparative analysis of China's and India's recent export performances. Asian Econ Pap 7(1):1–30
Kinoshita Y, Campos N (2003) Why does FDI go where it goes? New evidence from the transition countries, William Davidson Institute working paper, no. 573. International Monetary Fund, Washington, DC
Lal S, Streeten P (1977) Foreign investment, transnationals and developing countries. MacMillan, London
Markusen JR, Venables AJ (1999) Foreign direct investment as a catalyst for industrial development. Eur Econ Rev 43:335–356
Mukherji R (2008) Special economic zones in India: recent developments and future prospects, ISAS working paper, no.30. Institute of South Asian Studies, Singapore
Nasrin S, Baskaran A, Muchie M (2010) A study of major determinants and hindrances of FDI inflow in Bangladesh. DIR research series working paper no. 144, iAalborg University, Denmark
Nataraj G (2007) Infrastructure challenges in South Asia: the role of public-private partnerships, ADBI discussion paper, no. 80. ADB Institute, Tokyo
National Council for Applied Economic Research (NCAER)-Holcim (2010) Seeking efficiency and excellence in the implementation of infrastructure projects in India. NCAER, Delhi
National Involuntary Resettlement Policy (2003) Ministry of Labour, Sri Lanka
National Transmission and Dispatch Company (2006) Quarterly reports, Lahore
Noel M, Brzeski WJ (2004) Mobilizing private finance for local infrastructure in Europe and Central Asia: an alternative public-private partnership framework, World Bank working paper, no. 465. Washington, DC
Palit A (2009) India's foreign investment policy: achievements and inadequacies. FRI Centre, Paris
Planning Commission (2001) Report of the task force on employment opportunities. Planning commission, Government of India, New Delhi
Rahman A (2012) Foreign direct investment in Bangladesh, prospects and challenges, and its impact on economy. Asian Institute of Technology, Khlong Luang
Rugman AM (1986) New theories of the multinational enterprise: an assessment of internalization theory. Bull Econ Res 38(2):101–118
Sahoo P (2004) Fiscal federalism in India: a review. Asian Econ Rev 48:4
Sahoo P (2006) FDI in South Asia: trends, policy, impact and determinants, Asian Development Bank Institute discussion paper series, no.56. Asian Development Bank Institute, Tokyo
Sahoo P (2012) Foreign direct investment in India: unfinished agenda. In: Philippa D (ed) Economic reform processes in South Asia: toward policy efficiency. Routledge, New York, pp 109–136, Australian National University
Sahoo P, Nataraj G (2008) FDI in South Asia: policy trends and perspectives. Gitam J Manag 1(1):35–77, Gitam Institute of Management, Vishakhapatnam, India
Singh R (2010) Delays and cost overruns in infrastructure projects: extent, causes and remedies. Econ Political Wkly 45(21):43
Termination of Employment of Workers Act (1971) Ministry of Labour, Sri Lanka

Transparency International (2010) The corruption perceptions index, Berlin
UNCTAD (2012) World investment report. United Nations, New York
Virmani A (2004) Foreign direct investment reforms. Occasional policy papers, ICRIER working paper no. 131, New Delhi
World Bank Group (2010) Investing across borders. Washington, DC
World Economic Forum (2010) The global competitiveness report. Geneva, Switzerland

Index

P. Sahoo et al., *Foreign Direct Investment in South Asia*, DOI 10.1007/978-81-322-1536-3, © Springer India 2014

F

J

K

Q

R

MIX
Papier aus verantwortungsvollen Quellen
Paper from responsible sources
FSC® C105338

If you have any concerns about our products,
you can contact us on
ProductSafety@springernature.com

In case Publisher is established outside the EU,
the EU authorized representative is:
Springer Nature Customer Service Center GmbH
Europaplatz 3, 69115 Heidelberg, Germany

Printed by Libri Plureos GmbH
in Hamburg, Germany